INTERNATIONAL YEARBOOK
OF POLITICAL BEHAVIOR RESEARCH

General Editor: HEINZ EULAU, STANFORD UNIVERSITY

This volume was edited under the auspices of the Institute of War and Peace Studies, Columbia University.

Other books from the Institute are:

ALFRED VAGTS, *Defense and Diplomacy: The Soldier and the Conduct of Foreign Relations* (1956)

SEYMOUR MELMAN, editor, *Inspection for Disarmament* (1958)

WILLIAM T. R. FOX, editor, *Theoretical Aspects of International Relations* (1959)

KENNETH N. WALTZ, *Man, the State, and War* (1959)

SAMUEL P. HUNTINGTON, *The Common Defense: Strategic Programs in National Politics* (1961)

WARNER R. SCHILLING, PAUL Y. HAMMOND, and GLENN H. SNYDER, *Strategies, Budgets, and Defense Politics: Three Studies in the Making of National Security Policy* (in press)

Changing Patterns of Military Politics

CONTRIBUTORS

Philip Abrams, CAMBRIDGE UNIVERSITY

Martha Derthick, HARVARD UNIVERSITY

Raoul Girardet, INSTITUT D'ÉTUDES POLITIQUES

Samuel P. Huntington, COLUMBIA UNIVERSITY

Harold D. Lasswell, YALE UNIVERSITY

Laurence I. Radway, DARTMOUTH COLLEGE

David C. Rapoport, COLUMBIA UNIVERSITY

Changing Patterns

of

Military Politics

EDITED BY SAMUEL P. HUNTINGTON
COLUMBIA UNIVERSITY

THE FREE PRESS OF GLENCOE, INC.
A DIVISION OF THE CROWELL-COLLIER PUBLISHING COMPANY

printing number

2 3 4 5 6 7 8 9 10

Library of Congress Catalog Card Number: 61–18255

Preface

THE THEORETICAL ESSAYS and empirical studies brought together in this third volume of the *International Yearbook of Political Behavior Research* are devoted to an important problem, the function of violence in the quest for survival and the new roles of the military in politics. It is a problem that calls for both theoretical innovation and ingenuity in research. The revolution in weapons systems and the world revolutionary situation of the last two decades have brought about such drastic changes in the environment of domestic politics that much of the traditional lore about civil-military relations can no longer be taken for granted. The theoretical formulations and empirical researches reported in this volume attest to the possibility of bringing scientifically viable modes of analysis to a topic that, until recently, has been largely treated in normative and speculative terms.

The materials included here also belie the charge sometimes made against the newer theoretical and empirical tendencies in political science that they deal in trivia and neglect the "really important" problems of politics. Preoccupied as they seem to be with methods and techniques, political behaviorists and political sociologists, so the charge goes, tend to cultivate areas of research where access to data is easy, regardless of whether the problems involved are important or not. In short, the critics allege, behavioral researches on elections, community politics, legislative processes, and so on, do not "contribute" much to a "solution" of the "great issues" of politics.

It is perfectly true that much current behavioral research is concerned with topics that, in many respects, are not earthshaking. But why? This is so, not because empirical researchers take delight in methodological elegance for its own sake, but because they believe that a science of politics, to deserve the name of science, must build from the bottom up and cannot build from the top down. An empirical science is built by the slow, modest, and piecemeal cumulation of theoretical generalizations and empirical analyses. There is little glory to be had, for instance, in the patient analysis of mass political behavior; but the hundreds of studies—some good, some not so good—of electoral behavior that have accumulated in the last sixty years allow us today to make statements whose truth value has a reasonably high degree of probability.

Whether the political behavior of the democratic mass electorate constitutes a significant area of political inquiry is, of course, a matter of judgment. The "great issues" of politics, such as freedom, justice, or authority, are, indeed, important topics, but they are topics at the very apogee of the political system.

7

They are not beyond the reach of empirical investigation, but before they can be tackled successfully, the groundwork must be laid. This is all that one can hope for in the present stage of development in political science—an early stage, in spite of Plato, Aristotle, and all the other great thinkers who have influenced our notions of what is "important" in political investigation.

The question whether an Aristotle's concerns should be our concerns cannot be answered by an appeal to Aristotle. It can only be answered by resort to the crucible of our own experiences in the real world of politics. If our own experiences lead us back to the classical definitions of what is important, all to the better; if they do not, little is lost. This is not an argument against the classics, but an argument against the assumption that the great problems of classical political theory are the only problems worthy of examination.

Two volumes have so far appeared in this series: *Community Political Systems,* edited by Morris Janowitz, and *Political Decision-makers: Recruitment and Performance,* edited by Dwaine Marvick. Like these predecessors, this volume assumes the necessary unity of political theory, empirical research, and scientific method. Our readers might be interested in the general theme set for the next volume, edited by two members of our Advisory Board, Seymour M. Lipset and Stein Rokkan: the impact of sociocultural cleavages on the development and functioning of party systems and on the distribution of popular support for parties in different political systems. Scholars are invited to communicate with the general editor about future volumes.

Stanford, California   *Heinz Eulau*
May, 1961   GENERAL EDITOR

Contents

Contents

Changing Patterns of Military Politics

The New Military Politics

BY *SAMUEL P. HUNTINGTON*

THE FIFTEEN YEARS after World War II saw a proliferation of writing on military affairs in the United States and, to a somewhat lesser extent, in Great Britain. In the immediate postwar years this research and writing was largely devoted to recording and interpreting the experiences of World War II. Increasingly, however, as the bibliography at the end of this volume indicates, scholarly attention was directed to the more immediate and continuing problems of the Cold War and the broader academic and theoretical concerns which these problems stimulated. Scholars focused upon the problems of integrating foreign and military policies, the methods of strengthening civilian control in the defense establishment, the implications of nuclear weapons for national policy, the requirements of a deterrent strategy, and the nature of limited war. In both the World War II and Cold War phases military forces and violence were seen primarily as instruments of governments in international politics. By the 1960's, however, the recovery of old powers and the emergence of new ones, the rapid pace of economic development in advanced societies and of social change in less developed ones, were fundamentally altering the political scene. The United States, as Gene M. Lyons suggested, was evolving a "new civil-military relations."[1] This development was only one aspect of the new roles of violence and of military elites in world politics resulting from the balance of terror, technological advancement, the decline of empire, the processes of modernization, and the increased importance of general and regional collective-security arrangements.

In most modern industrial societies the changing functions of the military establishment seemed to produce significant tensions and frustrations within the officer corps. The traditional military officer—the "generalist" skilled in the command of troops in battle—was caught between the technician, on the

I wish to acknowledge my gratitude to the Institute of War and Peace Studies for making it possible for me to edit this volume and to prepare my contributions to it. I am also grateful to Mr. William E. Jackson, Jr., for his able and thoughtful assistance in research and editing.

one hand, and the guerrilla, on the other. The frustrations of the French army in Indochina and Algeria shaped its role in the crisis of May, 1958. The shrinkage of the British Empire and the pressures of technology caused stresses and strains within the British officer corps. The American officer corps went through the ordeal of the Korean War and a subsequent slow decline in status and steady tightening of civilian control. Among the services the Army suffered the most, and the frustrations and exasperation of its officers were clearly revealed in the memoirs of Generals Ridgway, Taylor, Gavin, and Medaris.[2]

The likelihood of direct armed conflict between the United States and the Soviet Union seemed to decline in the 1950's. At the same time, the threat of nuclear war tended to become more familiar. In these circumstances, the clarity and immediacy of external requirements shaping the size and character of the armed forces weakened; and the impact of domestic considerations, the pressures of industrial, regional, and popular groups, in influencing policy seemed to increase. The "military-industrial complex," or "defense lobby," became a new focus of concern. The political character of the armed services also changed. Their political evolution paralleled that of the National Guard described by Martha Derthick in this volume: as their functional role declined in importance they entrenched themselves and constructed elaborate political "castles" to insure their continued existence.[3] Counterbalancing these tendencies was the increased popular interest in disarmament and the formation of agitational and propaganda groups to mobilize public sentiment in favor of disarmament or arms control. The development of military-industrial vested interests, on the one hand, and of "mass" (in style if not in scope) movements for disarmament, on the other, posed new constraints on the formulation of military policy.

Abroad, the most prevalent forms of violence were civil wars, revolutionary wars, and coups d'état. Military elites frequently played a major role in stimulating social change, and rapid change, whether pushed by armies or civilian groups, was usually accompanied by violence. The Cold War, in a sense, was still being fought, but it was being fought within the boundaries of several dozen different states, and the control of the two major governments principally involved had been notably weakened. The initiative in the use of violence within the territory of a state normally rested with groups indigenous to that territory. The strategy and tactics of revolutionary war were very different from those of the traditional intergovernmental war. For the great powers the problem was how to bring one's strength to bear without directly fighting another government, how to intervene in the political-military warfare in another state without appearing to do so. In a world where other forms of political violence are much more prevalent than direct intergovernmental violence, it must also be assumed that other types of military forces and of civil-military relations will replace the more familiar forms.

The degree to which governments were losing the monopoly of violence was reflected not only in the extent to which nongovernments had assumed the initiative in employing violence within the territory of states, but also in the extent to which the exercise of violence on a broader level was conducted under the auspices of international organizations. NATO, the Warsaw Pact, the United Nations Command in Korea, and the United Nations force in the Congo all represented efforts by several governments to cooperate in the maintenance and the use of force. Traditionally the study of international relations was divided between international politics, focusing on war and diplomacy, on the one hand, and international organization, focusing on "peace" and disarmament, on the other. By 1960 these lines, if ever valid, had certainly lost their relevance. Arms control and disarmament were a principal focus of diplomatic negotiation among the great powers, while a general international organization was attempting to use military force to pacify the Congo.

The purpose of this volume is to explore some of these new developments and to advance concepts and hypotheses for their analysis. Its approach is both theoretical and empirical. The opening essay discusses the shift in the locus of violence from international politics to domestic politics and analyzes two forms of violence prevalent in the underdeveloped areas, revolutionary war and the reform coup d'état. Harold Lasswell then reconsiders the "garrison-state hypothesis," which he first advanced over twenty years ago, reformulates it in terms of new concepts, and concludes that, unfortunately, it is still relevant to the analysis of world politics. In another theoretical essay, David Rapoport offers a broad typology of civil-military relations— the nation-in-arms, the praetorian state, and the "civilian-and-military state" —and analyzes in depth the historical manifestations of the nation-in-arms and its social and political prerequisites. Laurence I. Radway presents the results of his direct observation of military behavior at the NATO Defense College and in several NATO headquarters, focusing particularly upon the means and the limits of cooperation in organizations composed of representatives from nations vastly disparate in military power. In his essay translated from French for this volume, Raoul Girardet analyzes the background of the "13th of May" in the unprecedented problems of French civil-military relations in the Fourth Republic. Also concerned with the decline of empire and the rise of democracy and technology, Philip Abrams shows the effects which these developments have had on the class position and behavior in retirement of Britain's military officers. In her study, based in large part on previously unavailable documentary sources, Martha Derthick analyzes the impact that the changing requirements of American defense in the nuclear age have had on the political behavior and power of one of its most traditional military organizations, the National Guard.

Rare is the symposium which is not attacked by reviewers for lacking unity and focus. This symposium is peculiarly vulnerable to such a charge: the topics covered range from the military system of Sparta to the organizational arrangements at SHAPE, and the techniques employed vary from soaring hypotheses on the role of the garrison state in today's world to detailed analysis of the career lines of British officers. In this sense the essays have neither common subject nor common method. Hopefully, however, they do serve a common purpose in suggesting some of the opportunities for fruitful research in the new military politics of the 1960's.

NOTES

1. Gene M. Lyons, "The New Civil-Military Relations," *American Political Science Review,* 55 (March, 1961), 53-63.

2. See, in addition, the discussion of military frustrations in Morris Janowitz, *The Professional Soldier: A Social and Political Portrait* (Glencoe, Ill., 1960), *passim,* but esp. chap. 20.

3. See my "Interservice Competition and the Political Roles of the Armed Services," *American Political Science Review,* 55 (March, 1961), 40-52.

Patterns of Violence
in World Politics

BY *SAMUEL P. HUNTINGTON*

I: The Changing Locus of Violence

"AN ARENA IS *military,*" say Lasswell and Kaplan, "when the expectation of violence is high; *civic,* when the expectation of violence is low."[1] For three centuries in the West international politics has been viewed as a military arena, and the domestic politics of nation-states have been thought to be civic arenas. Continuing this pattern, after World War II the expectations and apprehensions of international war, particularly war between Communist and Western states, were high. In practice, however, international violence was relatively infrequent. The Korean War was the only major prolonged interstate war between 1945 and 1960. Previously, of course, much longer periods of time had passed with even fewer interstate wars. These, however, were also periods of relative harmony with few significant clashes of interest between states. The fifteen years after World War II were marked by intense international conflicts, not only between the Soviet bloc and the West, but also between many other states over local issues. Nonetheless, with a few exceptions, governments did not resort to war. Never before in human history, one might say, were such high expectations of interstate violence accompanied by so little interstate violence in actuality.

The willingness of governments to resort to interstate violence presumably is affected by considerations of domestic politics and calculations of international gains. The decision to go to war or to take action that seriously risks war is seldom made casually.[2] In the past, when governments "blundered" into wars they did not want or could not win, the result was usually caused not by a refusal to act in a rational manner but by deficiencies in knowledge concerning the intentions and capabilities of other states. As long as governments choose war or peace in terms of their own interests and sometimes miscalculate those interests, interstate war is never impossible.

After 1945, however, the evolution of international politics produced new inhibitions reinforcing the reluctance of governments to resort to violence. In the past interstate wars were almost always associated with changes in

17

control or influence over territory. They were the natural concomitant of the "territoriality" of the nation-state.[3] In the mid-twentieth century, however, prospective gains in territorial control began to decrease in value compared to the risks and the costs involved in procuring them. Governments became more willing to live with disputed boundaries, unsettled claims, and irredentist hopes. In part this was due to the existence of nuclear weapons, and in part also it was the result of improvements in international communication and organization, which made more visible any resort to violence and provided mechanisms for avoiding violence or bringing it quickly to an end. Increasingly, in effect, the territorial status quo became stabilized and even sanctified beyond the ability of any one state, however powerful, unilaterally to change it. The destruction of Hiroshima and the humiliation of Suez were strong deterrents to the resort to force.

The decline in the likelihood of intergovernmental violence was marked by a change in the nature of the Cold War. In the early years of the struggle between the Soviet Union and the United States bipolarity prevailed, and the conflict between the two powers and their allies was largely over territory. A gain in territory (e.g., China) for one side was a direct loss for the other. In the mid-1950's, however, bipolarity began to decline, and the struggle between the two great powers shifted from territory to the "peaceful competition" of economic development, military build-ups, scientific achievements, and diplomatic successes. The relevant model for world politics was less a two-person zero-sum game than a multiperson nonzero-sum game. A gain for one country did not necessarily mean an equivalent loss for another. A finite limit existed on territory, but there were no limits on the goals which a government might set for itself in expanding its production, developing its military strength, and exploring outer space. All these activities served as substitutes for the actual recourse to violence.[4] In the international competition for prestige resort to violence was often a sign of weakness or failure.

As a result, the conflict between the major powers tended to become regularized or stabilized. The periodic threats made by one government or the other to destroy this stability were in themselves an index of its pervasiveness and value. The relative military power of the major states still remained decisively important. It was important, however, more for its contribution to Cold War diplomacy than for its potential contribution to hot war victory. In the early years of the Cold War statesmen on both sides seemed primarily concerned with ending the international deadlock. Increasingly, in the 1950's, they seemed more concerned with preserving it lest a worse fate befall them.

The inhibition of direct intergovernmental violence contrasted with the frequency and variety of violence in the domestic politics of the colonial territories and independent states of Latin America, Africa, the Middle East, and southern Asia. These were the principal military arenas in world politics. The Korean War was rivaled in either duration or intensity by the Chinese civil war, the Indonesian war for independence, the struggle between the French and the Viet Minh in Indochina. Insurrection, terrorism, or civil war occurred in Greece, Malaya, the Philippines, Kenya, Cyprus, Algeria, Cuba, the Congo, and Laos. In the Republic of Colombia 100,000 persons were killed in civil strife between 1948 and 1953.[5] In other Latin American countries, and in many Middle Eastern ones, coups d'état were a recurring phenomenon. The year 1960 could well be labeled the "year of revolt":[6] Korea, Turkey, the Congo, Cuba, the Dominican Republic, Ethiopia, Vietnam, Laos all shared in the pattern in one way or another. In Moscow and Washington strategists plotted and replotted the probable course of hypothetical wars between the Soviet Union and the United States. In the underdeveloped areas of the world, however, violence was an immediate actuality. The dominant pattern was not interstate war in the sense of sustained violence between the forces of two or more governments roughly comparable in structure and function, if not in power. Instead, it was insurrectionary violence, in which a nongovernmental body—a clique, a party, a movement—attempted to overthrow and to supersede the existing government. Territorial boundaries served not as the focus of conflict but as its parameters.

The frequency of violence in the domestic politics of the underdeveloped areas reflected the prevalence of rapid social and political change. "Social revolution," to quote Lasswell and Kaplan again, "occurs within a short time span only by the exercise of violence."[7] In the late 1950's the international situation was commonly described by such words as "stalemate," "deadlock," "equilibrium," and "balance." Within the principal countries of the West and even within the Soviet Union domestic politics was often spoken of in terms of "the absence of issues," "the end of ideology," "the apathy of the masses," "the prevalence of pragmatism," "other-directedness," and "organization men." In the underdeveloped areas, however, the key words were "development," "growth," "modernization," "westernization," "transition," and "independence." Here were the principal causes of insurrectionary violence.

II: Differences between Intergovernmental and Antigovernmental Violence

The classic theory of intergovernmental war was formulated by Clausewitz. When he said that war was a continuation of policy by other means, he meant that it was a continuation of foreign policy. He was concerned with the "war of a community—of whole nations and particularly of civilized nations. . . ."[8] For Clausewitz war was an instrument of governments and an interaction between governments. "War," he said, "is thus an act of force to compel our adversary to do our will. . . . Each of the adversaries forces the hand of the other, and a reciprocal action results which in theory can have no limit." Clausewitz's theory of war was dualistic, concerned solely with the interaction of two contestants. His analysis of the relation of military force to politics postulated a system of objective civilian control. His was the military theory of the nation-state, reflecting eighteenth-century practice and anticipating nineteenth-century developments. It is only partially relevant to intrastate war. Intrastate war is also the continuation of policy by other means, but it is the continuation of the policies of antigovernment and government within a common territory and society, each endeavoring to win support from at least some of the same groups. The patterns of intergovernmental war reflect the processes and structure of international politics; those of antigovernmental war reflect the processes and structure of domestic politics.

Intergovernmental war is initially symmetrical. The war begins between two independent governments, and it ends when one government succeeds in imposing its will on the other or when both governments conclude that their interests will no longer be served by continuing the struggle. The abstract pattern of insurrectionary war, on the other hand, is asymmetrical. It begins with a government confronting a nongovernment (institution, clique, movement, or party), and it ends with a similar relationship, although perhaps with the positions of the participants reversed. In the interval a symmetrical phase may occur, but prolonged symmetry means civil war in which two governments contend for authority within a single state. This closely resembles intergovernmental war. The American Civil War, for example, was a struggle between two governments each exercising effective authority over well-defined populations and territories. It differed little from the normal international war. A successful coup d'état, on the other hand, moves directly from one asymmetrical phase to another. The frequency of antigovernmental violence reflects the extent to which antigovernments monopolize the initiative in resorting to violence. They exist in greater numbers and variety than governments; possessing fewer responsibilities, they are restrained by fewer inhibitions. The distinctive characteristics of antigovernmental war stem from the fact that it is waged between qualitatively different types of organizations, each of which has its own liabilities and advantages.

In intergovernmental war the initiative is normally presumed to rest with the stronger of the two contestants: a three-to-one superiority, according to the traditional military maxim, was necessary to pass from the defensive to the offensive. In this sense, as Clausewitz maintained, defense was the stronger form of warfare because it could be sustained with weaker forces. In intrastate war, however, this relationship is reversed. As in nonviolent domestic politics, the offensive is the strategy of the weaker and the defensive that of the stronger. The strategic initiative always rests with the antigovernment, and larger forces are required by the defensive government than by the offensive clique or party. The offensive is the stronger form of warfare. In international warfare the offensive is the result of material superiority, while in domestic warfare the offensive is a means to material superiority. Inferiority can be converted to superiority, however, only because of the fundamentally tripartite nature of antigovernmental war as contrasted with the duality of intergovernmental war.

Abstractly, two general types of competitive situations can be distinguished: those in which the two parties interact directly and attempt to secure their aims by strengthening themselves and reducing the strength of their opponents and those in which the two contestants compete indirectly by attempting to win for themselves the support of third parties. The former situation, to adapt Spykman's terminology, involves "direct action," the latter "political action."[9] In actuality, of course, any competitive situation contains elements of both. To the extent, however, that only two parties exist, politics becomes impossible. Two men on a desert island can bargain or fight, but they cannot politick; when the waves wash up a third, however, politics begins. In competition between any two of the three, inherent differences in strength and cunning will still be important, but the extent to which one or the other can secure the support of the third will also be important. The classic recurring situations of politics always involve this tripartite relationship: two parties appealing for the vote of an electorate, two lobbyists attempting to influence legislators, two lawyers contesting before a judge, two states attempting to make an ally out of a neutral. In most interstate wars each participant has an interest in encouraging neutrality or belligerence in other powers. If, however, the support of a third party is essential to the victory of either of two participants in an interstate controversy, neither side is likely to risk war until it is assured of that support. In domestic violence, on the other hand, the essence of the conflict is the appeal to third parties. The direct action of the opponents upon each other, particularly in coups d'état, remains important, but the decisive characteristic of the struggle is the effort to gain the support of those who initially are neither friend nor foe. Apart from a prolonged intergovernmental civil war, the dichotomization of population and social institutions is seldom complete. All the distinctive methods of revolutionary war are devoted to the appeal for third-party support, and even in a coup d'état the great advantage of the quick seizure of the government is the opportunity it gives the insurrectionists to appeal to the uncommitted: the first act of the leaders of any successful coup invariably is the issuance of a manifesto demanding the support of the populace for "their" new government against the sinister forces of the counterrevolution.

The contestants in interstate wars are governments, and their goals may be limited to the acquisition of a particular piece of territory or some other specific value, or they may be total, requiring the elimination or complete subordination of the opposing government. Insurrectionary war, on the other hand, is almost always total. The government aims at the elimination of the challenge to its authority; the insurrectionists aim at the capture or destruction of the government. Thus, the political character of domestic war, in the competing appeals of the contestants to third parties, tends to be stronger than that of interstate war. On the other hand, negotiation and compromise between the contestants, which often characterize intergovernmental war, are normally lacking in domestic wars. Neither side wants to recognize the legitimacy of the other, and negotiations, much less agreements, imply such recognition. Armistices and peace treaties are possible between governments, but rarely between governments and antigovernments. When they do exist, they are generally recognized as temporary in nature, similar to the "political truces" which in national emergencies momentarily suspend partisan competition in constitutional democracies. When discussion does take place between domestic contestants, it usually results in the surrender of one or the other.

Antigovernmental war encourages civil-military relations different from those stimulated by interstate conflict. Other things being equal, the more a state achieves a system of objective civilian control the more effective it is in providing for its external security and in conducting foreign wars. Domestic war, on the other hand, demands subjective civilian control. In particular, in the post–World War II period the strategies of deterrence and of limited war not only required types of military forces that were of little use in internal wars, but they also tended to demand a relationship between military institutions and the government opposite to that required by internal war. In terms of type of military force, deterrence and limited war demanded reasonably small, ready, professional "constabulary forces," in Morris Janowitz's happy phrase.[10] In terms of military relations to the government, both the deterrent force and the limited war force had clearly defined missions and had to be highly responsive to the political leaders of the government in the performance of these missions. In domestic war, on the other hand, the political and military roles of the principal actors are merged on both sides, and political and military means become indistinguishable. In a coup d'état generals play political roles and governmental leaders, if they are able, exercise military command. In domestic war, moreover, the targets of both contestants are political institutions, social groups, and the general population. Both insurrectionaries and the government attempt to arouse these groups on their behalf. The employment of arms, like the exercise of the franchise, becomes a concomitant of citizenship. Thus the military forces which are employed and the nature of their leadership, on both sides, tend to be directly opposed to that required for interstate wars. Traditionally, the European powers made a relatively sharp distinction between the colonial army and the metropolitan army.[11] Certainly, it is an open question whether a government can maintain simultaneously within the same territory the systems required for both international war and domestic war. As Raoul Girardet has demonstrated, the change in function from interstate to domestic conflict may have drastic effect upon the attitudes of military officers toward their government and upon their amenability to the traditional forms of objective civilian control.[12]

III: Varieties of Domestic Violence

Different forms of government are associated with different forms of war. The decline of limited war and the rise of total war normally has been linked, for example, with the shift from absolute monarchy to democracy. Even monarchies, democracies, and totalitarian dictatorships, however, share much in common as governments, and the variations in the forms of war that they wage are neither numerous nor extensive. Insurrections, on the other hand, may be launched by the most varied groups, from a small junta of top military officers to a fanatic revolutionary party. Insurrectionary wars, consequently, seem to exist in an almost endless variety of forms. Perhaps for this reason the temptation to catalog them is virtually irresistible. Lasswell and Kaplan speak of palace revolutions, political revolutions, and social revolutions.[13] Bonnet distinguishes among *guerres civiles, guerres de libéra-*

tion, and *guerres révolutionnaires. Guerres civiles* are subdivided into riots, insurrections, pronunciamentos, and revolutions. *La guerre révolutionnaire,* in turn, is a compound of *la guerre de partisans* plus *la guerre psychologique.*[14] Stokes, in his analysis of violence in Latin America, identifies *machetismo, cuartelazo, golpe de estado,* and *revolución* as means of direct action, and *imposición, candidato único, continuismo,* and election as outwardly peaceful means of obtaining power which "rest upon a foundation of force."[15] In his volume on Latin American violence Lieuwen discusses *caudillismo,* "predatory militarism," coups d'état, and social revolutions.[16] Other writers speak of subversion, *émeutes,* general strikes, and assassination, and almost everyone attempts to draw a line between national revolutions and social revolutions. The variety of forms reflects differences in the nature of the participants, their relations with each other, and the political culture of the society in which they exist.

Historically the classic form of domestic violence in Europe was the urban revolt or revolution in which the principal focus was the seizure or attempted seizure of power by one class or social group through violence directed primarily against the established government in the capital city. For this Gallic tradition, epitomized by Halévy's "Insurgent," 1789 was the model.

There were [in the words of D. W. Brogan] the June Days of 1848; the resistance to the Coup d'Etat of 1851; the Commune of 1871. There were the less dramatic or less dramatized days of 1848 in Berlin and Vienna; there were riots and risings in the Romagna, in Valencia; there were the great strikes—and their bloody consequences, Fetherstonhaugh and the battle between the steel workers and the Pinkerton gunmen hired by Carnegie and Frick. There were Moscow and Petersburg in 1905; Paterson and Lowell; the 'Wobblies' and the mutineers of the 17th Infantry at Montpellier; all the tradition of insurrection and defiance that runs continuously from the first Fourteenth of July. . . .[17]

At the end of the line, there is Petersburg again in 1917. This type of insurrection reflected the politics of bourgeoisie, proletariat, and industrialism. A distinctive mark of the nineteenth century, it is out of date in the middle of the twentieth century.

After World War II politics in the underdeveloped areas centered about the struggle for independence and the processes of modernization and development. These were the principal causes of the two dominant forms of insurrectionary violence in these areas—the revolutionary war and the reform coup d'état. The struggle for independence often took the form of revolutionary war. The processes of modernization and westernization often required either revolutionary war or a succession of coups d'état.

IV: Revolutionary War and Group Alienation

Revolutionary wars of the post-World War II period included the later phases of the Chinese civil war, the struggle between the Viet Minh and the French in Indochina, the guerrilla war of the Communist rebels in Greece, the Hukbalahap rebellion in the Philippines, the jungle fighting in Malaya, the Algerian insurrection, and the Castro revolt against Batista.[18] Revolutionary war is linked with the end of colonialism, agrarian movements, and

the process of community definition and state creation. The difference
between it and the old European urban revolution is the difference between
the Chinese revolution and the Russian revolution.

Revolutionary wars occur when the government is distant—politically,
socially, and even geographically—from a significant counterelite. Recourse
to revolutionary war is a sign that the counterelite has failed to penetrate
the existing political structure. Colonial revolts, consequently, often take the
form of revolutionary wars. The base of the colonial government in its home
territory is out of reach of the nationalist counterelite, and this distance is
normally reinforced by ethnic differences between the colonial rulers and the
native population. Where revolutionary wars occur in noncolonial areas,
similar obstacles usually prevent the permeation of the government by the
counterelite. In the Philippines, for instance, the Hukbalahaps first attempted
to achieve their goals through peaceful means, electing seven members of
the Philippine legislature. When the legislature refused to seat them, the
Huk leaders returned to the countryside to precipitate revolt.

Divorced from the existing political system, the counterelite attempts to
develop a parallel structure independent of the government. Its goal is
usually the overthrow of the entire existing political and social system. A
long, arduous route to power, revolutionary war can only be pursued by
dedicated parties or movements sustained by a coherent ideology or sense of
mission. The war usually begins in an area distant from the capital and the
main centers of governmental power. If successful, the instigating group
gradually expands the locus of its authority, acquires more and more of the
attributes of a government, and eventually exhausts and overwhelms the
previously existing government. Lenin, it is reported, once said that "no
revolution of the masses can triumph without the help of a portion of the
armed forces that sustained the old regime."[19] The successful revolutionary
wars in Asia and Africa and the Castro revolution in Cuba are exceptions
to this rule. Revolutionary war proceeds on the premise that the government
controls the armed forces of the state and that it is necessary to develop
distinct revolutionary armed forces to employ against the state. In a successful revolutionary war a party creates an army, which, in turn, brings into
existence a government.

The decisive aspect of the revolutionary war is the contest between the
counterelite and the government for the support of a communal or socio-
economic group that is imperfectly integrated into the existing political
system. The causes of the alienation of the group may stem either from the
refusal of the government to recognize its distinctive characteristics and
problems or the relegation of the group to a secondary position in society.
As Lucien Pye has suggested, alienation often has its roots in the rationalism
of modern government.[20] The doctrines of equality and individualism undermine the ties of the community to the government. The abolition of the Arab
bureaus in Algeria was justified on the grounds that no distinction should
be drawn between Frenchmen of different faiths. The Chinese secretariat in
Malaya was emasculated because there "were no separate corps of officials
to deal with Malay or Indian problems, and it bordered on the invidious to

treat the Chinese as a special case."[21] In each case these actions symbolized an apparent indifference by the governing authorities to communal differences and hence encouraged feelings of alienation in the affected groups at the same time that they reduced the ability of the government to counteract them. Just as the educated Chinese in Malaya resented their "restricted citizenship," the Indochinese resented their "second class citizenship." Similarly, in the Philippines, "For too many years the government had been set apart from the common people in the farm lands of Central Luzon. . . . At the end of the war the peasants felt no obligation to support the government nor to be loyal to it in the struggle with the Huks."[22] The decline in identification and communication between communal group and the governmental authorities opens the group as a target for the counterelite.

The counterelite attempts to win the target group through terrorism and persuasion. In the "normal" intergovernmental war violence is directed primarily against the enemy; it is a means of reducing his numbers and of undermining his will to resist. In the initial phases of a revolutionary war, however, the counterelite directs its terrorism and violence primarily against the members of the target group. The aim of the violence is not to eliminate the forces of the government but to win the members of the target group. In Algeria between November, 1954, and April, 1957, the rebels killed 891 European civilians and 3,438 members of the French security forces but 5,576 Moslem civilians. In Malaya through June, 1957, the insurrectionists killed 106 Europeans, 226 Indians, 318 Malayans, and 1,700 Chinese civilians. In the first year of the Kenya emergency the Mau Mau killed eleven Asians, twenty-one Europeans, and at least 704 Africans. In Cyprus the EOKA killed three Greeks for every two non-Greeks.[23] In the Philippines the Huks killed farmers, burned homes, and raided villages in efforts to build up their support among the peasants. Similarly, the Viet Minh penetrated the Tonkin delta and established a codominion with the French, the one ruling by day and the other by night, through "its two most useful weapons, nationalism and terror."[24] Since the terrorism of the counterelite is useful only in the effects it has *pour encourager les autres,* it frequently includes blatant brutalities and atrocities. The elimination of prominent members of the target group who refuse to cooperate with the rebels convinces other members of the group that the only prudent course is to buy safety by contributing money to the rebels, furnishing them with information, or cooperating with them in other ways.

Simultaneously with their use of terror the counterelite and its military forces also employ persuasion. Propaganda and psychological war are the partners of terrorism. In Malaya, for example, Lucien Pye found that virtually all the surrendered Communist prisoners interviewed emphasized the importance of propaganda, identifying it with politics.[25] While the motivations of the counterelite may be ideological in character, the appeal to the target group is normally couched in the nationalistic or economic terms which are most meaningful to the target group. The revolutionaries particularly attempt to create and to maintain in the target group a sense of the ineptitude and weakness of the established government and a belief in the ultimate victory of the revolutionary group. The appearance of strength must be cultivated at the sacrifice of all else; a "bandwagon" psychology is essential in winning the target group.[26] In reply, the government attempts to convince the target group that it has the will and the strength to stamp out the insurrection. To win supporters in the target group, the government must guarantee not to abandon them at a later date. If it once breaks its word, it creates a doubt which will haunt it continuously. In a dualistic intergovernmental war the sense of inferiority, of fighting against great odds, may inspire great effort. In a tripartite revolutionary war, however, the decisive factor is the support of the target group. The members of the target group, in turn, want to be on the winning side. Whichever side can convince the target group that it is winning is in fact winning.

Terrorism, Brian Crozier argues, is the weapon of the weak.[27] It is a weapon, however, which is effective not against the strong but against the vulnerable. Though sporadic murders and bombings would never suffice to destroy the forces of the government, they may suffice to win the active or passive support of the target group. The protection of the target group against the terrorism may well strain the government's resources or impose upon it a burden that it does not wish to bear. The peculiar strength of the counterelite derives precisely from the fact that it is *not* a government and that it *is* pursuing an offensive strategy. Dramatic differences in strength usually exist between the antigovernmental and governmental forces. In Malaya, at their top strength, the Communists had 5,500 fighters in the jungle, while the British mobilized against them over 40,000 regular troops plus 100,000 men in auxiliary and constabulary forces. In Indochina the Viet Minh came out of World War II with slightly over 10,000 men. By the last year of the war their forces numbered 300,000 to 400,000 troops, including local militia, but the French Union forces were still more numerous. In March, 1956, FLN military strength in Algeria totalled 29,050 men, more than ever before, while French forces included about 200,000 men at that time and more than twice that number five months later.[28]

To carry out its efforts to conquer the target group, the counterelite and its military forces require a reasonably secure base of operations. One great weakness of the Hukbalahap movement was the inadequacy of the relatively restricted and heavily populated farm areas of central Luzon as a base for revolutionary operations. In Malaya the jungle furnished a base for the Communist guerrillas so long as they could procure food and supplies from villages and other settled areas. In Cuba the rugged terrain of the Sierra Maestrae furnished Castro with a base for operations against the peasants. In all three of these cases the rebel bases were within the territory of the government the rebels were attempting to overthrow. If a base can be established upon external territory, secure from governmental attack, the revolutionary movement has a much greater chance of success. Furnishing such a base for supplies and training purposes is the greatest assistance a foreign government can give a revolutionary movement. If the territory of the foreign government is contiguous with that of the target government, this assistance may be of decisive importance in the outcome of the revolutionary war. The withdrawal of Tito from the Comintern helped end the Greek war at the same time that the Communist victory in China insured the continuation of the Indochinese war. The Algerian Nationalists originally received extensive assistance from Egypt and then, after its independence, from Tunisia. Since a revolutionary war is a war of attrition, a relatively secure base is essential for its successful prosecution. A colonial power has an inherent advantage in fighting against a revolutionary movement that lacks a contiguous external base. On the other hand, a revolutionary movement with such a base has an inherent advantage in fighting an independent government without a home territory to draw upon. In the latter case, substantial support from allies, as in Greece, may be essential for the government to maintain itself. If the colonial government is secure in its home base and the revolutionary forces also possess a secure contiguous external base, it is possible that the war may, as in Indochina, drag on indefinitely with neither side able to force a decision.

Eventually, of course, if it is to achieve its ultimate goal, the revolutionary counterelite has to establish "liberated" base areas within the contested territory. As it gradually expands its locus of control, the revolutionary movement takes on more and more of the functions and characteristics of a government. Along with the collection of taxes and supplies from a liberated area, it also organizes the population into local militia units. The establishment of such units for the revolutionary forces, as for their opponents, is essential to free the mobile, "regular" forces for offensive operations in other areas. Terrorism gives way to guerrilla war and then to full-scale war.[29]

The reaction of the government in a revolutionary war normally goes through two phases. At first the government tends to treat the insurrection as a traditional problem for the police and the military. It minimizes the threat of the revolutionary forces and confidently proclaims that the "brigands" will be quickly eliminated and order restored. In 1946 the Philippine government declared that it would exterminate the Huks within sixty days. General Boucher confidently announced in the summer of 1948 that he would quickly clean up the Malayan guerrillas.[30] The government retains confidence in its superior conventional military forces, and it attempts to use those forces in the conventional fashion. The continued success of the revolutionary forces, however, precipitates a crisis within the government. It now recognizes that the revolution requires not only a much larger and different military effort to suppress it but also an integrated political-economic effort to counter the appeals of the revolutionaries to the target group. It also recognizes the need to overhaul its organizational structure dealing with the rebellion and to merge political and military responsibilities in a single individual. In November, 1952, for example, Oliver Lyttleton emphasized that the three great needs in Malaya were to unify civil-military authority, to secure Chinese cooperation in the antiguerrilla campaigns, and to organize Chinese militia units for the self-protection of the loyal Chinese population. Similarly, in the fall of 1950, the French were forced to the realization that "an effective end must be put to the antipathy between French civil and military authorities" in Indochina and that new efforts must be made to win the support of the Vietnamese in the struggle against the Viet Minh.[31]

As the government's response moves into its second phase, the new supreme political-military director of the effort plays a critical role. He not only concentrates in himself the direction of the war on all fronts, but he also dramatizes the determination and ability of the government to carry through the struggle and to maintain the safety of its supporters. In varying degrees this critically important role was played by Magsaysay in the Philippines, Templer in Malaya, Papagos in Greece, and de Lattre de Tassigny in Indochina. Above all, the leader plays the role of the politician in campaigning for the support and the confidence of the target group. Templer and Magsaysay devoted large portions of their time to touring the disturbed areas, restoring direct communications with the target group, and demonstrating personally the interests of the government in the well-being and safety of the target-group members.

The director of the counterrevolutionary effort may be a civilian cabinet officer (Magsaysay), a military theater commander (de Lattre), or military commander and civilian governor (Templer). Irrespective of his formal position, however, to be successful he must effectively exercise complete control of the counterrevolutionary effort. Magsaysay, for instance, insisted upon the unification of the Philippine Constabulary and the military forces, previously in separate departments, under a single chief of staff. Like Hoche in the pacification of the Vendée, he must be a "skilled politician as well as soldier." Magsaysay, for instance, although a civilian, personally commanded units in the field. The essential element is the vigor, determination, and ability of the individual, not his previous background or experience. Like the great colonial soldiers Bugeaud, Galliéni, and Lyautey, he must play both political and military roles; and, as Lyautey said, it is not the label but the man that matters, "the right man in the right place."[32]

The crucial step in the change in the approach of the government toward the revolutionary war is the recognition that the decisive aspect of the struggle is not the defeat of the enemy forces but the reconquest of the confidence of the contested population. To win the population, it is necessary to know the population, to win an audience with it, to detach it from the revolutionary forces, and eventually to control it.[33] The first necessity is for the government to convince the target group that it can provide for its security. This is the military job. Then, however, it must reintegrate the target group into the existing community. New organizational units devoted to this end provide help. In Algeria in 1955, for example, the government established the Special Administrative Sections to work with the Algerian Moslems and to carry on the activities which before 1945 had been performed by the Arab Bureaus. A nongovernmental group, the Malayan Chinese Association, founded in February, 1949, played an important role in combatting the appeal of the Communists to the Malayan Chinese and in bringing about their reintegration into the Malayan community. In the Philippines civil-affairs officers were appointed to undertake the "important tasks of interpreting the army to the people and of winning civilian support for the army activities against the Huks." The basic goal is to stimulate favorable attitudes toward the government on the part of the target group. In Malaya Templer taught the police that "in the long run their most important task was not to catch the terrorists but to persuade the public to look upon them as friends." In the Philippines Magsaysay ruthlessly suppressed police terrorism against the peasants and instituted a campaign of "attraction and fellowship."[34]

The reintegration of portions of the target group into the community may require extensive physical movement and resettlement. In Malaya, for instance, thousands of "squatters" making a meager living on government land close to the jungle became a major source of support and supplies for the guerrillas. One decisive action of the government in its struggles against the guerrillas was the movement and resettlement of these "squatters" in new villages, where they were provided with adequate work, land, and protection. According to one French officer the three most effective methods of pacification were the "tache d'huile" of Lyautey, the establishment of forbidden zones in which all nongovernment personnel were presumed to be enemies, and the regrouping of the population. In Cambodia, in 1952-1953, thousands of peasants were regrouped to provide for their own security and welfare.[35] In the Philippines Magsaysay created the EDCOR farms in Mindanao for the resettlement and rehabilitation of the Hukbalahaps. Significantly, one of the principal attractions of EDCOR to the rebels was the promise of peace and security which they offered.

The conduct of an effective counterrevolutionary action by a government thus requires a major change in the leadership, attitude, and functions of the military forces. The armed forces of the state become an instrument of persuasion as well as an instrument of coercion. The military become the chain which binds a potentially disaffected social group to the broader community. As one student of the Philippine anti-Huk campaign observed:

> The EDCOR farms created a radically new role for the army. No longer were the armed forces limited to defending the nation and destroying the enemy. The army was to serve the people in a new way—constructively and creatively. It would rehabilitate the Huks and restore them to the nation as loyal productive citizens.
>
> A foreign news correspondent [observing the EDCOR villages] . . . said, "I have seen many armies, but this one beats them all. This is an army with a social conscience."[36]

As Girardet makes clear in his essay in this volume, the French Army in Algeria not only developed nonmilitary functions and organizations but also a political program based on the continuing French presence in Algeria and social, economic, and political equality for the Moslem population. This "social conscience" of the French Army contrasted with the indecisiveness of the French government and the self-interested devotion to the status quo of the French colons.

As a result of the weakness of the defense in revolutionary war, the security of the target group can be protected only by the mobilization of the group itself. Militarily speaking, the formation of local militia units for this purpose is absolutely essential, as the regular military forces of the government would never suffice to guarantee security. One French officer has estimated that at least a ten-to-one superiority is necessary for effective internal defense, and in some areas of Malaya it was necessary to have a ratio of sixty-five armed men to every known terrorist.[37] Local militia units not only serve to re-establish confidence and security within the target group but also tend to cement its commitment to the side of the government. By 1952 the British in Malaya had organized over 244,000 home guards for the protection of the villages. In the Philippines and Indochina similar units were found to be indispensable.[38]

The goals of the conflicting parties and the importance of maintaining confidence in victory generally render nugatory any efforts to arrive at truces or agreements between the government and antigovernment forces. Between 1946 and 1948 the Roxas and Quirino Administrations in the Philippines attempted to reach a peaceful settlement with the Huks. One three-month truce ended "in bitter fighting," and a subsequent suspension of hostilities came to naught when the Huks refused to surrender their arms. Efforts to work out a basis for cooperation between the Communists and the Nationalists in China inevitably failed. Repeated negotiations between the French and the Viet Minh in Indochina did not produce any basis for agreement. In 1955 efforts to arrange a peaceful settlement in Malaya also broke down. In most of these instances the government was willing to offer a general amnesty to rebels who would surrender their arms, abandon their revolutionary activities, and resume normal peacetime employment. The rebels, on the other hand, normally were willing to abandon temporarily the military struggle, but not to surrender their arms or to give up their organization and its revolutionary aims. For them the truce or armistice was a shift in tactics but not in goal. On the other hand, any compromise by the government or agreement with the revolutionaries inevitably would raise questions in the minds of members of the target group about the determination of the government to maintain itself and to maintain order. As Jacques Soustelle remarked about Algeria:

> If the conviction that France will remain in Algeria is not inculcated in everyone, no Moslem, no matter how closely he may be bound to us by heart or by interest, will remain at our side. . . . Any political movement, any statement, any article in the press giving the impression that we will come to terms with terrorism—in other words, that the terrorists will some day be in a position to settle outstanding scores—drives the Algerian Moslems further from us.[39]

The decisive aspect of revolutionary war thus is the struggle for the loyalty of the vulnerable sector. In a sense, the war is conducted like an agonizing and bloody electoral campaign. If the counterelite can establish and maintain itself as the leader of the alienated sector, it has won its battle. If that sector is insufficient to maintain a state, continued strife is inevitable. If a territorially defined and viable state is feasible, succession from the old political community is the only solution. Victory for the government, in turn, can only be achieved by the reintegration of the alienated group into the over-all community and its participation in the political system.

The ability of a government to react successfully to a revolutionary war depends upon the perception and political strength of its leaders. The operations required in the second phase of the war often run counter to traditional ideas and established interests. The more detached a government is from the society disrupted by revolutionary war, the more able it will be to surmount these obstacles. An imperial government, for instance, may develop a broad view of the relations among the various groups in the colonial society and possess the ability to impose upon that society the social, economic, and political reforms necessary to reintegrate the target group into the community. A non-imperial government faced with revolutionary war may be unable to deal effectively with the war because it depends upon the very groups which the counterelite is challenging. In such circumstances the guidance and discipline of an allied government may be necessary to institute the measures required to win the revolutionary war. The British government was able to handle the Chinese insurrection in Malaya much easier than a Malayan government could have. On the other hand, divisions of opinion in the home country of the imperial government may hamper the ability of that government to fight the war. If these divisions make the government unable to devise at the political level a strategy for the conduct of the war, subordinate groups, such as the French Army in Algeria, may well attempt to assume that responsibility.

Many French writers have called revolutionary war the most probable form of future conflict. It is, however, the product of peculiar conditions. The decline of colonialism removes its best breeding ground. The revolutionary wars of the late 1940's, moreover, were in many respects an outgrowth of World War II: the insurrectionary counterelites usually began as anti-Axis guerrillas and accumulated weapons and experience which they used in the postwar period.[40] In southeast Asia the tactics of the Communist parties were shaped by the Chinese Communist victory; the revolutionary wars in the Philippines, Malaya, Indochina, and the attempted insurrections in Indonesia, Burma, and India, all reflected the Communist line of the moment. That line may again, of course, endorse these tactics. In the independent states of Asia and Africa, however, this hardly seems necessary. Their governments are often too weak to require it, and easier routes to power exist through propaganda, infiltration, and coup d'état. The Cold War competition of the major powers, however, could lead them to intervene to strengthen incipient revolutionary movements or tottering counter-revolutionary governments. Such interventions would then increase the ability of both sides to wage a prolonged revolutionary war.

Revolutionary war is most likely in a society occupying an extensive territory and divided between different communities and races in which one group predominates in the government. Potentialities for revolutionary war exist in many Latin American countries: the "Prestes column" of the 1920's in Brazil could well be the embryonic prototype of more elaborate movements to come. Conceivably the struggles between settler governments and African natives could also take this form. In South Africa, and possibly elsewhere, however, the lines may become so tightly drawn that the violence will take the form of direct intercommunal warfare rather than political competition between government and counterelite for support from the same group.

V: Reform Coups and Modernization

In contrast to revolutionary war, a coup d'état can only be undertaken by a group that is already a participant in the existing political system and that possesses institutional bases of power within that system. In particular, the instigating group needs the support of some elements in the armed forces. In a revolutionary war the insurrectionists build up strength by fighting the government; in a coup they acquire strength by taking over the government. The last and least important step in a revolutionary war is the first and the decisive step in a coup. A revolutionary war lasts years. In a coup, on the other hand, "Everything probably depends on the first two hours."[41]

In and of themselves, coups, like elections, strongly resemble each other. Coup is distinguished from coup, not by the techniques by which power is seized, but by the nature of the groups that seize it and the uses they make of it. V. O. Key, Jr., has suggested a distinction between critical elections and routine elections; so also there are coups which usher in momentous changes and those whose results are hardly perceptible.

At least three types of coups can be distinguished. In the *governmental* coup, or "palace revolution," the leadership of the government is changed, but no significant change takes place in the social structure or in groups and institutions participating in politics and supporting the government. Like the cabinet crises of the Third and Fourth Republics, governmental coups reflect underlying stability. At the other extreme, the *revolutionary* coup ushers in fundamental changes. It differs from a governmental coup not in the initial seizure of power but in the postcoup efforts to make basic social and economic changes and to alter the underlying distribution of power within the political system by eliminating or subordinating some groups and adding or strengthening others. In Egypt in July, 1952, for instance, the Free Officers originally planned only a "modest *coup d'état*." Once having overthrown the government, however, they found themselves impelled to expand their authority and make more radical changes.

By January, 1953 what had begun as a coup turned into a revolution. No longer was the old political system to be tolerated; no longer would the traditional social and economic structure remain intact.[42]

Thus, the seizure of power took on many characteristics of a revolutionary coup. A coup that proceeds into a full-fledged revolutionary phase usually involves additional violence by the revolutionary government against the islands of social, political, and military resistance within society. Often the result is civil war. While a revolutionary war is revolution from the outside in, a revolutionary coup is revolution from the inside out. The revolutionary war is a war of attrition against government and society; the revolutionary coup is a blitzkrieg against the government and a war of attrition by the government against society. A third type of coup, the *reform* coup, falls somewhere between the other two. A combination of military and civilian groups seizes power intending to make reforms in the political, economic, or social structure. They usually do make some reforms, though they do not instigate a convulsive revolutionary process. Instead, the coalition responsible for the coup usually begins to disintegrate after a few years. New alignments are formed with opposition elements. The momentum of change slows down, and in due course another coup takes place, with a new coalition coming to power dedicated to making different changes in the system.

In the underdeveloped areas of the world the governmental coup was the traditional means by which leadership was changed. The nineteenth-century history of Latin America was dominated by palace revolutions, which were not "real" revolutions. Similarly, in the Middle East Arab and Ottoman military chiefs often deposed their rulers without changing the political or social structure.[43] In both areas, however, governmental coups became less frequent in the twentieth century. In Latin America in the last decades of the nineteenth century and the first years of the twentieth fewer coups occurred and military men were less often leaders of the government. It seemed for a time as if the old pattern of governmental coups had been broken and that democratic and constitutional institutions were clearly emerging. Then in the second quarter of the twentieth century this tendency was reversed, and coups began to increase in frequency. "Argentina, Brazil, and Chile, for example, all relatively peaceful in the first quarter of the twentieth century, were unusually turbulent in the quarter-century following the great depression."[44] The amount of time that the presidency in the twenty Latin American republics was occupied by a military man rose markedly from 28.7 per cent in the decade 1917-1927 to 38.5 per cent between 1927 and 1937, 49 per cent in 1937-1947, and 45.5 per cent in 1947-1957.[45] In the Middle East the twentieth-century period of reform coups was inaugurated by the Young Turks in 1908. Shortly after freeing themselves from foreign rule or dominance, countries normally began to experience frequent coups d'état. Coups were a sign of independence and the real beginning of the processes of modernization and development. Iraq experienced seven coups between 1936 and 1941 and two more in 1952 and 1958. Four coups occurred in Syria between 1949 and 1952. Egypt's first coup after full independence from British influence came in 1952; a few years after independence, reform coups also took place in Pakistan, the Sudan, and Burma.

Reform coups tend to follow a dialectical process resembling the swings in the political pendulum in a constitutional democracy.[46] *Radical* reform coups are followed in a few years by *conservative* reform coups. The radical coups are usually led by army officers, middle-class civilians, leaders of reformist political parties (where these exist), and, possibly, labor leaders. Military leaders usually have a crucial role in the radical coup. The army is more exposed to Western influences than other groups in society; its officers usually include a high proportion of able, energetic, nationalistic, and upwardly mobile individuals from middle-class backgrounds; it is the one social and governmental institution capable of unified, effective, and disciplined

action.[47] While the higher ranks of the army may be affiliated with oligarchical and conservative elements, the field-grade officers frequently have close
ties with nationalistic, middle-class, civilian leaders. In some instances lawyers and teachers may shift to military careers in order to further social and
economic changes. In societies where civilian politics is corrupt and stale-
mated the army often appears to be the one organization capable of getting
things done. Their own success in accomplishing military and engineering
projects may stimulate in the soldiers the confidence that they can also solve
broader social problems.

The radical reformers are almost always highly nationalistic, progressive,
authoritarian, and developmental-minded. They also tend to be contemptu-
ous of politics and the politician. In some cases this is manifested in an
apolitical, technocratic, managerial approach, glorifying the uncorrupt administrator who stands above party and is devoted solely to the national
good. In other instances the contempt of politics becomes a more explicit
contempt for the institutions of parliamentary democracy as they formerly
existed in that country. The armed forces, it is said, must guide the nation
through a "tutelary" or "transitional" phase, after which a purified democracy will be inaugurated. In these instances the leaders of the reform coup
have no permanent political substitutes for democracy—they still adhere to
the cliches and rallying cries of the democratic ideology—but they argue on
a pragmatic basis that the operation of democratic institutions must be
temporarily postponed.[48] Reformers in a third category go beyond this to
espouse an explicitly antidemocratic political ideology. This was particularly
true in Latin America, where corporatist, semifascist ideologies were often
popular with military reformers in the 1930's and 1940's. These young
officers, in the words of Lieuwen:

became the sponsors of fundamental change and reform, the underminers of traditional
institutions, the proponents of public-welfare measures. Democratic political institutions
were of less concern to them. Indeed, they were often the leading advocates of militarized,
authoritarian government and were apt to speak scornfully of "decadent" democracy.

In other instances, such as Venezuela and Guatemala, some military reformers were linked to groups with leftist and socialist ideologies. The particular location of the reformers in the traditional European spectrum,
however, was generally meaningless. In some respects Peron was a fascist
and in others a left-wing socialist. The reform coup of 1943 in Bolivia was,
as Lieuwen concisely puts it, "authoritarian and even Fascist in form, social
and even proletarian in content."[49] Where does a Nasser or a Kassim fit in
the traditional left-right categories? Whatever form it assumed, the ideology
of the radical reformers was seldom spelled out explicitly and in detail. In
practice the reformers tended to be eclectic and pragmatic.

Each coup which brings in a new group of leaders, like each American
election which brings in a new administration, usually produces a brief
"honeymoon" period in which the leaders of the coup enjoy widespread popularity and support. This does not last long, however, for the coup arouses
expectations which cannot be satisfied; once the old government has been

ousted, conflicts develop among the various elements which supported the change. The objectives of the coup are found to be mutually contradictory; the expansion of the military forces conflicts with new social welfare programs; and the acquisition of weapons from foreign countries conflicts with efforts to achieve greater independence from them.[50] When fissures of this nature develop among the supporters of an administration in the United States, the leaders of the administration work out compromises where possible and, where impossible, carefully choose the groups they wish to pacify and those they must antagonize. The administration also knows definitely that it will continue to occupy governmental office for a fixed length of time. The radical reformers in power after a coup d'état, on the other hand, work under different conditions: their tenure is indefinite, and the prerogatives and temptations of office breed in the leaders of the radical regime the graft and corruption that characterized the old regime. The longer they stay in office, the more grievances and conflicts among their supporters accumulate, and the more likely they are to be thrown out of office by another coup led by another coalition of civil and military elements. This fate can be avoided or delayed only by the continuing mobilization of new supporters for the government. The relatively narrow scope of politics thus becomes an opportunity rather than a restriction for the leaders of the coup if they are not prevented by their social and economic attitudes and interests from taking advantage of it. By appealing to peasant, working class, and regional groups, the leaders of the coup offset losses elsewhere, maintain themselves in power, and enhance their ability to carry out reforms in economic development, land reform, and social welfare.

Strong pressures thus exist to lead a radical coup in a revolutionary direction. Often the first manifestation of these tendencies prompts a conservative countercoup. On the other hand, if the radicals do succeed in expanding the scope of politics, they also succeed in creating for themselves new sources of support. The more revolutionary and authoritarian the radical dictatorship, the broader its appeal and the more widespread the sense of participation by previously apolitical groups. Peron aroused a new sense of "Dignity and self-respect" in the workers. In Colombia, Rojas Pinilla

turned the clock forward on social achievement for the masses. He gave them status and a sense of their importance, if only because his government has emphasized their welfare. . . .

In this sense, paradoxically, the military dictator is making a substantial contribution toward democracy. . . .

Ultimate accomplishment of this process may require many Rojas Pinillas. . . . But the military dictatorships make their necessary contribution, a lasting one with their emphasis upon substantive democracy. Nothing can be the same after they have come, spoken to and for the masses and gone their way.[51]

Broadening the arena of participation seldom accomplishes more than a delay of the time when the opposition to the radical regime is able to carry off a conservative reform coup. If the scope of the political arena is not extended, the position of the radical leaders becomes more precarious, and the pendulum move quickly swings back in a conservative coup. Conservative coups are also dedicated to reform. While the leaders of the radical coups emphasize nationalism, land reform, and social welfare, those of the conservative coups stress legitimacy, fiscal responsibility, order, civil liberties, and democracy. Usually, the conservative coups are carried out by a combination of military and upper-middle-class or oligarchical elements. They attempt to put the brake on change, but they are seldom able to undo it.* After a period in power disillusionment again sets in. Younger military officers and progressive civilians begin to think of reform and development rather than stability and fiscal integrity, and the forces gather for a radical coup, which starts the process over again.

The alternation of radical and conservative reform coups was a common feature of Latin American politics after 1930. In Bolivia, for instance, a reform coup occurred in 1943, a conservative coup in 1946, and another semirevolutionary reform coup in 1952. In Venezuela, radical reformers seized power in 1945. The strong leftward tendency they inspired prompted a conservative coup in 1948. In 1958 another reform coup occurred and the radicals came back into power. The role of military men in reform coups depends less upon the radical or conservative nature of the coup than upon the nature of the civilian leaders and political organizations also supporting the coup. In Venezuela the conservatives relied largely on the military, and in 1953 General Jimenez came to power in a conservative dictatorship. Military officers participated in the radical coups of both 1945 and 1958, but the ability of leaders such as Betancourt and the organized strength of the Acción Democrática reform party meant that the military played a smaller role in the regimes following radical coups than they did in the regimes following the conservative coup. In Colombia, on the other hand, the situation was reversed. Both the Liberal and the Conservative Parties were predominantly conservative in outlook; the radical coup of 1953 was promoted by the military and produced the dictatorship of General Rojas Pinilla. After he was ousted by a conservative coup in 1957, in which military elements participated, the civilian leaders of the two political parties resumed the direction of the government.

The Latin American experience suggests that, while the military are not exclusively the defenders of the entrenched oligarchy, neither are they exclusively the harbingers of modernization. Prolonged military participation in politics inevitably means that the military reflect the divisions, stresses, and weaknesses of politics. Modernization is not the product of any one particular group, however "modernized" that group may be in comparison with the rest of society. Rather it is the product of coup and countercoup in which military elements play important roles in inaugurating both conservative and radical regimes. The desire for reform produced the 1958 coups in Asia and the Sudan; the process of reform will demand many more.

---

*The fact that radical coups against an entrenched oligarchy usually promise "reform" and conservative coups against a strong-man popular dictator usually promise "democracy" explains why each coup is hailed in the Anglo-Saxon world as ushering in a new age.

Each radical or conservative change in direction itself tends to be a complex event moving through several phases. In moderated and abbreviated form this pattern resembles the same phases through which major revolutionary upheavals usually proceed. Often several anticipatory attempts at coups d'état come before the actual seizure of power by the insurrectionists. These are signs of the shift in political coalitions: like by- or midterm elections in a democracy, they are warnings of the more fundamental changes to come. The critical seizure of power is then usually followed by one or more consolidating coups in which the original tendencies of the first coup are further strengthened. Following this, the momentum of reform usually subsides unless the leaders of the regime attempt drastically to expand their sources of support. In Egypt the conspiratorial efforts of the middle-class military reformers dated from World War II. The Free Officers Group was formally organized in 1949. A coup originally scheduled for March, 1952, was postponed. In July, however, as political restiveness increased, the Free Officers seized power. During the next eighteen months the coup moved through its consolidating phases: the Wafd, Communist, and Moslem Brethren opposition elements were successively eliminated, and in April, 1954, Naguib, the popular moderate leader behind whom the more conservative elements attempted to rally, was displaced by Nasser.[52]

In Argentina several efforts to overthrow the conservative government were made before the Group of United Officers led by Peron eventually ousted President Castillo in June, 1943. In October, 1945, Peron, with the help of labor, consolidated his power and removed many of those officers who had participated in the original coup. In September, 1951, conservative military groups attempted an unsuccessful revolt against Peron. Another effort, made when Peron was embroiled with the Church in June, 1955, also failed. Finally, the conservative officers captured power and removed Peron in September, 1955, and General Eduardo Leonardi became president. Leonardi, however, attempted "to follow a moderate policy" and "was attacked for his hesitation in 'de-Peronizing' the army and for his alleged favoritism of reactionary Catholic elements in the provisional government." Two months after he took office, he was ousted in a consolidating coup which brought General Aramburu to power.[53] Similarly, in Guatemala several efforts were made to remove the traditionalist regime of General Jorge Ubico before he was finally overthrown in June, 1944, and replaced by a moderate government led by General Pone Valdes, "who tried to protect the old order." Four months later a consolidating coup overthrew Valdes and eventually brought to power the radical administration of Arevalo.[54] An almost classic account of a consolidating coup is afforded by Alford Carleton's description of the relation between the March, 1949, coup in Syria of Colonel Husni Za'im which overthrew the government of President al-Quwwatli and the August, 1949, coup of Colonel Sami Hinnawi which ousted Za'im:

It gradually came to light that the second coup d'état was, in a real sense, merely the fulfillment of the original intention of the first. Those who had been Za'im's associates in the overthrow of the al-Quwwatli regime had to be rid of him before they could accomplish the original purpose of the first conspiracy, which was to unseat those who had proved themselves incompetent in the administration of the state and the conduct of the Palestine war, and to replace them in civil authority by those who had been the most upright and able critics of the old regime.[55]

In a similar pattern, young officer reformers in Bolivia overthrew the government in May, 1936, and created a Socialist Republic headed by Colonel David Toro. This regime introduced a number of reforms, but in July, 1937, "Lt. Colonel German Busch, who had engineered the coup which put Colonel Toro in power, overthrew Toro." Busch's government, in turn, "continued and intensified the general policies of the Toro administration."[56]

The Middle Eastern and Asian reform coups usually involved little bloodshed. In Latin America after World War II extensive violence occurred only in Colombia, Bolivia, and Cuba. Violence was limited because government was weak and politics small. In some instances, also, civilian leaders of the government invited the military to step in. So long as the participants in politics were relatively few in number and constituted in themselves a closely knit group, violence among them was not likely to be extensive. In Burma, for instance, military and political leaders were closely linked by marriage.[57] The long-run tendency of reform coups, however, is to activate more groups politically and to broaden participation in politics. Inevitably, this will affect the processes by which governments and policies are changed. As the political system becomes more complex, coups become more difficult. The army no longer can dominate politics. Too many groups participate in the political process and are able to exercise an effective veto over the choice of rulers. If an effort is made to override their interests, they may retaliate with their own forms of violence or coercion. General strikes, for instance, played major roles in the overthrow of regimes in Guatemala in 1944, in Haiti in 1946 and 1956, and in Peron's consolidating coup in Argentina in 1945.[58] When numerous groups participate in politics, he who wishes to secure power needs a broader base than is normally responsible for the classic coup. Kapp could be stopped by a general strike, but not Hitler. Similarly, the tradition of the *pronunciamiento* in Spain was broken in 1936. The revolt of the army produced not a coup but a civil war as labor, radical, Catalan, and other groups came to the support of the government. In the more radical of the reform coups workers' militias were often created either to aid in the seizure of power against elements of the regular army or to counterbalance the regular army after the seizure of power.

A succession of reform coups thus eventually tends to undermine the possibility of coups. Changes in power and policy require either complex bargaining among a large number of groups or bloody civil war. As the scope of politics is broadened, violence becomes less frequent but more virulent. As Dankwart Rustow has pointed out:

A century or two ago, vezirs might be banished or executed, sultans deposed or murdered: yet the average craftsman, villager, or nomad would scarcely notice any change. Today, by contrast, any political assassination or *coup d'état*—at times even a mere election— tends to be accompanied by extensive police or even military action, by mass arrests and deportations, by the suspension of newspapers, and by political trials. Instability, once a mere ripple on the surface, now engulfs the entire society.[59]

The democratization of government in a society in which violence is a key part of government also means the democratization of violence. The coup d'état—the limited war of domestic violence—may be replaced by the revolutionary war or other violent insurrection involving numerous elements of society. Conceivably, the conservative elements may retreat gracefully before the demands of the emerging groups, thereby permitting processes of peaceful change to develop. If they do not, the decline in the role of the military in society and government may well be accompanied by an increase in the role of violence.

Western observers often stress two key goals for the underdeveloped areas—economic development and modernization, on the one hand, and political stability, on the other. The compatibility of these goals, however, is very limited. Great Britain, to be sure, industrialized with relatively little internal strife, but even in the United States the process of modernization required the largest war of the century between 1815 and 1914. The likelihood that the nations of southern Asia, the Middle East, Africa, and Latin America can modernize their social and economic life without violent political dislocations seems relatively remote. Economic and social change requires political change. Without a constitutional tradition of peaceful change some form of violence is virtually inevitable. In the underdeveloped areas the alternatives, broadly speaking, are not constitutional change or violent change, but gradual change through a succession of reform coups d'état or tumultuous change through revolutionary wars or revolutionary coups d'état. The enforced absence of change, political "stability" without coups d'état, is often only the breeding ground for worse forms of violence. In Mexico, for instance, while General Porfirio Diaz ruled with an iron hand from 1877 to 1911, the ownership of the land became concentrated in fewer and fewer hands, and the plight of the peon was unrelieved. Diaz kept power for himself and order for his country for thirty-three years at the price of completely obstructing social and economic reform. The break, when it came in the overthrow of Diaz with relatively little bloodshed in the coup of May, 1911, released forces which perpetrated a decade of revolutionary upheaval and violence. Similarly, in other Latin American countries the longer entrenched and the more firmly opposed to change were the old regimes, the more the coups by which they were toppled tended to develop along radical or revolutionary lines. The colonels' revolt of 1943 in Argentina overthrew a traditionalist regime that had dominated the country since 1930. The long tenure of General Jorge Ubico as dictator of Guatemala beginning in 1931 ended with an extreme radical coup in 1944. Forty years of peaceful, civilian, oligarchical rule in Colombia ended in 1948 with five years of civil war in which over 100,000 people lost their lives. Batista's domination of Cuban politics from 1933 to 1959, except for a few years in the late 1940's, produced revolutionary war and Castro. The long reigns of the Trujillo family in the Dominican Republic (since 1930) and the Somoza family in Nicaragua (since 1936) suggest that their demises probably will be followed by revolutionary developments.

The alternative to social revolution on the Mexican or Cuban model appears to be a progression of reform coups. Reform coups are the products of the drives for westernization and modernization. Frequent coups are a sign of change and progress. Not all coups, to be sure, produce reforms, but virtually all reforms are produced by coups. Frequent reform coups d'état should be viewed not as pathological, but rather as a healthy mechanism of gradual change, the nonconstitutional equivalent of periodic changes in party control through the electoral process.

VI: International Tension and Domestic Violence— The Doctrines of La Guerre Révolutionnaire and Indirect Aggression

Various attempts have been made in the West to interpret and explain the violence in the politics of the underdeveloped areas. One common interpretation sees the rise of the new forms of domestic violence as directly related to the decline of the old forms of intergovernmental violence. In its most general form, the argument that a decrease in the frequency of intergovernmental conflict is likely to increase the frequency of domestic violence usually assumes that mankind's propensity to fight remains roughly constant. War is inevitable, and if it becomes unprofitable in one locale, it reappears in another. As a general truth, however, this proposition is not valid. To be sure, some relationship exists between the internal and external conflicts of a state, and external conflict does tend to increase internal unity and cohesion.[60] It does not, however, follow that external peace stimulates internal conflict, and the students of conflict have produced no significant evidence to show that such a relationship exists. Sweden and Switzerland have enjoyed both internal and external peace for decades. Governments, on the other hand, may attempt to stave off internal war with a nongovernment at home by instigating external war with a foreign government abroad. To the extent that the new inhibitory factors on interstate wars tend to close off this course of action, they also tend to make it more difficult to avoid domestic violence. Governments, however, are fairly ingenious. As alternatives to foreign wars as unifiers, they may resort to more intensive domestic action to suppress the embryonic conflict, in which case "police state" measures are the result of the absence rather than the presence of external conflict. In addition, governments may engage in nonviolent, peaceful adventurism, in which an external enemy is identified and castigated and serves as a target for group hostility, although the government carefully refrains from resorting to violence. The government may instead go to some lengths to provoke the opposing government to use violence first. Also, the reduction in interstate wars moderates one of the causes of domestic strife. "Civil war," as Sir George Clark observed of the seventeenth century, "was often a sequel to external victory . . . [and] a consequence of external defeat."[61]

While there may be no necessary general relationship between the inhibition of interstate violence and the prevalence of intrastate violence, this does not exclude the possibility of a relationship existing between the two in the special circumstances of the mid-twentieth century. That such a relationship does exist is a key assumption of the French doctrine of *la guerre révolutionnaire* and the American concept of indirect aggression. For both theories the new forms of domestic violence are primarily methods of intergovernmental conflict.

The French doctrine of *la guerre révolutionnaire* was in many respects the counterpart to the American doctrine of limited war.[62] The American doctrine was a reaction to a traumatic military experience in Korea, the French doctrine to similar experiences in Indochina and Algeria. To American thinkers the logical result of the balance of terror was limited war; to French military men it was insurrectionary war. While American theory distinguished between general war involving thermonuclear weapons, on the one hand, and limited war with conventional or tactical nuclear weapons, on the other, French theory drew a threefold distinction. "La guerre classique," the traditional form of general war, was now highly improbable. The two relevant types of military action were "la guerre nucléaire" and "la guerre révolutionnaire."[63] The former, the French emphasized, was likely to include all forms of interstate war; it was expensive, destructive, and relatively unlikely. While American theorists saw limited war as the most probable form of future Soviet military action, French writers assigned a similar role to *la guerre révolutionnaire*. In both countries it was argued that this new phenomenon required a major reorientation of military thought and new military doctrines. Yet, while the novel features of the new form of warfare were emphasized, in both countries extensive efforts were also made to develop its historical precedents. In both countries also it was emphasized that the new form of warfare was peculiarly suited to Marxist-Leninist theory and practice.

The parallels in the development of the doctrines of limited war and *la guerre révolutionnaire* should not obscure significant differences in the substances of these doctrines. The doctrine of limited war was a pure theory of intergovernmental war. The model for it was derived from the eighteenth-century world of territorial nation-states in which absolute governments exercised strict control over their military forces and used them as instruments in their diplomacy, and in which the struggles among the states were normally over specific pieces of territory and did not involve either the existence of the state or the overthrow of its political and social system. The basic model for the French doctrine, on the other hand, was not eighteenth-century Europe but twentieth-century China. While the limited-war theorists harked back to Clausewitz, those of *la guerre révolutionnaire* invoked Mao Tse-tung. *La guerre révolutionnaire,* they emphasized, was total war within a society. In it, to be sure, war was the instrument of politics, but its distinguishing characteristic was the intermingling of economic, political, and military means. The theory of limited war, in many respects so classically military, was in large part articulated in the United

States by civilian social scientists. The theory of *la guerre révolutionnaire,* on the other hand, involving the intimate mixture of political and military roles, techniques, and forces, was to a much larger extent the product of professional military officers.

The theorists of *la guerre révolutionnaire* recognized that it was a form of domestic war. It was, however, they insisted, a product of interstate conflict. They argued that it was primarily an instrument of one government, the Soviet Union, against another government, France, waged through satellites and political instruments. "The Algerian rebellion," one official French document stated, "is incontestably a movement inspired and actively supported by foreign countries which interfere impudently in the internal affairs of France."[64] *La guerre révolutionnaire,* Claude Delmas said, is the means whereby one state can make war against another without provoking general conflict and without even appearing to be resorting to war. The peculiar nature of *la guerre révolutionnaire* (guerrilla warfare plus psychological warfare) bore the imprint of the doctrine and tactics of international Communism. As Delmas declared, "la guerre révolutionnaire n'existerait pas (ou en resterait au stade de la guerilla) si les parties communistes n'etaient pas des instruments de la politique soviétique."[65] In some cases the French thinkers suggested that *la guerre révolutionnaire* was always the instrument of Communists; in others they argued that even where it was not the product of Communism the Communists always benefitted from its use; always, however, they maintained that the methods of *la guerre révolutionnaire* were inspired by Communist theory and practice, and that the Communists were the instruments of the Soviet Union.[66] Having linked the origins of *la guerre révolutionnaire* with the deterrence of intergovernmental wars and the nature of it with Communist theory and practice, the French thinkers inevitably were drawn to argue that every manifestation of *la guerre révolutionnaire* was the product of Communist action on behalf of the Soviet Union. The French military thus arrived at the conclusion shared by many civilian leaders of the government that in Algeria as in Indochina the real enemy was international Communism.[67]

Like the doctrine of *la guerre révolutionnaire,* the concept of indirect aggression was stimulated initially by the struggle with the Communist movements of southeast Asia. The Manila pact of September, 1954, provided that the parties would cooperate not only "to resist armed aggression" but also "to prevent and counter subversive activities directed from without against their territorial integrity and political stability." Although the operative terms of the pact in Article II were directed primarily at what Professor W. Macmahon Ball has called "subversion from without," the actual antisubversive activities jointly undertaken by members of the pact have been largely directed at "subversion from within." Committees and a staff established under the pact help to coordinate the antisubversive efforts of the members and to provide for the exchange of information.[68] The invocation of indirect aggression as a justification for direct American counteraction did not come until the 1958 coup d'état in Baghdad and the American intervention in Lebanon. Here the evidence of subversion from without was much more definite. American action was justified, the President argued, because the "Cairo, Damascus and Soviet radios" had encouraged an insurrection against the established government of Lebanon and the insurrectionists were being supplied with "sizeable amounts of arms, ammunition, and money and by personnel infiltrated from Syria to fight against the lawful authorities." The aim of these actions was to "overthrow the legally constituted Government of Lebanon and to install by violence a government which would subordinate the independence of Lebanon to the policies of the United Arab Republic."[69]

The doctrine of *la guerre révolutionnaire* began with the result—the struggles in Indochina, Algeria, and elsewhere—and argued that the Soviet Union and its subservient international Communist movement were in large part causes of this result. The doctrine of indirect aggression, on the other hand, began with the causes—the means by which one government can encourage violence against another government—and then argued that these causes could produce calamitous results. "Through use of inflammatory radio broadcasts; through infiltration of weapons, agents, and of bribe money," Mr. Dulles said, "through incitement to murder and assassination; and through threats of personal violence it becomes possible for one nation to destroy the genuine independence of another." Toleration of indirect aggression, he warned, would lead to a third world war.[70] Thus, while the doctrine of *la guerre révolutionnaire* stressed the extent to which Communist influence was responsible for actual revolutionary wars, the doctrine of indirect aggression stressed the extent to which one government, without resort to force, can produce revolution in another. The existence of an external base of support beyond the territory of the target government is, of course, a major aid to revolutionary forces. The basis for the revolution, however, must exist within the society in which it takes place. The techniques mentioned by President Eisenhower and Mr. Dulles can only serve to encourage and to support already existing antigovernmental forces in the target country.

The doctrine of indirect aggression tends to underestimate its pervasiveness and to overestimate its effectiveness. If "indirect aggression were to be admitted as a legitimate means of promoting international policy," Mr. Dulles declared, "small nations would be doomed and the world would become one of constant chaos, if not of war." Any change of government in any country, however, whether by violence or otherwise, presumably affects the interests of the major world powers. Governments attempt to encourage favorable changes in foreign governments and to prevent unfavorable ones. The pervasiveness of indirect aggression in this broad sense is, however, no testimony to its effectiveness. Because all domestic violence has implications for interstate conflict, it cannot be concluded that all domestic violence is caused by interstate conflict.

The tendency to overestimate the ease with which the Soviet Union can subvert or overthrow foreign governments leads to the conclusion that the United States can also profitably employ such tactics. "In the perfection of the instrument of subversion," one writer has said, for example, "the Soviets may have fashioned a form of unconventional military action capable of achieving victories as great as any expected from the more conventional forms of war." From this he concluded that "Subversion is not a form of action reserved for use by the Soviets alone; it can be fully as powerful if turned against them."[71] The Administration which Mr. Dulles served, however, came into power committed to a program of indirect aggression—liberation and political warfare—against the Soviet satellites. Its protestations were sufficient to make the Soviet Union until 1957 a leading advocate of UN condemnation of indirect aggression.[72] Its accomplishments, however, are a significant index of the effectiveness of the tactic.

Insurrection and subversion are primarily the weapons of indigenous antigovernments. Foreign governments, of course, may encourage antigovernments. Intervention by one government against another, however, has the potentialities and the limitations of intervention by outside personnel and money in a local election campaign. Though it can influence the result, it cannot create support where the basis for that support does not already exist, and it cannot reverse a drastically unfavorable balance of forces within the contested area. Intervention on behalf of an established government, moreover, is usually easier than intervention against it. Traditional liberal thinking has often been criticized for analyzing war and international relations in terms of the ideas and categories of domestic politics. The doctrines of *la guerre révolutionnaire* and indirect aggression, on the other hand, tend to apply to domestic political struggles the assumptions and concepts of international politics. Domestic violence, obviously, is influenced by the intensity and nature of international conflict, but it cannot be explained *simply* as the result of that conflict.

Foreign governmental intervention more often is the result of domestic violence than is domestic violence the product of foreign intervention. The longer the domestic violence continues, moreover, the more likely are foreign governments to become involved on one side or another. The Soviet Union initiated neither the Indochinese and Algerian insurrections nor the Castro revolution, but once these became established facts of political life, it could hardly be expected not to capitalize upon them. Thus, a quick coup d'état is more likely to minimize the involvement of external powers and maximize international stability than a prolonged revolutionary war. From the Western viewpoint, even a coup that topples a friendly government, such as the Kassim coup of 1958, but that installs a government with whom one can negotiate, might be preferable to an unsuccessful coup degenerating into extensive civil strife, which inevitably would involve the Soviet Union and the Western powers.

VII: Violence and Transnational Community

While the principal manifestations of domestic violence cannot be explained only by reference to *international* politics, neither can they be explained on an individual basis without reference to the general patterns of *world* politics. Outbreaks of domestic violence tend to occur in waves. In his study of Latin American politics Lieuwen identifies one wave of radical reform coups beginning with Peron's conquest of power in Argentina in 1943 and including coups or revolts in Bolivia in 1943, Ecuador and Guatemala in 1944, Brazil in 1945, El Salvador and Costa Rica in 1948, Panama and Bolivia in 1952, and Colombia in 1953. In addition, reformers came to power peacefully in Venezuela and Peru in 1945. Overlapping the reform wave was a progression of conservative coups: Venezuela and Peru in 1948, Haiti in 1950, Cuba in 1952, Guatemala and Brazil in 1954, Panama and Argentina in 1955, and Colombia in 1957.[73] In other waves of domestic violence the individual manifestations were much more closely grouped in time. In 1948, as the Communist line in Asia shifted, revolutionary wars or insurrections began in the Philippines, Burma, Indonesia, India, and Malaya. In 1956 anti-Soviet disorders shook the eastern European satellites, particularly Hungary and Poland. In 1958 military coups d'état took place in Iraq, the Sudan, Thailand, Burma, and Pakistan. In 1960 student demonstrations and riots helped to overturn the existing regimes in South Korea and Turkey, to cancel President Eisenhower's visit to Japan, and to stimulate the abortive insurrection of the Algerian colons.[74]

The reasons for these waves of violence undoubtedly vary. All of them, however, reflect the shrinking of world politics, the similarity of political conditions and forces in different countries, and the extent to which events in one country may affect those in another. At least three possible explanations exist for the waves of violence. First, they may be the result of common direction. This was certainly the case with the Communist-inspired revolutionary wars and insurrections of 1948 and 1949. Presumably it could be the case again if the Kremlin should decide that insurrection on a broad scale was a desirable way of achieving its objectives in the underdeveloped areas. Common direction, however, will not explain most of the waves of violence in domestic politics. Nor will the alternative extreme explanation of isolated parallelism, that is, the emergence in different countries of similar but unrelated situations that lead to similar and almost simultaneous coups or domestic wars. Undoubtedly, the processes of evolution in newly independent countries do follow certain broad common channels. But even if the paths of development were much more closely parallel than they are, this would still not completely explain the waves of violence. Parallelism does not necessarily imply simultaneity.

In addition to similarity of political condition, emulation is also necessary to create a wave. The power of example, the influence exercised by the "pace-setter," is a critically important result of the improvement in worldwide communications. A successful coup or insurrection by one party or group in one country inspires similar parties or groups in other countries to similar action. The conditions breeding insurrection or coup d'état must be present in these other countries, while the action of the "pace-setting" country indicates that the time may well be ripe. The success of Peron in Argentina stimulated radical military reformers in other Latin American states. The revolt in Bolivia a few months later was "obviously an echo of the events in Buenos Aires."[75] Similarly, the fall of Peron in 1955 stimulated the efforts to remove Rojas Pinilla in Colombia. The defeat of the French in one revolutionary war in Indochina directly encouraged the launching of another in Algeria. The successful toppling of Syngmann Rhee's government by student, civilian, and military action in 1960 demonstrated that the United States would not intervene to uphold an unpopular ally against a popular uprising and directly encouraged students, liberals, and soldiers to undertake similar successful action in Turkey.

A wave of violence presupposes a degree of transnational political community, involving some similarity of political conditions in the different countries and some influence by the political events in one country on the political events of another. A successful coup by conservative groups in Venezuela may stimulate action by conservative groups in Peru, but it is not likely to produce any comparable response in the United States, France, or Pakistan. In this sense, Peru and Venezuela are part of a political community from which the other three countries are excluded. On the other hand, a swing to the right in the United States may be the product of conditions that also produce a shift to the right in Canada, and the change in the United States may hasten the change in Canada. Or a military coup in Pakistan may serve as a model for comparable coups in other southern Asian states, but it is not likely to be relevant to political developments in Italy, Japan, or the Congo. Revolutions (and other forms of domestic violence reflecting changing political tides) are seldom exported, but they are often imitated. They can only be imitated, however, in countries where the necessary raw materials already exist.

The dominant forms of violence of each age reflect the politics of the age. The violence of the seventeenth century reflected the decline of the Hapsburg Empire and the conflicts over religion. The limited wars and colonial wars of the eighteenth century were the natural products of the national monarchies of the old regime. The nineteenth century encompassed insurrections devoted to liberalism, democracy, and social change, on the one hand, and renewed colonial wars on the other. The first half of the twentieth century saw nationalistic rivalries and expansion produce two world wars. The rapid political and economic change in Latin America, Africa, and southern Asia has produced and will continue to produce its own distinctive patterns of violence. This violence may take the form of revolutionary wars or reform coups, and it may assume still different forms. In the new states traditionalist elements are likely to reassert themselves and to challenge the nationalist leaders who led the fight against the colonial power. Wars of secession and integration are likely between the regions of artificially defined "nation-states." In Africa intertribal wars are still possible, and intercommunal wars between white settlers and natives seem unavoidable. Governments which have achieved their independence through revolutionary war or other forms of violence have their own distinctive problems in breaking the patterns of violence established in the pre-independence era.[76] All of these forms of violence are likely to involve military forces and civil-military relations very different from those usually associated with interstate wars along European lines. Most violence will be civil violence in that it occurs within the accepted boundaries of particular political units. All violence will be civil violence in that it occurs within the great society of world politics in which almost all nations and governments recognize a common interest in minimizing intergovernmental war and in which domestic violence in one country resembles and is influenced by the patterns of violence in other countries belonging to the same transnational political community.

For the future, the "general mêlée" of the seventeenth century may be a more applicable model than the calculated wars of the eighteenth. The distinction between intergovernmental and domestic wars may fade, with violence becoming more pervasive, more dispersed, and less within the control of governments. In a sense, vast areas of the world may evolve in the direction of Europe at the beginning of the seventeenth century when

wars were not continuations of religious or dynastic or any other policy by the use of organized force, but collisions of communities. Some of these communities were the imperfect and improvised assemblages of civil war, others were the comparatively complete societies called monarchies or republics. They sometimes blundered into their struggles and sometimes went into them methodically, with their eyes open, through the regular procedure of negotiation, ultimatum, and declaration of war; sometimes they managed hostilities equally methodically, but sometimes their forces, even if they did not become mutinous or barbarous, were not servants at all but were moved by a will of their own. Peace sometimes came by rational stages, but sometimes by exhaustion and anarchy. Any component part of society might break loose and smash or obstruct any other in its movements.[77]

As in the seventeenth century, however, the proliferation of new forms of violence may herald the emergence of new and more stable political institutions.

NOTES

1. Harold D. Lasswell and Abraham Kaplan, *Power and Society* (New Haven, 1950), p. 252.
2. See, e.g., T. Abel, "The Element of Decision in the Pattern of War," *American Sociological Review*, 6 (December, 1941), 853-859. The assumption that decisions to risk or to provoke war are carefully calculated was, of course, basic to the entire strategy of deterrence pursued by the United States after World War II.
3. See John H. Herz, *International Politics in the Atomic Age* (New York, 1959), Part One.
4. On the conditions under which arms races may substitute for war, see my "Arms Races: Prerequisites and Results," *Public Policy* (Yearbook of the Graduate School of Public Administration, Harvard University), 8 (1958), 41-86.
5. See Vernon Lee Fluharty, *Dance of the Millions: Military Rule and the Social Revolution in Colombia, 1930-1956* (Pittsburgh, 1957), pp. 2, 234, 250.
6. *New York Herald Tribune*, Dec. 6, 1960, p. 24.
7. Lasswell and Kaplan, *op. cit.*, p. 274. See also Quincy Wright, *A Study of War* (Chicago, 1942), I, 256-257.
8. Karl von Clausewitz, *On War*, trans. O. J. Matthijs Jolles (Washington, 1950), pp. 15-16. Cf. Herz, *op. cit*, p. 60.
9. Nicholas Spykman, *America's Strategy in World Politics* (New York, 1942), p. 13. See also Simmel's comments on the dyad and the triad, *The Sociology of Georg Simmel* trans. and ed. Kurt H. Wolff (Glencoe, Ill., 1950), pp. 135-169.
10. Morris Janowitz, *The Professional Soldier: A Social and Political Portrait* (Glencoe, Ill., 1960), ch. 20.
11. See Maury Feld, "A Typology of Military Organization," *Public Policy*, 8 (1958), 3-40.
12. See his essay, *infra*, pp. 123-129.
13. Lasswell and Kaplan, *op. cit.*, pp. 274-275.

14. Gabriel Bonnet, *Les Guerres insurrectionelles et révolutionnaires* (Paris, 1958), pp. 34ff.

15. W. S. Stokes, "Violence as a Power Factor in Latin American Politics," *Western Political Quarterly,* 5 (Summer, 1952), 445-468.

16. Edwin Lieuwen, *Arms and Politics in Latin America* (New York, 1960), *passim.*

17. D. W. Brogan, *The Price of Revolution* (New York, 1951), pp. 19-20.

18. This discussion deals with the *phenomenon* of revolutionary war. For analysis of the French *doctrine* of *la guerre révolutionnaire,* see *infra,* pp. 40-44, and the two excellent discussions of Raoul Girardet, *infra,* pp. 127-134, and Peter Paret, "The French Army and La Guerre Révolutionnaire," *Journal of the Royal United Service Institution,* 104 (February, 1959), 59-69.

19. Quoted in Lieuwen, *op. cit.,* p. 134. See also Katherine Chorley, *Armies and the Art of Revolution* (London, 1943), p. 23.

20. Lucien Pye, *Guerrilla Communism in Malaya* (Princeton, 1956), ch. 15.

21. Lennox A. Mills, *Malaya: A Political and Economic Appraisal* (Minneapolis, 1958), pp. 48-49; Michael K. Clark, *Algeria in Turmoil* (New York, 1959), pp. 8, 131.

22. Alvin H. Scaff, *The Philippine Answer to Communism* (Stanford, 1955), p. 135; Mills, *op. cit.,* pp. 54-55; Ellen J. Hammer, *The Struggle for Indochina* (Stanford, 1954), pp. 71-75.

23. Clark, *op. cit.,* p. 453; Mills, *op. cit.,* p. 51; D. H. Rawcliffe, *The Struggle for Kenya* (London, 1954), p. 93; Brian Crozier, *The Rebels: A Study of Post-War Insurrections* (Boston, 1960), p. 53.

24. Hammer, *op. cit.,* p. 292.

25. Pye, *op. cit.,* pp. 182ff.

26. *Ibid.,* pp. 8, 67-69; Clark, *op. cit.,* pp. 6, 133; Robert A. Smith, *Philippine Freedom 1946-1958* (New York, 1958), p. 142.

27. See Crozier, *op. cit.,* pp. 159-191, for an enlightening analysis of the successes and limitations of terrorism as a weapon.

28. Pye, *op. cit.,* pp. 91, 96n.; Mills, *op. cit.,* p. 53; Hammer, *op. cit.,* p. 287; E. L. Katzenbach, Jr., "Indo-China: A Military-Political Appreciation," *World Politics,* 4 (January, 1952), 205-206; Clark, *op. cit.,* pp. 299, 307.

29. See Girardet, *infra,* pp. 130-137; Crozier, *op. cit.,* pp. 127ff.

30. Scaff, *op. cit.,* p. 28; Harry Miller, *The Communist Menace in Malaya* (New York, 1954), pp. 92-93.

31. Katzenbach, *loc. cit.,* 192-193; Mills, *op. cit.,* p. 61.

32. Jean Gottmann, "Bugeaud, Galliéni, Lyautey: The Development of French Colonial Warfare," in Edward Mead Earle (ed.), *Makers of Modern Strategy* (Princeton, 1943), pp. 240-241; G. J. Younghusband, *Indian Frontier Warfare* (London, 1898), pp. 54-55; Scaff, *op. cit.,* p. 36; Smith, *op. cit.,* pp. 154-157.

33. Ximenes, "La guerre révolutionnaire et ses données fondamentales," *Revue militaire d'information* (February-March, 1957), 19-20.

34. Girardet, *infra,* pp. 135-137; Clark, *op. cit.,* pp. 8-9; Mills, *op. cit.,* pp. 63-72ff.; Scaff, *op. cit.,* p. 36; Lt. Col. T. C. Tirona, "The Philippine Anti-Communist Campaign," *Air University Quarterly Review,* 7 (Summer, 1954), 50.

35. J. Hogard, "Guerre révolutionnaire et pacification," *Revue militaire d'information* (January, 1957), 19.

36. Scaff, *op. cit.,* p. 38.

37. Col. Nemo, "Suggestions pour l'établissement d'une doctrine," *Revue militaire générale* (April, 1958), 490; Mills, *op. cit.,* p. 54.

38. Mills, *op. cit.,* p. 54; Tirona, *loc. cit.,* 54.

39. Quoted in Clark, *op. cit.,* p. 6; Scaff, *op. cit.,* pp. 28-30; Crozier, *op. cit.,* p. 16.

40. See Crozier, *op. cit.,* pp. 106-107.

41. Capt. D. J. Goodspeed, "The Secret Army," *Revue militaire générale* (October, 1957), 333.

42. Keith Wheelock, *Nasser's New Egypt: A Critical Analysis* (New York, 1960), pp. 21-22.

43. See George I. Blanksten, "Revolutions," in Harold E. Davis (ed.), *Government and Politics in Latin America* (New York, 1958), pp. 119-121, 141-45; R. H. Fitzgibbon, "Revolutions: Western Hemisphere," *South Atlantic Quarterly,* 55 (July, 1956), 263-279; M. Khadduri, "The Role of the Military in Middle East Politics," *American Political Science Review,* 47 (June, 1953), 516-517; E. Kedourie, "Soldiers and Politicians in the Middle East," Paper presented at Seventh Round Table, International Political Science Association (Opatija, Yugoslavia, September, 1959), pp. 1-2.

44. Lieuwen, *op. cit.,* pp. 55-56, 28-35.

45. Computed from figures in R. H. Fitzgibbon, "Armies and Politics in Latin America," Paper presented at Seventh Round Table, International Political Science Association, (Opatija, Yugoslavia, September, 1959), pp. 8-9.

46. This discussion of reform coups is based primarily upon Lieuwen's illuminating analysis, *op. cit.*, chaps. 2 and 5.

47. Dankwart A. Rustow, *Politics and Westernization in the Near East* (Princeton, 1956), pp. 8-9, 13, 26, 31-32; Khadduri, *loc. cit.*, 517-519; G. J. Pauker, "Southeast Asia as a Problem Area in the Next Decade," *World Politics*, 11 (April, 1959), 341-342; Lucien Pye, "Armies in the Process of Modernization," Unpublished paper, M. I. T. Center for International Studies, July, 1959, pp. 6-19; John J. Johnson, *Political Change in Latin America* (Stanford, 1958), pp. 13-14; Lieuwen, *op. cit.*, pp. 126-129.

48. For examples of these two types, see Pye, "Armies in the Process of Modernization," p. 28; Lieuwen, *op cit.*, p. 138; J. S. Badeau, "The Revolt Against Democracy," *Journal of International Affairs*, 13 (Spring, 1959), 149.

49. Lieuwen, *op. cit.*, pp. 79, 126-127.

50. J. C. Hurewitz, "Exploding Population and Politics in the Postwar Middle East," Unpublished manuscript, 1960, pp. 63-64.

51. Fluharty, *op. cit.*, pp. 316-317. See also Fitzgibbon, *loc. cit.*, 265ff.

52. See Wheelock, *op. cit.*, pp. 12-36.

53. Lieuwen, *op. cit.*, p. 73.

54. Blanksten, *loc. cit.*, pp. 138-39. In this essay, Blanksten analyzes the Mexican Revolution and "Near Revolutions" in Guatemala and Bolivia in terms of stages derived from Crane Brinton, *The Anatomy of Revolution* (New York, 1938), and Lyford P. Edwards, *The Natural History of Revolution* (Chicago, 1927).

55. Alford Carleton, "The Syrian Coups d'Etat," *Middle East Journal*, 4 (January, 1950), 10-11.

56. Robert J. Alexander, *The Bolivian National Revolution* (New Brunswick, N. J., 1958), pp. 25-26.

57. Pye, "Armies in the Process of Modernization," p. 22.

58. George I. Blanksten, "The Politics of Latin America," in Gabriel Almond and James S. Coleman (eds.), *The Politics of the Developing Areas* (Princeton, 1960), p. 498.

59. Rustow, *op. cit.*, p. 17.

60. See Georg Simmel, *Conflict*, trans. Kurt H. Wolff (Glencoe, Ill., 1955), pp. 87ff.; Lewis A. Coser, *The Functions of Social Conflict* (Glencoe, Ill., 1956), pp. 87ff.; Wright, *op. cit.*, I, 253ff.; R. F. Murphy, "Intergroup Hostility and Social Cohesion," *American Anthropologist*, 59 (December, 1957), 1018ff. Cf. David Rapoport, "Praetorianism" (Ph.D. Thesis, Univ. of California at Berkeley, 1960), pp. 85-86, 155ff., 230.

61. Sir George Clark, *War and Society in the Seventeenth Century* (Cambridge, 1958), p. 20.

62. For analyses of the French doctrine, see Girardet, *infra*, and Paret, *loc. cit.* The literature on *la guerre révolutionnaire* is immense. Between 1956 and 1960, almost every issue of the *Revue de défense nationale*, the *Revue militaire d'information* and the *Revue militaire générale* contained something on the subject. Among leading expositions are: Claude Delmas, *La guerre révolutionnaire* (Paris, 1959); Gabriel Bonnet, *op. cit.;* *Revue militaire d'information* (February-March, 1957); *Contre Révolution: stratégie et tactique* (Paris, 1958); J. Hogard, "Guerre révolutionnaire et pacification," *Revue militaire d'information* (January, 1957), 7-24. The first three items include helpful bibliographies.

63. See, e.g., Général d'Armée Jean Valluy, "Le corps des officiers devant la Nation," *Revue militaire générale* (December, 1958), 591-611; Delmas, *op. cit.*, pp. 9, 17; Gen. Paul Gerardot, "La renaissance militaire et le problème militaire français," *Revue militaire générale* (February, 1958), 173-195.

64. 1956 Supplement to dossier on Algeria prepared for French UN delegation, quoted in Crozier, *op. cit.*, pp. 130-31.

65. Delmas, *op. cit.*, p. 44.

66. See e.g., Gen. Coche, "Armée et guerre subversive," *Revue militaire générale* (March, 1959), 367-399; Contre-Amiral Peltier, "La pensée militaire soviétique," *Revue militaire générale* (December, 1957), 649-679; Chef d'escadrons Louis Pichon, "Caractères généraux de la guerre insurrectionnelle," *Revue militaire générale* (July, 1957), 158-186; *Revue militaire d'information* (February-March, 1957), 25; Delmas, *op. cit.*, p. 50.

67. Paret, *loc. cit.*, 67.

68. M. Margaret Ball, "Seato and Subversion," *Political Science*, 11 (March, 1959),

25ff.; W. Macmahon Ball, "Political Re-examination of SEATO," *International Organization,* 12 (Winter, 1958), 21-23.

69. Dwight D. Eisenhower, Message to Congress, July 15, 1958, *Department of State Bulletin,* 39 (August 4, 1958), 182.

70. John Foster Dulles, "Foundations of Peace," Address, Veterans of Foreign Wars, New York, N. Y., *Department of State Bulletin,* 39 (September 8, 1958), 375f.

71. Theodore Wyckoff, "War by Subversion," *South Atlantic Quarterly,* 59 (Winter, 1960), 35, 45.

72. See Geoffrey Barraclough, "What Is Indirect Aggression?" *The Listener,* 60 (September 18, 1958), 403-405. For a stimulating analysis of the relations between internal and external conflict, see George Modelski, *The International Relations of Internal War* (Princeton University, Center of International Studies, Research Monograph No. 11, May 24, 1961).

73. Lieuwen, *op. cit.,* pp. 63-65.

74. See the fears expressed in London of the tendency toward "government by students," *New York Times,* June 17, 1960, p. 11.

75. Lieuwen, *op. cit.,* p. 65.

76. D. E. Ashford, "Politics and Violence in Morocco," *Middle East Journal,* 13 (Winter, 1959), 11-25. See also R. A. LeVine, "Anti-European Violence in Africa: A Comparative Analysis," *Conflict Resolution,* 3 (December, 1959), 420-429.

77. Sir George Clark, *op. cit.,* pp. 73-74.

The Garrison-State Hypothesis Today

BY *HAROLD D. LASSWELL*

THE GARRISON-STATE hypothesis was first published about a quarter of a century ago.[1] The object of the present exercise is to consider the significance of the hypothesis in the light of scholarship and of the flow of history to date. The plan of discussion is this: (1) to consider certain points of method and terminology; (2) to examine the prospects for the continuation or discontinuation of the expectation of violence, which is a fundamental factor assumed by the garrison construct; (3) to explore the internal structure of decision within the several nation-states during future years; and (4) to draw implications for the guidance of science and policy.

I

The simplest version of the garrison-state hypothesis is that the arena of world politics is moving toward the domination of specialists on violence. The hypothesis offers a characterization of significant patterns of the past and future, thereby providing a provisional orientation within the flow of events "from what" "toward what." If we take the mid-nineteenth-century nation-states of European culture as the point of departure, it is meaningful to say that the most important elites were specialized in the exercise of business skills, and skills of symbol management, official administration, and party organization. Skills in the management of violence (or, more generally, of extreme coercion) continued to play a prominent role. Nevertheless, their subordination is indicated by the degree to which spokesmen for armies, navies, and police forces justified their appropriations by emphasizing power as a base of wealth, rather than wealth as a base of military-diplomatic power. Post-Napoleonic Europe was progressively absorbed in enrichment through the expansion of industrial society and the further decline of feudal values and institutions. The garrison-state construct proposes a model in which the sequence marches from the relatively mixed elite pattern of the nineteenth century to military-police dominance in the impending future.

With regard to method, the garrison-state formulation exemplifies one of the five intellectual tasks common to all problem solving and hence to the

51

solution of problems of politics. The five tasks are the clarification of goal, the description of trend in the realization of goal, the analysis of conditioning factors, the projection of future development, and the invention and evaluation of policy alternatives. The garrison-state construct obviously belongs primarily to the third and fourth of the intellectual tasks, since it deals directly with trend and projection.

It is worth noting, perhaps, that the garrison-state conception was originally put forward for the purpose, in part, of emphasizing a methodological position which had been outlined by the writer in *World Politics and Personal Insecurity*.[2] I was underlining the fruitfulness of comprehensive hypotheses about the manifold of future as well as past events—after the manner of Marx and other evolutionists—while rejecting the claim of such comprehensive formulations to be called scientific. A "developmental construct" is not limited to the extrapolation of trend curves, nor does it fail to take into account the available supply of scientific data or generalization. A construct such as the garrison state is a means of orientation *in time* toward the most significant features of the total configuration of events. Although comprehensive propositions about past-future configurations have often been labeled "scientific," as Marx and Engels called their bourgeois-proletariat formulation, it is misleading to do so, since their current degree of confirmation in regard to future events is too low to justify the use of the symbol of "science." Hence the word "construct."

Problems of policy are oriented toward the future, and part of the technique of rational decision is to adopt procedures that expose all assumptions about the future to the discipline of explicit consideration. To formulate or to evaluate a developmental construct is to engage in the use of problem-solving procedures.[3] Among political thinkers the developmental method can be most effectively employed in choosing problems of study, in the clarification of goals, and in the invention and evaluation of policy.[4]

In devising constructs, care must be taken to adhere to the distinction between expectation and preference. The garrison-state hypothesis is put forward as a matter-of-fact statement of expectation. The contingencies referred to, however, are perceived as welcome opportunities by some and as catastrophic challenges by others. In estimating the likelihood of future events, every candid person knows that there is a strong tendency to exaggerate the probability or the improbability of whatever contradicts his conscious or unconscious value orientation. Part of the procedure of problem solving is to search for covert as well as overt preferences and to give explicit consideration to the possibility of bias. In my case this precaution is of no little importance, since my preferred goal is to participate in activities that have promise for the eventual success of a universal order consonant with the requirements of human dignity.[5] Hence I have always regarded the possible coming of a garrisoned world with apprehension. I would like to help prevent this outcome by suitable policies—or, failing this, to encourage policies that humanize the garrison as completely as it can be.

Concerning terminology, a few points are worth mentioning. I use "state" in the conventional sense of jurisprudence and political science to designate a body politic that, when viewed in the context of the world arena, possesses a high degree of formal authority and effective control. Some scholars define terms so that "totalitarian" political systems are not entitled to be regarded as possessing true legal order. To the extent that garrison "states" are totalitarian, on these definitions, the proper terminology, following *Power and Society,* is garrison "rule."[6] I adhere to the earlier label partly because it is well established, and partly because, as presently will be seen, I do not limit the construct so drastically.

Many terms were, and are, available in place of "garrison." Among the considerations that led me to choose "garrison" was that I wanted to include "military" and "police," leaving the two words available as subcategories. Since in common usage "garrison" has strong military connotations, the expression "garrison police state" is sometimes employed to emphasize that all coercive specialists are included.

The present review of the construct must begin with an outline of the equilibrium conditions of a garrison system. Enough knowledge of the past is at hand to enable us to devise at least a rough working model of this kind. We formulate the fundamental conditions of a garrison system as follows: (1) the power elites value power enough to resort to large-scale coercion when they regard such coercive strategies as useful to the maintenance of their ascendancy; and (2) the elites accept the expectation that the retention of power during at least the immediate and middle-range future depends upon capability and willingness to coerce external or internal challengers.

Since the garrison construct is an aggregate hypothesis, it refers to the dominant characteristics of the entire arena of world politics, thereby going beyond the circumstances of a particular body politic. A garrisoned world is a military arena—not a civic arena—in which resort to extreme measures of coercion is regarded as a persisting state of affairs, or as a chronic danger.

We shall work within the frame of reference provided by these abbreviated models despite the disadvantage that they do not include definite specifications concerning the degree to which demands and expectations regarding power are affected by such factors as civilization, class, interest, personality, or level of crisis. To present a detailed model would involve the discussion with many more categories and formulations than we can touch upon within the limits of the present inquiry. We shall first concentrate upon the examination of the variables likely to affect the expectation of violence, the broad factor whose crucial role is stressed in the highly generalized model sketched above.

Note that the garrison-state construct does not stipulate whether the decision process internal to the state is characterized by narrow or wide participation in the making of important decisions. Hence the garrison is not "by definition" nondemocratic. This is left to empirical inquiry. However, my initial concern for the garrison system grew out of apprehension regarding the future of democracy and of large-scale violence. Although it was not my intention to assert that democracy and military activity are always and everywhere incompatible with one another, I did intend to suggest that in the light of historical and analytic knowledge there were ample grounds for concern about the viability of democracy under conditions of chronic war and threat of war or violent revolution. My concern was heightened by new factors in the environment of democratic systems—namely, the explosive growth of modern science and technology and the connection of these developments with the control of large population and resource basins suitable for huge capital accumulation. It seemed probable that the dynamism of Germany and Russia was largely to be understoood in terms of the destructive implication of the introduction of scientific and technological factors into a divided world arena.

The rise of totalitarian or near-totalitarian systems in Russia, Germany, Italy, and Japan was confronting the traditional strongholds of relatively free government and society with challenges of enormous gravity. Regardless of the immediate outcome of the rivalries and conflicts that were in the foreground twenty-five years ago, I was impressed by the cumulative impact of profound transformations in the structure of world societies, transformations that were not likely to be reversed by short-range wins or losses sustained by particular coalitions in the world arena. My hypothesis was that the Marx-Engels construct of universal felicity after an epoch of world war and revolution is dangerously oversanguine, the more probable outcome being a world of ruling castes (or a single caste) learning how to maintain ascendancy against internal challenge by the ruthless exploitation of hitherto unapplied instruments of modern science and technology. My view is the same today, though, as indicated above, I continue to regard it as inadmissible to use the term "inevitable" in referring to comprehensive future developments and regard preventive measures of policy with some confidence.

II

It it apparent that the garrison-state construct depends in large part upon the assumption that the expectation of violence (of extreme coercion) will continue, either in the form of a divided and mutually apprehensive arena in world politics or, in the case of a universal state, within the internal arena of the new order. We begin, therefore, by examining the prospects for the continuation or discontinuation of the expectation of violence.

Will the possibility of mutual destruction provide sufficiently strong incentive to bring about world unification by consent? If it is more widely recognized that politics as at present organized precipitates coerciveness, will identifications with the nation-state system grow weaker, enabling movements toward world unity to succeed? On balance is it probable that the expectation of violence will increase, decrease, or remain the same?

THE SHADOW OF DESTRUCTION

A recurring ground for hope of world unity and peace among advocates of a voluntarily unified world community is the destructiveness of contemporary weapons. In the last 200 years the appearance of new scientific and technological advances has been accompanied by a fresh round of prediction that war has now at last become so awesome that no thinking man could possibly take the risk of involving his people in a new conflict. Pacifists thought they saw the handwriting on the wall for humanity when balloons soared into the sky, carrying the possibility of a new and over-whelming front against armies, military bases, and cities. In turn, the air-plane, long-range artillery, and especially poison gas seemed to hold the key to frightening men into a better world. Today it is commonplace to hear—and to hear from some heads of states—that nuclear war is un-thinkable.

No one denies that mankind *can* be destroyed by bombs or gas. But the problems that confront responsible officials are couched in less simple terms. They are not faced with a single button marked "To destroy humanity, push here." The many policy alternatives available at any given moment blur the picture. The following questions serve to indicate the complexity of the "choice map" of top leaders:

Since we and our opponents both recognize the ultimate disaster that can befall us, is it likely that anyone will take the irrevocable step?

Is it not probable that the measures adopted in any immediate crisis will be designed, not for total, but for partial destruction?

Is it not likely that whatever measures are initially launched will be less effective than expected owing to equipment failures and human error, as well as to sabotage and instantaneous counteraction?

If we continue to hold out a little longer in our negotiations to reduce and limit the most destructive categories of weapon and weapon use, is it not likely that we will obtain better terms of agreement, in the sense that the arrangements agreed upon will provide more security, and also that we have a greater voice in inclusive administrative bodies?

If I seem too eager to agree now will it not weaken my power position at home by suggesting that I am willing to give too much in return for concessions whose true worth cannot be accurately appraised in advance?

POSSIBLE CHANGES IN IDENTIFICATION

The scope of action available to a political leader at a given time depends in part upon the intensity of identification with the established order that prevails at various levels. Is it likely that identifications will be affected by the perpetual mobilization to a degree that makes it "good politics" for leaders to reorganize the existing structure of the arena of world politics in the direction of a united world order attained by consent rather than by coercion?

Analysts of modern civilization have called attention to a phenomenon that is practically unheard of in folk societies although found in some city-centered civilizations of the past.[7] The phenomenon is alienation, by which is meant nonparticipation in the perspectives and behaviors appropriate to nation-states, and the carrying of nonparticipation to the ultimate of self-destruction. Included among nonparticipation patterns are practices which may be part of traditional culture, as when worldly things are abandoned in order to live the life of a recluse for the purpose of meditating upon trans-empirical matters.

Many scholars have been impressed by the evidence of alienation in the modern history of Western Europe.[8] A principal factor is alleged to be the breakdown in the ideological unity of Christendom, a breakup traumatically expressed by the willingness of Christian powers to form coalitions with the infidel and by the Protestant Reformation. It is conjectured that an additional factor is the unsettling impact of scientific knowledge upon man's image of himself and the world in which he lives. A "personal" God has dissolved into macrodistances or microphenomena equally alien to the cosmologies of the prescientific age. Mass and energy distributions are not yet integrated with the "subjective events" that seem so near yet so remarkably private and unique in human experience.

Investigators point to a variety of factors connected with social change that confront adults with problems of adaptation with which they are unable to cope by reason of the failure of childhood environments to provide the equipment required to enter the adult world with appropriate problem-solving capabilities. This failure to cope, reflected especially in the phenomenon of suicide, has been the focal point of many researches.[9] Investigators have examined the consequences of geographical mobility, which often fails to provide adults or children with a steady "supporting" configuration. Studies have also directed attention to social mobility, the rise or fall of individuals and groups in the class structure of society. Here again exposure to cross-pressure frequently works havoc with the minimum of stability required for early socialization or later continuation.

It is also recognized that our civilization specializes in the rapid obsolescing of old interests and the rapid rise of new ways of thinking, talking, and doing. Within the same ideological and territorial unit, and at the same class level, individuals are perpetually shifting occupations and leisure-time activities. New scientific and technological innovations draw attention to new sources of raw material and energy, or stimulate the invention of novel goods and services and of modified modes of production, merchandising, and utilization. Or the lead is taken by a new control device that makes it seem advantageous to merge plants, to revamp organizational structures, and to reassign personnel. The point of innovation may be a new accounting technique that alters the tax vulnerability of an organization and favors its survival. In any case, the social environment is complicated by operational networks that confront individuals with new patterns of attention and perspective.

The phenomenon called alienation is an extreme form of response precipitated by the clash of norm with norm or of norm with normlessness. It is possible that the spread of schooling, of travel, and of mass media of communication is having results quite different from that sought by the manipulators of communication as an instrument of policy. For instance, despite great apparent differences in the key symbols, slogans, and doctrines of socialism, Communism, and capitalism, the impression may be gathering strength that in all essentials everybody is talking about the same basic pattern of life.[10] Among articulate spokesmen for contemporary nation-states everyone seems to profess human dignity and freedom as an ultimate goal. Everyone favors peace and security, and everyone fosters the sciences and the technologies of production and destruction. Practically everyone endorses a rising standard of living, including social security against unemployment, accident and illness, old age, and related vicissitudes. Almost everyone seems to endorse the recognition of individual merit and to deplore discriminations based upon caste. Nearly everyone appears to advocate freedom to choose friends and intimates and to found a family. In the face of those overwhelming harmonies of goal, differences seem opportunistic, related to the timing of various stages in meeting the problems that arise in modernizing and industrializing peoples of various degrees of backwardness.

I summarize these points because they indicate why it is to be expected that in some states individuals will withdraw their willingness to fight for the preservation of the traditional autonomy of the nation-states or blocs to which they belong. Is it likely that these developments will be important enough to put an end to world rivalry and in so doing to weaken the forces that foster garrison states?

It is probable that the perspective referred to will be more frequent in the industrial countries of the non-Soviet than the Soviet world. The Soviet world has leaped ahead sensationally in ways that strengthen the sway of its central myth. More prosperity in the older countries is welcome, but it is "old hat." It evokes less pride than it once did.

We do not expect "peace at any price" movements to gain influence quickly in the United States in view of the likelihood that most alienated individuals will be recruited from among Americans who are least motivated to join active political programs of pressure-group and party agitation and organization.[11] Furthermore, any new movement will be obstructed by the opposition of established leaders who sense that such movements are potential threats. It is perceived that if "peace at any price" groups were to obtain the support of the Soviet leadership—as they undoubtedly would— Soviet leaders would work with and through them to the disadvantage of other elements.

If in the older industrial nations "peace at any price" movements begin to win significant support, it is safe to predict that police measures will be strengthened against "subversion." The "political vacuum" created by withdrawals of identification may be occupied, therefore, not by anticoercive elements, but rather by persons and programs having a militantly nationalistic coloration. As a means of heightening differentiation from the Soviet-centered world, nationalistic symbols would probably be elaborated and embellished by "religious" symbols (such as "atheistic communism").

It is probable that liberal political leaders would respond to future evidence of general disenchantment by seeking policies capable of firing the imagination of the rising generation at home and abroad. But foreign aid programs, for instance, suffer from the doubts and scruples of liberal regard for autonomy. By raising the cry of foreign interference the established elites of receiving countries are able to obtain exemption from effective supervision.

American leaders, for instance, have been embarrassed by this strategy and have tended to leave local cliques of landlords, officers, and officials free to enrich themselves without making a commensurate contribution to economic and social development. By perpetuating sources of discontent that can be exploited by rival world political elements the growth of stable and responsible government is precluded.[12]

The conclusion is that withdrawals of identification with politics, insofar as they gain enough initial strength to threaten the unity of older non-Soviet powers, will provoke policies of the garrison-police-state type.

THE OVER-ALL EXPECTATION OF VIOLENCE

We turn to the future of the over-all expectation of violence, recognizing that some points made in the preceding analysis of alienation are also pertinent here. We begin by replying to the question: By what broad paths of change is it conceivable that the world military arena can be transmuted into a civic arena? (1) By a general war that establishes the supremacy of one of the polar powers without damaging the victor to a degree that leaves him unable to hold the dominant position against a coalition of the remaining powers; (2) by limited wars that expand one of the polar powers without precipitating a general war and that establish such a position of supremacy that the other polar power throws in the sponge and becomes a satellite; (3) by policies short of active war that expand the effective domain of one polar power with the results outlined in (2) above; (4) by a fusion of the effective elites of the polar powers in order to protect themselves from further weakening their position for the benefit of other powers (the fusion could be effective if implemented by ultimatum and active pressure); and (5) by a fusion of effective elites, recruited from many powers in addition to the polar powers, who would establish unity largely by consent.

From past experience we know that one limitation of forecasters is their inability to free themselves from the assumption that the conspicuous scientific and technological features of their time are permanent. Recognizing that a major characteristic of science to date is the tremendous advantage of world powers that have great concentrations of capital at their disposal, we now ask whether technology can change so drastically that instruments of production and destruction are likely to be produced with small-scale outlays? Further, will the tremendous advantage of offensive weapons be nullified by the perfecting of defense? At present there are no convincing signs of basic revolutionary innovations.[13]

It is not to be overlooked that the growth of vast administrative networks under centralized and even largely automatized direction may have the seemingly paradoxical result of making top control spots more vulnerable than before to individual and small-group strategies of power seizure.[14] The patterns of control are continually transformed as new activities require more prompt and refined means of linkage with established and emerging operations. The networks of communication and decision become more elaborate—that is, more centered and subcentered. If small platoons are prepared to make simultaneous assaults upon key panels of control, the chances of success are good enough to risk, especially in times of general stress. Far from relaxing garrison-police conditions, such possibilities confirm the importance of eternal vigilance as the price of maintaining established elites in power.

In considering the future, we do not underestimate emerging technologies connected with "brain machines" and with experimental embryology and genetics. Mechanized robots are not only of potential importance as defensive guards or offensive elements. We are on the verge of producing machines that are capable of devising complex strategies of action and possibly—as Norbert Weiner suggests—of relegating mankind to a subordinate role.[15] At present it appears equally likely that a machine-run globe would be divided along present-day lines or that it would achieve unity. The same point applies to advanced forms of life that may be developed by experimental biology. And we do not dismiss as absurd the possibility that living forms which have developed elsewhere impose themselves here and inaugurate the "discipline from without" that mankind has been unable to attain from within.[16]

Can a communications revolution occur in which world elites voluntarily subject themselves to an ethico-political training that motivates the self-regulating, cooperative efforts necessary to actualize a global order of human dignity? Can such a reconstruction begin at the top (or with mid-elite elements) and lay the foundation for voluntary unification of demand, expectation, and identification?[17] Desirable as these developments are, we cannot at present view their chances with much hope.

III

The preceding examination of the prospects of terrifying the world into voluntary unity, of weakening local identifications for the benefit of an effective universal allegiance, and of weakening the expectations of violence points to one conclusion: the outlook is dim. Hence the precondition of the garrison-state outcome is likely to be fulfilled.

The garrison construct goes further: it characterizes the principal changes in intrastate power that are likely to result from factor combinations that tip the internal equilibrium toward narrow rather than wide power sharing and that favor the self-perpetuation of an elite specialized to the planning and implementation of coercive strategies of power.

Within the Soviet bloc of totalitarian powers the garrison-police construct is highly approximated, though it cannot yet be said with certainty that the ruling families have as yet consolidated themselves into a self-perpetuating caste. I shall not enter into a detailed discussion of the excellent literature now available for estimating the future course of development within the Soviet bloc as it relates to the wider sharing of effective power. I assert only that the garrison construct is more in harmony with the dynamics of totalitarian systems than are alternative hypotheses.

More critical for the future is the course of evolution within advanced industrial nations having traditions and customs of popular government.

In previous expositions of the garrison conception we have projected the sequence of change that results when emphasis moves from wealth or other values and is placed upon power.

Perpetual apprehension of war keeps the accent upon the consideration of power measured as fighting potential. The common goal of maintaining national freedom from external dictation is perceived as requiring the appraisal of all social values and institutional practices with state-power considerations in view. Economic values and institutions are drawn into the preparation of weapons and thereby subordinated to power. Scientific skill and education are requisitioned for research and development. Public enlightenment is limited in the name of military secrecy. Public health is fostered by programs designed to conserve the human resources that figure in military potential. Family and ecclesiastical institutions are given encouragement so long as they interpose no ideological or behavioral obstacles to national security. Institutions of social class and caste are remodeled to the extent that national vulnerability is believed to be at stake.

THE FUNCTIONAL PHASES OF DECISION

In this connection a distinction is to be drawn between those individuals, groups, and structures that are functionally specialized to violence and those that, at any given time, are conventionally recognized as military or police. The growing accent upon power and the institutions of power that occurs in periods of chronic mobilization typically works to improve the position of the uniformed professionals (when the base line of comparison is the precrisis period). At the same time, the comprehensiveness of the problems relating to modern war and war preparation tends to bring about a different result. Party politicians and other group leaders make themselves felt in the planning and execution of strategy; and scientists, engineers, and managers with nonmilitary backgrounds move into the complex and often high-level activities of state and society. The total decision process is carried on with a shifting balance between old and new elements at every phase. In examining the seven functions, we are guided to some extent by occurrences to date,[18] supplemented by the expectation of high levels of continuing and intermittent crisis that we have justified in the earlier part of the paper. In the final part of the present discussion we shall draw some policy implications from the interpenetration of old and new elements in the decision process.

The *intelligence* function is the obtaining and interpretation of information pertinent to decision. In a mobilized world the specialist on violence is in a preferred position, since he seems professionally more qualified than anybody else to give the estimates required in making the translation of "change in general" into "fighting potential." Laymen can listen with understanding to scientists and engineers who discuss the state of research and development at home and abroad, but for policy purposes this testimony must be fused with knowledge of how these activities and results are integrated with military resources organized in particular ways and affected by specific traditions of strategy. War games and exercises provide the specialist on weapons with a basis for making inferences that must be accepted in the last resort as the equations to be built into computing machines engaged in simulation programs. Also, we must depend upon these specialists to guide the delicate operations by which it is sought to penetrate the enemy's wall of secrecy for the sake of uncovering clues to intention and capability.

Perpetual mobilization makes it plausible to extend the scope of the function of the political police to include more thorough investigations of the present loyalty of personnel and of personnel vulnerability under hypothetical future contingencies. These contingencies include inducements offered by opposing powers and the more subtle effects of deprivations connected with a fluctuating state of tension and combat. The political-police function at home merges with the work of those who are seeking to find vulnerable spots in the personnel of foreign powers.

The intelligence function includes the invention and evaluation of strategic programs in the light of formulated goals and of the available body of trend and scientific knowledge, critically projected into the future. All questions of goal, no matter how seemingly trivial at first glance, can be plausibly shown to have a bearing upon the security position of the community.

The *recommending* (promoting) function in the decision process includes the advocacy of courses of action. Hence it goes beyond the presentation of plans to the bringing of pressure to bear upon critical points of action. In the United States, as in many other countries, specialists on violence are traditionally accepted as professional advisors rather than advocates. Hence in the rough-and-tumble of party and pressure politics specialists tend to be looked upon as special pleaders for high expenditure on behalf of provocative policies from which they obtain special benefits. While world crisis continues, however, this evaluation is likely to be modified, as the community comes to believe that proposals relating to strategy have little weight unless they have some measure of professional support. Hence, party leaders find it wise to align themselves with military figures, who are initially treated as advisors but who gradually intervene in public debate as policy advocates in their own right. Thus the scope of permissible participation by the military increases, and the path is cleared for confidence-inspiring personalities among the violence specialists to become candidates for nomination and election. Since the making of military policy evokes interservice differences, struggling factions reach out for elements in the community at large with which they can join in tacit coalitions to support controverted positions. Party and pressure-group leaders, journalists, scholars, and others will be drawn into these blocs.

Another decision function is *prescription*. At this stage, rules, whether constitutional, statutory, or administrative, are made for the guidance of policy. In Western countries the bodies charged with the prescribing function have been overwhelmingly civilian, subject to the modification that "veterans" are at an advantage after a war has vanished into the distance and the veterans are somewhat obsolete as soldiers. Perpetual crisis now brings older military specialists and newer specialists who are scientists into regular advisory contact with prescribers, and it is safe to say that the deliberations of political bodies are likely to be regarded with some disdain. They have much evidence of time-serving, ignorance, evasion, and general irresponsibility; and this provides a "moral" basis for the possible assumption of authority by the military during moments of severe crisis.

The *invocation* stage of decision is of very direct importance to police specialists, since they are traditionally regarded as the principal agents of the community in performing this function. To invoke is to characterize conduct provisionally as a deviation from prescribed norms. During times of crisis loyalty norms are added to the standards of intercrisis peacetime society. Hence the political-police function flourishes, affording opportunities for specialists in investigation to multiply their numbers and to extend their influence upon personnel selection. The casting of doubt upon the integrity of individuals becomes an instrument by which unscrupulous or credulous members of the political police are often able to rise in power and to appear indispensable to the central elite nucleus.

After invocation comes *application,* which is a final, not a provisional, judgment of conduct. Courts, for example, are organs of government that are highly adapted to the applying function. Whenever police evidence is turned down, courts cause some frustration among the police and often become targets of cumulative resentment. Political police officials are continually edging toward the pre-emption of judicial functions.

The *appraisal* stage of decision is the conducting of "autopsies" on the connection between policy goals, the means employed, and the results achieved. Those who obtain facts pertinent to appraisal are strategically situated, since they control many of the inferences upon which judgment depends. Since policy groups do not like criticism, they exert continual pressure to insure exemption from adverse appraisal by controlling the appraisers. The point is not only to escape criticism, but to do so by providing a scapegoat. For instance, the effort is often made to show that alleged military failures are not failures by the military but are properly attributable to legislative limitation, civilian administrative confusion, and the like.

Finally, we speak of the *terminating* function, which puts an end to arrangements which apply the prescriptive framework, and also to prescription themselves. Termination is often a matter of freeing individuals from obligation (or refusing to do so) and hence provides many points of leverage in the social process, especially in civilizations rather than folk societies where contract takes the place of custom.

Glancing over the seven functions, it is clear that specialists on violence are already located at strategic phases of intelligence, invocation, and application, providing bases from which they are in a position to edge toward wider spheres of effective control as crisis continues.[19]

POLITICAL SOCIALIZATION

The foregoing examination of the decision process has indicated how crisis accentuation of state power tends to subordinate all social values and institutions to considerations of military potential, and how as a result, military and police specialists are placed in advantageous positions within the decision process. We cannot terminate the analysis without giving more direct attention to the socialization process (the process of political education). Can we foresee any connection between changes in the perspectives entertained by young citizens as they move toward full participation in the body politic and the rise or fall of garrison states?

The idea that the future of politics depends in part upon the success or failure of political education is no novelty among political thinkers.[20] Many of the generalizations put forward by Plato have been confirmed, broadened, or modified by modern social and behavioral sciences. Plato was explicit in assigning the chief role in bringing about altered perspectives to the parental generation. He spoke, for example, of the "exaggeration" of an accepted ideal by the elders and sketched the political cycles that result therefrom. Assume, for instance, a community whose chief preferred value is wealth; Plato's proposition is that exaggerated stress on wealth—as in the encouragement of saving and investment—provokes a demand on the part of youth to enjoy life by greater consumption, leading in turn to self-indulgence in superfluities, and in a later generation to self-indulgence of the antisocial lusts characteristic of unconscious sexuality and aggression. The end of the cycle is tyranny.

In modern civilization specific sequences similar to these have often been described. Families which focus upon material accumulation are confronted by the rebellious potential of the young, which often leads to rejection of the family-wide goal in order to obtain more egocentric gratification in the form of expenditures on immediate enjoyment. Since a life pattern of egocentricity provides no generalizable norm of responsible conduct for the young, the next generation achieves no superego or ego ideal strong enough to enable the individual to "contain" the extremes of sexual and aggressive conduct referred to above.

Affluent "economies" appear to favor expenditures for egocentric enjoyment. Thus, in industrialized societies the family loses many functions connected with the transmission of cultural norms, which are left to such auxiliary institutions as schools, neighborhoods, and the mass media. The communications industry is particularly dominated by economic considerations and encourages consumption expenditure by exploiting the most exciting appeals, which are largely sexual and aggressive. Owing to the growth of economic concentration, these merchandising appeals spread to the local retailer and penetrate deeply into the body politic.

We sum up these tendencies by saying that the passage from group involvement to egocentricity fosters subsequent passage from "superfluous" enjoyment to sexual and assaultive excesses. These trends are furthered by *failure of superego formation* from (1) *absence of models who are group-oriented* toward such goals as accumulation for family wealth, political power, religious eminence, or medical distinction and (2) *conflict of models as a result of geographical and social mobility*. (These factors often support one another.)

Having recognized the strength of the forces working toward ego indulgence, we must not overlook the possible improvement of educational technique when a problem is fully perceived. Many elements are then stirred into intense activity in the direction of restoring a former equilibrium or of bringing a new and more satisfactory state of affairs into existence. It is true that the subdividing, mobile, and affluent civilization which we know in the United States has not mastered the technique of socialization; hence, uncounted millions of young people are as yet ineffectively challenged to lead significant lives that are contributory to the good of the commonwealth. But we have formidable instruments of communication at our disposal, and there are great reservoirs of aspiration and competence in our civilization. Possibly we can reverse trends toward egocentricity and successfully cultivate personality systems in which identifications are effectively oriented to include the larger community.[21]

A danger in such programs is that they will try to rebuild social consciences by encouraging militancy directed against the stranger (the "other"). Undoubtedly the most ancient and successful means of integrating an individual ego into a more comprehensive self-system is by using the traditional syndrome that includes the expectation of violence, the ethical demand to sacrifice for the common good, and identification with a community less comprehensive than all mankind. Perpetual crisis puts a premium upon appeals of this character and upon acquiring the social discipline symbolized by the folklore that presents the soldier at his best. In this way political power is renewable as a primary social value in rivalry with affection (family), well-being (comfort), skill and enlightenment, and wealth and respect when these values are pursued through the institutional forms of civilian life.

We have recently been reminded, if such reminders are needed, that young people are predisposed toward the submersion of the narrow ego into the larger self of great social movements that foster action and sacrifice.[22] It is also evident from psychiatric and psychological knowledge how deep are the demands to escape from guilt, "self-contempt," feelings of weakness and related deprivations by plunging into social programs of vast scope. But it is never to be forgotten that everyone does not become sexually or aggressively ego-indulgent all at once; on the contrary, increases in a countermores direction generate tendencies toward restoration of the mores. With rare exceptions, the completely egocentric personality is not met with in fact. He is a "theoretical limit." No matter how flamboyantly ego-indulgent the individual may be, intimate investigation almost always shows evidence of conflict with less egocentric tendencies within the personality as a whole[23] These considerations strengthen the chances that movements on behalf of social responsibility will succeed after periods of drift in the opposite direction.

Can the specialist on violence provide the model of social responsibility capable of mobilizing the latent propensities of the young in modern societies? It is already evident that in industrial society the specialist on violence is not condemned to the role of thug as he was in some of the disdainful

images perpetuated by the scholars of China. The professional preparation
of the fruits of science, can the culture of science itself be more widely
ulum of training has been greatly transformed under the pressure of changes
that stem from modern science, technology, and ideology.[24] Despite the
cleavages generated within the armed services by the rapid tempo of professional renovation, it is possible to point to officers who have attained distinction in their own right as contributors to the new technologies. A far
larger number has achieved enough competence to establish easy working
relations with outstanding men of science and scholarship.

IV

CIVILIANISM VS. MILITARISM

We come finally to the point of asking by what policies we can maintain as many as possible of the effective institutions of a free society despite
the improbability of moving soon into a world relatively free of the chronic
threat of serious coercion. From the point of view of the strategy of human
dignity the most promising trends to encourage are "civilianism," the movement that to a degree we can say is developing counter to "militarism." If
we understand by "militarism" the permeation of an entire society by the
self-serving ideology of the officer and soldier,[25] we can speak of "civilianism" as the absorption of the military by the multivalued orientation of a
society in which violent coercion is deglamorized as an end in itself and is
perceived as a regrettable concession to the persistence of variables whose
magnitudes we have not as yet been able to control without paying what
appears to be an excessive cost in terms of such autonomy as is possible
under the cloud of chronic peril. As the perspectives of society become
adapted to contemporary levels of risk, together with a common acceptance
of the military is not frozen in a sacrosanct mold. On the contrary the curric-
understood and applied to problem-solving *procedures* throughout society,
including the decision process?[26]

The perception that scientific model building and data processing, when
adapted to any recurring set of problems, call for the suspension of final
commitment until appropriate assumptions have been explored in disciplined
fashion, pertinent data obtained by appropriate methods, and interpretations
evaluated by a rigorous procedure—all this indicates the diffusion of the
scientific pattern throughout civilization. One implication is that physical
scientists, for example, will never betray the culture of science by committing
themselves to opinions on political and social matters without having
examined the pertinent context with proper discipline.

However Utopian this may be, in the visible future the dynamic equilibrium of politics will work in favor of civilianism to the extent that people
—that is, large populations, including the lower classes—continue to be posi-
tively valued for military purposes. Hitherto the dependence of arms production upon a huge labor force has been a factor making for a degree of
democratization. This trend has gained importance as a result of the modern
socialization of risk among all members of the population, whether military

or civilian. However, in a technology run by automation the labor force may begin to appear redundant as the disadvantages of a human labor force become more obvious, especially its vulnerability to discontent and hence to the appeal of ideologies counter to the established system of public order. To the extent that mere numbers are perceived as endangering the resource base of a nation-state, demands will be furthered for such policies as effective birth control and the substitution of robots for people.[27]

Up to the present the huge techno-scientific advance in the United States during recent years has greatly retarded the factors making for a police polity of internal repression. It has been possible to supply consumer goods in increasing abundance and to introduce automation at a rate compatible with existing techniques of expansion, re-education, and relocation. In the absence of sudden peaks of crisis the forum providing news and debate has been open to movements to protect civil liberty against disastrous assault or erosion. Despite revelations of the thinness of our subculture of civil liberty,[28] the forces of infringements have been rolled back on some fronts.

The process by which a garrison is civilianized is likely to make rather subtle transformations in the "nucleus elites" of the future. The following questions point toward new elite patterns through a fusion of the skills which are representative of the highly developed specialties of modern civilization:

Is it likely that effective elites will be recruited somewhat outside, though partly inside, the traditional framework of the armed forces? For example, will a new elite emerge that is initially composed of officers, physical scientists and engineers, administrators, party and pressure-group leaders, public relations specialists and lawyers, who gain acceptance as the most realistic and creative individuals in coping with the total decision problem?

Will the traditional services contribute to, while failing to dominate, the new class that emerges in the interstitial positions created within our ever complicating social process?

Will the culmination be a truly civil garrison where anyone resembling the traditional soldier or policeman is as out of date as horse cavalry?

Pertinent to these queries is the evidence brought together in the contemporary study of elites in large-scale industrial societies. The modern decision process appears to function through shifting coalitions composed of formal and tacit representatives of the plurality of groups and persons formed by exposure to and interaction with the complex symbolic and material subdivisions of our civilization. Persons rise to top eliteship who have the personality structure and skill patterns adapted to the task of maintaining internal acceptance within a constituency while engaging in coalitional activities with persons of corresponding aptitude and position. For example, data are now available for distinguishing the "nuclear elite" within the broad elite structure of the armed services of the United States. The problems that arise in operating large-scale organizations in our techno-scientific age tend to converge as one nears the center of formal authority and effective control, and hence to reduce the differences in perspective and operational strategy from one top level to another.[29]

The structure of the elite differs in nations of low industrialization and modernization from the pattern described for the United States; it also diverges in totalitarian polities. In many contemporary nations it is possible to recognize legacies of myth and technique from political systems formed under pre-industrial conditions, such as "oriental despotisms,"[30] in which centralized bureaucracies leaned heavily upon coercive instruments of power. It is also possible to identify political institutions dating from the period in which, under an umbrella of formal centralization, the effective control usually resided with rulers of component territories, who also depended upon coercive means of maintaining their rule against the center and against further dispersion to subcenters.[31] Similarly, we perceive the survival of patterns once current in a feudal society in which rule was not neatly articulated with large contiguous territory, although power relations were fundamental features of the whole society.[32] Furthermore, we sometimes become aware of perspectives persisting from brief or long experience of city-states.[33] In the latter we recognize the close connection between banditry and trade, but we also perceive the strength of the urban subdivision of the social environment as a factor in shaping civilizations in place of folk societies. In peasant villages—and these are spread over a sizable part of the globe—we now see, not a folk society cut off from wider arenas, but social formations resulting from the centralizing consequences of expanding urban-based civilizations.[34] Among the active folk societies of today—in various stages of disorganization and reintegration in civilization—it is rewarding to trace the extremes of emphasis or de-emphasis upon central authority and control.[35]

Wherever we examine the situation thoroughly, we find that a potent influence is the tendency to introject the standards set by the largest and most successful bodies politic in the arena of global politics. Often the focal point of local discontent is among the military, some of whom are pace-setters in comprehending the technology, science, and total culture of the principal powers. In view of the tendency toward "diffusion by partial incorporation" of the pattern of the top powers, we are justified in saying that it is by no means out of the question that military education may aid in producing a generation of top professional elements who are multivalue-oriented.

Within the Soviet world the elite structure has remained tenaciously in favor of the formal principle of civilian supremacy; hence, the Party continues to be the principal ladder up the authority and control pyramid. Within the Party, of course, it is the specialist upon the political-police function who has an advantage, since central power elements look to the police to protect them from the challenges that arise in a totalitarian system. Established elites in such a system typically consider themselves endangered by decentralization, deconcentration, democratization, pluralization, and de-regimentation. It has been indicated above why it is unlikely that existing top-elite components will regard it as advantageous to put an immediate end to the present divided structure of world politics.[36]

In the light of our previous discussion, we conclude, however reluctantly, that the garrison hypothesis provides a probable image of the past and future of our epoch. We would prefer it to be a self-disconfirming hypothesis. The master challenge of modern politics, therefore, is to civilianize a garrisoning world, thereby cultivating the conditions for its eventual dissolution.[37] The discipline acquired in the process may make it possible for mankind to accomplish what it has never been able to achieve before—namely, to create and perpetuate a universal public order of human dignity. So long as there is a gleam of hope for this culminating outcome of man's history, there is hope for life itself.

NOTES

1. My first publications employing the term were in 1937 and 1941. A summary and critique is to be found in Samuel P. Huntington, *The Soldier and the State* (Cambridge, Mass., 1957), pp. 346-350.

2. Harold D. Lasswell, *World Politics and Personal Insecurity* (New York, 1935), ch. 1. For a compendium of my characterizations of the construct, see H. Eulau, "H. D. Lasswell's Developmental Analysis," *Western Political Quarterly,* 11 (June, 1958), 229-242.

3. The allusion here is to the distinction between principles of content and of procedure. The first may be illustrated by the proposition that all rational thought requires goal clarification; the latter by the statement that in a problem-solving process it is important to find a place on the agenda for the clarification of goal.

4. See my discussion of "Strategies of Inquiry: The Rational Use of Observation," in Daniel Lerner (ed.), *The Human Meaning of the Social Sciences* (New York, 1959), ch. 4.

5. Compare M. S. McDougal, "Perspectives for an International Law of Human Dignity," *Proceedings American Society of International Law* (1959), 107-132.

6. Consult Carl J. Friedrich and Zbigniew K. Brzezinski, *Totalitarian Dictatorship and Autocracy* (Cambridge, Mass., 1956). For the definition of "rule," see Harold D. Lasswell and Abraham Kaplan, *Power and Society* (New Haven, 1950), p. 208; "regime" is defined at p. 130. The latter refers to formal authority, the former to effective control. "Law" is both authoritative and controlling.

7. V. Gordon Childe emphasizes the fundamental importance of the invention of cities for the emergence of civilization. The invention is tentatively located in a few river valleys about 7,000 years ago. See his *New Light on the Most Ancient East* (London, 1935) and later publications. Also Robert Redfield, *The Primitive World and Its Transformations* (Ithaca, 1953).

8. Tomás G. Masaryk, *Der Selbstmord als sociale Massenerscheinung der modernen civilisation* (Vienna, 1881); Emile Durkheim, *Suicide* (Glencoe, Ill., tr. 1951).

9. Andrew F. Henry and James F. Short, *Suicide and Homicide* (Glencoe Ill., 1954).

10. The impression is supported by such official acts as proposing and ratifying the Universal Declaration of the Rights of Man, and by the results of content analysis of the language of politics. For background see Herschel C. Baker, *The Dignity of Man* (Cambridge, Mass., 1947) and the data reported in the Stanford studies of political symbols by Lasswell, Pool, Lerner and others.

11. Indications of the connection between alienation and political participation are found in Robert E. Lane, *Political Life; Why People Get Involved in Politics* (Glencoe, Ill., 1959). See also William Kornhauser, *The Politics of Mass Society* (Glencoe, Ill., 1959); Eugene Burdick and Arthur J. Brodbeck (eds.), *American Voting Behavior* (Glencoe, Ill., 1959).

12. The complications of economic development are shown in studies such as Berthold F. Hoselitz (ed.), *The Progress of Underdeveloped Areas* (Chicago, 1952); Simon S. Kuznets *et al., Economic Growth: Brazil, India, Japan* (Durham, N. C., 1955); Gunnar Myrdal, *An International Economy: Problems and Prospects* (New York, 1956); Albert O. Hirschman, *The Strategy of Economic Development* (New Haven, 1958).

13. The reference is to more sweeping transformations than the spread of nuclear technology although this gives rise to complications. See *The Nth Country Problem and Arms Control* by the National Planning Association (Washington, 1960), which includes a technical annex by W. Davidon and others.

14. A theme that occurs in some writing on strategy; for example, Ferdinand O. Miksche, *Atomic Weapons and Armies* (New York, 1955).

15. The current developments in the science and technology of machines are summarized at intervals in *Science* and *Scientific American*.

16. See my projections in "Men in Space," *Annals of the New York Academy of Sciences,* 72 (April, 1958), 180-194.

17. Attention should be called to new techniques of training that, if used for parochial purposes, may work against more comprehensive perspectives. Consult F. Skinner's novel, *Walden Two* (New York, 1948), and his *Science and Human Behavior* (New York, 1953).

18. For indications see: Ralph S. Brown, *Loyalty and Security; Employment Tests in the U.S.* (New Haven, 1958); Comment, "School Boards, School Books, and the Freedom to Learn," *Yale Law Journal,* 59 (April, 1950), 928-954; Note, "Government Exclusion of Foreign Political Propaganda," *Harvard Law Review,* 68 (1955), 1393-1409; Robert K. Carr, *The House Committee on Un-American Activities* (Ithaca, 1952); Walter Gellhorn, *Security, Loyalty and Science* (Ithaca, 1950); Eleanor Bontecou, *The Federal Loyalty-Security Program* (Ithaca, 1953); Edward A. Shils, *The Torment of Secrecy* (Glencoe, Ill., 1956); Charles V. Kidd, *American Universities and Federal Research* (Cambridge, Mass., 1959); Solomon Fabricant, *The Trend of Government Activity in the U.S. Since 1900* (New York, 1952);F. S. Hoffman, "The Economic Analysis of Defense: Choice Without Markets," *American Economic Review,* 49 (May, 1959), 368, and discussion; James R. Schlesinger, *The Political Economy of National Security* (New York, 1960); Eli Ginzberg and Associates, *The Ineffective Soldier* (New York, 1959), 3 v.; Huntington, *op. cit.,* Part III; National Manpower Council, *A Policy for Scientific and Professional Manpower* (New York, 1953).

19. Existing data concerning participation by coercive specialists in official elites are fragmentary not only in regard to composition but, more importantly, in perspective. The Second *International Yearbook of Political Behavior Research,* edited by H. Eulau and D. Marvick, is devoted to the methods and results of elite research to date.

20. Herbert H. Hyman, *Political Socialization* (Glencoe, Ill., 1959); Lasswell, "Political Constitution and Character," *Psychoanalysis and the Psychoanalytic Review,* 46 (Winter, 1959), 3-18.

21. The systematic study of juvenile delinquency has led to the invention of group as well as individual strategies for dealing with the problems involved—e.g., Fritz Redl and David Wineman, *Children Who Hate* (Glencoe, Ill., 1951)—and the strategies involved in capturing gangs for socially approved activities.

22. Friedrich and Brzezinski, *op. cit.,* ch. 4.

23. Consult *American Handbook of Psychiatry,* especially vol. 1 (New York, 1959).

24. Gene M. Lyons and John W. Masland, *Education and Military Leadership: A Study of the ROTC* (Princeton, 1959).

25. This is the conception employed by Alfred Vagts in *A History of Militarism* (New York, 1937).

26. The task of integrating the scientific outlook with our total civilization appears more urgent and formidable than ever. See C. P. Snow, the physicist-novelist, whose phrase "the two cultures" stirred up lively discussion. Note his "Reply to my critics" in *Encounter,* 14 (February, 1960), 64-68. Also see *Daedalus, Journal of the American Academy of Arts and Sciences,* 89 (Winter, 1959), the issue devoted to "Education in the Age of Science."

27. Lurking in the background is the threat of "Machiavelli, M. D.," to which I referred in *World Politics and Personal Insecurity.* Luckily the top elite in Nazi Berlin and Communist Moscow was not recruited from individuals possessing enough knowledge of science and technology to discover the more destructive potentials. See also my "Political Science of Science: An Inquiry into the Possible Reconciliation of Mastery and Freedom," *American Political Science Review,* 50 (December, 1956), 961-979.

28. Notably Samuel A. Stouffer, *Communism, Conformity and Civil Liberties* (Garden City, N. Y., 1955).

29. Morris Janowitz, *The Professional Soldier; A Social and Political Portrait* (Glencoe, Ill., 1960), especially ch. 8 and Part VII.

30. Karl A. Wittfogel, *Oriental Despotism: A Comparative Study of Total Power* (New Haven, 1957).

31. Sally F. Moore, *Power and Property in Inca Peru* (New York, 1958). This book corrects the image of Inca society, law, and politics as a supercentralized system. See also Edwin Lieuwen, *Arms and Politics in Latin America* (New York, 1960).

32. Rushton Coulborn (ed.), *Feudalism in History* (Princeton, 1956).

33. Miriam Beard, *History of the Business Man* (New York, 1938) summarizes the data for the Mediterranean world of the fifth century B.C. and of 1500 A.D.

34. Redfield, *op. cit.*

35. Note especially John Middleton and David Tait (eds.), *Tribes Without Rulers; Studies in African Segmentary Systems* (London, 1958).

36. For details see Simon Wolin and Robert M. Slusser   (eds.), *The Soviet Secret Police* (New York, 1957); Merle Fainsod, *Smolensk under Soviet Rule* (Cambridge, Mass., 1958); Nathan C. Leites and Elsa Bernaut, *Ritual of Liquidation* (Glencoe, Ill., 1954); Boris Meissner (and John S. Reshetar), *The Communist Party of the Soviet Union* (New York, 1956).

37. See in this context Huntington, *op. cit.,* and in Janowitz, *op. cit.,* the discussion of "the constabulary concept" in the last chapter. There is a legitimate place for professionals who specialize upon sanctioning policy. I view this as a potential fusion of military, police, correctional, judicial and related skills. See Richard Arens and H. D. Lasswell, *In Defense of Public Order; The Emerging Field of Sanction Law* (New York, 1961).

A Comparative Theory
of Military and Political Types

BY *DAVID C. RAPOPORT*

War is only a part of political intercourse, therefore, by no means an independent thing in itself.
CLAUSEWITZ

IN A REMARKABLE but half-forgotten essay Friedrich Engels convincingly demonstrates that the dominant political characteristics of nineteenth-century states were clearly reflected in their military establishments.[1] His discussion suggests an important possibility, and one which few scholars in the nineteenth and twentieth centuries, including Engels himself, ever explored in detail—namely, that no adequate theory of comparative civil government is complete without a collateral hypothesis about military forms. Although this position may appear radical, an analysis of various types of military experience should at least throw some interesting light on comparative politics. A useful but little-employed way to study armies is to focus directly on the political functions they perform.

An army can serve the state in three major ways: it may be an instrument of foreign policy, it may be employed in domestic partisan politics to supplement police units, or it may perform general nonpartisan administrative functions that could conceivably be carried on by associations not organized for combat purposes. In this last category the most important function of the army occurs when the military establishment is a national school where the citizens can learn appropriate civic virtues and important technical and administrative skills that may contribute to the maintenance and/or improvement of their community.

While most armies in history have performed or could be called upon to perform all these major functions, the extent to which certain armies have been absorbed with one task or another has varied enormously—a preoccupation which stems from basic political causes and produces fundamental constitutional consequences. In short, many of the "laws" that govern politics in a particular state can be deduced by analyzing its military institutions.

Most of this essay is devoted to the "nation-in-arms," a state which uses

military training to educate its citizens. The other two types have been discussed in more detail elsewhere,[2] but summaries of those findings are presented here since they throw into greater relief the salient features of the
nation-in-arms and help provide the basis for a more comprehensive theory
of military-political experience.

I: The Praetorian State

The world is a garden, the fence of which is the dynasty. The dynasty is an authority
through which life is given proper behavior. Proper behavior is a policy directed by
the ruler. The ruler is an institution supported by soldiers. The soldiers are helpers maintained by money. Money is sustenance brought together by the subjects. The subjects are
servants who are protected by justice. Justice is something familiar (harmonious?) and
through it the world persists.   ATTRIBUTED TO ARISTOTLE[3]

In South America . . . the republics depend on military force. Their whole history is a
continued revolution. . . . Only force and voluntary subservience are principles of
action; and the forms which are called Constitutions are in this case only a resort of
necessity, and are of no protection against mistrust.   HEGEL[4]

Originally the Praetorian Guard was simply an elite military unit that
Augustus established to shield his person and government against domestic
unrest. During the course of imperial history, however, the Guard acquired
great independent power. It openly blackmailed governments that could not
survive without purchasing its loyalty, and it set up and deposed emperors,
often selling itself in the process to the highest bidder. In direct proportion
to the growth of the Guard's domestic significance, its capacity for war
seemed to wane. Thus, the term "praetorian" has come to have several
meanings.[5] It refers to soldiers hired by a government to police an unruly
population, but it also suggests that the loyalties of these soldiers are not
fixed, for they often overturn governments they were hired to defend. The
term finally is associated with venality, corruption, and military incapacity
or cowardice. In effect, a praetorian state is one where private ambitions are
rarely restrained by a sense of public authority or common purpose; the role
of power (i.e., wealth and force) is maximized.

Many observers before our century discussed the praetorian syndrome,
invariably describing it as the last stage in a state's necessary historical development—the era when public authority disintegrated. They argued that
the division of labor necessary to produce sufficient wealth to pay a professional administration and army also withered the social capacity to cooperate
for collective enterprises. To survive, government had to depend upon its
coercive instruments, and praetorianism was the inevitable result.

As all traditional accounts emphasize, the ability to administer and compel
in a praetorian state is always greater than the capacity to promote social
discipline. When it becomes impossible to control outlying areas, they become
infested with bandits or break off as independent states: witness the history
of most Arab empires and of Latin America in the nineteenth century. In
any case, the dominant position of those who command wealth and violence
is evident. To reverse the current terminology, a modern praetorian country

is not an "underdeveloped" but an "overdeveloped" land. Compared to most states prior to the twentieth century, it possesses vast technical resources, but sources of power cannot be used or even regulated for public purposes. Even when the government's agents appropriate the nation's wealth, most of it slips back into private purses.

The traditional accounts diverge on one specific matter: Montesquieu and Ferguson believed that despotism was necessarily linked with praetorianism; Tocqueville and Maine insisted that modern military insurrections would issue from democratic states. But, in fact, even though praetorianism flourishes in periods when "egalitarian" ideologies alone confer legitimacy, it is not associated with a particular governmental form, for a praetorian state cannot sustain the institutional base for either democratic or despotic principles. Thus, in the modern world those countries that are most democratic or those that are most despotic (totalitarian dictatorships) are least likely to be praetorian. On the contrary, praetorian countries frequently alternate "quasi-democratic" and "quasi-despotic" regimes. Furthermore, most ancient despotisms had non-praetorian and praetorian periods. In the latter the sovereign's *de jure* privileges were still intact, but his *de facto* powers depended on his own personal vigor; some rulers were able to produce public order, but others were overwhelmed by an egalitarian chaos.[6] In sum, continuous public instability makes it impossible to define the organization of public life in juridical or institutional terms; the most one can do is suggest major conditions that affect the struggle for power.

A praetorian society has a small, extremely wealthy oligarchy and a large, poverty-stricken mass—a sociological condition which both highlights and intensifies the ineffectiveness of state policy. Whether the state proclaims democratic or despotic principles, it must promise some measure of equality and cannot legitimize the existing distribution of wealth. The rich man, therefore, must attempt to protect his property by subverting the integrity of the state's administrative agents. On the other hand, the hatred of the poor lacks true moral fervor, for the mass cynically distrusts all public authority and will not submit to the restraint and sacrifices necessary for fundamental reform.

To the outside observer praetorian politics seem "formless," for the government of the day is not sustained by strong sentiments or well-disciplined social groups that enable it to weather adversity or to pursue consistent policies. Even governments which appear reasonably secure will fall suddenly in response to a slight change of circumstance. In the absence of impersonal loyalties the political significance of individual talents is maximized. Usually only a strong personality can secure momentary stability, but he rarely produces the institutions to confirm an appropriate successor.

Swollen, rootless, and *idle* urban mobs complicate the problem of governing. The incentive to work is lacking even where opportunity is available, for the fruits of creative labor cannot be protected by law. Economic potentialities constantly deteriorate; capricious law enforcement discourages capital accumulation. The breakdown of standards is apparent everywhere, especially in educational institutions.

Governments are most often overturned by violence, though there are usually few casualties, since not many will risk their lives to oppose or support a government during crisis. The army is the most fruitful source for political intrigue, and the government conspires to promote its military supporters, while the opposition attempts to curry favor with the most strategically placed military men. The officer corps invariably attracts two distinct political types—the political adventurer willing to gamble all in a dangerous stroke and the petty bureaucrat anxious to hold his rank in successive regimes and, therefore, reluctant to proceed vigorously against a rebel group. The rank and file who must suppress urban riots are drawn from politically "innocent" groups; in the modern praetorian state they originate from the rural peasantry, and in the ancient world they were usually foreign barbarians.

The political situation makes it impossible to organize an army with real fighting qualities. Little *esprit de corps* cements the officers together, and officer and enlisted man frequently display contempt and hatred for each other. Behind defensive barricades the army may be able to hold its own, but little ability is displayed in the field. The state prefers to avoid "entanglement" and to serve its foreign ends through conspiracy and bribery; it will fight few wars in any case. Thus, the belligerency of the ancient despotisms waned as they grew increasingly praetorian, and in the modern world it has been the states of Latin America which have most successfully kept international peace.[7]

It should be emphasized that the desire to avoid war is not simply an expression of military inadequacy, for praetorian states are often surrounded by primitive peoples or much weaker neighbors. Yet even a successful military campaign (except when led by the chief of state) introduces an extra element of uncertainty in domestic politics. The Roman emperors restricted their armies for good reason: war could and often did produce rival candidates for the throne. Almost every Latin American war was followed by a series of coups in *both* the victorious and vanquished states. Such minor operations as the dispatch of a Brazilian division to Italy in World War II or a Colombian battalion to Korea resulted in a revival of military conspiracy in states that had been comparatively stabilized for some time.

II: *The Civilian-and-Military Polity*

In (free states) . . . a man puts not off the citizen when he enters the camp, but it is because he is a citizen and would wish to continue so that he makes himself for a while a soldier.   BLACKSTONE[8]

Sire, among the inhabitants of this town, and your majesty's troops, I could not find so much as one executioner; they are honest citizens and brave soldiers. We jointly, therefore, beseech your majesty to command our arms and lives in things that are practicable.
                                                   VISCOUNTE DORTE[9]

In the contemporary world the best examples of this state-type are in the West—England, the United States, Germany, Denmark, Belgium,

Holland, and the four British dominions settled by Europeans. It should be emphasized, however, that some Western states are not members of this type, while some non-Western states are. Japan has a civilian-and-military polity, but Switzerland and, to a lesser extent, Sweden are nations-in-arms, while Spain and Portugal are praetorian states. France presents a special picture, for since the Revolution her armies have contained strong elements of all three state-types.[10]

The major function of the army in the civilian-and-military state is to support the nation's foreign policies. Internal political stability is a product of group equilibrium, and the armed forces cannot be used easily to suppress domestic discontent without running the risk of provoking major resistance from elements of the population—a resistance that would disrupt the *essential* nonpartisan basis of army cohesion and also destroy the state's source of military reserves. Whereas the praetorian army needs few reserves, and its size is determined primarily by the money to "hire" personnel, the army in a civilian-and-military polity will often have to expand rapidly to fight wars, and it must appeal to the citizen's patriotic sense to augment its strength.

The military obligation in this type of state is limited; it falls with varying weight upon different citizens, and, indeed, many do not have to serve at all. Most citizens are expected to meet some military obligations at least during emergency periods, though often an entire generation will not have had much military experience. Thus, in contrast to the nation-in-arms, a military education is not an essential ingredient of civic training. The citizen probably regards army service as an unwelcome, albeit sometimes necessary, interruption in his normal career, so that his government is cautious in extending the military burden, often trying to make the duty more palatable by increasing the civic advantages of those who serve. These civil-military principles were first established in Europe's medieval period; since that time they have been expressed in different institutional forms as the details of various constitutional arrangements changed, the bases of citizenship broadened, and new external threats developed.

In contrast to most primitive political establishments, the European medieval kingdom was unique. It did not require military service from all those who exercised civic privileges; the clergy, for instance, did not bear arms but still formed an important element of every medieval parliament. Moreover, the military obligation was carefully limited, it fell most heavily on the fief-holder, but he had to contribute only an annual forty days inside the realm, the freeman was obliged only to come to his sovereign's aid when the community was attacked, but local militias rarely exercised and were even less frequently used, the burgher was encouraged to maintain the community's defenses with his purse rather than his sword. Finally, no one was bound to aid the king in imperialist adventures; it was necessary to entice men to volunteer for overseas expeditions by paying them in coin. An aggressive war, therefore, was often difficult for the monarch to finance without securing the taxpayer's explicit consent to provide additional revenue—a consent which was rarely given without concessions from the crown in return.

In the civilian-and-military polity, unike the praetorian state or the nation-in-arms, an enormous build-up or deterioration of the military establishment is invariably related to the waxing or waning of an external threat. The Western medieval king was unable to make his subjects realize the advantages of peacetime training and, when war came, hastily assembled and ill-coordinated levies, supplemented by specially hired mercenaries, took the field. Despite the obvious inconveniences such practices produced, particularly when the money to pay mercenaries was not always immediately available, it is doubtful whether a fundamental change would have taken place if the Swedish armies, organized largely on nation-in-arms principles, had not suddenly threatened to overwhelm Europe.

As it was, the final solution to the Swedish threat was determined at least as much by internal political possibilities as by military logic. Though many men, such as Machiavelli, Lipsius, and Harrington, realized that the most efficient possible military organization would be modeled along Roman or Swedish lines, the task was impossible for most European states without both a fundamental reorientation of the Western ethic and the confiscation of most domestic real estate, so that the state could subsidize or encourage worthy soldiers. The compromise achieved illustrated the character of Western political life. An extraordinary type of standing army was created, which commanded the support of the major civilian groups because it more than any other type of military organization seemed consistent with traditional constitutional obligations and privileges.

Outside the West, standing armies were the principal domestic prop of civil government, and therefore all ranks, especially the more important, contained mercenaries. The European monarch's internal security and authority, on the other hand, enabled him to encourage an officer corps composed of noblemen whose "honor" prevented them from entertaining ideas of military conspiracy and whose natural exclusiveness made them an admirable instrument to discipline mercenary recruits confined to the enlisted ranks. Perhaps for the first time in history mercenaries were subjected to an impersonal authority and welded into an effective war machine. In home territories the army was augmented by militias of insufficiently trained freemen. The merchant was willing to increase his tax share in lieu of a personal military contribution.

The most recent stage of Western political-military development came as a result of the French Revolution. France, by introducing an effective conscription program, partially achieved the military advantages inherent in a citizen army—that is, increased reserve strength, better morale, and superior tactical mobility. Other Western countries in time adjusted to the new "military necessity," but, instead of developing a nation-in-arms formula as the Swiss did, they devised a much more cumbersome and expensive system —the "cadre-conscript" army.[11] During times of reduced international tension a small cadre force is maintained that is adequate for minor difficulties, and that can also be utilized to train quickly a mass of conscripted civilians to

serve for limited emergency periods. Alongside this establishment the traditionally ineffective militias persist. The cadre-conscript formula was maintained in the nineteenth century in part because it relieved the citizen of
overseas service in imperial territories—a practice which reflected the feudal
feeling that the freeman should not bear military burdens unconnected with
home defense. (The same attitude survives today in those British dominions
where a soldier will not be sent abroad without his consent, and in the
American practice of paying special bonuses for overseas service.) However,
the chief reason for the continued persistence of the system through to the
twentieth century lies in the traditional reluctance of the civilian to devote a
portion of his everyday life to military affairs.

III: The Nation-in-Arms

They were dirty and selfish. They carved their names on their shelves and cots and
wouldn't let us approach them. They would never loan another man the use of their shoe
polish. But if they needed anything they never hesitated to steal from a buddy. They
tattled to superiors and would fight at the slightest provocation and sometimes with no
apparent provocation.
                ISRAELI COMMENT ON JEWISH RECRUITS FROM PRAETORIAN COUNTRIES[12]

In times of peace these men should be trained in military discipline from their youth
up . . . after the example of the ancient Romans. The Romans did not even expect free
maintenance for their pains much less the right to loot, rob, beat up and murder
civilians as troops now do. A camp with them was a school of honour, of sobriety,
chastity, justice and virtue, and no one was allowed to avenge his own injuries or take the
law into his own hands.   BODIN[13]

A.   PRELIMINARY CONSIDERATIONS

Most writers since the time of Blackstone, especially in the Anglo-
American world, have held rather rigid preconceptions concerning the "inherent character" of military institutions. Thus, while the nation-in-arms
(which uses military training as the chief civic bond) is perhaps the most
commonly discussed, it is also the least understood state in modern military-
political theory.[14] Few thinkers have examined the relevant historical
materials or considered the comments of earlier writers. Men whose fundamental philosophies are as different as those of Herbert Spencer and Harold
Lasswell have agreed that a military people is usually governed by a despot
whose domestic authority is secured through an excessive use of violence
and an elaborate centralized administrative apparatus.[15] A similar picture
seems deeply entrenched in the popular mind and is certainly reflected in
many conventional histories of civil-military relationships.[16] But this image
seems distorted; it certainly should be questioned, for most states which
stressed the civic value of a military education have an entirely different
constitutional syndrome, and the one instance which seems to confirm the
dominant preconception best, Ottoman Turkey, most probably took its
despotic shape from other sources.

Probably the greatest barrier to a comprehensive theory of the military
is the tendency to contrast the character of military and political action.

We commonly maintain that "politics," especially in a "democratic" community, involves relationships between "equals"—it implies compromise and persuasion to reconcile groups which can rarely destroy each other. War, on the other hand, is resolved through the application of brute power in which one contending group is utterly crushed. The successful military organization, consequently, will have a clear hierarchical form, emphasizing the superiority of the officers and the unquestioned obedience of the lower ranks so that a maximum pressure can be exerted at any given point. The role of coercion is evident in every aspect of the military framework, and in states well constructed for war there is little room for politics, especially of the democratic variety. This approach, however, obscures much more than it clarifies, by inducing us to take for granted just what is most difficult and necessary to explain—the common elements in any formal organization that give it the strength to withstand continuous pressures to disintegrate.

All humans have a capacity for formal organization, but more often than not this ability remains latent. Although our college textbooks tirelessly and tritely repeat that man is a "social" or "group" being, the obvious fact is that he also has many antisocial or antigroup interests. Even the most perfectly organized communities will contain some men who are unwilling to accept much social control. More important, we can find countless instances in our anthropological literature of whole peoples lacking a sufficient sense of authority to insure domestic peace and collective action—the basic minimum for both a state and an army—and even the most superficial student of history can list an impressive array of societies that somehow lost the capacity they once had for war and government. Writers in an age which had a more penetrating political imagination than our own usually spoke of peoples who had an apolitical and an amilitary life as being in a "state of nature." But since the eighteenth century we have steadily lost all sense of man's ungovernable dimensions. Perhaps only the pathetic picture of confusion in today's so-called underdeveloped nations will finally enable us to define once again the psychological essentials of organization[17]—a task which Bagehot insisted lay beyond the political understanding of modern man.

... Plato and Aristotle ... had not had time to forget the difficulties of government. We have forgotten them altogether. We reckon as the basis of our culture, upon an amount of order, of tacit obedience, of prescriptive governability which these philosophers hoped to get as a principal result of their culture. We take without thought as a datum what they hunted as a quaesitum.[18]

In tracing the origin of states, especially prior to the nineteenth century, one cannot help noticing that there is an important relationship between the organization of a people's military and civil capacities—a relationship which is so striking that Bagehot could insist with some justice that at least in the "early ages of man . . . war makes nations." Only continuous conflict against the "outsider" provides an opportunity for the development of social discipline making feasible for the first time a "rigid, definite, concise law" binding individuals directly, the indispensable basis of government.

Bagehot overstated his brief, but we have ignored him for other reasons. Perhaps we are reluctant to admit that military training might have some significant, even indispensable, general social utility. Otherwise, it would seem difficult to explain why it has taken more than two centuries for a prominent anthropologist to repeat Montesquieu's circumspect statement that the ability to direct military operations and the talent for government generally evolve at the same time in a people's history—both being necessary manifestations of a common will to maintain unity.[19]

One certain test of . . . adequate military organization is a sense of tribalism which will prevent fighting inside the we-group.[20]

Most Californians were absolutely non-military. They possessed none of the traits requisite for the military horizon, a condition which would have taxed their all but non-existent social organization too much. Their societies made no provision for collective political action. When a terrier bites a spaniel, the other spaniels *as spaniels* do not enter the fight, and the Californians felt much the same way.[21]

If the behavior of subpolitical people is any criterion, abolition of the strong tribe or state might indeed mean the abolition of war on a grand scale, but it would also mean the abolition of the longer periods of peace and the larger areas of peace which the strong state affords. When there is no war-or-peace declaring authority, there is no peace at all.[22]

. . . war is an essential part of the societal complex, perhaps one of its strongest links and certainly one of its clearest reflectors. The relationship of efficient social organization in the arts of peace and the arts of group conflict is almost absolute whether one is speaking of civilization or subcivilization. Successful war depends upon teamwork and consensus both of which require command and discipline. Command and discipline furthermore, can eventually be no more than symbols of something deeper and more real than they themselves.[23]

It is impossible to study civil and military government, much less the relationship between the two, without emphasizing that the sustaining sentiment of a military force has much in common with that which cements any group of men engaged in politics—the willingness of most individuals to bridle private or personal impulses for the sake of general social objectives. Comrades must trust each other's ability to resist the innumerable temptations that threaten the group's solidarity; otherwise, in trying social situations the desire to fend for oneself becomes overwhelming.[24]

Politics and war are complex rational actions; they require teamwork and planning. Men must be trained, labor must be specialized and co-ordinated, and provisions must be made to allocate resources to meet likely contingencies that could split the group. In an army the necessary quest for unity is expressed in the unrelenting effort to inspire respect for authority. However, since authority can be abused, fomenting internal strife and antagonisms, the most effectively organized armies try to preserve authority by limiting it through a strict code of discipline that defines leadership and obedience, supraordination and subordination. In a state the esteem for law performs the same unifying function that respect for discipline does in an army, and the most authoritarian state is always the one in which *law* governs all social activity.

In sum, the demands of war and politics can be so similar that if it is possible to teach a man to be a good soldier, he can also be taught how to be a good citizen. Needless to say, by the same token, the good citizen should find it easy to become the good soldier. In all periods of history many states, especially those which require the full participation of the citizen body in politics, utilized the military experience as the best way to educate the citizen to his public responsibilities. Thus, practically every political theorist from Plato to Rousseau, except Hobbes and Locke, touched on the civic value of a martial education, and few would have found much to criticize in Harrington's repeated insistence that the internal stability and equality of a republic depended most of all upon the maintenance of a system of universal military education.[26]

B.   HISTORICAL INSTANCES

The Classical City-States. The origin of political life in Greece or the establishment of the city's authority over the anarchic and violently competing impulses of a primitive Homeric people is linked with the creation of a *formal* or consciously conceived system of education in which large-scale military exercises were the chief ingredient.[26] The city-state's stability was preserved as long as the citizen remained a warrior, and the polis' final corruption is associated with the use of mercenaries or the decay of its school for citizenship.

The ancient Greek had to develop his cohesive sentiments and skills by direct participation in state-promoted activities, for his city permitted little scope for competing religious and political jurisdictions. Citizens even found it difficult to collaborate to form self-governing commercial associations, because enterprise for mere profit was deemed unworthy of a freeman. It led him to serve the slave, the lodger, and the stranger.[27] As a consequence, the state could not afford to leave the citizen to his own devices lest his talent for association deteriorate utterly:

Thus in the Greek republics the magistrates were extremely embarrassed. They would not have the citizens apply themselves to trade, to agriculture, or to the arts, and yet they would not have them idle. They found, therefore, employment for them in gymnic and military exercises; and none else were allowed by their institutions.[28]

The reforms of Lycurgus in Sparta perhaps represent one of the best Greek efforts to find a stable political life. "Every act of the Spartan was weighed with reference to its probable effect upon the state; the entire educational system was but a formal training for effective citizenship."[29] Little was left to chance; such "natural" groups as the tribe or family had scant opportunity to develop cultural functions. The entire job of "political socialization" was performed under direct state supervision, every adult citizen had pedagogical responsibilities, and every child had a state-designated tutor.

Children from the ages of seven to eighteen resided at public barracks, where they learned to read and write and to participate in certain essential social activities such as sports, dancing, and military drill—where all individual movements were governed by order or rule. On his eighteenth birthday a boy became a "cadet" for two years to study the more complex and arduous disciplines associated with war. His next ten years were spent on active military duty, and not before this period was complete could he exercise the full privileges of citizenship. At that time he was at last permitted to visit the marketplace occasionally, where he would be exposed to activities not directly supervised by the state.

It should be stressed that Spartan training was not an education that emphasized personal submission only. Every boy at various periods alternated in exercising superior and inferior roles, for the Spartans believed (according to Plutarch) that it was impossible to learn how to command properly without knowing how to obey, and vice versa.[30] Mutual criticism was encouraged, provided it was offered in an orderly manner with an evident desire to improve the group's cohesion. The quality of her civic education enabled Sparta to command Greece's most effective army. Likewise, it sustained her much admired internal harmony and her prestige as Greece's most law-abiding state.

Athens, too, was a nation-in-arms. Traditionally she has been understood as the classical world's most "liberal" state, the center of Greek intellectual life. Indeed, she deserved her reputation, but only because her government took *less* interest in public education than that of Sparta did and permitted numerous *private* schools founded for military and gymnastic purposes to develop in other directions.[31] Athens tolerated nonmilitary studies, but until the city declined only graduates from the public war-schools were permitted to become citizens and assume the military obligation that lasted forty years. Thus, the Athenian adolescent began his training at sixteen; two years later he became an Ephebi (or a candidate for citizenship) and served for two years in the army. The Ephebi status was superseded after the recruit passed a series of military tests witnessed by the entire citizen body at a great public liturgy stressing the significance of the occasion. Successful aspirants for citizenship received a shield and a spear, whereupon they took the oath of allegiance which underscored the military aspect of Athenian public life:

I will never bring reproach upon my hallowed arms nor will I desert the comrade at whose side I stand, but will defend our altar and our hearths, single-handed or supported by many. My native land I will not leave a diminished heritage but greater and better than when I received it. I will obey whoever is in authority and submit to the established laws and all others which the people shall harmoniously enact. If any one tries to overthrow the constitution or disobey it, I will not permit him, but will come to its defence single-handed or with the support of all. I will honor the religion of my fathers. Let the Gods be my witnesses, Agraulos, Enyalias, Ares, Zeus, Thallo, Auxo, Hegemone.[32]

Athens established no public schools except in connection with her military needs; the family alone decided how much formal education (as we understand the term) the young Athenian required. Even in its most democratic moods the state never saw fit to make certain that its citizens possessed a minimum standard of nonmilitary enlightenment.

The Roman state bore significant resemblance to the Greek polities, though it varied much in specific detail; Rome in particular shouldered little direct responsibility in training its youth for war. No public schools of any sort were maintained,[33] and private educational institutions were scarce and ill-attended until the third century B.C. A boy's instruction was supervised directly by his father[34] until at the age of sixteen or seventeen he could assume the *toga virilis,* (the symbol of citizenship) and leave home to enlist for a military campaign.

Whereas the Greek subjected himself to military service to qualify for citizenship, the Roman acquired citizenship in order to enjoy the greater privilege of becoming a soldier. The Roman enlisted willingly and was not conscripted except in the unusual instance of dire and immediate state peril. The army attracted him as a steppingstone to a political career, since every public office had a military function and candidates for even the lowest elected position had to serve in a minimum of ten campaigns. A most important source of wealth lay in a share of war booty, but it should be emphasized in this respect that the Roman during the Republic did not simply seek personal gain. He was not a common mercenary who would jeopardize his unit's safety by breaking ranks to seek private plunder, nor would he conspire against his fellows and his state for a larger share of loot. The spoil of victory, he acknowledged, belonged to the political community. If the Roman sought wealth, he achieved it only by being devoted to an inflexible code of law and discipline. War to him was more properly a religious calling; the ritual of devotion was discipline, and material rewards awaited those inspired by true moral fervor.[35] The myth that Mars spawned Romulus was significant; early Roman history appears to be a never-ending series of bloody conflicts. From the day the city was founded until Carthage was finally subdued, "it seems likely that . . . the Romans spent more time in war . . . than they did in any other occupation whatsoever."[36]

Ottoman Turkey. War was as important for the Ottoman Turks as it was for the Romans. Originally, the Ottomans formed merely one of many Ghazi communities—quasi-monastic military-religious communities under the leadership of a war chief, or *emir,* living on the edge of the Christian world. The Moslem faith provided the initial basis for union, and a never-ceasing crusade against the infidel determined the specific character of mutual obligations. But a common life could not be maintained without a finely calculated balance that allowed each warrior a portion of the conquered land ample for subsistence but insufficient for diversion. Thus, a leader who was unable to achieve significant military truimphs was normally abandoned by his followers; on the other hand, a Ghazi state which conquered vast domains too early in its development found it always difficult to induce its soldiers to renew the onslaught against the nonbelievers. Only the Ottomans overcame both these problems,[37] and their success was largely the result of an early recognition that the subjugated territories had to be administered strictly according to a code of impersonal principles. Each warrior was entitled to some land, but its value varied with the significance of his military contribution; as a consequence, the popular enthusiasm for war was sustained by a solid economic underpinning.

The Ottoman conquests, unlike those of Rome, could not be managed without immediately strengthening the hand of the victorious *emir* or sultan; for, by the laws of Islam,[38] the soil of a prostrate nonbelieving country belonged to the conquering army, and the sultan alone had the privilege of temporary disposal. Inasmuch as Ottoman armies were massive organizations constantly refurbished by new recruits from less vigorous Moslem lands, the necessary exhaustive assessment of military merit after each campaign could not be made without the early development of a large, well-trained, and wholly devoted administrative staff. And since the Koran limited the sultan's disciplinary powers over free-born Moslems but gave him almost unlimited authority over slaves, the government of Turkey in a short time was composed almost entirely of slaves.

By virtue of these extraordinary circumstances, the Turks were able to create one of the most remarkable, efficient, and pliant ruling classes ever known. The sultan had a free hand to select, educate, promote and punish his human tools according to their competence and loyalty. He could begin training them at an early age, shutting them off from all outside influences until they were deemed fit to assume responsibilities. For good reason, the entire establishment has often been called a "school," with permanent students whose performances were constantly evaluated as they moved from grade to grade to learn the various arts of war and government necessary to keep the empire intact.[39]

War and government were the central concerns of the vast slave corps, and each slave was normally involved in both activities:

> On the military side, this (slave) institution carried on war abroad, repressed revolt at home, kept itself in power, and preserved sufficient order in the empire to allow a busy and varied economic and social activity. On the governmental side it supplied itself with funds, regulated its own workings—which was no small task—kept the operations of the other institutions in order, and enforced the law. The high official of the government held high command in war. The generals of the army had extensive administrative duties . . . , the management of departments of state, or the government of provinces.[40]

> War carried practically the whole government into the field. . . . Substitute officials had to be left behind to attend to what public business was absolutely necessary.[41]

Switzerland. Many "liberal" philosophers have related the genesis of despotism among the Turks to their continuous involvement in war. The conclusion rests on very suspect evidence; but when it is furthermore adduced as one proof in the general argument that war always stimulates autocracy, it is demonstrably false. The Roman experience is a much more common one, despotism originating when the state loses its imperial appetites and war capacities. War was a less important cause of the Turkish constitution than the facts that the Ottomans had no settled political formula before they expanded, that the Koran severely restricted their creative faculties, and that their armies grew constantly in size. When, however, a military community is small and its principles of government are fixed before conquests are made, the state gravitates toward a democratic constitution. It is not surprising therefore to find important features of the ancient world's

pattern emerge in the Swiss Forest Cantons from the thirteenth to the sixteenth centuries.[42]

Since the Swiss were fundamentally untouched by the feudal order that
dominated most of Europe, they were able to give a state form to the
primitive, and therefore casually organized, Teutonic warrior community
(Hundertschaft) by making military training compulsory for all men between
the ages of sixteen and sixty. A citizen was obliged to furnish his own arms
and to find sufficient time for the constant military maneuvers and raids
that, together with politics, constituted the community's chief public business. Much more like Rome than Athens or Sparta, the Swiss city required little precitizenship military training; the citizen developed his
associative skills as a member of an actual fighting team, and he lacked
the gymnasia, the common meals, and the athletic competition of the Greeks
as substitute outlets for his energies. The only voluntary associations encouraged, except perhaps the church, were marksmanship clubs, which
stimulated practice with war weapons.

The decline of the Swiss system of universal military education began in
the mid-sixteenth century. It was accompanied by a partial disintegration of
the Confederacy, which was basically a military alliance, and increasing
internal dissension in the separate cantons. A waning of the democratic
spirit was evident also, for oligarchies entrenched themselves in many
states.[43] Switzerland, it is true, remained a nursery for excellent soldiers,
since the appetite and talent for war are not lost overnight, and most European princes made ample use of her mercenaries. But her own fighting
strength constantly deteriorated as the "better classes" were reluctant to
assume heavy personal burdens. If the confederacy remained independent,
it was mostly because the various members of the European balance-of-
power system found it to their advantage to keep her free of entanglement.
When Napoleon finally destroyed that balance and invaded Switzerland, resistance to his armies was feeble and tragically inept. For the first time in
modern history the country was occupied, and in nearly two decades of
savage repression her citizens learned once again the political indispensa-
bility of her military institutions.

The revival of Swiss unity and the rebirth of democratic institutions, as
almost every text on Swiss history emphasizes, came as a direct result of the
renewal of common military obligations. Even though the cantons refused
in the post-Napoleonic period to accept a single government, they were
willing to adapt certain principles of medieval training to modern conditions
and to place canton army units under the command of national officers.
Thirty years later, in the Sonderband War, when most army units in the
face of secessionist sentiment remained loyal to federal officers, it was clear
that a central government was feasible in a land where regional, ethnic and
religious diversity might well have made a common life impossible:

The revolution . . . in 1815 is . . . significant. It was not a generally centralizing constitution which, transforming an alliance into a Confederation thereby incidentally unified its
military institutions. It was on the contrary, the universally recognized need for an improved system of national defence which imposed unification, in the military sphere,

upon a group of statesmen very reluctant to consent to any limitation of cantonal sovereignty in any other matters. It was most emphatically not the Confederation which nationalized its army in Switzerland in 1815, but the army which far in advance of all other federal institutions was the main factor of the general centralization which came about a generation later.[44]

The role that the army still plays in fostering common unity and public purpose is so well understood in Switzerland that a prominent leader of a pacifist organization could say:

Should armies ever entirely vanish . . . it seems to me that we in Switzerland ought merely to do away with ammunition, our military organization being otherwise the best school of civic virtues and of sane patriotism and the best system for developing both physical strength and that sentiment of solidarity which should inspire all those who are united together for the realization of one and the same idea.[45]

Israel. Although the "outsider" may be startled to hear that the Swiss who have governed themselves almost continuously for 600 years may still need to use the army as an instrument of public education, he will more easily understand the crucial civic importance of Israel's military establishment. Without universal military service Israel would probably find it impossible to achieve a minimum standard of citizenship for individuals from forty diverse lands who outnumber the native *sabra* by almost two and a half to one. Indeed, even with a military establishment that "provides the only point on which all citizens merge under one system, one command and one objective" a durable national life, in the last analysis, may still not be feasible.

A comparison of the Swiss and Israeli training patterns[46] suggests the different magnitude of their common problem and thus the different roles the two armies play in producing the citizen. The Swiss officer has far less to do than his Israeli counterpart, for the Swiss recruit prior to induction has had ample opportunity to develop some familiarity with modern technology, an appreciation for his country's history, some admiration of his army's outstanding traditions, a little experience in the difficult art of association, and a profound respect for the symbols of authority. As a result, the recruit is a partially finished soldier before he enters the army; there is thus no difficulty in limiting his initial training period to four months, in finding a military specialty related to his actual or intended civil occupation, in depending upon his sense of duty, after he has been released, to practice military skills in his free time as a "civilian," and in restricting "refresher"-course time to 260 days in his *first* eighteen years of military service.

But the Israeli officer has a far more complex task. Often the recruit has few useful modern technical skills, and frequently his attitudes toward authority were shaped in foreign states where distrust and the shirking of responsibility were the dominating features of public life. At the very least, the Israeli army must begin the educational process for more than half of its recruits, and before formal instruction can start, deeply entrenched anti-political attitudes must be destroyed. For these reasons, the Israelis need an initial training phase and refresher courses that are, respectively, nine and two times as long as their Swiss equivalents. Even with these "advantages" the Israeli government also finds it necessary to sponsor many youth groups organized along military lines so that the army's task is reduced to manageable proportions.

Before a Jewish immigrant inductee has completed his tour of duty, he learns to speak, read, and write Hebrew. He will perhaps for the first time in his life become familiar with the Bible—"Israel's history book . . . from which an Israeli habitually quotes and to which he refers when seeking a precedent or a comparison, a metaphor or a simile."[47] He will attend religious services and eat food prepared according to ancient dietary laws, practices he may never have engaged in before. On his innumerable route marches he will be taught the details of the small country's geography and the historical incidents connected with them. He may learn to farm; he will certainly participate in reforestation and road-building programs and will help administer public welfare activities. He will be given an opportunity to exercise command and to instruct recruits. Under army auspices he can attend nonmilitary schools to gain new skills and knowledge that may make him more valuable in civil society. All of this education is necessary for the Israeli army to utilize in the most effective fashion the recruit's fighting capacity.[48]

Paraguay. Israel, unlike most nations-in-arms, deliberately uses a military medium to encourage the spread of appropriate habits and technical skills necessary for the development of general material prosperity. But she is not unique in this respect; the Jesuit fathers successfully attempted a similar project more than three and a half centuries ago in the La Plata River region.[49] Under their guidance the primitive, peaceful, and defenseless Guarani Indians were encouraged to establish a series of small semi-autonomous city-states so that they might learn to protect themselves from the unending slave hunts promoted by the Spanish and Portuguese and the more warlike savages of the area. But in inducing the Guarani to accept a political life, the fathers utterly transformed the aboriginal personality: the Indian proved willing to accept a severe discipline for his existence. In a short time the missions became the most orderly, prosperous and best defended areas in all Spanish America. The experiment lasted for more than 150 years and was revived for another fifty during the nineteenth century.

Success was due in part to the Spartan-like thoroughness of the Jesuit lawgivers. Every aspect of the Indian's life from birth to death was subject to public regulation—a condition that was possible because each community tolerated no private property, limited its size, attained economic self-sufficiency, and isolated itself from the outside world. So strong was Jesuit authority, so complete was their control over the educational system, that the Order was able to maintain itself although there were only two unarmed Jesuits in each community.[50]

The Indian child's schooling began early; his subjects included religion, reading and writing, elementary mathematics, crafts, farming, military drill, and music—the last being especially important, since all industrial and military activities were carried on by bodies of men who discovered they were able to work more harmoniously as a team when their pace was determined by music rhythms.[51] Every adult male was enrolled in a company and de-voted a portion of his day to participating in the mass military exercises; in addition, he took his turn alternately as a sentinel, curfew warden, or police official. As among the ancients, magistrates were generally elected, and careful attention was paid to the military qualifications of the candi-dates, since most public offices had military functions. Thus, the garrison commander was the chief state official.

The underpinnings of the Indian communities were shattered in 1767 when intrigue at the Spanish court forced the Jesuits to evacuate the region. Within two decades most of the natives deserted the missions after watching their wealth and power disintegrate under a new exploiting administration sent from Madrid. However, when Spain in its turn was forced to leave the river area, circumstances were propitious for a Paraguayan political, econo-mic, and military revival embodying a curious combination of Jesuit, classi-cal, and Turkish principles.

Unlike the other Latin American states which filled the void left by Spain's collapse, Paraguay promoted *institutions* favoring a radical social, economic, and cultural egalitarianism.[52] The Spaniard was compelled to intermarry with the Indian and Negro, and for the most part the former was not permitted to participate in the military activities that were the chief avenue for personal advancement. The state owned most of the available land and leased it to the Indians, who assumed, in turn, appropriate mili-tary obligations. The army organized the country's educational facilities, obliging every male inhabitant to have some primary schooling and craft training. There were as a result few educational differences to separate the population, for there were practically no illiterates, on the one hand, and no secondary school graduates, on the other. The army was also the chief instrument of national economic development; military labor opened the country's mines and foundries, and it helped construct canals and roads including one of Latin America's first railroads.

Like its Jesuit ancestor, the "new" state strove instinctively to preserve its unusual internal arrangement by a policy of national isolation. The Catholic Church was put under domestic jurisdiction, and the nation was ringed with heavily armed garrisons. Few foreigners were permitted to enter Paraguay, and those who did enter were often not allowed to leave later. The natives were confined to the national homeland. Foreign trade was severely limited and like most internal commerce, remained a state monopoly.

In view of Paraguay's experience under the Jesuits, perhaps the most unexpected feature of the new constitution was the undisputed authority of its three successive despots. Although political theorists for a long time have noted that a strong sense of egalitarianism frequently nourishes despotism, in this particular instance one would nevertheless have been justified in antic-ipating a new variant of the classical polis. Indeed, Dr. Francia, the state's founder, did seem to desire a constitution modeled along Roman lines, though he suspected it would take the Indian at least a half-century to learn how to utilize republican forms properly. But, unfortunately, the circumstances that accompanied the nation's birth were more decisive than Francia's aspirations. Even in the Jesuit period, the Indian never had an opportunity to assume responsibilities that extended beyond the mission's boundaries, and for more than a generation before the Revolution the native had almost no scope for his political talents. Only the Creoles possessed the technical capacities to form a political elite, but they lacked sufficient self-discipline to constitute a government in their own interest, and they would not help design one which satisfied the Indian's yearning to return to Jesuit principles. If ever a government passed into the hands of a single man by default, this one did. In time, perhaps, Paraguay's egalitarianism might have produced a democratic polity, but before this could occur, the nation was involved in a disastrous war which put an end to her public order.

GENERAL FEATURES

The dominant ethic of a nation-in-arms is public service—*virtu*—and it is best expressed in military duty, a direct personal burden whose weight cannot be reduced substantially by the economic and social influence of the obligee. Those who are not required to serve cannot exercise full civic privileges. The women in Switzerland do not receive a military education; neither can they vote.[53] On the other hand, in Israel they do bear arms and, consequently, incur no political disadvantages. Before Israel's constitution was established, no nation-in-arms, however democratic or egalitarian its professed principles, permitted women to exercise public jurisdictions. Yet in the medieval period of the civilian-and-military polity, when privileges were narrowly confined, women could hold feudal tenure and public office, for a personal military obligation was not an essential qualification for citizenship.

The egalitarian sentiment manifested in the nation-in-arms' military posture also finds outlets in political and economic institutions, although the pattern in the latter areas varies much more widely than it does in military affairs. Government may either be radically democratic or thoroughly despotic, but it will not, as in a praetorian state, alternate between the two extreme forms; nor will its power suddenly wax and wane, depending on the personality of the sovereign. Public authority must be stable in order to pursue consistent education policies keeping vigorous the popular will to participate in state-sponsored activities. Government must prevent a maldistribution of wealth and privileges, for when no substantial "middle class" exists, the "rich are too fat and the poor too lean" to become enthusiastic soldiers. Thus, among the ancients the constant clamor for some measure of agrarian equality sustained the city's need for soldiers able and willing to equip themselves and the growing inability of sixteenth-century Ottoman sultans to make certain that land was distributed only as a reward for service diminished the fighting potential of their armies and created uncontrollable sources of wealth that were used to undermine the effectiveness of the state's administration. Israel's national life has strong socialist features and the economics of her *kibbutzim* may be profitably compared to that of the Jesuit communes. There can be little doubt that the dictators who ruled the Paraguayan successor state understood how to strengthen the nation-in-arms' solidarity. Witness the testimony of one who survived the demise of Francia's creation:

We were very rich, sir, we swam in wealth, we were happy. My native town of Ititimi then had twenty-four schools; now it has but one. There was not a citizen who did not possess a house, tools to work, and extensive plantings. We did not know hunger. We were a well-fed race, healthy and strong. We were happy and joyous, despite what is called our tyranny. . . . But the war came and we lost all. We fought desperately, because we loved our land insanely.[54]

If the Swiss have not found it necessary to regulate economic life as closely as other members of this state-type, it is because the development of commerce has not produced violent social extremes, and because the state has not been involved in war for a considerable period. But should the Swiss be obliged to fight, their present military system makes it mandatory for the government to administer the entire economy.[55]

One of the most unmistakable properties of the nation-in-arms is its highly developed military competence. The excellent fighting qualities of the classical city can hardly be questioned, and it is virtually impossible to explain satisfactorily the decisive victory of the tiny polis over the Persian empire without describing those conditions of citizenship which enabled the Hellenes to develop what Max Weber called "an incomparable military technique."[56] None of the large and wealthy, though unwieldy, contemporary empires could assemble an organization which could stand up to a Greek phalanx or a Roman legion. Indeed, despite the advantage of gunpowder, only the development of a "Protestant Discipline" in the seventeenth century enabled modern Western states to organize an army which might have held the field against a Classical force in its prime.[57]

The relationship between the ancient's military superiorities and his political life was understood by most philosophers between the Renaissance and the Enlightenment. Machiavelli, for instance, urged Florence to become a nation-in-arms in order to conquer and unify Italy, and Bacon noted the added strength England would gain by imitating the Roman military system.[58] A hundred years later Harrington wrote that the moment was perfect for the establishment of a British polis which would inevitably exercise world dominion.[59] Even in the eighteenth century Montesquieu insisted that the military exploits of monarchies necessarily suffered in many ways compared with those of the Classical republics.[60]

A similar picture of strength is evident in other nations-in-arms. The superior efficiency and the enormous striking power of Ottoman armies made the Sublime Porte the world's foremost power for many centuries; Bodin and Bacon were so impressed that they recommended some aspects of the hated Turk's political system to European princes.

The Swiss pikeman put an end to the feudal knight's sway; had the cantons enjoyed a single government, the Swiss probably would have conquered France and most of Europe in the early sixteenth century.[61] Instead, local rivalries and the lucrative possibilities in foreign mercenary service diverted the Alpine peasant's energies elsewhere. Switzerland's great nine-

teenth-century reforms, of course, have not been tested on the battlefield.
But foreign observers have shown great respect for the state's strength,[62]
and undoubtedly one reason that Switzerland has been able to remain neutral in modern Europe's quarrels is that she seems able to inflict severe
punishment on any invading army.

The Jesuit communities in the La Plata region also measured up to the
standard of military excellence usually found in a warrior state, and in
nearly a century of continuous war they put an end to the Spanish, Portuguese, and Indian slave-hunting expeditions. Though the Guarani never had
an opportunity to match their skill against trained European units, the
Spanish government was sufficiently confident of their quality to garrison
Guarani regiments occasionally in Argentina to ward off expected English
invasions.

Under the direction of her first three dictators, Paraguay, the successor
state to the Jesuit communities, became the strongest nation in South
America. It took the combined forces of Argentina, Brazil, and Uruguay
five bitter years to subdue her. Moreover, several contemporary military
observers have said that Paraguay would have easily defeated all her neighbors if Francisco Lopez, her last ruler, had not been insane or criminally
incompetent.

Finally, Israel proved in two wars that she is a match for any one of her
Arab neighbors (perhaps even all of them together), though she has far
fewer people as well as less wealth and war equipment than either Iraq or
Egypt.

There are, of course, specific reasons for the nation-in-arms' military
superiorities. Compared to its opponents, it is usually able to utilize a larger
number of trained effectives for decisive combat moments. Also, its armies
frequently possess better discipline and higher morale, which under certain
circumstances make tactical experiment a more realistic possibility.

Though most present-day observers are inclined to believe that the classical city was too small to survive for very long, the actual fact is that these
cities were capable of mobilizing comparatively large armies. Thus, Delbrück, the great German military historian, "discovered," to his surprise
and to the disbelief of many scholars, that the Athenians probably outnumbered the Persians at Marathon.[63] Long before, however, Montesquieu
had observed that the city easily put one-eighth of its free population in the
field while European monarchies strained themselves to outfit forces which
were only a hundredth of the kingdom's population.[64] Given the technological capacity of the ancient world, the city's forces were adequate for
defense. The Greek cities lost their independence, as Demosthenes indicates, not through inherent military inadequacies, but rather because their
systems of training were no longer universal. A similar development, according to Livy, made the huge wealthy empire of Augustus less able to
wage war than the smaller and more primitive Republic.[65]

Other nations-in-arms have a similar proportion of their populations
effectively trained for instant combat duty; modern Switzerland and Israel
have on occasion mobilized one-eighth of their inhabitants in forty-eight

hours. Despite the popular myths which portray nineteenth-century Paraguay and contemporary Israel as Davids in the midst of several Goliaths, these "tiny" nations were able to outnumber their foes on the battlefield. Population statistics are not reliable for the Swiss cities or the Ottoman empire. But the Swiss were able to assemble an army of 50,000 in the sixteenth century, the largest in Europe, and the Ottoman forces were substantially greater than the European until the basis for the Turk's military strength declined.

Military morale in this state-type tends to be exceptionally good, for service is deemed a privilege more than an obligation. Paramilitary training usually begins at an early impressionable age, and it is impossible to hold higher military rank without accepting increased personal sacrifices. Recruits are expected to attain high levels of achievement; even under trying circumstances those in authority will find little resistance to their commands. Conquered peoples and alien residents are not permitted to bear arms—a practice which differs markedly from that of the civilian-and-military state, which in the past recruited some mercenaries and subject peoples and at present conscripts noncitizens. The military establishment of the nation-in-arms, however, always remains the universal testing ground for public-spirited citizens. The ancient's desire to exclude mercenaries and to rotate military offices has modern counterparts in the efforts of Israel and Switzerland to reduce the professional or cadre military elements to a bare minimum and to appoint few men to high permanent military rank; the purpose in each instance is the same—as many citizens as possible must have opportunities to exercise higher command positions. Under such conditions military leaders come "naturally" from the most dedicated, highly educated, and socially significant elements in the population.

The state's constant demand on the "free time" of its citizens both reflects and sustains the population's vivid sense of social distinctiveness, giving rise to a strong national self-consciousness and exclusive political loyalties. In the ancient world "nationalism" was associated with participation in a state-sponsored religion, and the latter engendered sentiments so powerful that the Greeks, though they were closely bound by blood, culture, and history, were unable to create a voluntary political union larger than the city. The Roman national religion was, Polybius and Delbrück maintain, the basis for the Republic's military discipline, and Harrington was so impressed with the tendency of a nation-in-arms to produce a national religion that he predicted England would solve her religious tensions through universal military training.

Harrington's comment is suggestive, although it is obvious that a national religion is neither a necessary precondition nor a consequence of a nation-in-arms. Religion, however, in most instances, ever since the Classical period, has played an important role in shaping the character of this type of state. Turkish fighting enthusiasm depended largely on the continuous prosecution of the war against the infidel. The desertion of Bajazet's armies when he took the field against a fellow Moslem, Tamarlane, gave ample proof of this; only after the Sultan had sufficient personal economic and

administrative strength to dispense with the spontaneous support of the
Turkish masses could he attempt large imperial designs against other Moslem states. The Jesuits in Paraguay were forbidden by their religion from
shedding blood, but religion did not prevent them from acting as the
Indian's military instructors or from accompanying him in battle as chap-
lains. If the Indian dimly understood Catholicism's international implications, he must have been more impressed with the local meaning of his
padre's work. Furthermore, when Francia established the Paraguayan state,
he took special care to sever its religious ties with Rome, and religion became a Paraguayan national affair. Finally, for Israel the political significance of being the world's only Jewish state can hardly be overemphasized.

Only Switzerland obviously lacks the cementing force of religious
nationalism. For, as Machiavelli lamented, a genuine religious parochialism
was impossible in Europe after the "world-wide" dominion of Rome gave
birth to a universal religion. Still, the demands upon the citizens in a nation-
in-arms are so exacting that they will not be satisfied unless the population
has a vivid sense of common purpose and distinctiveness. Since Switzerland
can no longer play an independent role in international politics or ally herself with one of her neighbors against another without stimulating profound
internal cleavages along cultural lines, a likely precondition of Swiss unity
may be an "armed aloofness" that even prevented her from full participation in the League of Nations and from joining the U.N. Whatever the reason, she evidently does have a much more profound isolationist policy than
that of other "neutrals."

The high morale and intense exclusiveness characteristic of a nation-in-
arms is manifested in its war practices. Once war begins, it is usually waged
with a marked aggressive spirit. Conflicts tend to be "total," "scorched
earth" policies are not unusual, demands for "unconditional surrender" are
common, and often a nation will "ruin" itself rather than surrender. Thus,
the most successful warlike Classical cities (Sparta and Rome) refused to
permit defensive fortifications at home, for, according to Machiavelli, such
constructions *necessarily* undermined the aggressive spirit essential to
ancient armies. The mood of the ancient's wars so obviously stemmed from
his political style that Ferguson was moved to contrast them with those
prevailing in contemporary monarchies:

Upon the maxims of this government [monarchy] we apprehend a distinction between
the state and its members, as that between the King and the people, which renders war
as an operation of policy, not of popular animosity. While we strike at the public
interest we would spare the private: and we carry a respect and consideration for individuals which often stops the issue of blood in the ardour of victory and procures to
the prisoner of war a hospitable reception in the very city he came to destroy. . . .
They [the Ancients] endeavored to wound the state by destroying its members, by
desolating its territory, and by ruining the possessions of its subjects. They granted
quarter only to enslave. . . . When this was the issue of war, it was no wonder that
every fortress was defended to the last extremity.[66]

Many observers have remarked on the similarities of Swiss and Roman military fanaticism:

The Swiss have been compared with good reason to the Romans of the early Republic. In the Swiss, as in the Roman character, we find the most intense patriotism combined with a complete lack of chivalrous feeling or magnanimity. . . . In both the steadiest courage and the fervour of noblest self-sacrifice was combined with an appalling ferocity and a cynical disregard for the rights of all neighbors. Among each the warlike pride, generated by successful wars of independence led ere long to wars of conquest and plunder. As enemies both were distinguished for their deliberate and cold-blooded cruelty.[67]

Ottoman military enthusiasm was generated by the *Jihad,*

a doctrine of permanent war . . . [which] end[s] when the world at large constitutes one Moslem community. . . . Thus, strictly speaking every treaty of peace was in fact a truce rather than a peace treaty.[68]

Without the *Jihad* the Turkish army would never have possessed the ardor and efficiency which placed it far above other contemporary forces:

The silence, order and cleanliness of the camps, the absolute obedience enforced if need be by severe punishments and executions, the submissiveness to long marches, hard labor, and scanty food, the eagerness for battle, the joy in conflict, the recklessness of life, presented a perfection of discipline, self-control, and single-hearted purpose that seemed miraculous.[69]

The ferociousness of the Jesuit-led Guarani is well known, and under the second Lopez the Paraguayans' unrelenting desire to press the attack even when hopelessly outnumbered or in a good defensive position appeared entirely irrational to European military observers. But one foreigner suggested that this military "folly" might have had a sound political justification:

Perhaps Lopez thought it necessary not to let his men rest too long without fighting, lest they should feel he was afraid of the Allies.[70]

Only after four-fifths of the population was destroyed in five years of war was the remaining handful willing to surrender.

Finally, many have noted that Israel's army has a "curious mystique of militancy" symbolized in the tactical maxim of the Nahal, "When in doubt, lash out,"[71] or in the statement of Moshe Dayan, the army's recent commander, that he would not excuse a unit's failure to accomplish its mission unless it suffered 50 per cent casualties.[72] Moreover, the standard Israeli maneuver practice of rewarding the most aggressive individual, regardless of rank, with an opportunity to command his unit in the next war game may well be the institutional expression of Dayan's insistence that the proper command for an officer is "Not 'Go and do so and so!' but always 'Follow me!' "[73]

A well-organized nation-in-arms in the past has used its advantages of constant training and high morale to develop particular tactical superiorities. Most historical armies, for instance, have not been able to use infantrymen effectively, for men on foot will not stand steady in the face of charging horsemen or chariots unless they possess immense fire-power superiority or are placed behind strong fortifications. Yet the irony is, as almost every military writer since Aristotle and Xenophon has remarked, if the confidence of the footman in himself and his comrades can be developed to check the passion to waver or flee before the horse is upon him, the horse itself will be so unnerved in the instant before contact that there will be little difficulty in disposing of its rider. The same discipline necessary to sustain infantry can also be used to create a system of tactical maneuver indispensable to the infantryman's continued domination on the battlefield. But this achievement is impossible without repeated practice and a powerful will to conquer, and it is therefore necessary to stress the importance of their political systems in order to understand why the Greeks and Romans were the first peoples to use infantry well. When Rome lost its republican character, it gradually lost its facility to employ disciplined infantry, and it was not until the Swiss assembled their phalanxes a millennium later that any European people could employ infantry against cavalry in the open field. In the intervening period the Ottoman Janissaries were the only infantry worthy of the name. (They were incidentally also the first good Asian infantry.)

It is worth noting finally that the Jesuits made foot soldiers the backbone of their Indian armies. But under Lopez the Paraguayans often could not resist a cavalry charge, even though nineteenth-century technology gave them the fire-power advantages their fathers lacked. However, the entire Paraguayan military situation was so unusual that it is scarcely plausible. In the century between the Jesuit expulsion and the war against Brazil, Argentina, and Uruguay, no Paraguayan had combat experience. Francia, the army's founder, was innocent of war and is reported to have used Rollin's history of Rome as a textbook on organization, drill, and tactics.[74] While that work could help a novice develop a military organization, it seems hardly adequate for a tactical manual in the nineteenth century. Perhaps this combination of circumstances helps throw some light on the mystery which puzzled nearly every witness of the Paraguayan ordeal—the contrast between the Indian's excellent fighting qualities and his officer's patent inability to utilize elementary tactical and strategic advantages, two characteristics rarely found together in the same army. If Lopez had been less convinced of his own genius, the situation might have been remedied, for the really surprising aspect of this war was not that it took Argentina, Brazil, and Uruguay so long to defeat Paraguay, but that they were able to do so at all.

Another tactical advantage available to a nation-in-arms is the possibility of dividing its forces into small self-contained units to augment the army's general mobility and capacity to adapt to different fighting terrains. Hastily assembled citizen militias lack the training, and armies with many mercenaries lack the instinctive loyalties, to develop elaborate tactical subdivisions without essentially impairing the unity of command. But the Romans were able to master the difficult military geography of Europe by splitting their original phalanxes into legions, cohorts, maniples, and centuries. Europe had to wait for Gustavus Adolphus to build an army largely on nation-in-arms principles before any state could approach the Roman ability for tactical maneuver. Even though the eighteenth-century Western armies were commanded by loyal nobles, tactical dispersion on a grand scale was still difficult, for the ranks were composed of mercenaries. Subsequently, the *levée en masse* produced by the French during the Revolution made it necessary for the other Western states to utilize the military potentialities of the ordinary citizen. Although the modern nation-in-arms has no long-run advantage over its civilian-and-military contemporary in this tactical respect, the former still has an important strength which the praetorian state lacks. At least one major cause cited for Israel's recent triumph over Egypt was the victor's ability to diffuse military responsibilities effectively and the defeated's incapacity to do so.[75]

Inasmuch as the nation-in-arms possesses great military competence, enormous self-confidence, and exclusive nationalist tendencies, she in the past demonstrated little reluctance to engage frequently in hostilities. The Greeks and Romans have been reckoned as the most belligerent peoples in history,[76] and the Turks and Swiss before the eighteenth century were not far behind in aggressiveness. Paraguay initiated the only real war Latin America has known since Bolivar, and the pacifist-inclined modern European and Mediterranean Jew has developed a "new" militant personality in Israel. Yet the nation-in-arms does not always need to seek war as the indispensable stimulant to the vitality of the body politic. Paraguay flourished during its half-century of peace, and Switzerland's strength and cohesion has not been weakened by a determination to remain isolated from European hostilities since the French Revolution.

War can help increase the nation-in-arms' solidarity by making citizens aware of the necessity for maintaining their system of civic education, but other conditions can perform the same function. Undoubtedly, the realization that she lost her independence after her military system deteriorated and that she occupied an exposed position in the world's most belligerent continent contributed to Switzerland's determination to keep her military constitution intact. Although Israel's special identity as the only Jewish state and her desire to assimilate many immigrants with few common habits are incalculable factors buttressing her present constitutional life, the clear possibility of national annihilation seems the chief obstacle to Israelis who might prefer to reduce their civic obligations. When no such likelihood exists, and the state is surrounded by impotent neighbors, it may seek national isolation, as Paraguay did in the nineteenth century. But in the modern world isolation is unfeasible, secular and hedonist values are dominant, and it may become increasingly difficult for a nation-in-arms to find its necessary "moral equivalent" for war or for the threat of national extinction.

Even in earlier periods many citizens were reluctant to carry heavy military burdens once they came into contact with peoples whose obligations were less severe. And most states discovered that it was difficult to find another satisfactory civic education once a popular reluctance to attend the old school became manifest. Although the polis was able to reduce friendly contact with "outsiders" for a time after its foundation, the complete isolation Plato deemed essential for internal stability was impossible, since no city was more than a day's journey from its nearest neighbor. Parochial loyalties were at first strengthened by the annual wars, but gradually the inconclusive and bloody character of these conflicts induced more and more states to hire mercenaries to do their fighting. With this development the principal basis for civic training was lost, and the Greeks proved incapable of accepting a broader political ethic. Increased international contacts did not breed new loyalties; they merely weakened the desire to serve the tiny polis. Remnants of the warrior ideal prevented the citizen from pursuing commerce with dignity and from creating self-governing trade organizations. In sum, the Greek's capacity for association atrophied when he found military service too arduous; he was unwilling to submit to law, unable to respect authority, and too self-concerned to labor for a common purpose. Public office was no longer synonymous with private sacrifice and public service; it became instead the best available means for private enrichment through exploitation of public property. The war of each against all began.

The Roman school for citizenship lasted much longer, focusing much more narrowly on military matters and providing less opportunity for physical and mental diversion in the gymnasia. Moreover, since Rome did not require an elaborate adolescent training for citizenship, it proved easier to expand the size of the civic body to carry on war continuously without involving every member at any one time. Rome, therefore, had the power to conclude her wars, to wear her foes down; she was, as Machiavelli pointed out,[77] the one ancient city designed for conquest rather than defense. As long as she could find enemies worth conquering and as long as most Romans were needed for war, the Republic could survive. But when Mithridates was conquered, and most of the known world was under Roman sway, Sulla might well ask, "Now that the universe offers us no more enemies what may be the fate of the Republic?" Rome's praetorian age was about to begin.

IV: Conclusion

If it is good to know how to deal with men as they are, it is much better to make them what there is need they should be. The most absolute authority is that which penetrates a man's inner being, and concerns itself no less with his will than with his actions. . . . Make men, therefore, if you would command men: if you would have them obedient to the laws, make them love the laws, and then they will need to know only what is their duty to do it.   ROUSSEAU[78]

Few analyses of military institutions deal with the functions of the army in the political community. Yet when the military is examined from this perspective, various characteristics receive special meaning and form "new" logical relationships. Thus, in the civilian-and-military polity, despite the fact that the armies of the twelfth, sixteenth, eighteenth, and nineteenth centuries had many obvious formal differences, they shared more fundamental common elements that determined their internal structure, development, and efficiency. They were designed, first, to protect a special kind of state from aggression and, second, to serve its foreign policies. The military formula was, therefore, shaped by war needs and limited by a framework provided by a particular type of civic life. Developing technology and the social composition of the army had necessarily significant influences on organization and capabilities.

The scholar will find it less instructive to dwell on the formal organization, technology, and the social sources of recruitment in a praetorian army. The Praetorian Guard carried swords and was composed originally of Italy's finest youth, the Janissaries were slaves armed with muskets, and Argentina's officers come from the middle class and command tanks; but in each case the army is equally effective in policing the population and disposing of *de facto* governments. Similarly, in the nation-in-arms, provided the state can be defended, technology will have a small role in determining the character of the army, but the percentage of full citizens receiving an intensive military education is significant. When the entire civic population is well trained, the army develops an indomitable spirit and possesses a "democratic" quality, for military careers are allotted to the most talented, vigorous, and devoted citizens.

Military and political institutions are inseparable; in a certain sense they are mutually dependent variables. A change in the character of one produces a corresponding change in the other. The relationship between democracy and conscription in the West is well known. Less widely understood but equally significant is the Swiss experience. A return to a nation-in-arms policy and the unification of military institutions after the Napoleonic Wars constituted perhaps the most immediate cause of subsequent political union. But the military reform itself was feasible in the first place because the Swiss had a long and glorious history in addition to the bitter memory of a recent occupation. Moreover, before the cantons accepted a common government, the strength of their desire for unity was tested in the crucible of civil war.

It is essential to stress that both military and political institutions are manifestations of something deeper and more vital than themselves—a conception of community. A military innovator must be prepared to accept the possibility that civil life may have to be reconstructed to vouchsafe his military reforms. The continued persistence of Swiss separatism would probably have wrecked the national army. Many efforts have been made by modern praetorian governments to create a cadre-conscript army without simultaneously attempting to reconstruct public morality. But no "new" military establishment has emerged. Note one military analyst's estimate of the effect of "modern" training on one praetorian army. "The Egyptian officers were well-educated and . . . knew their jobs well," but they could not put "knowledge into practise"; they "disliked enduring hardship and tedious duty, took unkindly to campaigning and had little interest in risking [their] lives in battle."[79] Latin American armies have taken on a Western veneer under the influence of Prussian, French, and American military missions; nevertheless, they cannot be reduced when no threat of war exists. The only important substantive change is that the hand of the officer has been strengthened, and he, rather than the local *caudillo,* makes and unmakes governments. Could a different outcome have been reasonably anticipated? Was it possible for the Latin American officer to stay aloof from intrigue when civilians remained eager for conspiracy?

The nation-in-arms may offer an ideal model for those interested in "remaking" praetorian countries; the former's egalitarian principles can help resolve the latter's inherent ideological frustrations, and its institutions are comprehensive enough to embrace the necessary program of radical civic re-education. Nevertheless, prospects for most modern praetorian states are grim; few nations-in-arms have ever emerged from the havoc which praetorianism wreaks in public morality. The contemporary examples of Jewish and Swiss experience offer few parallels for many lands. Neither people had a praetorian experience; both had proud traditions and a recent great calamity that nourished an exclusive nationalism and then gave birth to a public order. But accidents of history have prevented modern praetorian state boundaries from coinciding with well-defined national sentiments. An Iraqi is almost as likely to support Egypt's ambitions as he is to sympathize with his own state's hopes. A decade ago a Bolivian might respond to the call of Buenos Aires, and today Havana might influence him greatly; only in fits and starts will he put the interest of La Paz first. A resident of Khartoum may be so attached to the cause of Africa that he will impair the unity of the Sudan. In contemporary times both Paraguay's policy of isolation to strengthen provincial loyalties and the Roman or Ottoman quest to find union in war would be impractical. The power of modern military technology and the influence of international bodies make even the belief that a small state's survival depends upon its own military efforts seem anachronistic except to those who have already preserved themselves in this way. Finally, the "world-wide revolution of rising expectations" intensifies the praetorian citizen's tendency to ask more from government than he is willing to grant in return and threatens, as a consequence, the search for stability. The brief recent Bolivian experiment with a nation-in-arms was a bellwether; from the start the militia was more prone to mutiny than to sacrifice. Few such states will be transformed; on the contrary, the number of praetorian countries could swell in the near future as dramatically as it has swollen in the recent past.

NOTES

1. Friedrich Engels, "The Armies of Europe," *Putnam's Monthly*, 6 (1855) 193-206, 306-317.

2. See my "Praetorianism: Government without Consensus," unpublished Ph.D. dissertation, University of California (Berkeley, 1960), to be published as *Praetorianism: Government without Authority*.

3. A statement supposedly made by Aristotle in *The Politics*. See Ibn Khaldun, *The Muqaddimah*, trans. and ed. Franz Rosenthal (London, 1958), I, 82.

4. G. W. F. Hegel, *Philosophy of History*, trans. J. Sibree (New York, 1899), p. 84.

5. The discussion in this paragraph depends upon the various definitions given to the words "Praetorian Guard," "praetorian," and "praetorianism" in *The New Oxford English Dictionary*, corr. and rev. (London, 1933), *Webster's New International Dictionary* (New York, 1949), and *Funk and Wagnalls New Standard Dictionary* (New York, 1949).

The best studies of the Guard are in French and German. See Marcel Durry, *Les Cohortes prétoriannes* (Paris, 1938) and his article, "Praetoria Cohortes," *Pauly Wissowa*, (Stuttgart, 1954) XXII: 2, 1607-1634. Cf. R. Cagnat, "Praetoriae Cohortes," in *Dictionnaire des Antiquites*, (Paris, 1875-1919), IV, 632-642.

I have been able to find only two modern discussions of the concept of praetorianism; both are in English. See F. J. Watkins, "Praetorianism," in *Encyclopedia of the Social Sciences* (New York, 1934), XII, 305-307, and S. Andrzejewski, *Military Organisation and Society* (London, 1954), pp. 104-107.

6. Gibbon very aptly describes the constitutional rhythms of a praetorian state: "[It] . . . floats between the extremes of absolute monarchy and wild democracy." *The Decline and Fall of the Roman Empire* (New York, 1899), I, 235.

7. See Alberto Lleras, "The Secret of Peace" in A. N. Christensen (ed.), *Evolution of Latin American Government* (New York, 1951), pp. 697-704.

8. William Blackstone, *Commentaries on the Laws of England* (Oxford: 1765), I, 13.

9. Justification of Viscounte Dorte in refusing to accept Charles IX's order to massacre the Huguenots in his province, in Charles de Secondat, Baron de Montesquieu, *Spirit of the Laws,* trans. Thomas Nugart, (New York, 1900), IV, 2.

10. I have not studied Norway, Austria, and Italy.

11. Western communities able to use a navy as the "first line of defense" found they could depend upon volunteers instead of conscripts to expand their cadres at least until the twentieth century. For a good analysis of the cadre establishment, see Frederick M. Stern, *The Citizen Army* (New York, 1957), pp. 1-55.

12. Observation of a native-born Israeli soldier on the early behavior of immigrant Jewish recruits from Egypt and Morocco, in Moshe Brilliant, "With a Patrol in Israel," *New York Times Magazine,* December 7, 1952, p. 22.

13. Jean Bodin, *Six Books of the Commonwealth,* trans. and ed. M. J. Tooley, (Oxford, 1955), V, 5.

14. Bacon was the first English philosopher to discuss "nation[s] that do profess arms as their principal honour, study, and occupation," and though his essay "Of the True Greatness of Kingdomes and Estates" was brilliant, it was ignored by subsequent commentators.

15. Cf. Herbert Spencer, *Principles of Sociology* (London, 1876), I, and Harold Lasswell, "Sino-Japanese Crisis: The Garrison State Versus the Civilian State," *China Quarterly,* 2 (Fall, 1937), 643-649; "The Garrison State and Specialists in Violence," *American Journal of Sociology,* 16 (January, 1941), 455-468; "The Interrelations of World Organization and Society," *Yale Law Journal,* 55 (August, 1946), 889-909; "The Threat Inherent in the Garrison-Police State," in his *National Security and Individual Freedom* (New York, 1950), pp. 23-49.

16. See for example Arthur Ekirch, *The Civilian and the Military* (New York, 1956) and Louis Smith, *American Democracy and Military Power* (Chicago, 1951).

17. The first major effort in this direction since the war is Edward C. Banfield, *The Moral Basis of a Backward Society* (Glencoe, Ill., 1958).

18. Walter Bagehot, *Physics and Politics* (New York, 1900), p. 18.

19. Montesquieu, *op. cit.,* I, 3.

20. Harry H. Turney-High, *Primitive War* (Columbia, S. C., 1949), p. 230.

21. *Ibid.,* p. 229.

22. *Ibid.,* pp. 231-232.

23. *Ibid.,* p. 235.

24. "Every member wishes to separate himself from the band when it is in danger. Indeed the wish to decamp is always strongest at just that point, the tactically critical point where the group is in greatest danger. The prime object of discipline and training is to prevent this." Hillaire Belloc, *Poitiers,* (London, 1913) p. 112.

25. James Harrington, *The Commonwealth of Oceana,* ed. S. B. Liljegren (Heidelberg, 1924), pp. 64-65, 82-87, 162-167.

26. George Counts, "Education: History," in *Encyclopedia of the Social Sciences* (New York, 1931), V, 403-414. Aristotle maintains that one *essential* characteristic of the polity is that all citizens bear arms, in *Politics,* 1265 a.

27. Guglielmo Ferrero explains the ancient's well-known reluctance to commerce in a different way; nevertheless, his comment also emphasizes the scant training this activity would give him for the exercise of public responsibilities.

". . . he has little liking for work and still less for subordination. He will work a little as an artisan or a trader if he is not subjected to control and he will resign himself to dependence on another as a retainer or arm-bearer, if he is thereby saved from working; but he will never voluntarily submit both to work and to be in dependence. He would rather beg or steal." *The Greatness and Decline of Rome* (New York, 1909) I, 28.

28. Montesquieu, *op. cit.,* IV, 8.

29. Elizabeth Weber, *The Duk-Duks, Primitive and Historic Types of Citizenship* (Chicago, 1929), p. 73. See also Plutarch, "Life of Lycurgus."

30. Plutarch, *ibid.*

31. Clarence Forbes, *Greek Physical Education* (New York, 1929), chs. IV and VIII.

32. "Athenian Ephebic Oath" trans. J. N. Taylor, *Classical Journal,* 13 (1918), 499.

33. ". . . as to the education of free-born citizens. This is a problem on which the Greeks have wasted much effort; but our institutions are opposed to any detailed universal system of public education, obligatory by law. In fact my guest, Polybius, maintains that this is the one point on which our institutions can be accused of negligence." Cicero, *de Rep.,* IV, 3. See also Weber, *op. cit.,* pp. 85-93; Counts, *loc. cit.;* Aubrey Gwynn, *Roman Education* (Oxford, 1926) ch. I.

34. An ideal Roman education conducted under the father's auspices is described by Plutarch in the "Life of Marcus Cato."

35. See Charles de Secondat, Baron de Montesquieu, *Considerations on the Causes of the Grandeur and Decline of Rome*, chs. 1-3, and 8-10; Hans Delbrück, *Numbers in History* (London, 1913) pp. 33-34; and Ernest Brehaut, "Occupational Development of Roman Society about the Time of Cato the Elder," *Essays in Intellectual History Dedicated to J. H. Robinson*, (New York, 1924), pp. 41-54.

36. Brehaut, *loc. cit.*, p. 49.

37. ". . . the Ottoman emirate remained the only real Ghazi state, the exclusive control and successful representative of the Ghazi movement whose renown spread far beyond its own borders and attracted the entire warlike youth of Anatolia and all those elements who were full of enthusiasm for religious war, for adventure, fame and spoil. The 'potential militaire' of this state was always larger than its own circumference (even after) the rapid growth of the latter. Thus the state must conquer, it must continue the Ghazi—the religious war." Paul Wittek, *The Rise of the Ottoman Empire* (London, 1938), pp. 45-46. The Ottoman state was a nation-in-arms for nearly three centuries; by the seventeenth century it exhibited marked praetorian features.

38. Joseph von Hammer, *Des Osmanischen Reichs Staatsversfassung und Staatsverwaltung* (Vienna, 1815), I, 340.

39. Albert H. Lybyer, *Government of the Ottoman Empire in the Time of Suleiman the Magnificent* (Cambridge, Mass., 1913), p. 71. See also Barnette Miller, *The Palace School of Mohammed the Conqueror* (Cambridge, Mass., 1941) and H. A. R. Gibb and H. Bowen, *Islamic Society and the West* (London, 1950), I, 45ff. At the time of Suleiman the Great, when the slave staff was near its peak efficiency, it numbered around 50,000; see von Hammer, *op. cit.* II, 181.

40. Lybyer, *op. cit.*, p. 91.

41. *Ibid.*, p. 90.

42. See Hans Delbrück, *Geschichte der Kriegskunst im Rahmen der Politischen Geschichte* (Berlin, 1900-1936), III, 563ff.; Julian Grande, *A Citizens' Army* (New York, 1916), "Introduction"; J. Christopher Herold, *The Swiss Without Halos* (New York, 1948) pp. 28ff., 42ff., and 113ff.; and Wilhelm Oechsli, *History of Switzerland* (London, 1922), ch. I.

43. Oechsli, *op. cit.*, pp. 250ff.

44. William Rappard, *Collective Security in Swiss Experience* (London, 1948), p. 77.

45. An unidentified former General Secretary of the International Peace Bureau, quoted by Julian Grande, *op. cit.*, pp. 106. An American pacifist offers similar testimony: ". . . what is barracks routine elsewhere is for the Swiss a school. The term they employ, *Rekrutenshule*, is significant of their essentially pedagogical approach to all problems that confront them, the military no less than those of civil life . . . .

"It is no easy matter to estimate the effect of Swiss military training upon citizenship in later life. No doubt it is profound, partly because of its universality. One often hears the remark in Switzerland, that the recruit school is like the public school, virtually every male citizen having attended both. Of course public school attendance lasts much longer; but on the other hand, the recruit school brings the manhood of the country together at a very impressionable age and under conditions that foster comradeship. Any two Swiss from whatever part of the country who have completed their training have something in common to talk about for the rest of their lives and they do talk about it frequently and with much gusto." Robert C. Brooks, *Civic Training in Switzerland* (Chicago, 1930), pp. 147, 150. See also Stern, *op. cit.*, pp. 155-175.

46. Not much material is available on the Israeli army for one who does not know Hebrew. Outside of numerous newspaper articles, I have consulted the following works: Horace M. Kallen, *Utopians at Bay*, (New York, 1958), chs. VI and VII; A. Kravi, *The Israeli Armed Forces* (Tel Aviv, 1957); Robert Henriques, *A Hundred Hours to Suez* (New York, 1957); Edgar O'Ballance, *The Sinai Campaign* (London, 1956); Ben Halpern, "The Role of the Military in Israel," mimeographed paper at Rand Corporation, in "Conference on the Military in the Underdeveloped Countries" (1959), to be published; and *Israel and the Middle East*, 5 (1955), nos. 1 and 3.

47. Henriques, *op. cit.*, p. 12.

48. Prime Minister Ben Gurion has explained the educational work of the army in this way: "To become a fighting nation we must first become a nation. But we are still only a collection of tribes . . . . At least our youth are being moulded into a nation." Quoted by Moshe Brilliant, *loc. cit.*, p. 22.

49. Montesquieu, *Spirit of the Laws*, IV, 6; Pelham Horton Box, *The Origins of the Paraguayan War* (Urbana, 1927), II, 289ff.; Sir Richard Burton, *Letters from the Battlefields of Paraguay* (London, 1870), pp. 33ff.; R. B. Cunninghame-Graham, *A Vanished Arcadia* (London, 1924), pp. 177ff.; René Fülöp-Miller, *The Power and Secret*

of Jesuits (New York, 1930), pp. 276-302; Magnus Mörner, *The Political and Economic Activities of the Jesuits in the La Plata Region* (Stockholm, 1953), pp. 152ff.; and George O'Neill, *Golden Years on the Paraguay* (London, 1934).

50. The size of the communities varied, and scholars still dispute the minimum and maximum figures represented, the most frequently given being between 2,500 and 7,500.

51. René Fülöp-Miller *(op. cit.,* pp. 283-289) characterizes the Jesuit enterprise as a "musical kingdom," since music accompanied practically every common activity. Although music may have been particularly significant in Paraguay, it seems to have been also important to most nations-in-arms and to early military developments elsewhere. The Greek philosophers were well aware of this, and the Turks included the study of music in the educational curriculum for the sultan's slaves. Moreover, in Europe the superiority of the Swiss in the fifteenth century and the final establishment of modern infantry tactical units by Maurice of Nassau in part depended upon the revival of military music, which enabled men to march in step.

52. Many specific details of the system which Francia and the two Lopez despots implemented in Paraguay have been lost to posterity, since most of the state's administrative records were destroyed. Furthermore, a great many matters are still disputed by present-day scholars, for the policies the three rulers pursued aroused strong passions among those who originally recorded them. Nevertheless, it seems to me that the main outlines of the state are clear. My description above depends mostly upon Box, *op. cit.,* R. B. Cunninghame-Graham, *Portrait of a Dictator* (London, 1933); Burton, *op. cit.,* Mörner, *op. cit.;* Philip Raine, *Paraguay* (New Brunswick, 1956), pp. 79-195; J. R. Rengger and M. Longchamp, *Essai historique sur la revolution du Paraguay* (Paris, 1827); George Thompson, *The War in Paraguay* (London, 1869); Lewis W. Bealer, "Francia," "Carlos Antonio Lopez," and "Francisco Solano Lopez" in A. C. Wilgus (ed.), *South American Dictators* (Washington, D.C., 1937), pp. 58-77 and 136-173, and Thomas Carlyle, "Dr. Francia," in *Critical and Miscellaneous Essays* (London, 1859), IV, p. 249-295.

53. Swiss males who are unable to fulfill their military obligations are required to pay a tax proportionate to the size of their income. They are not deprived of their civic rights as a consequence.

54. Quoted in Raine, *op. cit.,* p. 194.

55. Stern, *op. cit.,* p. 173.

56. Max Weber, *General Economic History* (London, 1923), p. 324.

57. The "military revolution" of the period was in part initiated by a "rediscovery" of classical military textbooks by political theorists like Machiavelli and Lipsius.

58. See "Of Empire" and "Of the True Greatness of Kingdoms and Estates."

59. Harrington, *op. cit.,* p. 197.

60. Montesquieu, *Considerations . . . ,* ch. 3.

61. Rappard, *op. cit.,* p. 15; Oechsli, *op. cit.,* p. 7 and ch. 4; Herold, *op. cit.,* p. 47

62. B. H. Liddell Hart, *The Defence of Britain* (New York, 1939), pp. 241ff., and Stern, *op. cit.,* ch. 13.

63. Delbrück, *op. cit.,* I, 39ff.

64. Montesquieu, *Considerations . . . , op. cit.,* ch. 3.

65. Livy, *History of Rome,* VII, 25; see also Montesquieu, *Considerations . . . ,* ch. 15.

66. Adam Ferguson, *An Essay on the History of Civil Society,* 3rd ed. (London, 1768), pp. 309-310.

67. Sir Charles Oman, *A History of the Art of War in the Middle Ages* (London, 1924), II, 253.

68. Majid Khadduri, *Law of War and Peace in Islam* (London, 1948), pp. 31, 96.

69. Lybyer, *op. cit.,* p. 108.

70. Thompson, *op. cit.,* p. 157.

71. London *Daily Telegraph,* May 5, 1960.

72. Henriques, *op. cit.,* p. 15.

73. *Ibid.*

74. Rengger and Longchamp, *op. cit.,* pp. 21ff.

75. Henriques, *op. cit.,* pp. 43ff., and 57ff.; O'Ballance, *op. cit.,* pp. 192ff.

76. Quincy Wright, *A Study of War,* (Chicago, 1942) I, 572. Professor Wright actually places classical civilization a close second to Babylonic civilization in his scale of "warlikeness," but includes in his indices irrelevant political characteristics. If a civilization's warlikeness is measured solely by the number of battles it fights, then Professor Wright's evidence indicates the classical states are far ahead at the top of the scale.

77. *Discourses,* I, 6.

78. J. J. Rousseau, "A Discourse on Political Economy," trans. G. D. H. Cole in *The Social Contract and Discourses* (London, 1913), p. 243.

79. O'Ballance, *op. cit.,* pp. 42-43.

Military Behavior in International Organization – NATO's Defense College

BY *LAURENCE I. RADWAY*

IN 1900 STATESMEN and general staffs could fairly assume that wars would be fought by national armies or loosely coordinated alliances. Though it is too soon to discard this assumption, it seems clear that highly structured coalitions or international "police forces" will be important forms of military organization in the future. Such multilateral security enterprises are but a special kind of cooperative system. Within them it is possible to observe a human problem familiar in small-scale organization. Participants are caught between a desire to subordinate their parochial ways and an inability to divest themselves of their separate identities.

My purpose is to examine this ancient dilemma as it is illustrated in the behavior of national military personnel in selected NATO institutions. The analysis centers on variables that create either divisive behavior and strained relations or integrative behavior and cooperative relations. Special attention is given to relations between American and allied military officers. The institution emphasized throughout is the NATO Defense College. Comparative references are also made to SHAPE, its subordinate Central and Southern headquarters at Fontainebleau and Naples, respectively, and the Atlantic headquarters at Norfolk, Virginia (SACLANT). But no effort is made to provide a complete or up-to-date description of either the College or the regional commands, or to evaluate their effectiveness, or to develop policy recommendations for the design and management of international military agencies.

The Defense College was established in Paris in 1951 by the North Atlantic Council to prepare personnel for NATO staffs and national ministries with NATO business. The NATO Standing Group was made responsible for immediate supervision. From fifty to sixty students were assigned by thirteen

I am grateful to the Social Science Research Council for supporting my research on this topic. Most of the material on which it is based was collected in 1957 by personal interviews or from unpublished memoranda.

NATO countries. About a dozen were civil servants. The remainder were officers, usually of the grade of colonel, lieutenant colonel, or equivalents. Staff and faculty members were drawn from several countries on a rotating basis. The course, which lasted slightly less than six months, consisted of lectures, committee work, discussion groups, and instructional tours to member nations.

Findings can be summarized quickly. Relations among officers assigned to the College were strained by political disagreements, national pride, and different economic, social, and cultural traditions. The fragility of the alliance made it difficult to counter these divisive influences by developing doctrine. For many reasons it also proved difficult to counter them by forging institutional, social, or professional bonds. But, despite these obstacles, "NATO spirit" was more evident at the Defense College than at regional military headquarters, where the game involved larger stakes.

I

At the time these observations were made, the members of NATO shared enough apprehension to maintain their military alliance. They were not, however, united by dramatic political goals or animated by ambitious economic or cultural objectives. It was not their declared purpose to federate, to develop a common foreign policy, to adopt a common language, to extend economic aid to the Afro-Asian world, to create a customs union, or to embark on a joint program to maintain full employment or a high level of social services. Some of the enthusiasm that had marked NATO's earlier years had evaporated. So had fear of imminent Soviet aggression. Member nations were divided or distracted by political issues within and without the area covered by their treaty—issues such as German rearmament, the European Defense Community, Indochina, Algeria, Cyprus, the Icelandic fisheries, and Suez. All members retained a veto power equal to or greater than that they enjoyed in the United Nations. Each sought to retain ultimate control over its armed forces. Except for Germany, each withheld some part of those forces from NATO's integrated commands. France had sent to Algeria troops previously stationed on the Western front. Great Britain had announced its intention to cut the Army of the Rhine. Several nations took unilateral action in reducing their military budgets or their terms of compulsory military service. All were plagued by doubts about the strategic policy governing the forces they were willing to contribute to the alliance. NATO continued to be sustained by a minimum of largely negative common aims. But its members were not fully agreed about the nature and seriousness of the danger confronting them, the best way to meet it, the importance to place upon it relative to other international problems, or the proper way to allocate burdens, places, and prerogatives among themselves.

Within the NATO Defense College these difficulties were reflected in jockeying for position, in open debate, and in national sensitivity that was expressed in a subdued manner or implied by elaborate efforts to avoid embarrassing incidents. National pride was evident in competition for places in the class and on the staff. The size of each class was limited to fifty or sixty students by the physical facilities that were available. Initial quotas were established with the advice of an *ad hoc* committee containing representatives of Belgium and Italy as well as the Standing Group powers, France, Great Britain, and the United States. Seven places were allocated to France, Great Britain, Italy, and the United States; five to Canada; four to Belgium-Luxembourg; three to Denmark, the Netherlands, Norway, and Portugal; and one to Iceland. Italy had insisted on parity with the Standing Group powers. Greece and Turkey, who entered the alliance later, were each given three positions. Germany, entering still later, asked for six positions but had to settle temporarily for four. Faculty posts were reserved exclusively to Standing Group nations at the start, but Italy again argued strongly for representation and secured it in the second class. Canada, Belgium, Germany, Turkey, and the Netherlands furnished instructors in later classes. A number of smaller countries also coveted the position of commandant when it was opened to non-Standing Group powers in 1956, and the matter had to be handled delicately to protect national pride.[1]

Although few members of the Defense College were familiar with such negotiations in detail, each was quite aware of the relative influence of his nation within the school. Each was also sensitive to ongoing disputes between his nation and other countries represented in the College. Within limits, students were officially encouraged to speak up on such disputes. The Suez crisis of 1956 provoked open debate between British and French students and their American colleagues. Several months earlier the Commandant had developed a committee problem on the Middle East with a specific intent of bringing out different attitudes toward colonialism. During their instructional tours the cross-examination of national authorities by the students was sometimes quite sharp. British ministers were asked by Greek colonels to justify their position on Cyprus. West German ministers were asked whether a Soviet offer to reunify their country would diminish their ardor for NATO.

It must be remembered, however, that the military students at the Defense College were members of a profession that has good reason to restrain public controversy. The physical setting in which they gathered tended also to inhibit private controversy. The *ad hoc* committee appointed to advise the Commandant-Designate in 1951 had recommended that students live together in SHAPE Village or a similar enclave. But it was impossible to find space quickly enough. Since both the Commandant-Designate and another member of the *ad hoc* committee were at that time in charge of defense colleges located in the École Militaire, they arranged to turn over to NATO a wing of the building that had been used to store old records. If the institution had been located in a great "country house," candid argument over the issues that divided its personnel might have continued long into the night. In the halls of the École Militaire candor often gave way to tact. Certain topics were either avoided or treated with restraint. Students did not incite argument over the wisdom of admitting Spain into NATO or the advisability of deploying German forces in Denmark. French officers were not pressed closely about the European Defense Community if they appeared reluctant to discuss it. At one time it was proposed to hold a formal discussion of French policy in Algeria, and to follow this with a discussion of the position of the Negro in the United States, but the suggestion was rejected; as an officer put it later, "We saw no reason to rub salt in open wounds." Two other small incidents suggest the care sometimes taken to preserve harmony: pictures of the Remagen bridgehead and the Nuremburg trials were removed from College walls prior to the arrival of the first contingent of German students; and opposition was expressed to adding Herbert Leuthy's *France Against Herself* to the library, because the book was felt to present an unfair picture of French government and society. A much more serious problem arose at the height of the Cyprus crisis, when it was not easy for the protagonists to extend a cordial welcome to each other's military officers. Two classes had to omit part of their instructional tours, and at other times Turkish and Greek officers did not accompany the student body on visits to each other's countries. (Greek forces were actually withdrawn from the NATO command at Izmir, Turkey, in 1958.) Some time also elapsed before German students accompanied the College to Denmark and Norway.

When members of the College did open up controversial issues, they frequently took the indirect course of putting guest speakers on the spot rather than spelling out their own views or cross-examining fellow students. Moreover, when an incident appeared to staff members to be particularly disturbing, they took steps to prevent its recurrence. A committee problem on relations between American troops and the surrounding French community was discontinued because discussion got out of hand. A lecturer on the Near East wore out his welcome by acid comments on Western policy. The first commandant asked his deputies to instruct visiting lecturers to avoid matters that might provoke "passionate" discussion or evoke "disagreeable memories." In a memorandum to his superiors he also noted that students were supposed to speak as experts, not as nationalists. In this way the desire to minimize clashes sometimes encouraged a retreat to the technical, particularly to shop talk about weapons and personnel policies.

II

A particularly sensitive point for allied officers was the ambiguous position of American personnel at the Defense College. Although their concern was not voiced loudly, it was important enough in the life of the institution to warrant detailed comment. The difficulty was that some American officers were perceived to be lacking in the personal stature appropriate to their easy assumption of leadership. American officers held high rank (no other nation selected an equally large percentage of full colonels), but they were considerably younger than most allied officers. They appeared less versatile, more narrowly specialized, and more likely to remain lowly "Indians" within their huge military establishment. Although they lived in better hotels and entertained more splendidly, they were perceived to be less well born, less well educated, deficient in essential historical knowledge, and deplorably weak in languages. The last was painfully obvious; no other national contingent so regularly enrolled so large a proportion of its members in the elementary class in French.

These perceptions generated an undercurrent of anti-American feeling among allied students because they coexisted with a lively sense of American national power. It was not understood that the stature of American personnel was to some extent a necessary consequence of that power. There was a paradox here. The very might of the United States gave its officers a dominant role in an enterprise in which they could not afford to get involved too deeply. In the larger treaty organization Americans took their leadership for granted. They said so in many ways: "We're the hammer." "SHAPE works because the U.S. takes up the slack." "We do 75 per cent of the work and check 99 per cent." In the Defense College, also, they felt that they had a unique capacity to conduct large operations. The American student who visited the École Navale next door could not help but notice that most of the books on its open shelves were in English. The United States, and to some extent Great Britain, had a unique familiarity with fleets, air forces, army groups, complex headquarters, heavy modern weapons, and elaborate logistical plans. Inevitably they adopted a paternal attitude toward the "Little League" teams fielded by Denmark, Greece, Norway, and Portugal. Special circumstances affecting the origin and administration of the Defense College also gave them a proprietary attitude toward the institution. General Alfred Gruenther had first suggested that a school was necessary, General Dwight D. Eisenhower had formally proposed one, and Professor Arnold Wolfers and General Paul Caraway had played important parts in organizing it. All four had been influenced by the example of the recently created National War College. Gruenther, who had served at the latter institution with Wolfers, invited him to Paris to help develop the Defense College's first curriculum. Caraway, who had also been there, was selected by name by Eisenhower to serve as one of the first commandant's deputies. Since the commandant himself held an additional post at SHAPE, he made Caraway "coordinator of studies" and delegated to him much of the work of organizing the institution. At the time of research Americans occupied the pivotal positions of commandant and executive officer of the College.

But to a degree unmatched by any other NATO country, the United States possessed both world-wide interests and a significant capacity to pursue them by independent action. From the perspective of Washington NATO appeared smaller than from Oslo, Brussels, Athens, or even London. Its Defense College, however useful, could not loom as large to the United States as to other member nations. In order to provide officers who might have modified the not always flattering image of American students, officials of the Defense Department would have had to give the NATO Defense College an overriding priority in their selection and assignment processes. This they did not do: on the contrary, American students were less senior than officers sent to our National War College, and they were selected after quotas for that institution and the service war colleges had been filled. The percentage of service-academy graduates among them (a sensitive indicator of status) was also relatively low.

Promotion and assignment records of American graduates of the Defense College were correspondingly unspectacular. During its first six years of operation (1951-1957) none of the College's American students rose to star rank. Although the data are not strictly comparable, it is significant that in the first eight years of the National War College's experience 50 per cent of its Army students, 42 per cent of its Air Force students, and 32 per cent of its Naval students achieved general or flag rank.[2] At the NATO College the record of American students also appeared less impressive than that of allied officers. Over two dozen of the latter became generals or admirals between 1951 and 1957. An Italian graduate became his nation's military representative at SHAPE. Five French graduates became generals. Danish graduates became commanders in chief of both the Danish army and air force. A Norwegian graduate became deputy commander of the Norwegian army. A Belgian alumnus became chief of Belgium's armed forces and member of NATO's Military Committee. Such assignments were understandable in countries whose armed forces were smaller and whose strategic policies were so intimately affected by NATO decisions. Yet the announcement of each such assignment was received with pride and joy at the Defense College, and the continued absence of American names did not pass unnoticed. The apparently more routine careers of American alumni could hardly enhance the reputation of American students. That reputation, in turn, fell sufficiently short of their power position to put them in an awkward position from which good will alone could not fully extricate them.

III

It is ironic as well as significant that the United States came to view the NATO Defense College as a cut below its own National War College. In 1951 General Eisenhower had communicated a proposal to the Standing Group for *both* a war college and a staff school, the former to be supervised by the NATO Council or the Standing Group, the latter to be supervised by SHAPE. But it was not deemed practicable to create two institutions. The War College that Eisenhower proposed was to be at the highest level. As examples of what he had in mind, he cited the National War College, the Imperial Defence College, and the Institute des Hautes Études de Defense Nationale. An institution of this kind would prepare already-trained personnel to study major issues of international defense policy—for example, specialization of functions within the alliance, sharing of defense costs, the relation of European integration to defense plans, and the coordination of security policies in non-NATO areas. However, the British preferred a staff school that would focus on such practical everyday matters as the structure of the alliance and the mechanisms of integrated staffs. Among other functions, it would serve as a tutoring bureau for smaller countries. General Eisenhower held out for his loftier concept, and when the French sided with him, the school was established at the higher level, with an appropriately ambitious curriculum. But the decision was not adhered to. The course was only half as long as courses at senior national schools. Moreover, within two years an *ad hoc* committee advisory to the Standing Group was expressing its concern over the language problem and the inability of some countries to supply senior officers even for so short a course. The difficulty of communication was in itself a formidable obstacle. English and French were the official languages of the College. Documents were prepared in both and lectures were simultaneously translated by skilled interpreters, as in the United Nations. All students were required to take one hour of instruction daily in the language in which they were weaker. Not more than 20 per cent of the students were truly bilingual. It was necessary to start with elementary problems if for no other reason than to give the class linguistic confidence. Even in the latter stages of the course men fluent in only one official language could not always scale analytical heights in bilingual committee meetings, particularly if they were held in small noisy rooms, and if they had been preceded by a "Tuborg" at the bar and an excellent French lunch with a carafe of *vin ordinaire*. The rare unfortunate who was fluent in neither official language had to smile his way through the program.

Variations in the size and power of member nations also made it hard to obtain a student body of uniformly high rank. Students ranged in age from thirty-four to fifty-two, and their ranks ran the gamut from major to brigadier general. Luxembourg and Iceland were unable to send any officers. West Germany, Norway, Portugal, and Turkey had to dip into lower ranks. Portugal often could not fill its quota at all. Canada and Belgium also fell behind. The British, who could have spared senior personnel more easily, persisted in their original concept of the institution. They assigned two or three times as many lieutenant colonels as the United States, and correspondingly fewer full colonels. In other words, just as differences in national ambitions made some countries compete for places within the College, so differences in national power made other countries unable or unwilling to take full advantage of the opportunities made available to them. Given a most heterogeneous student body whose members were unable to communicate easily, the Defense College was forced to operate somewhat below the level at which it had been constituted. It would be a caricature of the truth to suggest that this discrepancy between the norm and the fact greatly complicated relationships within the College. But it was clearly a frustrating matter for the commandants and their staffs, while for part of the student body it was a source of anxiety or a pretext for indifference.

IV

Differences in national administrative styles also created a problem for the College. Americans in particular had a distinctive style derived from the conditions under which they worked at home. Bureaucratic relations replace intuitive personal understandings in organizations whose members cannot deal on familiar terms. With its large enterprises and its high rate of personal mobility, the United States is the natural habitat of bureaucracy;

and American administrative style was much in evidence at the time of research, because the Defense College was headed by an American officer. Like all NATO commanders, he was reasonably free to determine the procedures of his headquarters, and like all he tended to follow the system to which he was accustomed. "Spit and polish" and deadlines became more important, the tempo of work quickened, warning bells were introduced to advertise the start of lectures, attendance was taken, organization charts were drafted, and the syllabus was expanded into a set of written pamphlets defining the aims and content of each segment of the course.

But European officers frequently felt that personal creativity and personal recognition were impossible in the system that Americans took for granted. Functions were too highly specialized, vertical and horizontal clearances too numerous, the editing of drafts too ruthless, authority to sign one's own name too closely held, and literary elegance too completely subordinated to prescribed formats and to "cliches the presence of which were obligatory in all papers."[3] On the other hand, Americans for whom the doctrine of "completed staff work" was an article of faith felt that French and other European officers were too reluctant to conclude their studies with firm and precise proposals for action, too slow to consult their peers, and too quick to go to superiors for advice on policy premises or on the way in which the problem should be formulated. Some allied officers still regarded a commander as a grand seigneur to whom one turned for fatherly advice. But the breezy guidebook prepared by SHAPE's American secretariat told new personnel, "Don't expect to sit on the boss's desk." Other Europeans for whom a job still carried a suggestion of private patrimony were told, "Every staff agency comments on all actions that influence its field of interest." It is not surprising to find a plaintive note in a memorandum prepared by a French officer for the guidance of his successor, also French, at a NATO headquarters dominated by American administrative traditions:

Here one rarely receives higher guidance regarding the position to adopt. Ideas do not circulate from top to bottom but from bottom to top. Problems move from section to section very slowly. Each man comments on them and then the problem returns to the officer responsible for the study or response, which officer then redrafts the paper. The paper goes back up the hierarchy until it eventually reaches the top. Sometimes one is called to discuss it at one of these echelons. Sometimes one sees the final product, generally unrecognizable. Sometimes one hears nothing further about it.

One effect of these differences in style was to create a divergence between administrative theory and practice. Officially, American officers became even more determined to maintain the prescribed standards of organization. Unofficially, all officers were impelled, by the very impracticability of these standards, to rely more heavily on informal organization. Much of this informal organization was based on nationality, but national contingents were so small that personnel also divided themselves into northern and southern blocs or English-speaking and Romance-language groups. These formed in the corridors, at lunch, and on social occasions. Official parties given by instructors or student committees were international; spontaneous gatherings more often were semi-international. Official channels were international, but officers competent in the same official language preferred to transact business with or through each other. What this meant in practice is suggested by a SHAPE directive on the transmission of documents to national ministries. Canada, Denmark, Great Britain, the Netherlands, Norway, and the United States received copies only in English. Other countries requested copies in approximately the following ratios: Germany, 11 copies in English: 1 in French; Greece, 10:2; Turkey, 9:3; Iceland, Italy, Luxembourg, and Portugal, 6:6; Belgium, 4:8; France, 1:11.

Up to this point the analysis of the NATO Defense College can be summarized by saying that differences in political aims, and in the character of underlying civilizations, resulted in some open debate, competition for place, delicate personal relations, a desire to avoid embarrassing incidents, a reduction in the level at which the institution could operate, a heavy stress on formal organization, and a parallel tendency to rely on unofficial organization to get things done.

V

The foregoing conclusion assumes that national differences were not overshadowed by commitments to large common policies or to the Defense College as an institution. It also assumes that identification with national groups was not seriously weakened by overlapping memberships in non-national groups. It remains to inquire to what extent these assumptions are valid.

The Defense College staff worked hard to give its students a common understanding of the threat confronting the West and of the larger purposes and policies of the alliance. But analysis of about 120 lectures and briefings in a typical course at the time of research reveals that 75 per cent were devoted to other matters:

33%   The political, military, and economic positions of NATO members or neutral nations. Lectures on neutral nations constituted about one-fifth of all talks within this category.

20%   European history, basic economics, social change, raw materials, plant facilities, public opinion, psychological warfare, diplomacy, other European organizations.

13%   The organization and procedures of NATO's military commands and its political, financial, and logistical agencies.

9%   Concepts of air, sea, and land power, and the nature, capabilities, and development of modern weapons systems.

Of the thirty remaining lectures and briefings, thirteen dealt with Soviet capabilities and intentions—including such topics as Soviet economic growth, military power, political theory, foreign policy, military psychology, military doctrine, and instruments of political subversion—or with more general aspects of Soviet society—such as Russian history, nationalities in the Soviet Union, the Soviet citizen, and the structure of Soviet government. Few of these were given by NATO officials, and no effort was made to provide a single approved view of specific Soviet aims. Five lectures dealt more authoritatively with the moral values of the West, the political origins and development of NATO, its current political problems, and its role in world politics. But these contained only somewhat abstract statements of purpose and policy. They stressed such matters as the common desire of all NATO members to preserve their territorial integrity and modes of life, the importance of cooperating to this end, the consistency of such cooperation with the aims of the United Nations, and the practical problems that stood in the way of peace and unity. Finally, twelve official briefings were given on the defense of the entire NATO area; the mission, military posture, and atomic weapons policy of the European command; the missions and plans of its four subordinate commands; and the defense of the North American, Atlantic, and English Channel areas. These briefings typically discussed NATO and enemy capabilities in the particular sector and the special problems facing each command in its effort to achieve maximum readiness. It was at this point that students received doctrine regarding NATO's settled strategic policies.

But the course as a whole transmitted relatively little common doctrine because there was very little to transmit. It was on this ground that the College's first Commandant had explicitly defended the plan to invite a different speaker to present "his" views each day. He notified his staff and his superiors that College instructors would not "teach" in the sense of offering "real courses of study" because NATO doctrine did not yet exist. The College's position here becomes clearer if the institution is viewed as a microcosm of the larger universe of education. Many civilian universities have turned to general education in a desire to transmit the heritage of the West or to recover a sense of purpose that allegedly obtained in an earlier day. Sectarian colleges, notably those identified with the Catholic faith, make more of an effort to transmit common doctrine than those not affiliated with a particular denomination, as do military schools operated by a single service. Service academies and war colleges miss few opportunities to instill a belief in the importance of air, land, or sea power. The National War College, on the other hand, must maintain something like an "equal-time rule" to protect all services, and it is considerably more vocal in disclaiming all intent to indoctrinate.[4] Because it represented so many nations as well as services, the NATO Defense College found it especially difficult to discover or lay down common principles. It was, therefore, particularly inclined to make a virtue of necessity. Students were exhorted to think for themselves. Faculty members were restricted to the role of moderators, facilitators, and consultants. Each member nation was given an opportunity to present an official statement of its military, political, and economic position. And a rough form of proportional representation was devised to allocate lecturers by nationality. Non-Standing Group powers provided slightly more than 25 per cent of all speakers. The remainder were drawn in approximately equal numbers from French, British, and American sources, with the French providing slightly fewer than the British and Americans. A few lecturers were drawn from non-NATO countries, such as India, Pakistan, Sweden, and Yugoslavia. The College rejected an offer to have a Spanish official lecture and was once turned down in an effort to get an Austrian official. Documents, books, magazines, lecture topics, and committee problems were taken from the national military colleges of several member nations.

As has been suggested, the most important exception to this general policy of calculated pluralism arose in the area of strategic doctrine. Both official NATO lecturers and Defense College authorities insisted on the "shield" theory of defense. This was the concept that NATO land power should be substantial enough to: (1) protect frontiers, air bases, and ports from probing actions, (2) provide advance warning of a general assault by requiring an enemy to concentrate his forces, and (3) delay such an assault until retaliatory operations could be undertaken. They rejected the view, taken by Sir John Slessor and other air-power enthusiasts, that land power should serve only as a "trip wire," or at best a "heavy plate glass," tampering with which would release a nuclear counterstroke.[5] But the Defense College could not permit its students to spend a major part of their time in sustained critical study of the "shield" doctrine without opening up a Pandora's box of fear, frustration, and mutual recrimination. The unilateral declaration of a massive retaliation policy by the United States had led many Europeans to conclude that they would be obliterated or abandoned in time of crisis. It also created enough doubt about the utility of land forces to discourage European politicians who were already reluctant to demand the sacrifices necessary to raise such forces. Their doubt, plus the delay in the activation of German divisions, the withdrawal of French troops to Algeria, a planned reduction in British forces, and shortened periods of conscription in other countries, had kept the size and effectiveness of forces below the minimum deemed essential to adequate defense on the ground. So intractable was this strategic issue, and so divisive in its implications, that the Defense College could not pursue it too far without jeopardizing the internal harmony it sought to promote.

It was easier to ask students to evaluate NATO's military organization or to propose political and economic reforms in the alliance. Inquiries of this kind had been encouraged from the beginning. General Eisenhower, in his first report as Supreme Allied Commander, expressed his hope that the NATO Defense College would "find the right answers to many questions that today are unanswerable."[6] One question he had in mind was whether smaller countries should specialize (in land warfare, tactical aviation, or mine-sweeping, for example) or whether each should continue to maintain a great variety of military forces. Students discussed this and other problems in their committees, which were directed to recommend measures to increase the unity and effectiveness of the alliance. Typical of the conclusions of such committees were recommendations to finance NATO training centers out of a common NATO budget and proposals to add a fourth member to the Standing Group on a rotating basis, in order to make it more representative of smaller powers. But the conclusions of student committees, composed of men who had little professional guidance and less time, could not be a substitute for firm policy handed down by higher echelon.

Although the Defense College staff thought some committee solutions suggestive enough to be brought to the attention of a wider audience, the Standing Group took the position that they represented exercises of a pedagogical value only. It tried to restrict their circulation and did not encourage other NATO agencies to take them seriously. This was also the position of the first Commandant. The second Commandant, however, encouraged Lester Pearson of Canada to request copies of the College's committee reports on NATO organization after Pearson had been designated one of the "Three Wise Men" responsible for reviewing NATO's functions. Selected reports were thereupon sent to the Palais de Chaillot. A member of the political secretariat who reviewed them there stated that their observations could have been made by a well-informed newspaper reader but that they also contained a few excellent suggestions already under consideration in the secretariat.

VI

Commandants and their staffs also encountered obstacles in their efforts to develop loyalty to the Defense College as an institution. A great deal was done to develop a common life for College personnel. Luncheon was provided daily on the premises, and a bar was maintained. Wives were invited to undertake group projects of their own and to attend occasional movies, lectures, and social functions at the school. Short trips were taken to points of interest in the Paris area. More important were the longer instructional tours, during which College personnel traveled together on a chartered plane, stayed at the same hotels, and saw more of each other socially, even though in the later stages of a tour, students would drift toward their language or national groups. The "old school tie" was worn at annual reunions, and alumni were encouraged to form local chapters at NATO headquarters and in national ministries.

Institutional spirit was also fostered by the common "hardships" to which personnel were exposed. All members had been uprooted from their professional and cultural homes. They were fully aware that their school operated on a slender budget. It was tucked away in an unobtrusively marked wing of a building 3,000 miles from its busy supervisors on the Standing Group. Students, and especially staff members, were hungry for evidence that the institution was appreciated by NATO and by their own governments. It was a great day for the College when the Secretary General or the Supreme Commander spoke to the student body, or when an official visit was finally paid by all of the Permanent Representatives to the NATO Council. It was a sad day when the Standing Group traveled to Paris without making a courtesy call. It was also a sad day when the Standing Group denied the College the authority to visit the United States,[7] or when it buried its annual reports, ignored its recommendations, limited its communication with the NATO Council, or refused to meet its requests for classified information. The Standing Group's feeling about the use of classified information by the

College seems to have been influenced in part by the bureaucratic rivalry that often exists between general staffs and war colleges. Students were not supposed to discuss operational plans or to receive classified information more sensitive than "Secret." Security precautions at the College were adequate and at the same time less stringent than at NATO regional commands or at the National War College, where there was greater reason for special care. Students found it particularly galling to be denied access to a basic document dealing with future NATO strategy when they knew that the document was used in all NATO commands and when they regularly heard references to it by guest lecturers during instructional tours. In this case, and with respect to reports on major NATO exercises, students had to be content with a general briefing given to them by their commandant.

While many of the makings of institutional spirit were present at the Defense College, so were many of the obstacles. The problem was larger than one of evoking the kind of sentimental affection that undergraduates develop for a residential college (and evoking it in a commuters' school that offered a half-year course to men in their forties). In this case the men held sensitive positions as members of the armed forces of sovereign nations. They had not chosen a career of service to the alliance or to its College, and they had sworn an oath to neither. They had merely been assigned to a school by their governments for a short tour of duty.

VII

To some extent preoccupation with national problems was modified by overlapping membership in non-national groups. The staff of the Defense College tried deliberately to create such groups in composing its student committees, each consisting of six men of different nationalities. This required French and German members, for example, to cooperate in assessing the menace of a third party that threatened both. Greek and Turkish officers had to join in analyzing the command organization in the Baltic, an area of vital interest to neither. The latter example suggests that the scope of the Defense College's interests—the breadth of its curriculum—carried to each national group the message that its dilemmas were not the only dilemmas. This was at least a gentle counterforce to ethnocentric views of the world.

The personal friendships that developed during the course may also be regarded as a form of cross-national association. Any hardheaded appraisal of the effect of physical propinquity on mature officers of different nationalities must acknowledge that some old prejudices were simply fortified, and that many casual ties were broken on graduation day. But others were maintained longer, particularly when the *"anciens"* found themselves assigned to the same NATO headquarters. Moreover, the understandings generated by friendship tended to outlast the particular association. On this point the testimony of NATO Defense College graduates resembled the testimony of war college graduates in the United States. An Italian alumnus, for example, would claim that he found it easier to transact business with a German officer because he had known him at the Defense College, or because he had worked in committee with other German officers, or because he heard German officials give authoritative statements of their country's problems and viewpoints. Armed with such knowledge, graduates also contended that they were less often startled or offended by the reactions they encountered in allied personnel. The potential importance of such claims becomes clear if it is noted that at the time they were made, five NATO Defense College graduates were assigned to the Standing Group, eight to the Northern Command, nine to the Palais de Chaillot, thirteen to the Central Command, twenty-four to the Southern Command, and forty to SHAPE. This was not an insignificant proportion of all officers of comparable rank at these headquarters. Of the 550 students who graduated in the first ten classes, roughly half were assigned to NATO organizations or to domestic agencies where they worked on NATO matters.

On the other hand, it is not easy to decide how much weight to give testimony concerning the value of friendships formed at the College. A skeptic might reasonably believe that allied officers at an integrated headquarters have some incentive to give reassuring responses to an itinerant American researcher, while a cynic might observe that international antagonists are not necessarily personal enemies. Moreover, the formation of genuine friendships at the College was limited by language differences, by the shortness of the course, by the departure of students for their hotels or apartments at 5:00 p.m., and, in a less obvious way, by differences in living standards and social customs. Not all nationalities are quick to bring new acquaintances into their homes, and not all produce "organization women" eager to mix with the wives of their husbands' colleagues. Almost every American officer who was interviewed in the course of this research testified that these factors had prevented him from getting to know French officers well.

Identification with fellow nationals was also modified only slightly by the growth of informal groups based on similar functions or professions. It is true that naval officers of different countries discovered that they had received similar training, that they used similar concepts, and sometimes that they had fought similar battles in domestic as well as international politics. Foreign service officers found a bond in their common tendency to criticize the political naïveté of military personnel; the latter, for example, assumed that large forces could be transported to Europe without creating political difficulties for host countries or without curtailing world shipping. Finance officials talked shop about the extravagances of their military countrymen. What some army officers referred to as "the international cartel of air power" was especially vocal. Protegé relationships existed between American air force officers and those of some smaller allied nations. Many of the latter had been trained under American auspices or at American installations: they wore their caps the same way; they affected the same slang; they used English in their air-ground communications; and they regarded the USAF's share of the American military budget as an ideal toward which their less enlightened politicians could properly inch their way. There was also some evidence of changes in protegé relationships; for example, Greek air force personnel officially retained British terminology to designate ranks but often used American terminology in ordinary speech.

Such professional alliances were reasonably important at SHAPE, at Naples, and at SACLANT. In such headquarters army officers were most concerned about the adequacy of the "shield." Air force and naval officers often disagreed strongly about the role of the Sixth Fleet in the Mediterranean. Naval officers, whose high level spokesman was the naval deputy at SHAPE, battled for a larger share of the money available for NATO infrastructure—roads, airfields, pipelines, ports, telegraph, and radio and radar facilities. Long arguments took place over the extent to which military aid programs should build air, sea, or land power in a given country. Indeed, American air force officers at Naples were fond of saying that their army and naval compatriots sought to reopen battles lost in the Pentagon by enlisting the support of allies overseas. And a very senior American naval aviator spoke in so uncompromising a tone to the NATO Defense College that he was not invited to repeat his message on sea power.

Yet outer limits were set to the development of functional alliances among military personnel by the predominantly land-force orientation of most NATO nations. Only the United States had the massive naval and air forces to support gorgeous interservice battles. A French colonel who had heard Admiral Mountbatten tell the College that leaders from Hannibal to Hitler had fatally underestimated sea power, testified, "To hear this in the École Militaire was for me extraordinary." To most nations military power meant land power. Within the student body and staff of the Defense College army officers were almost as numerous as naval and air force officers together. The first eleven courses contained 206 army officers, 124 air force officers, 120 naval officers, and 129 civilians. Moreover, the student body was so small, and its members divided into so many committees, that only rarely did two allied officers of the same service work together. Finally, it should be noted that only a fraction of the curriculum was devoted to military matters, that the school was not responsible for developing strategic policies, and that its staff did not seek to develop functional alliances as a counterweight to national groups. Some American officers actually testified that the service rivalries that had seemed so important to them in the United States began to pale in significance in the course of their encounters with allied personnel at the Defense College.

VIII

In 1951 the *ad hoc* advisory committee appointed by the Standing Group to assist the Commandant-Designate of the Defense College agreed that every student must be in the same category for security purposes. To exclude any national group from certain materials or studies, the committee felt, would at once destroy "the NATO spirit."

The fact that this advice was followed suggests that, despite all obstacles to the emergence of extranational loyalties at the Defense College, something called "NATO spirit" was stronger at this institution than at any of the regional military headquarters that were examined. In this context the phrase refers to the special constitutional morality of the treaty organization. The members of NATO professed to seek a form of association in which all partners were equally trusted and in which each received his due. Ideally, the weak would not exercise their right to veto anything, and the strong would not exercise their power to dominate everything. Certainly, the declared purposes of none of the member nations could be served by a hegemony exercised too blatantly by the United States alone or by the three Standing Group powers together. The NATO Defense College came quite close to striking the delicate balance that all claimed to desire, because its *mission* permitted it to come close. This was an educational, not a policy-making, enterprise. Because the institution neither formulated nor carried out official plans, the stakes in its decisions were small, and the irritants produced by economic and social differences could be endured with more equanimity. In short, the College was an ideal laboratory for experiments in international cooperation.

This difference between the Defense College and regional military headquarters was evident in many details. At the College, as has been noted, students enjoyed equal access to sensitive information. In the regional commands, where more highly classified messages circulated, countries more often made informal arrangements to keep some messages in national hands. The Defense College also made a greater effort to preserve equality in the use of official NATO languages. All documents were faithfully reproduced in both. It was a cause of official concern when the percentage of lectures delivered in French fell too low—below 30 per cent, for example. At regional commands other than Fontainebleau the language problem was "solved" at the expense of French pride by conducting business largely in English. The Southern Command at Naples, for example, requested that all SHAPE documents be forwarded in the ratio of fifteen copies in English to one in French. The Northern Command at Oslo received only English copies. At SHAPE itself at least five staff sections—Intelligence, Signal, Organization and Training, Annual Review, and Adjutant General—received copies only in English, and the Budget and Finance office received one copy in French to eight in English. The NATO Defense College, on the other hand, received the same number of copies in each language. Again, official visitors to SHAPE or Naples frequently received their official briefings from Americans. Defense College students were briefed by the foreign and defense ministers of all member nations, and they heard lectures from such noted French commentators as Raymond Aron, Georges Bidault, Bertrand de Jouvenel, Robert Schumann and André Siegfried. The administrative staff of the College included relatively few Anglo-Saxons. Of the seventy-two employees responsible for secretarial services, translation, maintenance, internal security, library and the like, fifty-six were French. The whole atmosphere of the College was more "Continental" than other NATO installations commanded by Americans. At SHAPE very senior Americans flew the flag of the United States in their offices. At Naples allied officers were surrounded by Pentagon-style office equipment, water coolers, and Waldorf salads. An Italian officer would surely feel more at home in the College across the Alps where the décor was more to his taste and the commandant flew a NATO flag.

In the forum of the Defense College it was also easier for the Standing Group powers to make concessions to other members of the alliance. Such concessions were evident in its curriculum and in its personnel quotas. The curriculum was by no means confined to narrowly military topics or to problems of Europe alone. Students discussed measures to implement Article 2 of the North Atlantic Treaty well before the NATO Council appointed a committee of "Three Wise Men" to turn their attention to that matter. They debated the wisdom of a NATO program of technical assistance to underdeveloped countries. They discussed the need for a planning staff to help the NATO Council anticipate political disputes. Before the Suez crisis emerged, student committees were analyzing NATO's interest in the Middle East. Other lectures touched on Pakistan, India, southeast Asia, and tropical Africa. To facilitate intelligent discussion of such topics, commandants sought to increase the number of civilians in the student body and on the faculty. They also wanted to bring experts from the Palais de Chaillot to the College and to permit students to attend selected meetings at the Palais de Chaillot. In each of these matters the Defense College had to combat the opposition of the Standing Group nations, and particularly of the United States. The Standing Group supervised the College with the aid of an international planning team composed of staff officers. At the time of research, the American member of this team was unaware that civilians constituted over 20 per cent of the College's student body (his guess was 1 or 2 per cent). The United States sent a single Foreign Service Officer to each class. Most other countries, including Great Britain, sent a larger number of civilians and selected them from a greater variety of ministries, such as Finance, Commerce, Defense, Justice, or Public Works. This undoubtedly reflected the greater impact of NATO on their national societies.

The American member of the planning team was also convinced that the curriculum should emphasize military problems rather than such topics as Suez or the Organization for European Economic Cooperation. Despite the earlier American insistence on an institution at the war-college level, this officer clearly viewed it as a staff school.[8] On the other hand, some non-Standing Group nations preferred a broader charter for the College because they preferred a broader charter for the alliance. Belgium, Canada, Italy, the Netherlands and Germany had already begun to insist that member nations utilize NATO machinery to consult more closely on a wider range of issues. Commandants were attentive to their views not only because they wished the College to operate at the highest level, but because they lacked responsibility for formulating NATO policy and therefore assumed fewer risks in expanding the range of their interests.

The manner in which personnel were allocated also indicates that the dominance of the Standing Group powers, and especially of the United States, was less obvious and long lasting at the Defense College than at regional military headquarters. In 1957 American, British and French officers occupied a large majority of positions at or above the level of section chief in the principal NATO commands. The percentages are given in the following table:[9]

Table

Command	U.S.	U.K.	France	Total
SHAPE	47%	21%	15%	83%
SHAPE Subcommands	40	20	8	68
SACLANT	67	13	3	83

Nor do these figures tell the entire story. In some cases Americans were placed in charge of every other echelon of an organization and tended to de-emphasize the importance of intervening echelons. This was true, for example, within the air force element of the Southern Command, even though most of the operational air units were Greek, Italian or Turkish, and even though these units constituted the greater part of their national air strength. The Americans held ten of the eleven positions in SHAPE's Air and Special Operations Section and at least one position in every other important section. A roster of key personnel throughout the entire alliance listed Americans in all fifteen of NATO's major installations. British personnel were listed in ten, French in six, and other nationalities in fewer. In some areas an American was placed in charge because other countries were reluctant to serve under each others' nationals. This was especially true of Greece, Italy, and Turkey throughout the Southern Command.

A different kind of distribution prevailed at the Defense College. As already noted, France, Great Britain, Italy, and Germany sent substantially the same number of students as the United States. Each of the Standing Group countries was entitled to assign an equal number of instructors, and a determined effort was made to secure a larger number from the other countries, even though in practice it proved difficult to obtain instructors from non-Standing Group countries other than Italy and Germany. Instructors were assigned to the College for two or more years, and many nations could not spare them that long. Even the position of commandant was opened to members at large. In the first six years it had been rotated among the Standing Group countries, and it would have been France's turn again in 1957. But by 1956 the other members of NATO had forced the creation of a committee of permanent military representatives to safeguard their interests. As a result of the pressure of this committee, the position of commandant, along with a limited number of other NATO positions of importance, was made available to non-Standing Group powers. Italy, Portugal, and Turkey expressed their readiness to nominate candidates, and Canada was also interested but could not make available an officer of the three-star rank required. Since all three countries were on the military representatives committee, and since Portugal's member was the very candidate his nation had nominated, the committee felt unable to make the decision itself. It referred the matter to the more detached Standing Group, which selected the Italian candidate. He was succeeded by Turkish and Belgian commandants.

Positions could be distributed more evenly at the Defense College because they carried less power; and because they carried less power, their incumbents were under less pressure to take cues from their national governments. To be sure, general officers of all nations were readily available in the Paris area, and the commandants encouraged them to visit the College during the course. It was also believed by some that the first contingent of German students had been briefed in advance of their arrival. But, in the nature of things, it was less important for Defense College students to seek external guidance, and it was less likely that national officials would seek to intrude with messages for the ears or eyes of their compatriots only. Such messages were not unknown at regional military headquarters. Moreover, at SHAPE and at SACLANT national ministries of defense maintained liaison offices to insure that their viewpoints were available not only to the Supreme Commander but to their own nationals as well. This was official practice, and a very practical line of reasoning was developed to make it consistent with the principle of an integrated staff. It was still considered improper for a staff officer to turn to his national military representative for instructions when he received a paper for comment. But he was supposed to know the viewpoint of his country well enough not to let pass without critical comment a recommendation that it would eventually oppose strongly. Such realism was essential at the heart of the alliance. Within the NATO Defense College the heat was off.

NOTES

1. See the discussion above at page 119.
2. See John W. Masland and Laurence I. Radway, *Soldiers and Scholars: Military Education and National Policy* (Princeton, 1957), p. 322*n*.
3. The phrase was used by a European officer who had served at the College.
4. Masland and Radway, *op. cit.*, pp. 373-375.
5. The Commandant of the NATO Defense College, an American army officer at the time this observation was made, was extremely forceful in his rejection of the "trip wire" and "plate glass" concepts.
6. Dwight D. Eisenhower, *First Annual Report, Supreme Commander, Europe* (Paris, April 2, 1952), p. 35.
7. Only once during its first decade was the College authorized to make an instructional tour of North America. It had long since visited every other area covered by the treaty organization.
8. See pages 107 and 108 above.
9. SHAPE subcommands include the Northern headquarters in Norway, the Central headquarters at Fontainebleau, the Southern headquarters at Naples, and the Mediterranean headquarters at Malta. The percentages for SHAPE are almost exactly the same as those that prevailed five years earlier.

Civil and Military Power in the Fourth Republic

BY *RAOUL GIRARDET*

I: Introduction

THROUGHOUT THE NINETEENTH CENTURY and during the first part of the twentieth, the definition of the relations between civil and military power in France was based on two simple and essential principles. The first was the complete subordination of military power to the authority of legal government. Summing up the tradition of French civil law on this matter, M. Duguit, a lawyer, writes:

The military must be a passive tool in the hands of government. The latter can only fulfill its mission if it has the military completely at its disposal, so that the government may use it as an unconscious material force. This excludes all possibility of military leaders in any way refusing to comply with governmental orders. . . . The state would no longer exist if military leaders were allowed to question its orders. The ideal armed force would be one that government could activate simply by pressing a button.[1]

This first fundamental principle logically led to the second essential rule—the military must never interfere in politics. At the beginning of the century it was taught at St. Cyr that, "The army's loyalty and devotion to legal government must be absolute. There is no other formula that would as securely safeguard the soldier's honor." Thus, the army must have no feelings, no opinions, and no inclinations; if these do exist, the army must be unaware of them and act as if they were nonexistent. During the nineteenth century neutrality, or rather political passivity, was considered one of the principal tenets of military ethics. In this way, an attempt was made to free the soldier from any doubt, interior struggle, or pangs of conscience. In time of political upheaval he would "stand by his flag," taking orders from his

Translated by Martha Finkelstein, Columbia University, from R. Girardet, "Pouvoir Civil et Pouvoir Militaire en France sous la Quatrieme République," paper, 7th Round Table, International Political Science Association (Opatija, Yugoslavia), September, 1959, and R. Girardet, "Pouvoir civil et pouvoir militaire dans la France contemporaine," *Revue Française de Science Politique*, 10 (March, 1960), 5-38. The editor is grateful to M. Girardet and to the editors of the *Revue* for permission to translate and publish this essay.

superiors, who in turn would defer to the final decisions of the Minister of War then in power. Thus, the political fidelity of the army would be at once revocable and perpetual. The military would be loyal to the state irrespective of changing governments. In short, the army should always be "la Grande Muette."[2]

These, then, are the two political principles which were strikingly brought again to the fore during the political crisis of May, 1958, which led to the downfall of the institutions of the Fourth Republic. The army refused to bend to the decisions of legal authority and directly entered the political scene. It was at the army's request and by its pressure that General de Gaulle was called upon to shoulder governmental responsibilities for the second time in his career. At the same time, political and ideological preoccupations began to hold an increasingly important position in the heart of the military community. The army tended to form its own opinions on a number of important contemporary problems, thereby refusing to continue its traditional role as an inert, passive mechanism. How can this abrupt change be explained? How can we interpret this sudden re-evaluation of some of the essential values upon which were based the political and social order of contemporary France? To discuss these questions is the purpose of this study, which is limited to the period of the Fourth Republic, from 1945 to 1958.

I have deliberately not attempted to analyze institutional mechanisms. Their functions have often been examined, and the Fourth Republic does not mark any important innovation in comparison with the preceding period.[3] I shall approach only indirectly the study of the social structures of the contemporary French army. Information in this area is rare, fragmentary, and scattered; however, I shall indicate that information which bears witness to the indisputable "social crisis" that the army of the Fourth Republic underwent—a crisis inseparable from moral and psychological "unrest." Finally, I shall in no way try to chronicle the various military "conspiracies" and semi-conspiracies that preceded, accompanied, or followed the episode of May, 1958. It would be premature to venture into a field where all the existing documentation amounts to a few journalistic accounts. In a more limited manner I shall endeavor only to follow and to interpret the *change of attitude* that has marked the history of the French army from 1945 to the present, a change of attitude with regard to government and to certain essential values. In the last fifteen years the French military has undergone a very great psychological, intellectual, and moral change; I shall attempt to investigate and outline the reasons for this change.

In effect, three factors seem to stand out:

1. The very grave psychological and moral repercussions that the French army has felt because of the colonial wars it has had to wage since the end of World War II.
2. The development by a few military theoreticians of a new doctrine of "revolutionary war," and the spread of this doctrine throughout the military community.

3. The French army's assumption of administrative power in Algerian departments and the transformation of Algeria into a "military province."

In the convergence of these factors lies the essential explanation for the gradual establishment of a new type of relations between civil and military power.

I shall use the word "army" as if this institution was completely homogeneous and corresponded to an internally undifferentiated social milieu. Needless to say, the army is not a "bloc," since within it there are numerous differences and even tensions. It might also be useful to make distinctions according to armies, rank, age, social origins, and "patterns of thought." Often contradictory intellectual currents exist within the army; the political leanings of its men are varied. A paratroop commander graduated from St. Cyr in 1939 would not have the same reactions as a general graduated from Polytechnique in 1912. I believe, however, that in the period which concerns us, and according to our plan of study, it is best not to attach too much importance to these differences. The trend which culminated in the present evolution of the army was undoubtedly, in the beginning, espoused by a minority, but its general direction was followed by almost the entire military community. By 1959 there existed in French military circles a sufficiently strong consensus on certain essential points, a sufficiently clear and effective unity of behavior and reaction, so that one could speak of an "attitude" or of the "army's point of view" without incurring any serious misconceptions.

II: "The Unrest of the Army"[4]

The Fourth Republic will necessarily hold an important place in the moral history of the French army: to many officers it was a period of re-evaluation. "Twenty years of war have changed us," states a "forty-year-old officer." Lacking assurance from those in a position to give it, the soldier has become a questioning man.[5] "For almost twenty years, without understanding why or how, France has been at war," says a member of the same generation. "But those to whom the country has given arms, those who kill and those who die have a right to question."[6] In fact, a complete revision of certain fundamental values has affected many military minds in the past fifteen years. This has incurred the often distressing repudiation of certain essential conventions, an often harrowing abandon of elementary postulates that for more than a century were the basis of the rules of military ethics. The old imperatives of the honor of the military, codified and handed down by the nineteenth century, no longer seem capable of answering the questions and problems which arise from France's situation in the middle of the twentieth century. Other rules are sought, other assurances are demanded with uneasiness and often in confusion. This moral revolution slowly has upset the customs and way of thinking of military society. And it is this moral revolution that constitutes the most often misunderstood but essential aspect of the "unrest of the army," which was noted by the French press in the last years of the Fourth Republic.

In order to understand this crisis, the very important heritage left by the World War and the occupation cannot be neglected. Since 1940, traditional principles of military ethics, notably that of total and absolute obedience to political power, have been suddenly questioned. How can the imperative of submission to legal power be invoked when three governments have simultaneously laid claim to the exclusive privilege of legitimacy? How can we distinguish between what is rebellion and what is loyalty since, by their contradictory use, they have necessarily lost all meaning? For the first time, the soldier has had to choose among many opposing duties.[7] In a moving book Air Commander Jules Roy evokes the drama of the army in Africa in November, 1942.[8] He writes of the divergences in the communiques from Vichy, Algiers, and London, of the orders, the doubts, the contradictory demands, and "the collapse of old disciplines which could no longer hold us together." "There no longer was any virtue," writes M. Roy, "which could be called discipline. At the same time, I was condemned not to rely on anyone." These lines seem to indicate the breakdown of the abstract, impersonal, legalistic concept of military duty as it had been defined in the nineteenth century. The fleet, scuttled at Toulon, had wanted to obey. However, it was condemned to disappear from the battlefields where the destiny of the world hung in the balance. On the other hand, those who erased the humiliation of 1940 were those who agreed to break the bonds of discipline, those who were seditious toward the established order. The existence of a wealth of references, memories, and experiences from this period could not help but count in the years to follow. After World War II had ended, the army, on the whole, did not feel it necessary to draw any definite lesson from these past events.[9] It even appears that the military kept silent about the moral crisis which they considered to be linked with exceptional circumstances that were unlikely to occur again. The right to vote, granted to the military by a decree of August 7, 1945, did not seem to prevent the army's return, during peacetime, to its traditional policy of nonintervention in politics. In fact, there was a wait of about six years, until the unfolding of the war in Indochina, before the problem of relations between civil and military power was brought to the fore by the army as a whole. Only then were new awarenesses and new attitudes more precisely and more systmatically defined.

TENSION WITH THE GOVERNMENT AND THE CRISIS OF AUTHORITY

In 1957, General Navarre, former Commander-in-Chief of the French expeditionary force in the Far East which was defeated at Dien Bien Phu, declared, "The real reasons for the defeat in Indochina are political."[10] This statement summarizes perfectly (in spite of its author's lack of popularity with his troops) the conclusion which the army seems to have drawn from its unfortunate Indochinese venture. A simple but unshakable conviction developed. After the Geneva armistice, the fighting men in Indochina placed the responsibility for the particularly bloody eight-year war which ended in humiliation on governmental policy, or rather the lack of it.[11]

Many blamed the government for improper handling of the war, the dispersion of governmental authority (Indochinese affairs were the concern of nine ministries), unclear decisions, lack of continuity in the definition, and the pursuit of a policy. The government was also blamed for never having supplied the expeditionary force with necessary technical means for successful conduct of the conflict, for the shortage of men, for the mediocrity and depletion of war material, and for the fluctuations in prestige.[12] The government was also reproached for never having stated any coherent or precise purpose for the war, and for having provided only very insufficient effort when victory seemed possible and then uselessly continuing the fight when the situation was irreparably compromised. Civil power was finally blamed for not protecting the fighting force from its "enemies from within," for not dealing severely with the divulgence of military secrets, and for having silently tolerated numerous financial dealings, all of which illustrated the scandalous chronicle of the Indochinese conflict. The army had been "stabbed in the back"; it had been betrayed more by the institutional disorder than by the weakness of men in power.[13]

There existed a feeling of betrayal by the government, and also a feeling of abandonment by the nation. The fighting force in Indochina felt it was carrying on the fight alone, on the margin of the French community; it was neither understood nor supported by public opinion. With bitterness and sometimes with morose delight, the army recalled all the facts which pointed to the nation's indifference or hostility: the campaigns by the extreme left against "this filthy war," the sympathy expressed by some of the press for the cause of the adversary, the secrecy surrounding the army's suffering, the clandestine atmosphere imposed on the embarkation of reinforcements and the return of wounded, the numerous harassments consciously or unconsciously inflicted.[14]

They wanted him to be alone, to fight alone [one officer writes, speaking of the position of the soldier in contemporary France]. They refused to dirty their hands less from scruples than from a sluggishness of mind, an obsession for peace at home and intellectual comfort. . . . If the whole business was to turn out badly, then the army would naturally take the blame. Thus, the soldier was sent to fight a war for which no one wanted to shoulder the responsibilities.[15]

I breathed the air of defeat, lived through the months feeling abandoned [a contemporary novelist, trying to retrace a psychological pattern, has an officer say]. We were appropriately beaten but not for lack of courage. However, we were ashamed of this unreasonable, ignoble war that our country's leaders had forced us to wage without foreseeing the fatality of its failure and our humiliation.[16]

This state of mind handed down by the Indochinese conflict—this bitterness, rancor, and humiliation—was to be aggravated even more by events after 1954, such as the abandonment of Morocco and Tunisia, the failure of the Suez expedition, the difficult and uncertain beginnings of the fight against the Algerian rebellion. A strong sentimental attachment bound the army to the Moroccan protectorate, which it considered its own creation. The discontinuance of the Suez operation was even more humiliating to the troops that had conducted it, since they were aware of having achieved a perfect technical success.[17] The atmosphere in which the task of pacification in Algeria was undertaken at last seemed tragically confused. A repetition of the errors of Indochina seemed inevitable. The army felt badly adapted to this mission; its daily efforts seemed inevitably menaced or compromised by the government's weakness.[18] "It would be a pleasure to be the victors every once in a while," declared a colonel in 1954 upon seeing the victorious troops of Viet Minh advance on the port of Hanoi. To many of the most sorely tried officers, who bore the essential weight of the fighting in Indochina and North Africa, the ethic of "useless service"—of gratuitous and total devotion to obedience (a principle often invoked by their elders)—was not enough to justify their sacrifices or give meaning to their work. "Success is the only military rule," states a publication read by young military personnel.[19] "Military servitude" is the motto of a sick poet. Servitude no longer exists; there is only success or failure. One does not study to serve but to win. This is the only way to serve with honor. These ideas are worth remembering: convinced that it would have to pay with its blood and honor for errors made by the government, the army found it absolutely necessary to substitute for the traditional duty of obedience *new imperatives based solely on the effectiveness and success of its fight.*

Therefore, it is not surprising that from 1953 to 1958 there was a considerable change in the traditional form of military discipline. On several different occasions officers publicly expressed disagreement with certain governmental decisions. In 1954 Marshal Juin, the highest official in the military hierarchy, took issue with the government project pertaining to E.D.C. and attacked it with violence. In 1956 General Guillaume, chief of the armed forces general staff, and General Zeller, chief of staff of ground forces, resigned in protest against the brutal "reconversion" of NATO divisions sent to Algeria by the government. In 1956 and 1957 sanctions were taken against Generals Faure and Bollardière, both found guilty of acts regarded as insubordination. Then came the resignation of General Dufourt, inspector general of the artillery, who scored certain appointments that he considered unjustified. Tensions were sharpest and most numerous at the very core of the military hierarchy. World War II, Indochina, and then the Algerian ordeal had created a young generation of officers for whom the values of obedience were visibly less important than they had been for their elders. These young officers had borne the principal weight of the fighting in the Far East and in North Africa, where the very violence of the fight had given them exceptional initative and had forced them to assume uncommon responsibilities. It was these young captains and commanders who most strongly expressed their feelings of anger and humiliation. However, it was not only the government, the regime, and its institutions that they held responsible, but also the high command, the unwieldiness and sclerosis of the military apparatus, and the conformism and routine into which many of their leaders had sunk. They tended to include the established political order and the structure of military society in their attack; as a group they condemned the men in power and some of their own chiefs. One may read the following in an inquiry into the "crisis in the army" published in December, 1956:

There is a general crisis of authority which manifests itself as much by a lack of discipline as by a lack of confidence in leaders. This has led to a serious rupture between generations. In the same direction, a feeling of failure and ineffectiveness in the face of the army's recent, present or future tasks has given rise to a desire for reorganization which in itself seems almost impossible to achieve.[20]

This break between generations, remarked by many other observers—this internal crisis in the military—added to the general feeling of discontent and fever, gave the French army in the spring of 1958 a very peculiar character, which, until that time, had hardly ever appeared in its history.

III: The Birth of a Revolutionary Force

The period from 1947 to 1958 saw not only the growth of constantly aggravated tension between the army and governmental power, but also what was at first a vague and later a precise change in the relations that traditionally united military society with the national community. Today the military is no longer integrated in the French social system as it was on the eve of World War II. A new way of life has come into being; new habits, new ways of thinking and feeling, have developed.

The first fact is the constant devaluation of the military profession. A comparison of a captain's pay in 1900 and 1950 shows a decrease from 161 to 95 gold francs.[21] This is an even more drastic reduction that it seems, since the added resources from which many officers' families benefited (other income, returns from landed property and real estate) also have been reduced considerably. Significantly, as reported in a recent journalistic account, a majority of the students at the Academy of St. Cyr want to marry a woman who has a job of her own.

The French officer cannot help but make bitter comparisons between his pay and that of foreign armies. It has been calculated that in 1953 a commanding officer in France earning 95,000 francs per month would have earned 120,000 if he were English, 220,000 if he were Russian, and 280,000 if he were American.[22] He also cannot help but feel at a disadvantage in relation to other civil servants. There is no doubt that the decree of January 13, 1948, which fixed the scale of civil service salaries, greatly lowered military classifications in relation to those of civil employees, both of which had previously been homologous. (The few modifications of internal details have not greatly improved the position of superior cadres.) It is true that substantial bonuses were added to the pay of the fighting forces in Indochina. But it is no less certain that the great majority of French officers feel condemned to a mediocre and impecunious existence. They are all the more distressed, since the devaluation of their material situation is accompanied by a parallel devaluation of their social prestige and moral standing.[23] An even graver problem, however, is the almost permanent *nomadism* of military personnel since World War II. Aside from colonial troops, the life of the professional soldier, under the Third Republic, differed little from that of any other public servant. It was not unusual to find officers whose entire careers had been spent in no more than three or four garrisons at home. Today the entire army has shared the fate once reserved for only the colonial officer. It is important to note that a large number of captains serving in

Algeria in 1959 had previously had two tours of duty of twenty-seven months
in Indochina and then a first tour of duty of two years in Algeria (without
prejudice for those who had spent several rather active months in Tunisia
or Morocco); they were then fulfilling a second Algerian tour of duty of at
least thirty months, according to official expectations. It can be estimated
that since 1947 these officers have spent an average of eighty-eight months
(including travel time) out of 144 outside of metropolitan France and
separated from their families.[24] For many officers who completed their studies
on the eve of World War II and who today are in their forties, the fighting,
interrupted only rarely, has lasted since 1939. This kind of existence most
assuredly has taken its toll on family life; there are long separations, problems
in the rearing of children, and the like. It is even more distressing in the face
of the grave housing problem confronting the career officer during his stays
at home. In 1957 a journalist estimated that 52,000 apartments were lacking
for military personnel. About twenty per cent of the officers assigned to
France would have to stay at hotels with their families; more than thirty per
cent (forty per cent according to Jean Planchais)[25] would be separated from
their families.[26] The inevitable consequences of such a state of affairs were the
inability of the military to establish or expand the circle of its social relations,
the breaking or loosening of certain traditional ties, and the creation of a
military "island" within the national community.

Thus, greatly cut off by its very way of life from the rest of the national
community, the military tended to withdraw into itself. It was gradually
forced to establish its own ethics, its own particular set of values in opposition to existing social standards. Many young officers did not hesitate to
express their contempt for bourgeois conventions, for luxuries, for the
pursuit of security and profit, as well as their pride in being different in a

I am not a clerk [a young military novelist has an officer in Indochina say]. I do not
country that, in their opinion, had lost its sense of grandeur and adventure.
They opposed their values to those of a "bourgeois" France.
wage war in an office from nine to five. Paid vacations do not interest me, nor does a
salary. I don't give a damn for an old age pension since I may be killed before I can
collect it. . . . I have no house to build in the suburbs or at the seashore and no garden
to tend on weekends. I have neither the time nor the opportunity to enjoy the luxuries
which have become the only goal in life for my compatriots. . . . I feel no bitterness
or regret. I love my country and my profession. This is perhaps the only thing which
has permitted me to escape from a nine to five existence, from weekends and from the
automobile showroom.[27]

The anger inherent in these lines is even more apparent in the fictionalized
account of one commanding officer of colonial paratroopers evoking the
life of his comrades in Indochina:

It was successively suggested that he sell aperitifs, nylon stockings, automobile acces-
sories, perfumes, watches. He consistently turned down these suggestions. He wanted
a job that would mean more than a salary. . . . [He] was not yet prepared to struggle
for existence in the commercial civilization of the twentieth century. . . .[28]

Schooled in an atmosphere of war, he also feels alien to the mass which
surrounds him.

Children leave school, women go shopping, a cop awaits relief, the delivery boy whistles on his rounds, auto horns assault your ears, the retired recount their memories. . . . We don't even know such people; we hardly see them. We can do nothing with them; we're not of the same world.

Finally, with a feeling of relief, the young officer sets off again for Indochina.

On second thought, [he later realizes] the stay in France was the most painful. His furlough in France was worse than the tour of duty in Indochina. War was more logical; he felt at home although on foreign soil.

Because of the vehemence of tone, the two preceding accounts are typical of extreme cases. In less aggressive and more subtle form, the feelings they convey, however, were shared by a great number of young army personnel.

We have drawn into ourselves [states a captain, writing of his experiences in Indochina]. We have lived close together and have become as sensitive and sore as whipped animals. How great was our despair at being rejected by our country and how great was our need for fraternity![29]

In the new French military literature of the 1950's one often heard an echo of the romanticism expressed by *Les Réprouvés (The Outcasts)* of Ernst von Salomon after World War I. It would be foolish to consider it just as literature. In effect, the voluntary, aggressive nonconformity affected by many young officers was linked with a gap between the important intellectual values commonly accepted by French opinion and the intellectual values by which the unity of the army is maintained. France embodied a curious paradox. In a conservative society—where class tensions were increasingly less violent and where the general trend was toward granting an ever greater place to the pursuit of material well-being and the need for security—the army in 1958, even more than the proletariat whose way of life was in the process of change, tended to appear as one of the most extraordinary forces, perhaps the only revolutionary one capable of menacing the established order.

IV: Facts and Myths of Revolutionary War

The growth of a revolutionary spirit within the French army is strongly linked with the war in Indochina. This conflict is equally inseparable from another important occurrence in the military history of contemporary France —the army's discovery of a new type of warfare—causing the formulation of a new doctrine which was soon to dominate the thoughts and behavior of its intellectual élite.[30]

Some of us who have returned from this war [writes an officer] look back on the recent past and find that no other period in our military career has shaped our destinies as much, because we never before felt the need to think about our problems, to reject the formulas given us and to uncover new ideas and solutions each time.[31]

The doctrine formulated by the French army since its Indochinese experience is that of *revolutionary war*. With this new doctrine, certain traditional values had to be re-examined, leading to a concept of the role of the military within contemporary society that was considerably different from earlier concepts.

THE TACTICS AND STRATEGY OF REVOLUTIONARY WAR

The elaboration of the doctrinal concepts of revolutionary war is a direct outgrowth of a study of tactical methods employed by the Viet Minh forces in Indochina. In effect, the army in Indochina was confronted by an unknown adversary which it could not defeat, in spite of recognized material superiority. The enemy had deliberately planned its strategy to thwart the French. The plan called for "war among the masses," in the words of Mao Tse-tung. Its main objective was the conquest of people, not the taking of territory or the domination of a battlefield. The victor was the one who knew how to take hold of a population morally, then materially mobilize its strength. To achieve this end, the enemy in Indochina employed very specific techniques which were completely effective. They were constant propaganda, systematic terrorism, the deliberate dismemberment of existing social structures, and the establishment of "parallel hierarchies," which slowly replaced the hierarchies of legal order and enslaved the population in an increasingly tight web of steel. The French army was forced to admit that in such a struggle military action should be secondary to psychological action, propaganda, the collection and exploitation of political as well as operational information, police action, liaison with the people, and economic and social action. The French army discovered that its men not only had to be experts in the use of arms, but also, and perhaps above all, had to be political agitators, organizers, and leaders of partisans. In the end, the qualities and methods of the ideological crusader were more effective in obtaining final victory than the qualities and methods of the soldier.

Theoreticians of revolutionary war have naturally come to include these tactical lessons of the war in Indochina in their general views on contemporary history and on the evolution of conflicts since 1945. It is evident to them that today the classical battle is no longer the only means by which a power may gain control of territory or even of an entire country. Revolts, coups d'état, and action by political parties are often more effective instruments of domination than is the direct intervention of bombers or tanks. Consequently, the defense of a territory no longer means the defense of frontiers from an enemy who perhaps would not attempt a breakthrough. Defense today must be against the political and ideological forces of internal subversion. Many believe that even a nuclear army is no more than an instrument of intimidation destined to protect the free development and continuance of revolutionary action.

At the end of the last war it might have been thought [writes Colonel Lacheroy, one of the principal interpreters of the new doctrine] that military art was assuming a new form . . . that we were moving in the direction of "push-button" warfare. However, since that time, French officers and soldiers have died daily for their country in some corner of the globe. These men were not confronted by a "push-button" war, but rather by varied forms of conflict, insurrectional uprisings, ideological warfare, in a word, by "revolutionary wars."[82]

Colonel Lacheroy continues:

Many officers among us feel that there will be no atomic war, perhaps no conventional war, but only revolutionary war. Alas, that is our destiny; we are already faced with it; we must act accordingly. . . .

Going even further, many are convinced that it is only by revolutionary war that the future of the world will be decided in the years to come.

What are the sources of the concept of a global strategy of revolutionary war expressed by these military authors? The example of Indochina convinced them of the fundamental unity of doctrine and direction of the Communist world. From the works of Soviet and Chinese military theoreticians, they have ascertained claims for the universal extension of Marxist-Leninist ideology. According to the theorists of revolutionary war, the West must look forward to permanent, many-sided, total, and universal aggression. "The Third World War," they state, "has begun"; and the fight is waged throughout all continents, within each country. In this struggle, the defense of European frontiers is of secondary importance. The enemy will circumvent them either through internal disintegration or by conquering Asian and African nations with its ideology. Liberal democracies should not only attempt to protect themselves against the possible menace of a frontal attack by Soviet troops.[33] It is rather against the expansion and penetration of a revolutionary political ideology and messianism that they should fortify themselves.

The army [writes an officer, speaking for some of his comrades] has learned to recognize its country's true adversary. . . . Although the menace remains abstract and distant for most Frenchmen, even the most lucid ones, the army has accepted its most immediate form, that of an invisible and omnipresent enemy, more deadly for its power of seduction and subversion, its propaganda and underground activities than for its actual weapon strength.[34]

Dominated by the concept of permanent, universal revolutionary war aimed at the ideological conquest of the globe, the new military thought tends to include the interpretation of all conflicts and tensions in the contemporary world within this doctrinal framework. The Algerian revolt is presented as a new but decisive phase in the Communist struggle for world domination. According to the new theory, the fight against the F.L.N. is not only justified as a defense of the rights of French sovereignty; it is also justified in the name of strategic imperatives which control the outbreak of a "third global conflict." There is no better example of this attitude than the remarks made by General Allard, commander of the army in Algiers, in a speech given at SHAPE on November 15, 1957:

Cleverly maintaining both interest and unrest brought about by alternating periods of peace and intimidation, of smiles or menaces, the U.S.S.R. has succeeded in focusing the free world's defense on one sole objective: to persuade the possible adversary to renounce total war. The Soviet Union thereby has concealed from many the fact that her main effort is not directed towards the East-West axis, but rather towards a vast curve enveloping China, the Far East, Southeast Asia, the Middle East, Egypt, and North Africa, thereby encircling Europe. This is now almost a reality; the one step remaining is to wrest Algeria from France. . . . Then the encircling and the isolation of the free world will be able to continue. We must also realize that the masterminds in the Kremlin are aware that the process of contamination must reach the Dark Continent and cross the Atlantic to South and Central America! What then will be the chance for survival of the peoples we represent. However, there is one obstacle to the realization of this plan which is less perfect than it appears. This obstacle is the determination of France not to be ousted from Algeria. . . . France had already attempted to stem the expansion of Communism in Tonkin. . . . The free world did not understand the importance of these attempts and they failed. Our last line of defense is Algeria.[35]

One must not forget, in reading this text, that General Allard, speaking to members of NATO, was trying to convince them of the need of a common cause in the battle being waged by the French army in Algeria. It is interesting, nevertheless, to note that the themes which he develops are the same ones discussed continuously in French military literature of the past few years.[36] The doctrine of revolutionary war defines the military missions of France in terms of a general interpretation of the international situation. It is within the framework of an ideological world crusade that this doctrine tends, explicitly or implicitly, to pinpoint and justify the action of the French army.

REVOLUTIONARY WAR AND THE POLITICAL VOCATION OF THE ARMY

From 1954 to 1958, four decisive years in the intellectual history of the army, the theory of revolutionary war spread rapidly in military circles. The expeditionary forces in Indochina were the crucible in which the new doctrine was formed. After their return from the Far East, some officers devoted themselves to the publication of their memoirs and their reflections. General Chassin, former commander of the air forces of the expeditionary corps and author of various works on Mao Tse-tung, is responsible, it seems, for the first studies on this subject, published in the October, 1954, issue of *Revue militaire d'information* and in the December issue of *Revue de défense nationale*. In June, 1955, Captain Souyris published an important article on the "self-defense of the masses" in the same journal. In December of the same year *Message des forces armées* made these significant remarks in its editorial:

The military must fully understand the techniques of the war imposed upon it; it must realize that these techniques are not at all like those employed in '40 and '45 nor are they the ones learned at military school. . . . Traditional warfare is not the only possible answer. The disciples of Lenin are masters in two other types of conflict. These are psychological war and revolutionary war; the latter is being launched right now.[37]

A few months later Commander Hogard published the results of his research in the *Revue de défense nationale*. Finally, in February-March, 1957, a special issue of *Revue militaire d'information* was devoted entirely to a discussion of the doctrine of revolutionary war.[38] From that time the army's intellectual élite, especially young officers, seems to have accepted the new idea. In every issue of the various military publications there is discussion or study of some new aspect of subversive, psychological, or revolutionary war. At the same time, new concepts were officially propagated in military echelons. In 1956 an Instruction Center in Psychological Warfare was created in Paris, where military specialists were trained. In 1957, courses in "psychological instruction" were instituted in all military schools. These courses include a thorough study of Marxist-Leninist doctrine, the techniques of its penetration, and methods of combating them. A completely new terminology has appeared in the military vocabulary. New trends of thought and new attitudes have taken shape.

The first consequence of the generalization of the concept of revolutionary war is the often uncertain and anxious search by young military personnel for the metaphysic of political conflict.

In the present war of ideas waged by Marxism [writes the spokesman for a group of officers] we cannot win if we have no truths in which to believe, no values to defend. Today, every officer is convinced of this. . . .

In the past, the nation needed men traditionally devoted to a career of arms. . . . Political preoccupations had no place in a narrowly specialized army. However, since the concept of war has changed—we are now faced with ideological warfare—the military must change as well. . . . It must be capable of establishing, effecting and assimilating a coherent plan.[39]

The search for an international doctrine capable of effectively opposing Marxist-Leninist theories, the pursuit of a system of values strong enough to unite and stimulate national energies, will henceforth play a great part in military preoccupations. Some, perhaps the majority, will attempt to define an ideology based on the exaltation of the traditional values of Western humanism: the dignity of man, patriotism, respect for spiritual values, the desire for justice and progress. (This is mainly the "doctrine" taught in courses on "psychological action" at the École spèciale militaire—that is, a synthesis of the ancient precepts of democratic idealism and the teachings of Christian morality.) Others overtly express their espousal of the principles of a strict type of Catholicism, finding the answer to the revolutionary menace in the establishment of an authoritarian, traditionalist Christian order which explicitly repudiates the postulates of liberal individualism.[40] Finally, others lean toward an anti-Marxist, as well as anticapitalist, national collectivism. Needless to say, there is much confusion and hesitation, along with many contradictions, in this systematic quest for a doctrine.[41] However, the mere existence of the quest is more important than the results it produces: it does not presuppose political commitment on the part of young officers; it does not involve any militant action from within a party or group. (Contrary to what has been written and said, adjustments of this sort occur only in isolated and rather rare cases. The military jealously wants to preserve its autonomy and avoid anything which might disrupt its unity.) It is no less true that the intensity of these doctrinal, ideological preoccupations has lead the military further and further away from the elementary and simply defined precepts on which was founded its traditional position of nonintervention in politics.

It is no doubt evident that from the point of view of political science the doctrinal schematization of revolutionary war, as it is expounded by military theoreticians, must necessarily incur many reservations. The first, and probably the most decisive, criticism is of its frequent assimilation of the methods and aims of subversive war. The same techniques do not necessarily have to be employed to achieve similar objectives.[42] Too much attention is given to these methods and techniques, to the detriment of a study of the political, sociological, and economic terrain in which they are employed. The techniques of subversive war may exploit or aggravate tensions inherent in certain political societies; however, it is difficult to say whether the techniques cause these tensions. When Colonel Lacheroy writes, citing the case of Indochina, "In the beginning, there is nothing,"[43] it is evident that he is silent about the internal conflicts inherent in any colonial society. Perhaps it may finally be said that the novel character of revolutionary war is less decisive than many have tended to believe. The history of the West offers many examples of this type of war, such as guerrilla warfare and the use of "fifth columns" to force the ramparts of cities without direct combat. Can we forget the tenor of the political ideology presented by the wars of the French Revolution or even by the "nationalistic" wars of the first half of the nineteenth century?

The basic originality of subversive wars in the second half of the twentieth century, however, must not be denied or underestimated. Of course, a theoretical analysis could reduce these wars to a certain number of elements that might be found to have been employed in the past. However, originality rests on a careful combination of all these elements and the systematic use of the methods of modern social psychology. The armies of the Convention propagated an ideology and, in their conquest of an enemy country, depended on that part of the population which had been won over to this ideology. However, their propaganda was relatively abstract. Destruction of the enemy forces and capture of territory were the first objectives. The Allies in no way attempted *first* to secure the masses, to encircle them, to ensnare them in the powerful and tight web of a totalitarian organization, to make of each individual, regardless of age or sex, an actual fighter integrated in and used by a politico-military system. Then, too, there is the close alliance of an ideology of universal scope with a massive centralized and disciplined political organization, also international in character. Soviet power is not the West's only adversary; the other, which cannot be divorced from the first, is Communism, a party and political ideology supranational in character. In present circumstances defense of national sovereignty for certain countries can no longer be organized purely on the basis of the menace of "foreign" war. The possibility of what is traditionally called "civil" war must be considered. This possibility not only raises particularly complex problems of military organization but also leads, however regretfully, to an inevitable revision of the old postulates of military devotion.

V: The Algerian Affair

The war in Indochina marked the beginning of a grave period of tension between civil power and the military. The precepts of revolutionary war gradually tended to draw the military away from its traditional policy of political nonintervention. Algeria, however, was the decisive affair in which the army was to stand up to the government. This event cannot be fully understood unless an important fact, which seems to have escaped the majority of political observers, is considered. That fact is the progressive establishment, between 1954 and 1958, of a veritable "military province" in Algerian departments, the progressive assumption by the army of almost complete authority and administrative responsibility for this vast territory.

THE MILITARIZATION OF ALGERIA

When the Algerian rebellion broke out at the end of 1954, the task assigned to the army was relatively simple: re-establish order—that is, suppress uprisings, and chase, destroy, or subdue the F.L.N. bands. However, since it was limited to a strictly military operation, the army's effort was doomed to almost irremediable failure. Deprived of information and cut off from any contact with the Moslem population, the "forces of law and order" wore themselves out thrusting at an elusive adversary. The experience of more than a century of colonial wars, the lessons of Galliéni and of Lyautey placed emphasis on the necessity of a policy of "pacification," closely coordinating military, psychological, and administrative action under one authority.[44] The Indochinese precedent, constantly evoked by the doctrinaires of revolutionary war, was an indication of the dramatic conclusion that awaited combat unadapted to the methods of the adversary. The F.L.N., like the forces of Viet Minh, conducted a war "among the masses." Instead of hoping to achieve immediate military coups, the F.L.N. attempted to spread the network of its political and administrative structures over the entire Algerian population. Therefore, the French goal should have been, not the pursuit of its guerrillas, but the destruction of its political organization through the establishment of an opposition, through substitution of another political organization. The government could not help but recognize the validity of these observations. The police and traditional judiciary apparatus, accustomed to handling occurrences of an average criminal nature, were ridiculously impotent in the face of the systematic practice of terrorism carried on by the F.L.N. Algeria had only known inadequate administrative institutions, and in many places the all-too-weak existing structures began to crack at the beginning of the rebellion. There was an almost complete administrative void. At that time, only the army was in a position to fill it. Thus, gradually, from 1956 on, under the impetus of M. Lacoste, the resident Minister, increasingly greater responsibilities were confided in the military. The result was that, at least on a local level, the army had within its authority almost all repressive and administrative power.

The most important innovations were perhaps the S.A.S. (Special Administrative Sections) and the S.A.U. (Urban Administrative Sections) created in 1956. They led, in fact, to the establishment of a new administrative sectoring that was superimposed upon existing districts without destroying them (prefects and subprefects carried on their work until the crisis of May 13, 1958). The commanding officer of the S.A.S., usually a captain, was entirely responsible for the administrative affairs of the district under his command.[45] His job was to take a census of the people, supervise them, and guide them. He supervised the economic development of the area, granting medical and social assistance. He also endeavored to reduce deficiencies in education.[46] This one man was mayor, teacher, and engineer. He directed and supervised the work of the medical staff and social workers under him, initiated work projects, levied taxes, established a small police force, and sparked local political activities. In 1958 there were more than 600 S.A.S. officers in Algeria, as a rule in areas cleared of rebel bands. Of course, in so-called operational districts most of the officers had to assume similar administrative tasks more or less empirically.

Faithful to the principles of "parallel hierarchies" dear to theoreticians of revolutionary war, the army also attempted to increase the number of organizations and groups under its supervision. In Algiers and its outskirts the fight against terrorism led to the establishment of a tight surveillance network based on the designation of some men responsible for whole neighborhoods and others for small groups of houses. But it was on the civic, moral, and professional level that the most interesting groups were formed. In every built-up area there were servicemen's canteens, places for gatherings and discussions, where the men could bring their sons. There were women's clubs led by social workers; even Moslems gathered there. The army even created and supervised trade schools; there were twenty-six of them by the end of 1957, with instructors coming from the *Centre de formation* at Dellys, which was itself established under military authority. There were even centers for the education of the future leaders of douars. Here basic administrative procedures were taught, along with enough military training to provide for the self-defense of villages.[47]

In line with this effort to hold the population together, the army created a powerful apparatus for the gathering of information and the direction of public opinion. The latter was supervised by the Fifth Division of the Tenth Military District, which, since the beginning of the rebellion, had worked unceasingly to expand its field of activity. Its beginnings were relatively modest. Loudspeaker and leaflet campaigns were employed to spread French propaganda. Then better methods were perfected. A corps of itinerant officers (O.I.) was created. Advisory groups of these officers, expert in psychological action, traveled from district to district. Military publications increased. Movies and, above all, radio were more widely used. All in all, extremely diversified methods of propaganda were employed by the army in Algeria. These tasks added to the reasons for the almost complete change in the concept of the officer's traditional role:

This army . . . which in '39 sadly abandoned its horses . . . to dirty its hands in the mechanics of tanks and machine guns, becoming accustomed to the smell of oil and gas, . . . was now plunged in a war in which these very tanks and guns would soon join the horses as museum pieces. The men now learned that they had to take care of the people, learn to swab mercurochrome, administer antibiotics and sulfa drugs, supervise the population, take the census, dole out work, talk of bulldozers, bridges and roads, highways, credit, enter into local politics, etc. . . . In a word, the army was the housekeeper of the nation.[48]

In fact, on the verge of the crisis of May 13, 1958, the army had not only supplanted civil administration in districts where the latter was incapable of handling its job, but the precepts of revolutionary war had also taken over from old colonial traditions, extending and developing them. With its newspapers, schools, teams of social workers, youth organizations, and women's clubs, the army tended to appear as an omnipotent party, even monopolizing public power in some regions of Algeria. The army had its own propaganda machine, and its own surveillance and repression system. At least on the local level, it controlled and animated the most dynamic elements of that part of the Moslem population that had escaped the claws of the rebellion. In short, the army had given Algeria many new institutions.

DETERMINATION OF AN ALGERIAN POLICY

How can we avoid concluding that techniques of psychological action and of rehabilitation of the people are not, and cannot be, politically neutral? In reality, the mere fact that the army waged "a war among the masses," or, in more traditional terms, substituted "pacification" for "repression," inferred, even to the lowest echelons of the military hierarchy, the recognition of the development of a *particular Algerian policy*. Of course, the need for an all-inclusive policy attacking the entire Algerian problem was not immediately apparent to military circles. For a long while many officers refused to see beyond the narrow limits of the task assigned to them. For a long time as well the army in Algeria waited for the government to define and propose this sorely needed policy.

Several of our comrades in Algeria [stated an editorial in *Message des forces armées* of August, 1956] have informed us of the difficulty of their position due to the complete absence of any governmental decision. In this psychological combat the army is asked to gain the popular confidence without the implacable weapon of a well-defined policy.[49]

It is quite evident that, because of the great division in political parties and public opinion, the government was powerless to promote the well-defined policy demanded by the above military editorialist. What was demanded was a plan of action for Algeria completely without ambiguity, containing a sufficiently broad outlook for the future. The government's indecision in this matter was not the only cause for discontent with civil power that existed in the military. The necessities of the struggle forced the army to determine this political program for itself. However, it does not seem, in spite of some assertions,[50] that there was systematic agreement or a coordinated and deliberate quest on the part of its officers. The methods of pacification and their logical implications gradually led to the almost spontaneous elaboration of a coherent Algerian policy based on several essential assertions.

The first of these was the continuing presence of the French on Algerian soil. The essential task of pacification was, in effect, to win over, or to win back, the adherence of the Moslem population, which was basically insecure, hesitant, vacillating, and dominated by concern for the future. The reservations created by this situation were due more to fear of compromise than to open hostility. Any vagueness as to the future, any ambiguity as to France's will to maintain her sovereignty, ran the risk of irreparably paralyzing any action aimed at persuading and involving the country. Therefore, every French officer serving in Algeria, in order to properly fulfill his mission, of necessity had to declare that those remaining loyal would never be abandoned. Because of this, it can be understood why the army had to disagree with the policy of "cease fire, elections, negotiations" as defined in 1956 by the government of M. Guy Mollet. This formula was not aimed at securing the future; it allowed for the greatest diversity of solutions and left the way open to all possibilities. The "pacifying" officer, bound by the daily difficulties of his task, was led to believe, on the contrary, that future security was the first and most important condition for the effectiveness of his work. He had to proclaim that any retreat was unthinkable. Any break in the expression of his will or in the manifestation of his resolve would greatly compromise the pursuit of goals he had been ordered to achieve.

It was not, however, just a question of obtaining the resigned or passive assent of the majority of the population. Even when secured, a guarantee of the continuance of French sovereignty was not enough to stand up to the mystique of the rebellion. Another faith and vision of the future had to be set in opposition to the faith and vision that sparked the adversary. This in turn led to a second, equally political, assertion: the need for the civic, economic, and social progress of the Moslems in Algeria. Since these Moslems were constantly dominated by a feeling of alienation from and frustration toward the population of European origin, the army thought that it would never win their deep faith or productively galvanize their energies and enthusiasm unless it offered them the concrete hope of a better and more dignified life. Thus, the army planned to concentrate on the most lowly, the outcasts.

France's future in this country, [writes *Contacts,* a journal of the Tenth Military District] "lies in its concern for the lowly, and they are many. . . . Instead of maintaining the traditional self-seeking or distrustful contacts with informed or lettered people, thereby creating a barrier between the masses and France, we should study the lives of the small people, the poor, those who have been exploited without our knowledge.[51]

An attempt was made to change the status of the Moslem woman and hasten her emancipation.

Little by little [continued *Contacts*] we shall interest the women in our present struggle, giving them cause to turn their backs on the rebels. We would explain that women were the most downtrodden section of the population, that our goal is for the betterment of all, particularly the most unhappy.[52]

Finally, a revolution of the Kemalist type, overthrowing old institutions and aimed at the destruction of traditional inequalities was proposed to the Algerian masses. A new Algeria would grow out of the struggle, an Algeria where all citizens would have identical rights and similar opportunities. It was said that the Algerians of tomorrow would be "completely independent Frenchmen."

The army was soon to summarize its vast program in one simple phrase, "l'Algérie française," and in one word, "integration." However, it would be a mistake to think that the officers using this word accorded it an extremely precise institutional meaning. A great diversity of opinion existed in military circles about the nature of future administrative ties which ought to unite Algerian and metropolitan departments. Some were in favor of complete assimilation, while others were aware of an Algerian "personality" endowed with its own institutions. In fact, as it was used by the army until May 13, 1958,[53] integration essentially corresponded to a synthesis of three major elements, the fundamental imperatives of military policy in Algeria: maintenance of French sovereignty, the attainment by the Moslems of full civil equality, and economic and social progress.

> Integration [writes *Contacts*] means the recognition by Algerians and their metropolitan brothers of the equal rights of all citizens of Algeria; it means the pooling of all the material resources of both Algeria and the mother country.

Understood in this sense, integration constituted the idea-force, the myth that the army intended to offer to the dreams of the Algerian masses and oppose to the mystique of independence. "Our myth," declares Colonel Lacheroy, "involves telling the Moslem, 'You will be like us.' "[54] This may lead to a misconception. It was not just cold calculation or a simple propaganda maneuver, but a profound desire by the army to achieve an ideal condition. This condition involved the complete abrogation of semicolonial statutes existing in Algeria until 1954, and the establishment of entirely new ties between Algerian and metropolitan departments. At this point, the military were quite far from their original task of re-establishing order. The army had set up a goal in the Algerian fight that, without expressly contradicting it, greatly transcended the goal sought by the government. On the basis of experience the army developed a complete, coherent Algerian policy closely linked to the imperatives and terms of the battle it had to fight. It was a fitting policy, defined by the army itself, which remained totally independent of the decisions of the government.

SENTIMENTAL AND MORAL INTERESTS

Above all, the pursuit of this Algerian policy was connected, within the ideological context of the French army, with a tenacious loyalty to certain strong and influential values. It must not be forgotten that the conquest of the French colonial empire, in the nineteenth century and at the beginning of the twentieth, was almost entirely the work of the army. It is not surprising that attachment to this empire occupied an important place in the moral patrimony of the French officer, that it was bound up with some of the most profound traditions inherited by the officer. Ties binding the army to the heritage of a colonial past were particularly numerous and strong in North Africa. How could this fund of memories, images, legends and collective pride be evoked? There were the legend of Lyautey and the great moments in the Moroccan epic, all living realities talked about at mess and taught at military academies. There was Algeria's role as a place of refuge from 1940 to 1943. The divisions that had fought in Italy and landed in France came to Algeria and found shelter. North African garrisons were a kind of sanctuary during the first years of the postwar period. The officers there enjoyed a higher standard of living and greater respect. Above all, there was great contact between the military and the Moslem population. Many officers had led North African units or fought at their side. Ties of friendship in battle, of respect and affection, developed and remained strong.[55] The army was also proud of having assured perfect equality of treatment within its ranks for both North Africans and Frenchmen.[56] Many such factors combined to grant North Africa a privileged place in the "sentimental geography" of the French army.

But there were graver considerations. The pursuit of the task of pacification ineluctably obliged the French officer to compromise a number of loyal Algerian Moslems with French authority, for which he felt directly responsible. To evacuate Algeria would amount to abandoning the loyal to the reprisals of the rebellion. To the officer who had granted his protection, this would mean forfeiting basic duties of loyalty and honor. Many men had already returned from Indochina with a feeling of guilt, bearing a heavy burden for having betrayed the commitments they had made to the Vietnamese partisans fighting by their side.

I knew a captain of the red hats [writes one witness] who was obsessed with the idea that he had lost his honor in Indochina because he had influenced hundreds of young Catholic Vietnamese to join him by repeating "we will never let you down," which he truly believed. At our departure the Viets had these young people shot for having believed the captain.[57]

In Algeria, where the basic task was to obtain active, militant allegiance of the population, the problem was posed in a more general way. It is not surprising that it finally had a determinant place in the minds of a great many officers.[58]

In this vein, there is no more significant example than this passage taken from the work of a former second lieutenant in the paratroopers, Jean Yves Alquier, where he relates his experiences as an S.A.S. officer. M. Alquier is about to return to civilian life. An old Moslem, once a fighter and now a douar leader is bidding him farewell:

Lieutenant [says the old man], I want to speak to you for the last time before you leave us. It's about the young people of my *mechta*. I made them return from Algiers at your request so they could work with you and the captain. As long as you were here, they had confidence in France. But now I fear she is abandoning us. . . . You know that if Algeria is given her independence, all those who worked with France will be murdered. So, here is my request. As a trusting friend, I ask that you swear that you will never abandon us, or that before leaving you will authorize the young people to go to work in Algiers or in France; they will be content there. I will stay behind with my sons and my people. . . .

Lieutenant Alquier then comments:

While the old chief awaited my decision, I thought about all the people in Indochina who had been killed for believing that France, after having fought at their side, would never abandon them. I thought of those in Tunisia who, loyal to the end, had disappeared without a trace since our departure; and of those in Morocco. . . . And once again I wondered if one day we would not have the death of all those we had rallied and then betrayed on our conscience.[59]

As it happened, Lieutenant Alquier refused to commit himself and allow the young people of the douar to leave for Algiers. But the promise that he dared not make that day was made by many who could not take any other stand without betraying their mission. In the eyes of many officers the policy of pacification led to the establishment of a contract with the Moslem population, a personally binding contract that they had no right to break.[60] Thus, it seemed impossible that the army should follow any policy other than the one to which the government had so deeply committed it. In consequence, the government lost the possibility of defining and imposing another policy. To the moral imperatives of obedience to legal government the army opposed other stronger imperatives, which grew out of the execution of the mission it had received.

It was a strange war, which, by its very form, led those who fought it to elaborate a policy committing them irrevocably to a particular path. It was an undertaking that conformed to the decision of legal government and was a legitimate outgrowth of national will; yet the struggle against the Algerian rebellion imperceptibly but irresistibly escaped the control of governmental authority. Under these conditions, it is hardly rash to assert that, by having developed all the logical consequences of the mission granted by civil power, the army finally arrived at opposing this power in decisive conflict. The army appears to have been borne along by the internal mechanism of the battle it was ordered to wage, a battle whose prime necessity and profound legitimacy seemed to be quite evident. Because the army suspected that a new government would try, in May, 1958, to force it to abandon a duty which had become part of its main existence, the army finally decided— against all its traditions and customs—to revolt, to stand up to the regime and impose its own law.

VI: Conclusion

The object of this study is not to record the crisis of May 13, 1958, nor is it to attempt to indicate the relative importance of the army's role in the forces that contributed to the downfall of the Fourth Republic. Was it an epilogue to an accidental period of tension between a regime whose authority was increasingly contested and an uneasy and discontented army? Or was it rather a pivotal date marking the advent of a new era in the definition of relations between civil and military power in contemporary France? These are the only questions we must ask regarding the events of May, 1958.

MAY 13 AND ITS SIGNIFICANCE

To answer these questions, it must first be stressed that the army's intervention on the political scene was in no way a traditional *pronunciamento*. The army had no intention of assuming complete power. Aside from a few officers who were ardently committed, almost no one considered installing a military junta to assume and exercise governmental authority. Nor was there any idea of supporting a party or particular political group by force of arms. The institution of "committees of public welfare," where military leaders sat with representatives of Algerian political movements, only corresponded to accidental and temporary necessities. There was no question of substituting another premeditated form of government or other institutions for those of the Fourth Republic. Strictly speaking, the army had no political program. Even the appeal to General de Gaulle appeared to those who made it only as an impromptu recourse in order to get out of a dangerous and continuing situation. "The army turned to General de Gaulle as the only person capable of resolving France's crisis and of assuming, for the greatest good, the highest post in the country."[61] In fact, the army's action might justifiably be compared to that of a pressure group (a pressure group endowed, however, with a particular power). It did not attempt to impose precise governmental formulas, but essentially endeavored to influence the formation of a policy.

Having obtained its immediate goals with General de Gaulle's accession to power, the army might have returned to the traditional limits of its duties. It did not seek to prolong its victory or enlarge the range of its political intervention. The army in no way endeavored to impose its men or machinery on the new regime. The Fifth Republic, an outgrowth of military insubordination, at no time took on the appearance of a military government. There is no doubt that a year after the "revolution" of May, 1958, feelings of bitterness and deception were often expressed in the military, notably in lower ranks. General de Gaulle's Algerian policy met with strong criticism. Although his intentions seemed in line with the plan for a French Algeria, he was reproached for his methods, his caution, and his temporizing empiricism, which were considered fallacious and dangerous. Many regretted that the new regime did not require that the entire country participate more actively in the war effort. Changes in command in 1959 and 1960 hurt many feelings and wounded many egos. The press continues to speak of the unrest in the army, and it is evident that discontent and doubt have far from disappeared. It is no less true that the prospect of a new May 13, frequently mentioned in some circles of the extreme right-wing opposition, does not awaken any echo, at least for the moment. It is also certain that the army sought (even without any governmental intervention) to divest itself, with success, of any compromise regarding political movements; it is now a question strictly of metropolitan and Algerian groups.[62] The army felt more satisfaction than regret when it assisted in the breaking up of the Committees of Public Welfare in Algeria in which its representatives had played an important role. Apparently the government of the Fifth Republic has today succeeded in rapidly and effectively re-establishing the traditional rules bearing on military power's subordination to legal power.

It is important, however, to stress that, although the army as a whole does not appear at present to question the obedience it owes to the new state, this is essentially a *reflected* obedience. All military authors, anonymous or otherwise, who have written since the events of May, 1958, agree in denouncing the old notion of passive obedience as definitely outmoded. We cannot simply return, they repeat, to the traditional concept of the army as a blind, inert tool in the hands of government, nor can we reinstate the principle of complete nonintervention in politics. A reply attributed to a young lieutenant serving in Algeria is quite significant; questioned by a foreign correspondent about whom he would obey if he were to receive contradictory orders from General de Gaulle and General Massu, this officer would have replied, "I will think it over."[63] These words are very similar to the formula, this one authentic, employed by a paratroop officer to define the new conditions of military obedience:

Obedience, taught us by our masters, is not the only rule for an officer. He has the right and duty to weigh all ideas. We have benefited from the lessons of 1940.[64]

The unfortunate consequences arising from the generalization of these principles, affecting the internal unity of the army and the effectiveness of the military apparatus, were not foreseen. The authors of these replies only take a stand on the level of political choices; on this level they are convinced of the army's fundamental unity on certain basic issues. They are or appear to be persuaded that the military would present a complete community of reactions, an unmarred cohesiveness in the face of any given challenge.

Thus, with respect to government obedience is reflected; it is revocable and *conditional*. As a matter of fact, the army acts as if, on the political plane, it had a kind of *veto power*. It considers itself authorized to use this veto on a governmental decision that might directly menace what the army believes to be the requirements of national destiny. Agreement on two cases where political intervention of the army could be considered legitimate seems to exist today within the military community. The first case would be the denunciation of French sovereignty in Algerian departments. The second would be the rise to power of the Communist Party; some say that even a popular front government with Communist support would be no more than the first stage of the establishment in France of a "peoples' democracy." In these two cases the army would be disloyal to itself, to its mission, and to its duties if it remained mute, submissive, and passive.

Such a resolution today sums up French political evolution within a set of totally new unwritten laws. However convincing this may be, there are still many ambiguities. What degree of autonomy for Algeria would give the army a right to speak of abandonment? Would the existence of a Communist-supported government legitimize insubordination? Some officers, well aware of these difficulties, hope to regulate the use of the new rights by the establishment of a kind of military council of order. As a product of the military, this body would represent the army in the government, airing its grievances, fears, or desires. Acting as a moral guardian, it would inspire the army in its attitudes and duties. In short, it would be the interpreter and director of the military conscience. The formulation of this project is still quite vague. However, its main idea corresponds to a concept, espoused by many of the new military generation, of the army's political role. The army must remain separate from government: it must not become involved in it or strive for power, but it must be capable, under certain circumstances, of directly effecting the execution of its permanent mission of national defense, of making its voice heard, and of looking after the fundamental laws of national destiny.

ANALYSIS

Thus, we cannot explain the new relations between political and military power simply by the crisis in governmental authority that marked the decline of the Fourth Republic. The great change in values which has upset the moral configuration of French military society may be historically significant. The change was brought about by the evolution of forms of war in the twentieth century and by the particulars of France's international position. There is a supplementary ideological note, increasingly accentuated by modern world conflicts, in the French army's repudiation of the old principles of nonintervention in politics and passive obedience. Until the eve of World War II, the concept of military duty was based on the past history of nineteenth-century European wars. These were waged between states of similar social and economic structure over conflicting political and territorial ambitions. In spite of numerous ideological implications, the second world conflict was still considered by the majority of officers as merely a new episode in Franco-German antagonism, as a third phase in a fight begun in 1870. In their eyes national imperatives remained separate from and superior to ideological considerations. To some it was always possible to fight for one's country without feeling the least sympathy for parliamentary democracy; in the same way, some members of the *Wehrmacht,* in 1945, might still have thought that they were fighting for the German nation and not for the National Socialist cause.

This way of thinking has almost completely changed today. The army is convinced that the battles in which it is engaged, or for which it is preparing, no longer correspond to traditional struggles between states. It is convinced that the stakes in conflicts where it has or will have to intervene are no longer the conquest of territory or the material supremacy of one state over another. A concept of life, the very idea of man's destiny, is, in the army's eyes, the main concern. Of course, the idea of independence and national grandeur continue to hold a fundamental place in the army's ethic. However, they are now part of a system of values which transcends them. In addition, the forms of combat experienced by the army, first in Indochina and then in Algeria, appear to have definitely demonstrated that superiority of material force is not alone sufficient to overcome the enemy. The first job is to win over the masses, to attract their minds and hearts. General Henri Zeller, army chief of staff, in 1957, said, "Since we are engaged in a global crisis and are confronted by definite adversaries, an army can no longer obey or sacrifice itself for words such as 'duty' or 'discipline' that are now completely lacking in meaning."[65] Since the clash of political credos seems to dominate the second half of the twentieth century, it is virtually impossible to keep an army (except perhaps an army of mercenaries) bound solely to the principles of obedience and discipline. The fundamental task is to find out whether there is agreement—in general, as well as in intensity of conviction— between the ideology adopted by the army and the ideology of the government on which the army depends.

This problem is presented to France in an especially serious manner in view of the country's very particular position in international affairs, notably because of the losing battle it has fought for almost fifteen years in face of the world movement toward decolonization. Since 1945, in Asia then in Africa, France has had to cope with a war that is both permanent and limited. The traditional line of demarcation between peace and war has become increasingly vague. France was "more" or "less" at war according to events. She was "more" at war in the beginning of the Algerian rebellion than during the Indochinese conflict; she was even "more" at war during the few weeks of the Suez expedition. These conflicts called for a greater military effort than was needed for the colonial expeditions of the last century. However, the government has never considered it necessary to mobilize more than a portion of the nation's resources and available material. The French army is in readiness for war at a time when the country continues to live according to the rhythm and modes of peace. It is an ambiguous situation with many invisible tensions for a liberal democratic government. It must not be forgotten that regimes of this type were unable to bear the burden of two world wars without temporarily suspending or modifying the normal functions of their institutions. The logical exigencies of the war in which they are engaged lead military men to question key aspects of the customary political activity in a democratic state. They consider these aspects to be incompatible with the proper conduct of war for which the army is responsible. Civil power, for its part, still remains bound to plurality and the free confrontation of political parties, while it must also continue to guarantee the maintenance of basic freedoms. Divided between the obligations of a state of war and the respect due the norms of a state of peace, civil power is faced with a dramatic contradiction. To a great extent the government of the Fourth Republic had to yield to the army's will in May, 1958, because it did not know how or was unable to resolve this contradiction.

Within this perspective, it is uncertain whether France's case is unique. The division of the globe into two ideologically opposed blocs, the forms and evolution of the Cold War, may place before other liberal democratic governments the same delicate problem of the simultaneity of a state of war and a state of peace. It is almost inevitable that tensions will arise between civil and military power. (The Korean conflict and some of its repercussions on American politics perhaps confirm this fact.) The ordeal will only be avoided or easily surmounted where there is deep national accord, where a nation is closely and consciously unified around a concept of its destiny and a vision of its future.

NOTES

1. Quoted by J. de Soto, "Pouvoir civil et pouvoir militaire," in *La Défense nationale,* Centre de sciences politiques de l'Institut d'Etudes juridiques de Nice (Paris, 1958). I depend on this excellent article for the historical part of this study.
2. For the development of the ethic of passive obedience, see R. Girardet, *La Société militaire dans la France contemporaine* (Paris, 1953), pp. 117ff.
3. Cf. the important collective work edited under the direction of Louis Trotabas, by Le Centre de sciences politiques de l'Institut d'Etudes juridiques de Nice. *La Défense nationale* (Paris, 1958). We refer mainly to the articles of J. de Soto, "Pouvoir politique

et pouvoir militaire," pp. 87ff; P. Weil, "Armée et fonction publique," pp. 183ff; J. Essig, "Les Aspects civils et militaires de la défense nationale," pp. 205ff.

4. This expression from the title of a book by Jean Planchais, *Le Malaise de l'armée* (Paris, 1958). At this time, it is the only complete work devoted to this subject.

5. "D'un officier de quarante ans," *D.E.M.A.I.N. (Bulletin de documentation et d'étude des méthodes et activités internationales)*, June 26, 1959.

6. P. H. Simon, *Portrait d'un officier* (Paris, 1958), p. 30.

7. An officer declared in my presence, "I ceased believing in the virtues of obedience one day in November, 1942, on a Moroccan beach, when I received two contradictory orders in the space of two minutes: one from my commanding officer for my platoon to join the American landing force, the other from my colonel to hold out to the bitter end."

8. Jules Roy, *Le Métier des armes* (Paris, 1948), pp. 180ff.

9. However, see the May, 1950, issue of *Esprit* in which several authors foresee the political commitment of the army on the basis of experiences during 1940 and 1942. The "revolutionary" tenor of General de Gaulle's "insubordination" act in June, 1940, is strongly stressed.

10. General Henri Navarre, *L'Agonie de l'Indochine* (Paris, 1957), p. 319.

11. In 1953 a military lecturer expressed the army's losses in Indochina: "An officer every day, a battalion every month."

12. Many officers also blame the ineffectiveness of military organization. But, on the whole, they hold civil power responsible for insufficiencies.

13. It is fitting here to quote extracts of the indictment of the political regime which terminates General Navarre's account of the war: "The first reason [for the defeat in Indochina] from which all others follow is the lack of a policy. From the beginning to the end, our leaders never dared tell the country that there was a war in Indochina. They did not know how to commit the nation to war, or how to make peace. They were incapable of defining a line of conduct regarding the Associated States, of holding to it and of imposing it upon representatives of France on the spot. They could only evolve solutions from day to day which were rendered useless by events. . . . Our leaders could not lend a national character to a conflict for which they were unable to define a purpose. Unable to indicate to the country the reasons for the war, they did not request sacrifices which might have won it. . . . What is more, they permitted the army to be stabbed in the back. They tolerated continuous treason from the Communist party and its collaborators. They allowed the press, assured of immunity, to attack the morale of the fighting men, to sap the spirit of the nation and to divulge military secrets. . . . The beatings about the bush, the errors, the cowardices accumulated in eight years are too numerous and too long in existence to be blamed solely on men or even on governments which succeeded to power. They are the fruits of the regime. They are a product of the very nature of the French political system." Navarre, *op. cit.*, pp. 320-321.

14. Two of many examples cited complacently by the military press. In 1951 the government officially made it known that blood collected by the Office of Public Health would no longer be used for the wounded in Indochina. It was not until July, 1952, that a law was passed granting the soldiers of the Indochinese conflict the status of veterans; it was first implemented eighteen months later.

15. "D'un officier de quarante ans" (continuation), *D.E.M.A.I.N.*, July 3, 1959.

16. Simon, *op. cit.*, p 110.

17. In 1957, a journalist reported the account of a paratroop officer, a veteran of Indochina: "Two years later [after Dien Bien Phu], chased from Morocco and Tunisia, where we had been masters for many years, disheartened by the Algerian problem, we were ordered to fight a classic battle, one without the threat of civil war, a military venture with precise orders, 'Overthrow a dictator.' The deception of the Suez operation was as great as the enthusiasm it had aroused. It is impossible to describe the discouragement of my paratroopers who were forced to leave Egypt and turn their backs on victory." *Réalités*, May, 1957, pp. 41, 105.

18. On the uncertainties which marked the action of the army in Algeria until 1957, see J. J. Servan-Schreiber, *Lieutenant en Algérie* (Paris, 1957); Roger Barberot, *Malaventure en Algérie avec le général Paris de Bollardière* (Paris, 1957); and the discussion that precedes *Ceux d'Algérie* (Paris, 1957), pp. 3ff. Military literature progressively changes its tone from the beginning of 1958.

19. *Message des forces armées*, July, 1954.

20. *Message des forces armées*, December, 1956. This issue is concerned with an inquiry into the crisis in the army as attested to by one group of officers. It should be noted, however, that the break between generations recurs with the events of May, 1958.

"This is no illusion," declares one officer to a journalist. "Ninety per cent of the subordinate officers, 50 per cent of the superior officers and 5 per cent of the high command are with us." *La Nation française,* May 28, 1958.

21. "Essai sur la structure sociale de l'armée française," *Les officiers, La Nouvelle critique,* No. 107 (June, 1957), p. 43ff. Although the article, as a whole, should be received with reservations, I have taken most of my information from it. See also Planchais, *op. cit.,* pp. 14ff.

22. "La Grande frustration du jeune officier supérieur," *Réalités,* May, 1957, pp. 36ff.

23. In this regard, two facts are significant: (1) The constant reduction in the number of applicants to the Academy of St. Cyr—2,452 applicants in 1939, 587 in 1951, 360 in 1954. The number of graduates from the Ecole Polytechnique also tends to be insignificant in the so-called educated ranks when, in the past, they were in the majority; in 1913 the percentage of captains of artillery graduated from Polytechnique was 53 per cent; it fell to 11 per cent in 1939, to 5 per cent in 1953, and to 1.5 per cent in 1958. (2) The ever-increasing proportion of army officers coming from the ranks. The percentage of captains coming from the ranks rose from 5.4 per cent in 1949 to 35.8 per cent in 1958 (*La Nouvelle critique, loc. cit.,* p. 55). Note also among the students of the Academy of St. Cyr the unusually large percentage of young men coming from military families—41 per cent in 1956, 42 per cent in 1957, 47 per cent in 1958. This is an indication of the withdrawal of military society into its own private sphere.

24. *La Nouvelle critique, loc. cit.,* p. 52.

25. Planchais, *op. cit.,* p. 18.

26. "There would be no crisis in the army today if we were able to find a place to live," an officer replied to a journalist in May, 1957. *Réalités,* May, 1957, p. 36.

27. Hubert Bassot, *Les Silencieux* (Paris, 1958), pp. 118-119.

28. Bertrand de Castelbajac, *La Gloire est leur salaire* (Paris, 1958), p. 29ff.

29. "Le Mal jaune," *Le Courrier de la nation,* August 7, 1958, p. 20 [written by a captain].

30. From the wealth of French military literature devoted to the definition of revolutionary war, special note should be made of: the February-March issue of *Revue militaire d'information,* 1957; Col. Ch. Lacheroy, "La Guerre révolutionnaire," *La Défense nationale, op. cit.,* pp. 307ff.; Claude Delmas, *La Guerre révolutionnaire* (Paris, 1959); a series of articles by Commander J. Hogard, *Revue de défense nationale,* 23 (December, 1956), 24 (January and February, 1957).

31. Lacheroy, *op. cit.,* p. 308.

32. In *La Défense nationale, op. cit.,* pp. 307ff.

33. Cf. Michel Déon, *L'Armée d'Algérie et la pacification* (Paris, 1959). The author reports (p. 7) the opinion of some of the men at Headquarters in Algiers. "A stand for a fortified Europe seems morally, materially and comfortably defensible, yet it does not consider the terrible Soviet theory of expansion. . . . Will there be an atomic attack tomorrow? It is not very probable. We do not see why the U.S.S.R. would run such a risk. In 13 years, the Soviet Union has succeeded, without firing a shot, in claiming millions of people from the West. These people, although not in its power, nevertheless gravitated towards the Soviet orbit and artlessly reacted to its propaganda."

34. "L'Armée est-elle fasciste?" *Le Courrier de la nation,* August 7, 1958, p. 12.

35. Quoted by Déon, *op. cit.,* pp. 7-8.

36. We quote a text in which *Message des forces armées* comments on the conclusion of a debate on the Algerian question at the U.N. in 1957: "At last, the Algerian problem has been posed clearly as a tactical phase of permanent revolutionary war. An awareness of this reality by responsible people in government and in the military, by French public opinion and, we hope, by all citizens of the free world, constitutes the first condition for salvation. It must now be clear, to even the most blind, that for years we have been engaged in a third world conflict. It is a conflict, a revolution, whose aim is the conquest of the world, a universal, continuous war which, on all fronts, interior as well as exterior, attests more or less "hotly," according to the tactics of the moment, to the fundamental incompatability of two concepts of man, to the out and out impossibility of coexistence of two types of human civilization." *Message des forces armées,* March, 1957, signed Milites (the collective pseudonym for a group of officers).

37. "La Troisiéme guerre mondiale n'aura pas lieu," *Message des forces armées,* December, 1955. An unofficial publication priding itself on its nonconformity with regard to the military hierarchy, *Message* is a good barometer of the opinions of young army personnel.

38. This issue was exceptionally successful; 50,000 copies were in circulation.

39. "L'Armée est-elle fasciste?" *loc. cit.,* p. 12.

40. There is no doubt that intellectual and moral action of this strict Catholic movement, *La Cité catholique,* has found a large audience in certain military circles.

41. There are many officers, however, who recognize these contradictions and admit the difficulty of surmounting them. Cf. Jean Brune, "L'Armée à la recherche d'une doctrine," *La Nation française,* June 10, 1959, an important article. "The drama of these young officers, hungry for an absolute, who . . . have understood that traditional nationalism must be enriched by new ideas, . . . rests in the cruel suffering they experience upon discovering that a solid doctrine would only permit them to grasp for [their] dream, and therein search desperately for basic ideals and still not find them. An army with colonels initiated in the techniques of revolutionary war, and of captains and lieutenants confronted with human misery, hates Communism before which it has retreated since Lang Son and Cao Bang. The army is also doubtful and suspicious of capitalism which seems to furnish material for subversive propaganda. Although the military is haunted by this repudiation of both Communism and capitalism, it can find nothing to oppose them, nothing to replace them. In this too hasty, too feverish and incoherent quest, the army runs the risk of falling into the most dangerous traps. While completely unraveling the most secret intricacies of the manipulation of the masses imagined by the Communists, the army has assimilated some of them. Even with a knowledge of the adversary's methods of conquest, the question of what to do still remains. Blind application of these methods would only pave the way for the enemy, or a least would lead to a degrading imitation, thus denying just those principles which the army was defending. In this lies the army's confusion." These lines merit special note since the author touches on the military in Algeria.

42. The official terminology of French military education distinguishes between "subversive war" and "revolutionary war." The latter is defined as "a doctrine of war expounded by Marxist-Leninist theoreticians and exploited by revolutionary movements of various leanings."

43. *La Défense nationale, op. cit.,* p. 319.

44. By way of example, this extract from a report drawn up by a district commander in August, 1956: "In order to end the army's blindness, it must, at all costs, re-establish contact with the Moslem population. Only in this way will the army be able to obtain precise information and act effectively. This re-establishment of contact requires the simultaneous initiation of purely military acts (intervention) along with acts of pacification. The force which pacifies on the one hand . . . and strikes on the other must be the same; that is, military authority. And the old authority cannot be the pacifier." The report concludes with an affirmation that "authority should be vested in the army, the only force capable of being judge and jury, of re-establishing contact, of conducting military action and pacification." Quoted by Roger Barberot, *Malaventure en Algérie* (Paris, 1957), p. 86.

45. The experience of an S.A.S. chief is treated in a book by J. Y. Alquier, *Nous avons pacifié Tazalt* (Paris, 1957).

46. In May, 1957, 418 military instructors were teaching 23,000 Moslem students. In the same month 650 work projects were being managed by the army.

47. For a broader study of this, see the work of Déon, *op. cit.,* pp. 120ff.

48. Barberot, *op. cit.,* p. 193.

49. It is curious to note that the military press, particularly the Algerian military press, most favorably received the various plans for laws for Algeria submitted to Parliament in 1956 and 1957.

50. For example, an officer writes: "As an active force in time of crisis, the army is obligated to palliate wavering authority on all levels." *Contacts.*

51. *Contacts,* March, 1958. The article is signed Captain X, S.A.S. commander.

52. *Ibid.* Needless to say, such an attitude is not shared by a great portion of the Algerian population of European origin, which, for a long time, was only concerned with defense of its personal interests. In fact, the army has always had to state its differences with this group. Cf. Simon, *op. cit.,* p. 145: "In Algeria, there are few fighters who think that only the condition of the Moslems must change. You can't fight for so many years without knowing the smell of a people's skin, without hearing its heart beat; the army does not wish to perpetuate the exploitation of the Algerian people or bind their lives to the paternalism of a Larondière (an enlightened colon). But, if most of my comrades agree to recognize the aspirations of the Algerian people as legitimate, there are some who give the rebels the moral credit for having embodied this legitimacy." All military literature devoted to the events in Algeria follows this line of reasoning. A great part of the French press has perpetrated a misconception by frequently confusing the goals of the army and those of the *ultras* in Algiers.

53. "Ce qu'est l'intégration," *Contacts,* July, 1958.

54. Quoted by Léo Hamon, *De Gaulle dans la République,* (Paris, 1958), p. 91.

55. For example, see Simon, *op. cit.,* for a description of the long friendship between a French officer and an Algerian noncommissioned officer. Similar cases are quite common.

56. Praise of the qualities of North Africans, and especially of the Kabyles and Berbers, is one of the frequent themes of French military literature. Cf. this extract from a recent circular "addressed to students of advanced military preparation in the Paris area." "We loved these people who were so close to nature. They are often faint-hearted, crafty, vindictive and even cruel, but their faults are more visible than ours. They do not have the advantage of a refined civilization, of officialdom, of the growth of a virtuous middle class, of securities with a fixed return." Quoted by Planchais, *op. cit.,* p. 21.

57. Alquier, *op. cit.,* p. 231.

58. The dishonor felt by the French army because of the abandonment, after the Geneva armistice, of the loyal populations of Tonkin and Laos, is another theme that constantly recurs in military literature devoted to the war in Indochina. Cf., among others, the account of the abandonment of a post in Tonkin, by Castelbajac, *op. cit.,* pp. 96ff. "Le Mal jaune," *loc. cit.:* "We can never forget the sight of a crowd of people hurling themselves into the sea in an effort to overtake our ships, and the memory of the many who drowned that day. . . . The Meos stayed with us the longest. One day they decided to form an underground and in a few months they learned the use of weapons, explosives and radio. With the armistice, the order came to abandon them along with the rest. This virtually turned them over to the Vietminhs who would no doubt exterminate them. The radios of the underground Meos continued functioning after the armistice and we remember all the messages they sent us." And the article concludes with an evocation of May 13, 1958. It states that the army revolted "because we are no longer willing to betray our pacts of friendship."

59. Alquier, *op. cit.,* pp. 270-271.

60. It is important to note that during the summer of 1958 at the time of the referendum campaign, this contract was solemnly renewed by the army. By asking the Moslems to vote "yes" to the constitution proposed by General de Gaulle, the army had committed itself to the assurance of permanent protection against the reprisals of the F.L.N. A correspondent in Algeria from *Le Monde* forcefully emphasized this. "This is without doubt the most serious and most honorable aspect of the referendum. . . . General Faure told us yesterday: 'I have just returned from a tour of Kabylia. The people often asked that I give my word of honor as an officer that France was here to stay and that she would never abandon them. I gave them my word. They asked me if I spoke in the name of General de Gaulle. I said yes.' This same question was asked of S.A.S. officers in dozens of douars, and the same answer was given." Phillipe Herreman, "L'Armée refusera à trahir la confiance de ceux qui ont voté 'oui'," *Le Monde,* September 28, 1958.

61. General Paul Ely, *Revue militaire d'information,* August-September, 1958. A separate study should be devoted to "Gaullist" penetration in the French army. It appears to be only quite limited. A feeling of deep attachment to General de Gaulle is expressed by a small group of officers who had served with the Free French from 1940 to 1943.

62. Cf. a long anonymous article, edited by a group of officers, "L'Armée est-elle fasciste?" *loc. cit.,* p. 19. (*Courrier de la nation* is a Gaullist weekly): "It should not be thought that the rank and file of the army is fooled by the military's often hyperbolic praise which, along with criticisms, has increased in the past two months. Having demonstrated the great unity of the army, the force that it represents incurs hope as well as fear. But having decided to act for the good of the entire nation, the army is scornful of, and will not let itself be used by a few fascists at home, nor does it intend to aid the *ultras* in Algeria. The army has no particular love for either of them."

63. Castelbajac, *op. cit.,* p. 2.

64. "Comment pensent les paras?" *La France catholique,* June 20, 1958, p. 5.

65. General Henri Zeller, "Armée et politique." *Revue de la défense nationale,* 24 (April, 1957), 514.

Democracy, Technology, and the Retired British Officer

BY *PHILIP ABRAMS*

In other words the pattern of an officer's career is anachronistic. It presupposes that the typical officer will be a public school man who after twenty years of service life can retire to manage his estates and interest himself in the public affairs of his neighbourhood. (Report of the Advisory Committee on Recruiting, Cmnd. 545, 1958)

I: The Military Profession—Face to Face with Democracy

STUDIES OF CIVIL-MILITARY relations have always found the British military profession mildly eccentric. Comparative accounts of the power struggle between civilian and military elites make relatively little use of British material.[1] It seems to be agreed that effective civilian control was guaranteed sometime in the seventeenth century by sanctions deeply rooted in the social structure. By making the military career a minor function in the life of a class which had already engrossed property-owning, entrepreneurial, and administrative roles, Britain avoided producing a self-conscious military caste interested in appropriating power and prestige to itself. As so often in British history, class lines were drawn in such a way as to score out the autonomy of other institutions.[2] Not even now have British officers reached the point of urging the existence of "purely military factors" outside the competence of the civilian—an "American principle," according to the *Economist,* denied by both theory and practice in Britain. This is hardly surprising, since practice has long tended to make the civil servant not only the constitutional superior of the officer but, often enough, his elder brother or cousin as well.[3]

But this very shelving of the graver political tensions of the civil-military relationship has itself tended to aggravate a number of social sore points. Thus, while there has always been a large number of soldiers in British politics and business, they have tended (unlike the American officers described by Morris Janowitz) to behave as members of their class rather than of their profession.[4] Officers of modest origin who might have been motivated to use rank or military status as a lever of power were usually deterred by the firm upper-class grip on the policies and social roles of the profession. The Army has, of course, long been a favored career of the respectable middle class, as well as of upper-class younger sons, but the former were not able, typically, to use the opportunities for social advancement and self-assertion normally provided by a strong professional organization.[5]

Traditionally, then, a service career meant different things for different social groups in Britain. The picture of the ex-officer in the eyes of the man in the street, of *Punch,* and of politicians of all parties was appropriately ambiguous. On the one hand, the retired officer was seen as a mandarin of civil life, a man whose "connections" carried him as a sinister *military* voice into the highest councils of industry and government. As such, he fits neatly into the picture, long popular with radicals, of a tight network of "controllers" bound together by family alliances, dominating each major institution of British life, and, through their personal contacts, drawing them together in a unified structure of power.[6] But the officer was also the slightly pathetic socially displaced person, reduced to the indignities of obscure retirement or demeaning civil chores—the salesman who cannot forget the habits of command, the familiar middle-aged advertiser chasing a "position of responsibility."[7] Indeed, he still appears frequently enough in both roles in Parliament. Conservative M.P's tend to stress the plight of the retired officer, to paint harrowing pictures of poverty and unemployment, while Labour Members hint at mass movements of ex-officers into government departments and armaments firms. Trade Unionists, arguing that in spite of nationalization the "old gang" is still running the basic industries, adduce supposed quantities of former officers now on the staffs of the public corporations. In reply to a Conservative statement in the House of Commons in June, 1956, that there was "some anxiety among officers, particularly brigadiers," about postservice employment, a Labour speaker asked whether this was to be taken to mean that there was now "no room in the ranks of the *normal* occupation of ex-Brigadiers"—namely, on the Conservative back benches.

The exchange perfectly illustrates the traditional ambiguity as to the social role of the retired officer—at once the upper-class man moving horizontally to new positions of power and the modestly retired professional man not helped by his career to climb to a point where he could grasp civil rewards and status to match his military dignity. The two views are not incompatible, of course. But the picture is further confused today by the belief that class has ceded to (or at least been balanced by) other factors as the effective determinant of postservice prestige and occupation—rank, for example, or technical skills that allow, say, a qualified young officer to move straight into a high post in an important aircraft, engineering, or shipbuilding firm. In so far as rank is held to carry its own rewards today, it is further supposed that there is therefore something like an autonomous *military* influence at work in British civilian affairs—an influence felt through direct political pressure and in the allocation of jobs and honors to former soldiers and in the growth of quasi-military or para-military organizations and associations.

These beliefs also find their expression in Parliamentary questions, in suggestions that officers from the technical arms are finding their way to both the buying and selling ends of key government contracts, or in suggestions that rank is being treated as an acceptable alternative to humbler but more appropriate qualifications—as, for example, when the Secretary of State for War is asked whether he:

Is aware that top ranking officers have no difficulty in finding appointments as they immediately become directors of one of the Big Five banks, although they have no banking experience?

And this assumption that the military career is at last being detached from its old dependence on the pattern of class relationships would seem to be a reasonable one. There is a good deal of evidence, too, for thinking that the "civilian alliances" of officers as such (as members of a profession, that is) are of greater consequence today than in the past, that in terms of both power and influence there may be a significant *military* element in contemporary Britain. There have, after all, been serious attempts made since 1939 to transform the functions of the armed forces as well as the structure of the society in which they operate. The traditional first role of the British military, "imperial policing," now occupies a dramatically reduced proportion of the available energies. Britain has become a country where "equality of opportunity" is the favorite political slogan of all parties. It would be very remarkable if the situation of the retired officer remained unchanged. But in considering that situation we must take note of certain relevant features of the *general* situation of the military profession in contemporary Britain. The meaning for the officer of at least three powerful pressures of recent years must be considered: the drive to democratize British society as a whole, the drive to democratize the military career, and the drastic redirection of the government's basic defense strategy since 1956.

The most obviously pertinent side effect of the growth of social and economic democracy since 1939 has been a marked decline in the relative attractions of service careers. As Britain becomes more and more "middle class"; as economic security, congenial work, and sophisticated technical skills become more and more a matter of course; as managerial and technological posts diversify and become more and more accessible to the talented in civil life—so the status of the officer tends to be deflated.[8] A traditional service career, particularly that of the regimental officer, offers few of the prizes esteemed by young people today; it offers few openings for technical intelligence, its managerial habits are not those of government or industry, its financial rewards are modest, many entrants must expect to be retired in mid-career to take their chances in other employments, and even the lucky ones who continue up the ladder are likely to meet frustration in the face of the ingrained traditions of "loyal subordination" and civilian control of policy. It is hardly surprising that a recent survey among university students found that, even with the purely financial disabilities removed, no more than 2 per cent were willing to contemplate a service career.[9] "The pattern of an officer's career is anachronistic." Professionalism is on the march in Britain. At least one experienced social analyst predicts a new ruling elite of university graduates and professional men in 1970. Ironically, the traditional service career, with its highly developed professional structure, would seem to be in the worst possible position to exploit this new enthusiasm of the young for professional skills, opportunities, and organizations through which to express their talents.

I should perhaps say a word here about the use of the word "profession" in this paper. By "profession" I understand not merely an occupation group with a fairly explicit career structure and fairly highly defined characteristic skills based on intensive training, but an occupation group also with something like its own characteristic values and attitudes, and one that offers its members, through movement up the career ladder, identity, position, and rewards in society at large essentially because of their membership in the occupation group. The "professional elite," therefore, is made up of those members of the occupation group in positions concentrating influence or power decisive for the profession as a whole or for society in general. By "elite profession," similarly, I understand a profession in which either the professional occupation itself or the eventual rewards of that activity involve participation in high-level general policymaking.

Morris Janowitz has suggested five hypothetical lines of change along which we may expect a military profession to be moving in a society developing as Britain is developing today. He suggests that the military will adapt (1) by modifying the "basis of authority and discipline" in the direction of more persuasive modes of control, (2) by narrowing "the skill differential between military and civilian elites" through the adoption of more and more advanced scientific techniques, (3) by widening the social field from which officers are recruited, (4) by modifying the career structure so as to make access to elite positions a reward for the highly competent performance of routine professional functions, and (5) by throwing up an increasingly "explicit political ethos" of its own.[10] In a sense, adjustment along these lines may be considered a necessity for a military profession anxious to function effectively in a socially democratic society, and it will be relevant to discuss the present prospects of British officers in this context. Objectively, the pressures on the services to adapt have been considerable, particularly in view of the avowed urgent need of the Army for high-calibre officer recruits. And yet, in relation to all but the last of Janowitz' five hypotheses —if we except the R.A.F.—development in Britain has been extraordinarily ragged and slow.

It is interesting to note that the R.A.F. is an exception. For here not only has the switch to "push-button" warfare done least harm to the public image of the usefulness of the service, but there has, perforce, been a narrowing of the technological "skill differential." And it is surely no coincidence that we also find recruitment on a much broader social basis, that there is at least serious argument in the Air Force in favor of a shift from "authoritarian domination" toward manipulation and persuasive management, and that there is an awareness of the attractions of a contemporary professional career pattern. Whereas the Army still seeks to recruit on the strength of its collective public role, "Guardians of the Peace," the Air Force is luring young men with prospects of personal social status expressed in modern professional terms: "From fighter pilot to top flight executive—Today's Top Job is the R.A.F." We shall see that this greater adaptability and technical "modernity" of the Air Force has also been mirrored in the fortunes of its retired officers.

In the older services the picture is very different. There is, of course, no lack of awareness that the social structure of the services and of society are at odds, nor of the steps that might be taken to restore some kind of congruity. Indeed, the problem is of urgent interest, since it relates to the issue of recruiting. Seen from the outside, the problem, for the Army at least, appears as an intolerable dilemma: the service itself has a profound distrust of democracy; yet it must operate in a thoroughly democratic society. To date the pattern is clear: the attempt since 1945 to democratize the senior services, to adjust their career patterns to the circumstances of a more egalitarian society, has, on the whole, been very effectively resisted.

II: Class, Status, and Recruiting

The Advisory Committee on Recruiting of 1958 suggested many ways in which the "conditions of service of officers" should be "modified in the light of social and economic changes." Some of these were fairly simple to effect and have been implemented by the government. Pay and pensions were brought roughly into line with those in the civil service. But, as the Committee's *Report* observed—and several social surveys support the view—financial rewards are not the major issue. The more fundamental suggestions were also the more controversial: namely, that the field of recruitment should be widened, the responsibilities of officers extended to a degree "comparable with those of civilian professional men," the numbers and opportunities of officers with advanced technical qualifications increased, and the whole career structure overhauled in a manner compatible with civilian professional expectations.[11] In short, the services were to be democratized and professionalized. Along with these recommendations, we may consider another long championed by Labour politicians—that the time has come to redesign the whole basis of authority in the services.[12] With this addition, the picture of conscious pressure to change in all but one of the directions Janowitz suggests is established. The extent of the development along the lines of his fifth hypothesis—the growth of a more explicit and flexible political ethos—is discussed below.

The period of Labour government saw a serious attempt to introduce a social equality of opportunity in service careers; there was to be a "one-ladder" system running from the bottom to the top: all officers were to start their careers in the ranks, to know and understand their men; sophisticated "man management" was to take the place of authoritarian discipline. The wartime experience of psychological testing to select officers provided a powerful argument against the traditional "two-ladders," "officers-and-other-ranks," point of view. A senior ex-War Office psychologist expressed the judgment that there was "a dangerous fallacy in the dichotomy of mankind into leaders and non-leaders."[13] As late as 1955 a Labour motion to remove the phrase "unbecoming to the character of an officer and a gentle-man" from the *Queen's Regulations*, was defeated by only fifteen votes—20 per cent of those voting with the majority being former regular officers. The Labour argument in this debate was that the words symbolized an aristo-cratic conception of leadership, set officers apart as a "different order of human being," and did not fit in with "the present day conception of individual relations": "we have to see that an officer's authority must rest on his being in every respect fitted for his job—plain competence at his job" —this, rather than dignity born of gentlemanly social qualities, should be the essential qualification of the modern officer.

The arguments of the *Report* of the Advisory Committee were less direct than this, but rather more substantial. The case was presented without ideological overtones. It was argued quite simply that in the Army's own interest (if it was to have any chance of "getting young men of the right calibre") the social base of the officer corps must be broadened. Analyzing the existing supply of recruits, the *Report* concluded that, like it or not, the existing field of recruitment was too narrow, that the restriction was arti-ficial and unnecessary, and that its nature was social—a bias against candidates from certain backgrounds and with certain accents. These views were presented modestly enough ("it does seem that the Army leans far too heavily upon the product of the old 'Army Class' of schools for its cadet entry"), and the recommendation that "the Army consider other sources of supply" was equally restrained. On the other hand, the statistical appendix to the *Report* made very clear the degree to which selection was still weighted in favor of traditional social groups—toward boys from Public Schools in the southern half of England, the traditional "gentry" territory in fact. Between 1947 and 1958, 990 schools submitted candidates for Sandhurst, and of these only 195 were Public schools; yet 35 per cent of the candidates came from twenty-one top public schools. Candidates from the latter were emphatically more successful than those from state schools (Table I).[14]

Table I. Candidates for Regular Army Commissions

	Total	Percentage	Passed	Percentage of Group	Failed	Percentage of Group
	583	100%	168	29%	415	71%
Public schools	354	61	129	37	225	63
Other schools	229	39	39	17	190	83
Southern schools	398	68	135	34	263	66
Northern schools	185	32	33	18	152	82

Again, we might mention here that a substantial majority of the group of university students mentioned above who were willing to consider a service career came from upper or upper-middle class homes, had been educated at public schools, and had Conservative politics; in 60 per cent of the cases they intended to go into the armed forces regardless of the financial dis-advantages.[15] Not only do the services incline to recruit from the traditional "officer" groups of society, but very few outside those groups seem to be interested in being recruited.

It is of course possible to reply—as the Army did reply to the Advisory Committee—that this weighting is legitimate, that the public schools produce candidates of a more suitable "type."[16] But this is to set up a circular argument of a singularly frustrating sort. If only certain select social groups and schools can provide suitable officer material and if these groups themselves are not able to supply officers in sufficient quantities, the recruiting problem cannot be solved.

Nevertheless, both on the issue of widening the field of recruitment and, though this is less certain, on that of shifting the nature of military authority from command toward consensus, the services appear for various reasons to have decided against democracy. The two issues would seem to be linked in many important minds by the common denominator of class. Thus, Air Chief Marshal Sir Philip Joubert deplores the passing of the traditional officer class:

> So long as officers came from homes about which there was an atmosphere of the unknown—"out of our class, chum!"—so long did they have that little something that inspired not only the respect, but the awe of the men. As soon as they came from the same class, however good they may have been at their job—they lacked this quality.[17]

Speaking in the debate on the "officer and gentleman" phrase, the then Secretary of State for War celebrated the mystery of military leadership with equal enthusiasm—"the status of an officer is intangible; the Army Council were unanimous about this"; again and again it was respect for the *status* of the officer that was invoked in the defense of the traditional concept.[18]

It would seem, in fact, that senior soldiers are no more willing to abandon the "two-ladders" structure today than they were when Lord Wolsely attacked it in 1869.[19] The government "comment" on the Advisory Committee's proposal to widen the field of recruiting was curiously evasive—"every effort will continue to be made to obtain suitable entrants from all suitable sources"—the effect of the verb "continue" being to deny the existence of the problem. And service voices urging democratization are very rare, the most frequent being those of exceptional personalities, such as Field Marshal Montgomery, who as early as 1946 insisted that the Army must adapt itself to "the social fabric of the nation," or Air Force officers.[20] Thus, an article in the *Journal* of the Royal United Services Institute in 1958 urges that the structure of the R.A.F., "minimum fighting men backed by maximum technicians," required an "entirely new approach" to the problems of authority and discipline. Functionally, more and more airmen are performing civilian jobs, military discipline tends to detract from "functional efficiency," and if the R.A.F. is to compete with industry it must provide a work atmosphere akin to that of civil air technicians—"one in which the men are treated as individuals and respected as such" based on "a new kind of self-discipline attuned to the needs of the nuclear age." But this article was perhaps adventurous even for the R.A.F., and it constantly insists on the uniqueness of the Air Force; the very title "How 'Military' is the R.A.F.?" is revealing.

More characteristic is an article written in 1952 by the editor of another leading Service journal, *Brassey's Annual*.[21] Surveying what he considers to have been a disastrous period of Labour rule, he insists that it is "time that equalitarian theory was swept away altogether from this sphere"—meaning the recruitment, training, and career of officers. Holding to the view that a "gulf is fixed" between officers and men, he notes with some satisfaction that, despite the prewar legislation, all the services have managed in effect to avoid making officers serve in the ranks while "observing the letter of the law"; for, he adds:

The atmosphere of the barrack-room is actively inimical to the tradition in which the potential officer must grow if he is to imbibe the essence of real leadership.

There has been a harvest of articles in the service publications attempting to distill "the essence of real leadership," to define officer quality, and to pin down the components of the "intangible" status of the officer; but it is the editor of *Brassey's* himself who goes to the heart of the matter. Having decided against "equalitarian" principles as the basis of the officer profession and being faced with a dearth of recruits from the traditional sources, the services have, and he quotes Lord Beveridge, "somehow to carry on an aristocratic tradition in Britain without the aristocrats." In civilian eyes the status of the officer today is not so much intangible as derisory; how, having saddled themselves with the problem of carrying on the aristocratic tradition, can the services reconstitute that status (given that gentle birth, even were there enough gentlemen, will not suffice in the competition with the new civilian goals)? They must, concludes the editor of *Brassey's*, compete effectively with other employers for recruits from *today's* top 10 per cent, the "elite of intelligence." Which means that the life of the officer must be restructured to fit the model of an up-to-date elite profession.

III: The "New" Officer

What steps the services themselves might have taken in this direction is not clear. But since 1956, under political pressure powerfully inspired by motives of economy as well as of strategy, some dramatic changes have been effected; and it is in this context that the fortunes of currently retired officers are most significant and will be considered.

Of course some considerable reforms were effected in the decade before 1956. The first postwar review of the Service Estimates furnished the opportunity to stress the need to professionalize the Army. Civil and military skills and posts were to be interwoven, there would be a "complete integration" of civilian and military personnel at every level in the Ministry of Supply, and officers would be qualified for these posts and for new technical openings in the Army itself by high-level courses at the Military College of Science.[22] But up to 1955 the framework of these reforms presupposed by government defense policy was a large and expanding corps of officers. Despite a reduction in retiring ages in 1950, the intention was always to increase the number of active officers. In 1952 appointments in static headquarters were thrown open to retired officers and arrangements were made for selected lieutenant-colonels and majors to continue serving up to fifty-five years. No substantial scaling down of overseas commitments was visualized. Where contraction was inevitable, service in Germany and later a variety of NATO and civil defense functions helped to take up the slack. The officers withdrawn from India were assigned to posts in the British Army. Soldier-bureaucrats were allowed to proliferate at Headquarters.[23] In 1955 the career-regular element in the armed forces, including officers, was absolute and relatively larger than ever. Despite the withdrawal from colonial and overseas garrisons after the war, the numbers of the defense forces in 1951 were about 205 per cent higher than in 1931—an increase which should be compared with the mere 11 per cent rise in the service professions as a whole. It is often assumed that the wholesale movement of ex-officers into civilian occupations was a postwar and postimperial phenomenon. In fact, it assumed new and major dimensions only after 1957. Despite seemingly powerful political pressures, the flow out of the services was kept at a traditional and "normal" level for a decade after the war. Above all, the suggestion that any major war of the future would be of the "push-button" type was resisted as long as possible. Although a resettlement service was established by the government in 1949 to help retired officers and other ranks find civil employments, it did relatively little business in the first seven years of its existence.[24] Rather, the old-style career structure was allowed to persist, creating as it did a severe bottleneck of middle-aged officers with poor prospects of promotion and worse chances of finding a nonmilitary job. Thus in 1954-55, according to *The Times'* military correspondent, of the 491 Regular officers of the Army who resigned voluntarily 104 were subalterns, 101 captains, 191 majors, 74 lieutenant-colonels, and a mere handful more senior officers. Of these only 22 per cent retired to take up civil jobs, but at least 179 of them had been passed over for promotion. The system was creating a superfluity of middle-grade officers. On the other hand, far more officers were retiring than was compatible with the government's "large Army" policy—2.4 per cent in 1954, as against a planned 1.5 per cent. Unless reasonable prospects of future employment within the services could be held out to such officers, they would presumably continue to leave at a high rate. The incidental effect of the defense reorganization of 1956-1957 was to make the best of the situation and accept the high rate of mid-career retirement. This, of course, did not solve the problem from the recruiting point of view; it merely shifted it. It now became imperative to hold out attractive prospects of a second career after retirement. Apparently it was thought rather easier to do this than to adapt the pattern of the service career itself (Table II).[25]

Table II. Promotion Prospects in the Army 1945-1954

Promotion	Chance
Major to Lieut.-Colonel	65%
Lieut.-Colonel to Colonel	54
Lieut.-Colonel to Major-General	15
Lieut.-Colonel to Lieut.-General	3.3
Lieut.-Colonel to General	1.6

The officer's career was not, of course, a major initial concern of that reorganization. The problem was rather to achieve effective central coordination of service policies and to set up once more the clearly defined chain of command in the organization of defense which had been allowed to lapse in the face of pressure from each service to pursue its own ends. The waste, chaos, and inability to make sensible use of new technical developments that resulted from this laxity were strikingly demonstrated in the Suez invasion in 1956. In that emergency a more or less *ad hoc* line of command was established, which entirely bypassed the service ministries. Duncan Sandys was appointed Minister of Defence in January 1957 with a specific brief to secure for himself as Minister the functions of initiative, coordination, and control of all "decisions in all matters of policy affecting the size, shape, organization and disposition of the armed forces, their equipment, and supply (including defense research and development) and their pay and conditions of service." This enterprise dovetailed with an attempt by some senior officers, notably Lord Mountbatten, to achieve integrated operational control by placing a Service representative in immediate contact with the Minister as his principal adviser. The White Paper of 1958, *"The Central Organization for Defence,"* constituted a steeply graded pyramid of control along just such lines: a powerful Minister working through Service and Cabinet committees and at his side, responsible to no one but the Minister, a powerful Chief of Defence Staff. A period of energetic development was envisaged based on the integration of service activities, increasing diffusion of technological roles, and the drawing together of civilian and military personnel.[26] Some officers would have gone much further in the direction of unification and the transforming of officers into technically skilled professional men. But, as one advocate of reform put it, "it would be foolish to ignore the great weight of reactionary but none the less sincere opposition to reform which is to be found in every great Public Service."[27]

The opposition among soldiers to modernization was particularly effective at this time, since it merged with resistance to the other still more fundamental policy change of these years—namely, the acceptance of nuclear weapons as the heart of British defense strategy. Whatever the motives for this reorientation, it served to expose for the first time, and in brutal light, the deficiencies of the existing officer-career structure. In deciding to reduce the over-all numbers of the armed forces by very nearly one-half within five years, to make drastic reductions in British overseas garrisons, to abolish in all but name the traditional regimental organization, and at the same time to put the services on an all-regular basis while prematurely retiring some thousands of currently serving officers, the government brought civilians, soldiers, and itself face to face with the anomalies of the officer's career and social situation. Little wonder that the immediate reaction of a "large number of devoted officers" was to express themselves as vehemently opposed to change. Anxieties and resentments that had been rankling for years now came to the surface. As one soldier put it, we have a new look for nuclear war, we must have a new deal for the officer as well:

The Services must improve the status of the officer. This has been steadily debased as the dead hand of socialism and democratisation has made itself felt in our national way of life.

Specifically, this author demanded a real career, real security in old age, and real opportunities for skill and enterprise.[28]

To a certain extent, of course, change along such lines was implicit in the major shift in policy and organization anyway. Between government pressure to achieve a modern professional force, highly mobile and exploiting all technical and scientific opportunities, and military pressure to enhance the status of the officer and cushion his entry into civil society on retirement, a good deal has been achieved in the last four years. On both sides there has been considerable enthusiasm for the shift to contemporary technology presupposed in the government decisions of 1957-1958.[29] A number of articles in the service journals have urged more extensive high-level scientific education for officers. The Advisory Commitee on Recruiting, in its turn, advocated increased technical training. Various scholarships have been introduced along these lines, although the Committee's further proposal that officers should be allowed sabbatical leave to follow long courses of a scientific, technical, or managerial nature has not yet been taken up. But within the Army at least one really decisive step has been taken; in 1959, with the reminder that "Science is becoming yearly more important to the Army," the Secretary of State of War announced that technical officers would be given access to the very highest appointments.[30] In view of the overwhelming importance of staff-college qualifications for promotion to the highest ranks the statement that the new ideal would be the combination of technical and staff-college qualifications must be considered a major concession to contemporary professionalism (Table III).[31]

Table III. Promotion and Staff College Training (senior officers 1955)

Rank	P.S.C.	Non-P.S.C.
General	10	1
Lieut.-General	15	2
Major-General	68	14
Brigadier	101	41
Colonel	322	110
Lieut.-Colonel	677	261
	1,193	429

No less apparent is the development of a certain political consciousness and of certain rudimentary forms of political activity among top service personnel. But, while this too may have been implicit in the new central structure and policy, it has hardly been greeted with the same enthusiasm by the government. There has, for example, been an extraordinary change in the content of the service periodicals in the last year or two. Traditionally the majority of articles in these journals were historical and tactical analyses of battles, discussions of discipline, service conditions and experiences, and flat factual accounts of new technical developments. Since 1957, however, the leading journals have been more and more given up to speculation and controversy on basic themes of international politics, the role of the military, and defense strategy and organization. The same is true of the lectures sponsored by the Royal United Services Institute. The case for and against nuclear disarmament in all its aspects has been vigorously debated among senior officers. There has been discussion of Sino-Soviet relations, of the organization of defense, and of the compatibility of Britain's NATO and Commonwealth responsibilities.[32] Most interesting perhaps, a small but influential group of civilian intellectuals, experts on strategy, has appeared; and these men have been welcomed by the services as allies and experts, the association finding expression now in the recently established Institute of Strategic Studies that specializes in high-level confidential discussions of policy issues between senior soldiers, top civil servants, and other highly qualified civilians.[33] An article in *Brassey's* in 1958 on "The Modern Relationship of Statesmen and Military Leaders" concluded that today "the able officer *must* assert himself as a co-partner in the business of strategy."[34] In 1958, too, the editor of the *Army Quarterly,* outlining a new scheme of "selection and training for high command," advocated one- or two-year courses on "cold war problems" and the "political background" of military issues. And in 1960 the tide of controversy and discussion finally produced a direct challenge from a senior officer to government defense policy.

In February of that year a lecture given by Lieutenant-General Sir John Cowley to an R.U.S.I. audience was published with the title "Future Trends in Warfare." General Cowley analyzed the logic of deterrent theory and found it nonsensical. His conclusion was not new, but it carried enormous weight, being based, as he said, on the "inside" knowledge of a man uniquely well placed to survey the whole armaments situation. The only conceivable sensible job for the military today, he concluded, was to act swiftly to "freeze" incipient wars long enough for the "statesmen to decide whether they really want to obliterate the human race." A challenge of such an "American" order to the tradition of civilian control was unprecedented. It came as "a breath of fresh air" to *The Times* it is true, but rather as a stab in the back to the Minister of Defence. But, in spite of the Minister's wrath, and although he won on the general issue that "future statements or lectures which bear on major defence policies of the Government must be cleared by me," the Army chiefs appear to have felt some sympathy for General Cowley; within a month of his lecture he was appointed to the Army Council.[35]

Some other manifestations of a growing political sense among officers are considered below; meanwhile, it seems safe to say that the development of the military "profession" is proceeding at a very uneven rate. In the terms of Professor Janowitz' five hypotheses, it would seem that, while there has been little change in relation to the field of recruitment or of the nature of military authority, there has been, at least in the last year or two, rapid movement in the direction of narrowing the "skill differential" between civilian and military professional men, at any rate at the top, and an equally marked tendency toward a "more explicit political ethos." If this analysis is correct, it would seem to suggest an interesting attempt to compromise between the class-dominated past and the professional future.

If such a compromise is to succeed the career pattern itself becomes the issue of most urgent concern. The variety of experts who have written on the problem of enhancing the service career with contemporary professional prospects—and this includes the members of the Advisory Committee of 1958—are agreed that the essential difficulty is that which we have already seen observed by the military correspondent of *The Times*—namely, the truncated career, the virtual redundancy within the services, of many officers of middle age and the great difficulty of obtaining alternative civilian employment. Again, it was the policy decisions of 1957 that made this an urgent and a public issue. The reduction in the over-all size of the forces made it impossible to continue to ignore the superfluity of certain sorts of officer which the old career structure involved.[36]

The White Paper envisaged the premature retirement in the following five years of some 8,000 officers—over and above the 17,000 who would retire in the normal way. More than half of them would come from the Army. Thereafter the rate of retirement was to continue at an unprecedentedly high level. As a proportion of the employed population, the number of officers was to be reduced from .13 per cent to .07 per cent. This meant a serious approach to the problems of resettlement in civilian life. It also meant—in the interests of recruiting alone—some sort of action to reduce the bottleneck effect in the middle ranks or, in so far as it is inevitable, to shift it toward a younger age group. The mid- or late forties is too late an age for the average untrained officer to take up a new job with any real expectation of promotion. And, as a writer in *Brassey's* observed:

In recent years there has been a growing tendency for young men seeking a career in the Services to assess the value of the training offered by the Services in relation to post-service employment.[37]

This was not to the advantage of the services, of course. In the words of the Advisory Committee on Recruiting:

They cannot afford to go into a profession where there is more than even chance that they will be retired at 45, an age at which their family responsibilities are often at their heaviest and at which their chances of obtaining another career are already dwindling.[38]

Further up the ladder the problem was only slightly less acute:

Even if they are better than average and reach the rank of brigadier or major-general, they may still be retired in their early fifties, with a pension which by itself would mean a significant cut in their standard of living, and with little chance of another job of similar *status*.[39]

In short, the decisive consideration in designing an attractive professional career structure is the prospect at the end of it. The White Paper of 1957 implied action in two directions: to rationalize the career pattern itself and to explore and open new paths along which the retired officer could expect to find positions compatible with his former status in civilian life.

IV: Postservice Prospects

THE RESETTLEMENT SERVICE

There has been much well-publicized activity in both of these directions since 1957.[40] The Defence White Paper of 1960 was largely devoted to the "human factor," setting out a new structure of pay and pensions—"my responsibility as Minister of Defence is to see that these young men who carry these immense responsibilities are paid on about a fair level with people in equivalent industries"—and formally announcing a new shape to the service career.[41] In future the release of middle-grade officers would be effected in the late thirties—which meant relatively rapid promotion up to about thirty-eight and then either a more or less guaranteed lifetime career of useful activity or "if he does not want that (the officer) can go out when he has a chance of making another life outside." Those who stayed in the profession—and service life was compared with some emphasis to "a skilled job in a profession" on this occasion—could now expect the career ladder to carry them to the age of fifty-five, though not, as one military spokesman said, "to sixty as some of us had hoped."

But, though this pattern is fairer to the average middle-aged officer, it does little in itself to persuade the potential recruit that twenty years in the services as a first career are not a waste of his energies and opportunities. Nor is the ambitious and capable soldier likely to welcome the prospect of retirement at fifty-five, however generous his pension. The successful re-settling of both groups remains the outstanding challenge to those who would create a modern military profession in Britain. And since 1957 the machinery of resettlement has been developed as dramatically as the career pattern itself.[42] The heart of this apparatus remains the "service" provided by the Ministry of Labour since 1949. But this has now been invested with a new prestige and strengthened by a network of contacts with powerful figures in the services, private industry, and government. Prior to 1957 the imagined stigma of the "Labour Exchange" still weighed heavily against the service, no more than 25 per cent of retiring officers being willing to make use of it.[43] Nor perhaps was its record of placings likely to encourage even those officers not troubled by any sense of the indignity of using the service.

In 1957, however, the service took a new lease on life. The retiring Vice-Chief of Air Staff, Sir Ronald Ivelaw-Chapman, was appointed Director of Resettlement, a new post, to coordinate the activities of the various service voluntary and governmental organizations involved in promoting the employ-ment of ex-Regulars—the most important of these for officers being the Officers Association. A system of liaison and cooperation among these various bodies was developed. Most important perhaps was the setting up of a Resettlement Advisory Board designed to be strong and influential of itself and manned accordingly with key industrial figures. Sir Frederic Hooper (Managing Director of Schweppes Ltd.) became Chairman of the Board, the other members being General Sir Charles Dunphie (Chairman and

Managing Director of Vickers Armstrong Ltd. and Director of the West-minster Bank), W. D. Goss (sometime General Secretary of the T. & G. W. U.), Sir William McFadzean (Chairman and Managing Director of British Insulated Callenders Cables and currently President of the Federation of British Industries), and J. McLean (Chairman of George Wills & Sons Ltd.). Mr. Goss concerned himself primarily with the employment of other ranks, and the main task of the other members of the Board rapidly became clear: to create an atmosphere favorable to the easy transfer of ex-officers to industrial positions.

On the advice of the Board and led by Sir Frederic Hooper, the Resettle-ment Service has for four years maintained a major propaganda campaign toward this end.[44] Soldiers had to be convinced that employment of an attractive nature was available. Employers had to be persuaded that the services could provide high quality and easily trainable personnel. This has been very largely an ideological matter on both sides—to break down pictures of blimpishness among civilians and to dislodge ingrained but outmoded conceptions of status among officers. Much effort has been put into dignify-ing the Resettlement Service. The Ministry of Labour has managed, albeit unintentionally, to conquer the myth of its own slightly low-class personality by working alongside and in cooperation with the influential and very re-spectable Officers' Association. Twelve regional committees have been set up, "each chaired by a distinguished local industrialist whose name carries great weight in his respective region." The Director of Resettlement has addressed many "gatherings of leading industrialists," Rotary Clubs, Chambers of Commerce, etc., as well as approaching

the leading authorities of all the nationalised industries and corporations such as atomic, coal, transport, B.B.C. and the like, to remind them of the new material on the labour market and to get concessions for the ex-regular where possible.[45]

Opportunities were "sought and obtained" to persuade employers by means of the press, radio, and television.[46] The Lord Mayor of London gave a reception in May, 1958, at which the Minister of Labour and the Chairman of the Advisory Board addressed "many representatives of industry, com-merce and the professions." The "job finder of the Officers' Association visited over 900 employers in the year 1958-1959.[47] In pamphlets distributed to employers the "special personal qualities" of the ex-officer are stressed. On the other hand, pamphlets addressed to officers emphasize the importance of commerce to the nation. Thus employers were advised, for example:

It is from retired officers that we should also be able to find . . . . many of the right type for the peculiarly exacting task of overseas representation. Good manners and appearance, an ability to mix, an appreciation of foreign customs and mentalities, some knowledge of world affairs and languages—all these qualities and skills are essential to the high level salesmanship upon which our exports depend.[48]

While, on the other hand, officers were reminded that:

on the success of the business world depends the way and standard of life of everyone in this country. There can be no sound defence policy, no value in compensation and pension payments, unless the country can depend on an overall successful industry and commerce.[49]

No one has been more active in these campaigns to enhance the prestige of commercial employments in the eyes of the officer and to make the officer acceptable to employers than Sir Frederic Hooper himself; his own company has pinned its American sales to the image, massively publicized, of the distinguished ex-officer. Commander Whitehead, the bearded Schweppes representative, is perhaps the superlative symbol of the ideal of the Resettlement Service, the dignified salesman.

Over and above this propaganda activity, however, a number of immediately practical steps have been taken.[50] Substantial grants, the so-called Golden Bowler, have been provided by way of compensation for premature retirement over and above the normal retired pay and terminal grant. Thus, a typical infantry major compulsorily retired at the age of forty after nineteen years service was offered a capital payment of £5,000, a terminal grant of £1,665, and retired pay of £555 a year; for colonels and equivalent ranks at fifteen years service the capital payment was fixed at £6,000. These tax-free capital payments are matched by smaller grants to officers retiring normally during the run-down period in recognition of the fact that they have to compete for jobs with the prematurely retired. A series of training and "reorientation" schemes have been set up to introduce the officer to civilian life. A number of articles and pamphlets have indicated the sort of jobs officers may reasonably expect and the best means of pursuing them. Ministry of Labour officials have toured service establishments talking to officers about civilian employment. And something remarkably like a military pressure group has emerged in Parliament to voice the problems and aspirations of the retired officer. Debates on general defense issues have been diverted to wring assurances of sympathy for the plight of officers from Ministers. A small group of M.P.'s, all Conservatives but not all ex-officers, have persistently put two or three themes dear to the heart of the retired soldier before the House.[51]

It is interesting to note in this connection again the importance of conceptions of status. While some Labour M.P.'s have been appalled at the commercial opportunities put into the hands of ex-officers by the new grants (one, for example, predicted "From Brigadier to Captain of Industry," as a common newspaper headline of the future), it would seem that many officers themselves hanker after more respectable employment. The suggestion, for example, that retired officers are uniquely suited to civil-service employments comes forward fairly frequently—"up to 45 in the Army and then in some other branch of Government service." Ministers are called on to scour their departments for suitable vacancies:

A large majority of these officers who have already spent a great deal of their life in public service would be particularly suited for employment in government departments.

While Labour Members have felt that far more officers may be finding their way into the civil service than is good for it, the prospect of an extended "public service" career may well appear to the soldier as one of the few possible ways of postponing the day when the notorious exchange

BUTLER. Sir, there is an officer and a gentleman waiting for you downstairs.
EMPLOYER. Oh, in that case show them both up.

—describes a brutal social reality.[52]

In spite, then, of the resistance of the older services to some of the implications of democracy, serious efforts to create a modern military profession in Britain are afoot. And these efforts are complemented by high-level pressure and forceful action to provide the retired officer with suitable rewards in terms of status and employment. But how effective is this energy expended on their behalf? Is the favor shown to traditional social groups at the point of recruiting also apparent at the end of the officer's career? And if so, is this social conservatism a significant obstacle to the business of enhancing that career with contemporary professional perspectives? What is happening to retired officers today?

THE DRIFT TO THE TOP

Service officers now number rather less than .1 per cent of the employed population. Yet, whatever their difficulties, retired officers can hardly claim to be unrepresented or underrepresented in the higher, decision-making levels of British civilian life. By contrast with their size as a social group they enjoy a considerable share of Parliamentary time and a very substantial share of Parliamentary personnel—some 9 per cent of present M.P.'s are former regular officers. Over and above explicitly military sections of our civil administration—such as the Service Ministries, and the Ministry of Defence, and the proliferating Civil Defence apparatus—into which officers now move in large numbers, openings have been found throughout the civil service for former soldiers.[53] The Commonwealth Relations Office, for example, employs three major-generals today: thirteen of the sixteen "historians" attached to the Cabinet Office are officers, and all three of the "narrators." Another seven retired sailors are employed as historians by the Admiralty. On an average, some 4 per cent of the top posts in a wide area of industry and civil government are now filled by ex-officers. In some industries—notably those most closely associated with government—the proportion is rather high. Retired officers holding consequential administrative or industrial posts comprise over 20 per cent of the entries in a *Who's Who in British Aviation*. Twelve of the nineteen major aircraft companies supplying the government number sixteen former officers among their directors or top executives. Twelve retired officers are in similar positions in the nine leading aero-engine firms. Several more are employed by firms allied to aviation as liaison or public relations officers. At the purchasing end roughly one in four of the air and weapons "directorate" of the Ministry of Aviation —which has taken over the main functions of the Ministry of Supply—are officers, from the Chief Aeronautical Adviser to the directors of the department of Research and Development.

Both in industry and in the apparatus of government a clear pattern for military intrusion has been set by the most eminent leaders of all three services. As the British exponent of General Mark Clark's "buddy system," we have Lord Mountbatten, reputed to have "talked" the Prime Minister into creating the supreme Defence advisory post—which he himself now holds.[54] Field Marshal Lord Alexander, after being Governor General of Canada, made a still more dramatic entry into politics as Conservative Minister of Defence. Marshal of the Royal Air Force Lord Douglas of Kirtleside, Military Governor of the British zone in Germany until 1947, has been director of one public corporation and is now chairman of another, B.E.A. Another Marshal of the R.A.F., Sir John Slessor, a staunch advocate of civilian control, is Vice President of the influential Institute of Strategic Studies and a director of Blackburn and General Aircraft, the firm that builds, inter alia, the controversial WA39 fighter. Another, Lord Portal of Hungerford, has all the positions of a major industrial magnate, with director-ships in banking, insurance, and the motor industry. Field Marshal Sir Gerald Templer, similarly, moved from his post as C.I.G.S. to the top of private commerce as director and chairman of the British Metal Corporation and director of leading insurance firms.

Field Marshal Lord Montgomery, though he holds no formal positions of power, has set a similar pattern for military activity and influence of another sort. His well-publicized amateur incursions into high-level politics and his visits to Moscow, Peking, and South Africa have been treated with remark-able seriousness by the press. At least one mass circulation paper regarded his private "summit" meetings as being no less important than those of official international diplomacy. And there is, generally, marked willingness to listen to the political and strategic prescriptions of retired soldiers, an apparent confidence among civilians in the wisdom born of military experi-ence—this despite the observation by the current Master-General of the Ordnance that technical change is now so rapid that the opinions of retired officers are virtually worthless.[55] The memoirs of retired soldiers are a regular feature of one leading "quality" Sunday paper. The market for such publica-tions is, currently, insatiatible; at the time of writing, autobiographical and biographical studies of living soldiers have been published at the rate of one a week for the last two months. A current peak-hour radio serial features the memoirs of a retired general. Literary, biographical, strategic, and even political essays by military men are now so commonplace that one reviewer of a small part of this diffuse public relations enterprise was moved to express the hope "that Sandhurst, Camberley and Aldershot are now training future generals not only in space tactics, but also for the essential rigours of the typewriter and the television camera."[56]

If we consider institutions rather than individuals, the impression of military influence is, at first sight, equally strong. The aviation industry is an extreme case, of course, but slightly over 4 per cent of the business leaders in the Directory of Directors are former officers.[57] This figure is confirmed by a large scale survey, "The Path to Leadership in Industry," sponsored by the *Daily Telegraph*, covering "the directors of all large commercial and industrial public companies." It appears from this survey that the regular armed forces were the first career choice of fifty-one of the 1,243 directors interviewed (4 per cent)—or rather more than 15 per cent of the whole group (322) who started their career *outside* business firms. Again, three of the twelve regional directors of the Federation of British Industries are retired officers. If we turn to the Boards of the nationalized industries—described collectively as "the most powerful group of business managers in the western world"—we find the retired regular officer equally well represented.[58]

This is perhaps the most controversial aspect of the situation of the retired officer in British eyes. On what criteria, it is often asked, are soldiers selected to run experiments in industrial democracy? What effect has this small but powerful military group had on the character of the public corporation? In 1951, 6 per cent of the full-time members of the twelve Boards, which between them control the lives of over two million workers, were former officers. Two years later the appointment of General Sir Brian Robertson as Chairman of the British Transport Commission provoked a flurry of concern about the qualifications and suitability of ex-soldiers for such posts. The *Observer* noted that only four of the fourteen B.T.C. members had had experience in railway management and suggested that one great advantage of military men in such positions might be their ingrained readiness to take orders from their political "superiors." *Punch* saluted Sir Brian as a "hero of our time," with a verse that began "There isn't a profession a soldier could feel grander in," and ended:

> In short, although the transport world I'm not an Alexander in,
> I am the very model of a modern railway mandarin.[59]

Whatever the facts, the myth of undue military influence in the nationalized industries is well established. Sir Brian Robertson is pointed out as a typical case, though it is not always clear what he is meant to be "typical" of. When the Acton Society Trust investigated the composition of the Boards in 1951, one of the four main criticisms before them was the charge that they were dominated by "retired admirals." In so far as the charge tied up with other complaints in a general picture of continuing control by the traditional ruling and employing groups, it clearly had real substance. But there is perhaps more to it than that. Thus, the N.U.R. journal, the *Railway Review*, has often stressed the strictly military *character* of railway administration under public ownership as well as pointing to the number of former officers in the hierarchy of that administration—although major generals are rather more in evidence than admirals.[60] And it is clear that Sir Brian Robertson, for example, does have a habit of applying military concepts to the human problems of the railways in a manner that might well be thought inappropriate to a supposed model of industrial democracy, or, indeed, to any sort of civilian enterprise. Indeed, the fact that the government accepted a "military" organizational model for the public corporations is perhaps rather more important than the fact—a corollary of the first—that it then appointed a number of former soldiers to run them. Thus, the B.T.C. is organized along quasi-military lines, with its "General Staff" and its "Staff College"—both, incidentally, administered by retired major-generals—and a quasi-military order of priorities follows naturally enough. "The staff consists, very importantly, of officers," says Sir Brian, and goes on to speak of the "recruitment of Officer material" as the "one direction more than others in which the whole of the undertaking needs to make progress." Including Sir Brian, three of the fifteen commissioners today are retired officers—selected, it would appear, one for his record as an administrator and a manager of men (though the railways have hardly been notable for an absence of trade disputes since 1953), one for his eminent social standing and contacts in private industry and finance, and only one for his technical qualifications and experience of transport problems. And this picture *does* seem to be typical of the so-called public sector of the British economy.[61]

In banking, another very controversial area, the military group is no smaller, though it is less easy to detect a military influence. Twelve retired senior officers now hold positions as directors of seven leading banking houses; they include three Field Marshals, an Admiral of the Fleet and a Marshal of the R.A.F.[62] Insurance and investment companies, again, make slightly greater use of officers from the highest ranks, shipbuilding and engineering firms rather less. In all, however, it is difficult to reduce the ex-officer group in the higher strata of industry and commerce to much below, or, as an average, to raise it to very much above, 4 per cent. Given the key nature of many of these positions, it could well be argued that this is a serious overrepresentation, that a service career provides an excessively smooth and well-worn "path to leadership" in other fields. But to do this we must explore the nature and grounds of these appointments in some detail.

First, however, we should note one other institutional area in which retired officers tend to cluster: the gallimaufry of ceremonial posts and semi-sinecures ringing the apparatus of British government. In view of the marked and conscious concern of the officer for status—as against more material rewards—it is worth observing that six years of socialism and the dwindling of Empire have done relatively little to diminish opportunities of this sort. Though the power that went with many of these positions has gone, the positions themselves survive and carry considerable residual prestige. Six out of 100 general officers to retire from the Army since 1955 have become governors and commanders-in-chief of Commonwealth countries—though the scale is reduced and the "countries" now tend to be diminutive islands rather than subcontinents. Another twenty-five of these officers enjoy positions of less military and social dignity as colonels commandant or deputy lieutenants of counties. And of the variety of posts attached to the Royal households and the ceremonial establishments of the central civil government, 108 are currently held by former officers. These posts range in character from the essentially decorative, such as harbinger gentleman-at-arms, to those with marginal social influence, such as press secretary to the Queen Mother, and those carrying significant social control, such as examiner of plays. All confer effective prestige.

Striking as this picture of officer access to elite dignities and positions may be, it tells us little in itself. How for example, does the present picture compare with that of the prewar years? It is not, of course, necessary to my argument that the proportion of officers highly placed in civil life should show an absolute increase over the 1930's. Indeed, given the decline of the officer group as a proportion of the employed population to a new low level, anything short of a decline of the number of highly placed ex-officers relative to the size of the officer corps would tend to support the only contention I am concerned to make here—that the advent of social democracy has not significantly impaired the elite prospects of service officers. Nevertheless, it would seem that in some areas at least retired officers have improved their position over the last three decades. Thus, whereas for the period 1919–1935 regular officers averaged some eighty times the representation in the House of Commons that their numbers in the whole society would justify, in the period 1945–1963 the degree of overrepresentation will be nearer 100. (In neither period of course has there been any significant "other rank" representation.)

Meanwhile, some further questions about the social success of retired officers present themselves. We must consider the social meaning of their success. Who are these officers socially? Are other groups aspiring to the same goals and being unduly excluded by their ascent? Is military status "in itself" carrying over into civilian prestige and honors—this, of course, would be the most convincing token of an efficient professional organization —or is the success of some officers to be explained on other grounds?

V: The Retired Officer: The Pattern of Re-employment

The material of the discussion that follows is drawn from three complementary investigations. The first is material based on a pair of surveys conducted by the Ministry of Labour among small samples of officers and employers who had had experience of the resettlement service. These surveys can hardly be treated as more than pilot investigations, although their findings are unambiguous enough. It is to be hoped that a more substantial inquiry will be carried out in the future. Secondly, I have made use of an analysis of the 1,658 officers retired since 1945 who are listed in the current *Who's Who*—and, in particular, of the 582 in this group who have entered new full-time positions. But, while an examination of this group does tell us a good deal about those who enjoy present eminence, it is, again, unreliable as a portrait of the officer corps as a whole: only the highest-ranking soldiers are included on the basis of rank, regardless of other social positions; lower ranks are entered only where there is a particular achievement or outstanding family connection to be mentioned as well. Thus, this sample does not allow us to contrast the social structure of the "re-employed" group with that of the services as a whole. And, to counteract this distorted representation of class and rank, my third and principal source is a group of 100 general officers of the Army to retire between September, 1955, and

September, 1959. This is a universe, not a sample, and has the advantage of exposing the issue of postservice position stripped of any but the actual factors of class and rank and of minimizing the influence of mere seniority in securing honors and jobs. It also eliminates a certain distortion of the larger picture set up by differences between the services, by the much greater use-value to employers of Air Force officers of all ranks, and by the continuing grip of the *corps d'elite* of the Army on certain honorific positions.

What does the retired officer want? Crude as it must be to reduce the varied motives of actual individuals to the categories of status and employment, it is clear that status and employment *are* major and explicit preoccupations of a great number of officers and that the most illuminating analysis of the retired officer will be in these terms. But this implies two major subdivisions of the officer group. While low-ranking officers are going to be interested in employment as well as status, and probably in the last resort in employment rather than status, the senior officer retiring on a more adequate pension will not feel the need for employment as such, though he may be attracted for other reasons to certain types of jobs. On the other hand, the feeling for dignity will be that much more ingrained in the normal senior officer. Again, officers with outstanding military achievements behind them, or guaranteed personal standing by birth or otherwise, will not feel the attraction of status-bearing positions so powerfully. The distinction in terms of rank being the more tangible of the two, it is in terms of two major rank groups that I shall discuss the retired officer here—broadly, of those below and above the rank of lieutenant-colonel or its equivalent.

What information there is about the lower-rank group comes mainly from the Ministry of Labour sources. It is a very tentative picture: such as it is, the impression of vague disappointment that one gathers from a study of these officers suggests that, while the immediate problem of finding jobs is being solved very efficiently, the long-term problem of providing a prospect of really attractive opportunities has become increasingly acute. At this level, anyway, there are few signs of any new powerful incentives to make the services one's first career.

Some 11,000 regular officers left the services between July, 1957, and March, 1959, the great majority of them majors, lieutenant-colonels, or the equivalent. Of this 11,000, 75 per cent registered with the Ministry of Labour, and of these almost 90 per cent had found jobs of some sort before the end of the same twenty-one-month period.[63] This is a very good record indeed. It seems likely that most of these who do not now register are either not particularly interested in finding civilian jobs (including many older officers) or are already provided with some personal contact or access to employment (including many upper-class officers). Even among those who do register, about a quarter of the 10 per cent that remain unemployed appear to want only minor additions to their pensions or jobs in particular districts where they have already determined to live. On the basic issue of providing employment of some sort the complacency of the Advisory Board's Progress Report is surely justified:

the registered unemployment figure is the one on which we must work in considering the size of the problem, and the comparative smallness of this figure, even including those who are not really in the employment field, leads us to believe that most officers who want jobs are finding them.

The tone of the Annual Report of the Officers' Association for 1958-1959, surveying the peak years of the run-down, is much the same, a confident record of solid achievement: 7,544 interviews, seven out of every eight prematurely retired officers in jobs, 810 other regulars placed, and a further 1,420 "self-placed after advice."[64]

However, there are signs that neither officers nor employers are quite as enthusiastic about the scheme as the resettlement authorities themselves appear to be. Employers are not quite as eager as they might be to take on officers. Officers are discovering a discrepancy between the jobs they imagine themselves in and those they actually get.

Inquiries among officers suggest that "business" is the favorite of the great majority of those looking for jobs, while about a quarter of them spread their choices among teaching, the civil service, and other professional activities. But this does not conflict with the impression of a reaction against business apparent in Parliament: it is the managerial, not the commercial, functions of the business world that most officers desire. An article in the *Army Quarterly* for January, 1960, "The Industrial Field of Employment for Retired Officers," confirms this view.[65] Officers tend to assume that "looking after men" in whatever context is somehow "up their street." Their favorite option in naming possible jobs is "Personnel Manager." Of the twenty conceivable positions this author mentions, only one is of a directly commercial character—and even that involves buying not selling. And yet by far the biggest single group of retired officers below the rank of lieutenant-colonel who have jobs is made up of those who are employed as salesmen of one sort or another.

Managerial openings are in fact few and far between. It is not simply that officers accustomed to a relatively autocratic pattern of leadership of large numbers of men are finding that both the scale and nature of authority in industry and commerce are different: very few jobs as leaders of the business world are being made available. Only twelve of 163 officers covered by the second Ministry of Labour investigation had found their way into "Personnel Work"; another fifteen held middle-management positions as works, plant, and depot managers, but this includes a number with technical qualifications; and, against this, we have to set sixty-three in "sales work of all kinds"—except the relatively dignified work of selling insurance; and a further twenty-nine employed in the lowest grades of management or in clerical posts.

Nor is this scaling down simply a matter of status: the majority of re-employed officers are having to accept quite considerable cuts in their incomes as well. Starting salaries tend to hover around the £800 a year mark—which for a professional man in mid-career is bordering on the insulting. In fact, of the 200 officers covered by the Ministry of Labour surveys, some 40 per cent started work at under £800 (Table IV). The average salary of the officers placed through the Officers Association in 1958-1959 was £717 (and £716 the year before).

Table IV. Starting Salaries of 200 Officers

Salary	Per Cent
Under £600	8
£600–799	33
£800–999	23
£1,000 and over	26
Not known	10

It should, of course, be emphasized that these are starting salaries only and that the officers themselves do not appear to object very strenuously to the cuts in income they are having to take. Nevertheless, taken in conjunction with the type of jobs actually, rather than ideally, available to re-settled officers, these figures do suggest a severe deflation of the hopes with which the resettlement program was launched. Half the officers questioned by the Ministry of Labour had received no increase at the end of their first year's employment. It would seem that an unduly high proportion of these officers are not in fact entering the managerial path at all—that their low starting salaries are not simply interim figures during "training," compensated for by handsome "prospectus," but rather a fairly realistic introduction to the level of work and income at which the business world is prepared to receive them. Of the officers placed through the Officers Association, 22 per cent have become "representatives or salesmen," again the largest single group; and here, in competition with men with increasingly elaborate professional qualifications and long experience, the chances of breaking into the arena of "top and middle management" toward which resettlement is implicitly oriented are dim indeed. It is true, of course, that middle-aged men with a decade or more of commercial experience behind them could not, by and large, be found at the salaries held out to officers. But it will hardly reassure the officer or the potential officer-recruit to be told that his one competitive advantage on retiring will be the relative cheapness of his labor. Coming from a profession where position and, indeed, personality confer status autonomously with little regard to income into a world where salary and the material tokens of salary tend to be more and more the explicit indices of personal worth, the officer's sense of virtual demotion may well be very acute. From the officer's point of view the meaning of resettlement is rapidly becoming clear; a new career implies starting at the bottom again, "performing clerical and manual tasks if need be."

Resettlement has also exposed the disparity between service and civilian work-experience and training. Service training, except in the technical arms, appears to be of negligible value in civilian jobs. The prized but abstract "officer qualities" do not translate into any specific industrial or commercial executive qualifications:

What are these personal qualities? In health the officer will compare favourably with a civilian of the same age. He has been well educated. He has a highly developed sense of loyalty. As a very young man he will have been responsible for the welfare of others twice his age, not to mention valuable armaments. He is skilled at making reports and dealing with documents. For much of his time in the Services he is likely to have been training men as well as leading them—a particularly useful asset when applied to modern industry.

Nevertheless, the consensus of opinion is clear. Personality apart, service experience and training tend to isolate the officer from the civilian world, not to prepare him for leadership in it. This has perhaps been the cruelest discovery of the last four years; the general sense now is of a significant (though not insurmountable) gap between the habits and values of civilian life and those of the services—a gap already clear to those authorities concerned with recruiting if not to the Resettlement Service itself.[66]

The pamphlets through which the Service first publicized its activities make clear the extent to which at first service training *was* expected to provide particular qualifications attractive to employers. Not only most officers but the sponsors of the Service as well apparently saw service experience as a genuinely useful if rudimentary training for industrial management; "the fruits of this training could usefully be transferred to a civilian occupation." While taking pains to disabuse officers of the notion that military skills in the field of the "management of men" are any qualification for personnel management, the Advisory Board goes out of its way to contradict the opinion of the 1958 Advisory Committee on Recruiting on the general point, and to insist in its Progress Report, despite the tone of the replies to the Board's own surveys, that the "two forms of life" are based "on the *same* principles of planning, administration and leadership." Deploring the "attitude of mind" favored by the Grigg Committee as being "most harmful to resettlement" and perpetuating "the tradition that regards Service life and business life as utterly dissimilar, if not antagonistic," the Board's Report boldly asserts, "military and economic strategy have much in common."

If we do no more than allow these two committees to cancel each other out, however, there is little objective evidence to support this contention of the Advisory Board. British trade unions at least seem to have a ready suspicion of "military" influences in management, and the Ministry of Labour, in suggesting a syllabus for the reorientation courses designed to ease the "considerable psychological adjustment" demanded of the average officer on entering the civilian world, laid marked emphasis on the distinction between service discipline and civil administration, noting not merely a general isolation of the officer from the "economic and industrial facts of life" but a more immediate ignorance of the changed social relationships of postwar Britain. Tutors were advised to emphasize that the "very crux" of civilian management is "the ability to keep in full and effective touch with departments *without interfering with the proper devolution of responsibility.*" Attention was drawn to the contemporary "human aspects of business" resulting from, for example, "changes in the public system of educational opportunity." The permanent impression is that, while there may indeed be similarities in the strategy of military and economic planning, the tactics, social relations and immediate objectives of each field are fundamentally dissimilar.

And the process of "psychological adjustment" has itself been a deflating one. While there are few reports of difficulty in adjusting to civilian life as such, the atmosphere of civilian work is clearly less easily tolerable. A main object of the reorientation courses was to overcome an "emotional prejudice against going into trade"; great weight was given to the role of leadership in business life; "our fate will be determined by the capacity of this leadership within industry and commerce." But, as we have seen, it is hardly as leaders that ex-officers of middle rank are entering industry and commerce. It would seem that the more flexible morality of the commercial world, and the ascendancy of the profit concept in particular, have come as something of a a shock to men trained in a more rigorous code of honor. And, though at one time the Ministry of Labour appears to have anticipated "a readjustment of ideas on the part of business men as well as on the part of officers," the necessity of this is not easy to see. Indeed, the Advisory Board itself ended its appeal to employers on a note of somewhat unreadjusted realism:

Employers now have the opportunity of acquiring first-rate recruits, men of broad outlook and mature experience, from a largely untapped source. We have no hesitation whatsoever in recommending their services as a most rewarding investment.

In short, although the material now available, and especially the two tiny Ministry of Labour investigations, is inadequate for any firm conclusion, it would seem safe to venture some tentative observations on the experience of resettlement. If anything the picture will be overoptimistic, as nothing has been said here of the subgroup of older officers whose position and prospects are the least encouraging of all. Of the 1,442 officers on the "Live Register" of the Officers Association at the end of September, 1959, 418 were over fifty and 134 were over sixty. Even the Advisory Board could hold out nothing but a "precarious future" to officers over forty-six, whatever their ability; and an officer-author in the *Army Quarterly,* answering the question, "Are there any prospects in industry?" was forced to reply for this age-group "Emphatically, 'No.' "[67]

But, setting aside this group, the picture that remains is one of sad anticlimax coming in the wake of the elaborate publicity and organization that has been set up to promote effective resettlement. The achievement to date, it would seem, though it has solved the immediate crisis of officer unemployment, has not measured up to the urgent problems of recruiting and professionalization that face the services today. On what grounds could one seriously urge any capable young man to spend twenty years in a service career when one can only promise him a cruel deflation thereafter? Reduced pay, reduced status, an unsympathetic "ethos," and a relative deficiency of such skills as might earn him promotion—it is not a prospect likely to appeal to any one. And a glance at the group of officers of these middle ranks who have found the new employment and have made their way into *Who's Who* confirms that that *is* the actual prospect facing most officers of middle rank at present.

It would be rash to speculate about the aspirations of officers as such on the strength of the group of 1,658 retired since 1945 and listed in *Who's Who*. The criteria of selection are both arbitrary and obscure. But we may speak with more confidence of the 582 members of this group who have taken up postretirement full-time occupations. By definition, they at least wanted employment or formal position of some sort. Whether any of the other 1,076 did, we cannot say. Again, by definition all 582 may be said to enjoy high social status, and in the case of the low- and middle-ranking officers at least this must be tied to something other than their military standing. And the lesson to be drawn from analysis of those below the rank of lieutenant-colonel is a simple but saddening one: that there is no better way to get to the top of English society than to start there.[68]

There are ninety-three such officers—18.5 per cent of the occupied group. Seventy-one of them are in top administrative or commercial positions. And of these, twenty-five come from indubitably upper-class family backgrounds. Another twenty-six are from upper-middle class families, and four of the twenty with middle-class origins had officer fathers—a not insignificant advantage.* Of this middle-class group six served in technical arms of the Army and two in the Air Force. In the upper- and upper-middle-class groups none had served in the technical arms and only two had been in the Air Force. But the most striking thing is the balance of the class groups themselves. In the retired group as a whole (1,658) the proportions are very different: 11 per cent upper class (184), 34 per cent upper-middle class (558), and 55 per cent middle class (916). In other words, for an officer of modest rank and without technical qualifications and experience to achieve eminence in civilian life, access to the civilian social elite on the strength of premilitary "background" is a major if not an indispensable advantage.

It is not simply that a disproportionate share of the top positions that fall to officers of these ranks go to the well-born. Rather, there is a sort of elite continuum that carries certain individuals through the hierarchy of any institution they choose to enter. Over 40 per cent of the officers from the two higher-class groups have immediate relatives in positions of the highest dignity or control, as against 5 per cent (one individual) of the middle-class group. Of the officers from the two higher groups, again, 56 per cent served in the *corps d'elite* regiments of the Army, a privilege extended to only two of the middle-class officers, both of them men with officer fathers. Similarly, the chances of officers of these ranks acquiring other major honorific positions in addition to their main occupation are rather more than four to one in favor of the higher social classes. And this general bias toward the upper social strata appears in the distribution of commercial and industrial no less than of political and administrative posts.

In short, at this stage at least rank and military status do not act as social equalizers. What can be done to redress the traditional balance, to make professional talent rather than social connection the source of the higher

---

*The criteria on which these class lines are drawn are discussed below, p. 178.

postservice rewards? Some kind of advanced technical training would seem an obvious possibility. The officers in the Ministry of Labour investigation seem to have found, contrary to expectation, that existing service training was of little value in civil life. But, on the other hand, none of them suggested that "Service training could have been slanted to be more useful in civil life without detracting from its Service purpose." If this is true, it will perhaps become essential to reconsider "Service purposes" with a view to effecting some kind of rapprochment between, for example, the principles of civil and military management. Several recent articles in service journals have suggested the introduction of technical and executive training into the career of even the regimental officer.[69] The officers in this particular group showed some considerable interest in the problem of prerelease training, one realist going as far as to advocate "five years of preparation for civil life" and another proposing that in "peace time the aim should be to provide an officer with sufficient time and stability to obtain civil qualifications by the time he is 40, with attachments to commercial or industrial firms the normal thing." This kind of quasi-feudal relationship between the services and business firms would no doubt be attractive to many officers. For, although it may not be, as one officer said, the job of the services to train "late-starter civilians," without such special advantages that is just what the average retired officer of middle rank is.[70]

The Ministry of Labour has in fact provided fourteen series of "reorientation" and business-training courses for officers since April, 1958. These are six-week courses of a fairly general nature designed to help officers to "switch their thinking from the military to the civilian pattern," but not to equip them for any specific job. Just over 2,000 officers have applied to take these courses in psychological adjustment, and, although neither officers nor employers could be said to be wildly enthusiastic about the courses, they do seem to have meant a slight improvement in an officer's chances of finding a well-paid post. Of the 752 who took the first six series of courses (and replied to a subsequent questionnaire), 90 per cent had found jobs of some sort (this figure is the same as in the whole group of officers of these ranks, of course), but of these only 315 were willing to reveal their new incomes. Assuming that this does not conceal a large group of very low salaries, however, it would seem that the courses have helped officers to renew their careers at incomes a fraction higher than those of their untrained colleagues: 125 of this group are in the top three salary brackets, eighty-four of them earning over £1,000 a year (but only six of them over £2,000). Again, the courses do at least seem to help officers to avoid the least dignified posts— those involving undisguised salesmanship. Thus, of one group of eighteen elder officers, while fourteen went into industry or commerce, only three took jobs of even a "quasi-commercial" nature.

But the groups involved are far too small to bear substantial generalizations. And even the most favorable interpretation could hardly suggest that these courses are solving or even grappling with the problems of deflation and disproportionate class opportunity that we have discussed. It is, indeed, by no means clear that these problems are capable of solution. The alternatives would seem to be either to change the training of officers and the nature of military management so as to equip officers *incidentally* for civilian success, or to change the ingrained status conceptions of the officer so as to allow the major who becomes a sales representative at the age of forty a sense of continuing social ascent. It is unlikely that the objective job market will improve or that the search for high-level openings in the business world will be much more fruitful in the future than it has been so far, however eminent its sponsors. But the deflation effect that now accompanies the transfer could be avoided if the officer came to regard himself as on a par with professional men on any other relatively unskilled executive ladder. This, of course, means an assault on the "intangible" status of the officer. And, given the social conservatism of at least the two older services, as manifested in their attitudes to discipline and recruiting, it would seem that this course is not really open to them. The other possibility is to transform the Army and Navy on the model of the Air Force into increasingly, and in the long run predominantly, technical forces. This would, of course, expose the orthodox regimental career as the professional poor relation that it is.

THE PROFESSIONAL ELITE

What of those officers who continue up the professional ladder?[71] Does rank come into its own as a path to civilian positions at a higher level? What sort of dignities and jobs are the typical civilian rewards for senior soldiers today? Of the 1,658 officers entered in *Who's Who* 851 have held or hold civilian posts or honors, and 582 can be said to have full-time postservice occupations. Of this group, 489 are above the rank of colonel, and it is these officers whose activities we must now investigate. First, however, a word about the classifications I have imposed on the group as a whole will be relevant.

I have used five class groups and four rank groups, breaking down the variety of posts held in terms of the social influence or control they confer and the nature of the activity they involve. The class categories are rather more exclusive than is normal, and no doubt quite a number of officers are placed in a lower group than they or their peers would consider suitable. This tendency to downgrade does, however, mean that any bias toward the higher social groups that might appear in the distribution of rewards will be understated rather than exaggerated. Thus the "upper-class group" includes only members of titled families or of first-generation collateral branches of such families. The "upper-middle class" includes only officers from families listed in Burkes *Landed Gentry* or whose parents were in the higher echelons of the more dignified professions.[72] All other professional, business or unspecified backgrounds have been treated as "middle class." Only one officer admits to having joined in the ranks and worked his way up. I have, however, used two other groups "upper-middle-class military" and "middle-class military," including those officers with immediate relations holding military rank respectively above and below that of colonel. The purpose of these two subgroups, of course, is merely to allow us to consider how far a military background itself helps an officer's advancement. In every case educational evidence has been used to check or complement class ascription based on parentage: "Eton and Sandhurst" brings a man with unidentified parents into the "upper middle class."

In terms of these very rough categories, the class balance of the whole group of 1,658 is, as noted above, more or less as one would expect: 184, 558 (217 and 341), and 916 (124 and 792); or 11 per cent, 34 per cent, and 55 per cent. This group as a whole may be considered the elite of the profession, though I shall suggest that we are in fact dealing with two not always complementary elite groups. Its social composition is already in striking contrast to the balance of the general population. Nevertheless, there is a rough congruity with that pattern in that, while only the higher social strata are included here, the shape of the group from top to bottom is of a fairly broad-based pyramid.

This being so, the spread of class groups among those 706 who are wholly retired, listing no jobs, no national or local sinecures or honorific positions, no posts in voluntary organizations, and no titles of honor beyond their service rank (or inherited family titles), is rather remarkable. Using again only the three main groups the figures are 50, 183, and 473, or 27 per cent of the upper-class group, 33 per cent of the upper-middle class, and 51 per cent of the middle class. And yet it hardly seems reasonable to suppose that middle-class soldiers are less eager for postservice jobs and dignities than their colleagues from higher social backgrounds—certainly not to this extent (Table V).

Table V. Proportion of Officers "Wholly Retired"—by Class

Class Group	Nos.		Retired	Percentage of Retired in Class	Percentage of Class in Retired Group
UC	184	(11%)	50	7%	27%
UMC	558	(34%)	183	26	33
MC	916	(55%)	473	67	51
Total	1,658	(100%)	706	100	—

The occupations and dignities of those officers who are or have been fully engaged in some new social role have been analyzed, in the first place, on fairly simple lines. For senior officers—especially under the new pension arrangements—the issue of employment as such is likely to be less important than those of influence, power, and interest. Their roles and activities are treated in the first place, therefore, horizontally, as top or minor positions. Here "top" includes posts at the level of directors or administrative-grade civil servants or high-level functionaries in organizations operating on a national or international scale; advisory posts and sinecures giving access to the center of government departments; general secretaries of voluntary organizations, again at national level; diplomatic and colonial posts in which the holder is the principal representative of the British government in that area; and so forth. "Minor" includes all other bureaucratic and executive functions, executive posts in leading business firms, directorships in smaller firms, posts in local government, honorific positions carrying less than nation-wide influence, etc. Each of these groups is further divided into three vertical compartments according to the type of control or influence exercised: government (meaning civil or military administration, including the administration of voluntary and business organizations and the nationalized industries), business (meaning the policymaking, investment and executive functions of industry and commerce), and professional (which includes a variety of posts involving nonmilitary professional skills in academic and voluntary organizations, financial, legal, and research activities, editors, bursars, and a fringe of more esoteric vocations, such as pig breeding).[73]

Finally, before we turn to the fully occupied group of officers, we should glance at those in part-time positions or employments and those holding posts or titles which are purely honorific. For it is here that the advantages of dignified social origins are most apparent. Of 100 leading positions in local administration carrying few duties and considerable regional influence, seventy-eight went to officers from the upper- and upper-middle-class groups. And here we may usefully apply the five "background" categories suggested above—"upper class," "upper-middle class (military)," "upper-middle class," "middle class (military)," "middle class"—and we shall find that the advantage of a military family connection or tradition is by no means insignificant. The figures for all five groups over 190 top part-time positions are 41, 34, 50, 19, 46, which, as percentages of the respective class groups means 23 per cent, 15 per cent, 15 per cent, 15 per cent, and 6 per cent—a distribution heavily weighted toward the higher social groups.[74]

Coming now to the group of 489 officers above the rank of colonel that I have called "fully occupied," we find that the advantage of upper-class origins is apparently gradually cancelled out as we approach the highest military ranks. Among colonels and brigadiers background and social connections still count heavily. Among major-generals the discrepancy is less obvious. And among soldiers above the rank of lieutenant-general or its equivalent social origins seem to make no difference. On the other hand, background does still seem to be important in enabling soldiers to reach these highest ranks: there are forty-eight generals and lieutenant-generals from the three upper groups, as against forty-four from the two lower. The rank of major-general, on the other hand, would appear to be the "normal" apex of the military career of the soldier from a middle-class background.[75] It is at this rank that the class balance is redressed and the middle-class group outnumbers the upper- and upper-middle group in about the proportion of the balance in the whole 1,658. Of the retired soldiers of middle-class origins in top jobs, 45 per cent retired at the rank of major-general; of the upper-class soldiers in top jobs, only 21 per cent were major-generals. Since this picture is reversed for lower ranks, and since the balance is equal for the higher ranks, it would seem plausible to infer that, whereas a soldier from a modest background cannot expect a reasonable chance of securing a top postservice position until he reaches the rank of major-general, an equally ambitious but better-born soldier can afford to retire considerably earlier; on the other hand, among those soldiers whose ambitions are concentrated within their profession and who continue up the career ladder, a balanced distribution of rewards tends to be blocked by the habit of preferring the well-born for promotion (this is certainly the case in the Army, possibly the case in the Navy, and probably not the case in the R.A.F.), (Table VI).

Table VI. Distribution of Ranks by Social Background
(for 342 officers in "top" positions only)

RANKS	CLASSES
i lieut.-general and above (and equivalent)	i upper
ii major-general (and equivalent)	ii upper-middle class (military)
iii brigadier and below (and equivalent)	iii upper middle
	iv middle class (military)
	v middle

Classes	Rank i	Percentage of Class	Rank ii	Percentage of Class	Rank iii	Percentage of Class	Total
i	12	29%	9	21%	20	50%	41
ii	21	42	15	30	14	28	50
iii	30	27	28	26	51	47	109
iv	8	34	8	34	7	32	23
v	33	28	54	45	32	27	119
Total	104		114		124		342

Looked at differently, the same sense of the failure of the professional structure to iron out precareer differences of social standing is equally apparent. While the class balance of this group of officers as a whole is fifty-one to forty-nine (already a slight shift from the balance of the *Who's Who* universe), forty-five to fifty-five, a breakdown of the distribution of top and minor or local posts held betrays a more marked top-heaviness. Moving from the lowest to the highest social group, there is a steady progression in in the percentage who have found themselves top positions. Of the 70 per cent of the whole rank group in such positions, 59 per cent are from the three higher class groups as against 41 per cent from the two lower, while the 30 per cent of local or minor occupations and dignities are distributed thirty-three to sixty-seven (Table VII).

Table VII. Distribution of Positions by Social Background

Classes	"Top"	Percentage of Class	"Minor"	Percentage of Class	Percentage of Group
i	41	83%	5	17%	10%
ii & iii	159	79	44	21	42
iv & v	142	59	98	41	48
Total	342		147		100%

When we consider the *type* rather than the grade of these officer occupations, the general statistical picture suggests that differences of class and rank have only slightly less effect. It seems that officers from the more obscure backgrounds tend to go into administrative rather than business occupations, benefitting more from official appointments than from social connections in the world of industry and commerce (Table VIII).

Table VIII. Type of Positions Held (top only)

Administration	Classes	Business	Professional
i	16	16	5
ii	31	13	6
iii	50	49	14
iv	15	8	—
v	61	43	15

And a glance at some of the actual positions held suggests some further and subtler distinctions. Thus, the twelve upper-class officers with ranks above lieutenant-general have held between them two colonial governorships, four banking directorships, two ministerial appointments, and thirteen directorships in leading oil, engineering, shipbuilding, motor car, and chemical firms. They include the Chairman of one public corporation, a former Secretary-General of NATO, a Labour peer, a Conservative M.P., a President of the Scottish Unionist (Conservative) Party, the Chairman and President of the British Council, and the occupants of a half a dozen outstanding honorific or ceremonial sinecures. Two-thirds of the group served in the elite regiments of the Army; none had experience in the technical arms; only two were in the Air Force; three have immediate relatives in positions of social, economic, or political eminence. A random group of a dozen of the fifty-four middle-class ex-major-generals in "top" positions manages to look rather different. There is one colonial governor among them, no cabinet ministers, and no directors of banks. There is one Chairman of a public corporation (technically qualified), and two other officers with technical service backgrounds have posts directing public services in former British colonies. In private industry the group holds among them eleven directorships—in chemicals, engineering, and the motor industry (but these are all shared among three individuals, two of them with technical service experience). One rear-admiral is employed by the Admiralty, another is a Regional-Director of Civil Defence. Another top civil defense job is held by a retired major-general. Two others hold high administrative posts in educational and welfare organizations. Half of the group served in the technical arms of the Army and Navy, none in the elite regiments; only two were in the Air Force. None have eminent immediate relatives. If we take another dozen officers with middle-class backgrounds, this time from the group of thirty-three above the rank of lieutenant-general, we get the same sense of movement into a rather different area from that commanded by the upper-class officers. While there are no officers from the technical arms of the Army and Navy in this group, there are five ex-R.A.F. officers in industrial or administrative posts to do with aviation or electronics requiring advanced technical skills. There is one colonial governor, a Director-General of the English Speaking Union, a Director of Civil Defence, a top administrative functionary of the B.B.C., and, spread among five members of group (including two of the five R.A.F. officers), nine directorships of private industrial and commercial enterprises. Again, none of these officers served in the *corps d'elite* regiments or has immediate relatives in top positions.

Looking at tiny groups in this way is, of course, an unreliable procedure. Nevertheless, I believe the impression one gets by doing so is accurate enough. It can be checked by considering one final, and more reliable, sample, before attempting some general comments on the situation of the retired senior officer as such.

Between September, 1955, and September, 1959, the retirement of 100 general officers of the Army was announced.[76] By looking at the fortunes of these men, we can get rather closer to the actual social quality of the highest levels of the military profession and to the actual influences at work in the distribution of postservice jobs and honors. The group contains eighty-one major-generals and nineteen officers above that rank. Divided into five class groups in terms of parentage, the pattern of the group from top to bottom is ten, eighteen, eighteen, thirteen, forty-one. The number apparently "wholly retired" is forty-one—though it may well be that a number of the more recently retired officers will take up new occupations in the future; the *Who's Who* information suggests that there is quite often a considerable gap after retirement. This group of forty-one divides by class into three, five, six, five, twenty-two—or about one-third of the three higher groups, as against half of the lower. The distribution of ranks between the class groups is more or less one to one except for an undeniable, but perhaps overemphasized, predominance of upper-middle-class (military) parentage among the generals and lieutenant-generals—incidentally, not one of these officers is in the "wholly retired" category.[77] And the distribution of positions reveals a similar marked but not dramatic weighting toward the higher social groups; the upper three class groups (46 per cent) hold sixteen top positions, the two lower groups (54 per cent) hold ten—and eight of these individuals served in one or other of the technical arms. Again, if we look at the nature of the actual jobs held, it is difficult to avoid the feeling that certain peaks within the area of top administrative and business positions continue to be commanded by the well-born.

VI: An Elite Profession?

In short, while the services, and particularly the Air Force, do to a quite appreciable extent provide an access to the higher levels of social control and influence in general, they serve far more, and particularly the Army, as a path for horizontal movement across the top of British society for members of those traditional "ruling" groups who start at the top and continue there. Despite the laments of a number of officers about the march of socialism and democracy, it would seem that there have been far fewer concessions to social equality here than in other professional groups; and to this extent the services are likely to prove a less attractive and less efficient professional body in the context of a modern society. On the particular question of post-retirement dignities and employments the traditional pattern would appear to have been significantly broken only in so far as less well-connected officers have been able to acquire advanced technical qualifications through their service career.

It would seem, then, that the military career in Britain still has two major social functions to perform—and to a quite significant extent these functions are mutually exclusive. Where Janowitz speaking of American soldiers can equate the elite of the profession with those holding the highest ranks, this is still not the case in Britain.[78] Over against the "horizontal" and properly professional elite group of the senior ranks is set what may be called a "vertical" elite, holding a vital area of all officer positions, concentrated in certain regiments particularly, and securing inordinate access to the ranks and rewards of the professional elite proper.

On the other hand, it would seem to be true, at least for the highest ranks, that a service career does offer a rather better prospect of postcareer honors, influence, and power for all comers than the average professional life; even allowing for the disparity between classes, how many other professions can boast of a 26 per cent transfer from their own top jobs to equally commanding positions in government, industry, and commerce? And it is even possible, now that technical officers have been formally granted access to the highest ranks, and as the services are forced to acquire an increasingly technological character, that discrepancies of career opportunity based on class will be ironed out—no doubt leaving the *corps d'elite* quite plainly performing unique and basically nonmilitary social functions. Already some newspapers seem to believe that the main purposes of the officers of the top regiments is to provide guided tours of London for debutantes.

Meanwhile, the present situation is a gloomy one. Officers seem to be passing into commanding positions in civil life at a rate quite fast enough to justify uneasy speculations about "military" influence. On the other hand, these positions are not distributed in a manner likely to attract the able boy from a modest home to a military career. And at the lower ranks, where this situation is more acute, it is fast becoming apparent to the outsider that the notion of "officer status" is something of a fraud. Traditionally the appeal of the military profession was that it conferred "status." But it did this largely by association. Those who dominated the profession enjoyed status in their own persons—for nonprofessional reasons—and a certain amount of dignity rubbed off on those who shared their professional life. The profession in itself confers neither status nor qualifications, and the heavily disproportionate success of those officers whose standing is based on their pre- or extracareer attributes in the pursuit of civilian positions is making this only too apparent.

One final point should be considered in this connection. A number of recent studies have argued the tight interlocking, through family associations, education, and clubs, of several segments of the British elite of affairs.[79] Moreover, it appears that the occupations so studied continue to draw very heavily on the families of the traditional social elite. The services seem to play their part in perpetuating this nexus. If we follow one or two lines of social connection running out from senior regular officers, we can cover a remarkably wide area of the power and authority in contemporary Britain.[80]

Thus, if we set out from Britain's most distinguished retired soldier, Viscount Alexander of Tunis, formerly Minister of Defence and Governor-General of Canada, we can in a mere two steps plunge ourselves into the heart of a very traditional-looking military high society. Lord Alexander has been, *inter alia,* a director of Barclays Bank (one of the "Big Five"), on the board of which, among other captains of industry, is Marshal of the R.A.F. Viscount Portal of Hungerford, who, in his turn is a director of the firm of Portal's Ltd., as at one time was Lord Ismay, another of Britain's most eminent military leaders and for some time Secretary-General of NATO. Lord Ismay has also taken part in the direction of the Big Five banks, having been on the board of Lloyds. We have thus a quite concentrated knot of soldier-financiers from whom we may pursue social connections in various directions. For example, among the many distinguished directors of Barclay's is G. W. Ff. Dawnay, scion of one of the outstanding military, commercial, and noble families in Britain, himself a former major of the Coldstream Guards. His brother, the 10th Viscount Downe is a colonel of the Green Howards. If we go back two generations, we find the eighth Viscount as Major General Dawnay commanding in 1879 in the Zulu War. The ninth Viscount was A.D.C. to Lord French from 1915-1918; and among his surviving nephews, cousins of the present Viscount, are Major-General David Dawnay, who retired in 1957 and is currently Clerk of the Course at Ascot, and has married a daughter of the sixth Marquess of Waterford; Vice-Admiral Peter Dawnay, Deputy Controller of the Navy and Flag Officer of the Royal Yachts, who has married into the family of the Duke of Buccleugh; and Lieutenant-Colonel Ronald Dawnay of the Coldstream Guards. These three officers number among their other cousins another Lieutenant-Colonel of the Coldstream Guards, now a director and chairman of the shipping company of Dalgety & Co. and director of a galaxy of other firms, including the influential Electrical & Musical Industries, and his brother Captain O. P. Dawnay, a director of Dawnay, Day & Co. (bankers) and of two insurance companies, private secretary to the Queen Mother and husband of a daughter of the eighth Earl of Glasgow. The Captain's father was yet another Major-General Dawnay, who married a daughter of F. W. Buxton, Esq., thus establishing a link with another only slightly less prominent family of soldiers, bankers and, in this case, brewers. F. W. Buxton himself married a daughter of the first Baron Lawrence, himself a distinguished general, and his own second daughter married the sixth earl of Chichester. Among his surviving nephews and great-nephews are Major H. E. Buxton; Major D. G. Buxton, retired as a local director of Barclay's Bank, and Major L. G. Buxton, a former national director of Barclay's. Sir Thomas Fowell Victor Buxton, the present head of the family, is a director of four brewing companies including Truman, Hanbury, Buxton & Co. His cousin John Fowell Buxon, Master of the Brewers' Company, is a director of the same breweries. Captains and majors of the elite regiments, J.P.'s and Deputy Lieutenants are scattered generously through every branch of the family. Another cousin Major Ivor Buxton, also director of three breweries, married a daughter of Colonel

Hugh Gurney Barclay; another, Alfred Fowell Buxton, held directorships of the National Provincial Bank and Alliance Assurance, and his son, Wing Commander D. A. J. Buxton, is a director of the Uganda Co. Commander Bernard Buxton, yet another cousin, married a niece of Viscount Alexander of Tunis. From this point we may follow the Barclay connection or that through the family of the earls of Chichester. If we choose the latter, we run upon another military and brewing family, the Whitbreads. Thus a son of Samuel Whitbread, sometime Civil Lord of the Admiralty, married a daughter of the third earl; his nephew Major Simon Whitbread is the present head of the family and a director of the family brewery. A cousin of the Major, Colonel W. H. Whitbread, is not only Chairman of Whitbread's but a director of twenty other brewing companies, of the Eagle Star Insurance, and, inevitably, of Barclay's Bank. And a granddaughter of Samuel Whitbread married into yet another family of officers and merchants, the Abel Smiths. And with this prolific and well-connected family we may close the present circle. The immediate relations Beatrice Whitbread acquired by marrying into this family include two lieutenant-colonels, a colonel, and a captain of the Grenadier Guards, a vice-admiral, and, at one remove, a general, a brigadier-general, a lieutenant-general, and a Governor of Queensland, Australia. Her husband is himself a director of a number of finance and merchant-banking companies. One of his uncles, Eustace Abel Smith, was a director of the second of the Big Five banks, in which this circle of families is interested—the National Provincial—on the board of which, incidentally, we now find Field Marshal Lord Harding. His son, Major Desmond Abel Smith of the Grenadier Guards, is, in turn, a director of the National Provincial Bank as well as of the British Petroleum Co., the Equitable Life Assurance, Dalgety & Co., and a variety of other leading companies; he is married to a daughter of General Sir Herbert Lawrence—the niece by marriage of F. W. Buxton. Among his many cousins we may mention at least one, Brigadier Alexander Abel Smith, director of the merchant banking house of Schroder & Co., of the Provident Mutual Life Assurance and of the increasingly powerful Pressed Steel Co. The family is linked independently by marriage to those of the earls of Glasgow and Chichester, and thus to the Dawnays and Buxtons.

There is clearly something more than a simple group of families here. The impression is of a community held together by many formal and informal contacts and shared experiences and enjoying influence, through the positions and association of many of its members, over important areas of British social and economic life. And the military career is not the least important of the common factors in the life of this community. It may well be as necessary as the network of marriages, the background of "family" businesses, and the shared education in preserving the common standards that hold these families together as a distinct, small, but powerful fragment of British society. If this is indeed the case, it may, of course, well appear essential from their point of view to hold off the full democratization of the military profession.

NOTES

1. Cf. Samuel P. Huntington, *The Soldier and the State* (Cambridge, Mass., 1957); Morris Janowitz, *The Professional Soldier* (Glencoe, Ill., 1960); Michael Howard (ed.), *Soldiers and Governments* (London, 1957).

2. E.g., Howard, *op. cit.*, and Huntington, *op. cit.*, p. 23.

3. *The Economist*, November 22, 1952; cf. M. Howard, *The Listener*, February 28, 1957.

4. Janowitz, *op. cit.*, p. 374.

5. Huntington, *op. cit.*, p. 36; cf. J. F. S. Ross, *Electors and Elections* (London, 1955).

6. Cf. "The Insiders," published in *Universities and Left Review*, Vol. I No. 2 (1957); Clive Jenkins, *Power at the Top* (London, 1959); T. Lupton and C. Shirley-Williams, "The Social Background of Top Decision-Makers," *The Manchester School*, January, 1959.

7. Cf. House of Commons, *Official Report*, February 9, 15, 1955; March 15, 1956; June 5, 30, 1956.

8. Cf. a correspondence in the *Observer*, September-October, 1960, on the assumption that the officer is typically "idle, feckless and drunken."

9. *Cambridge Opinion* (1959), undergraduate survey.

10. Janowitz, *op. cit.*, pp. 8-12.

11. *Report of the Advisory Committee on Recruiting*, Cmnd., 545 (1958).

12. Cf. House of Commons, *Official Report*, debates on the Army Bill through 1955; and E. S. Turner, *Gallant Gentlemen* (London, 1956).

13. Henry Harris, *The Group Approach to Leadership Testing* (London, 1949); cf. House of Lords, *Official Report*, May, 1948, debate on selection of officers.

14. Cmnd. 545 (1958), Appendix E.

15. *Cambridge Opinion, op. cit.* I am grateful to the sponsors of this inquiry for access to unpublished material.

16. *Government Comments on the Report of the Advisory Committee on Recruiting*, Cmnd. 570 (1958).

17. *Sunday Express*, February 26, 1956.

18. House of Commons, *Official Report*, February 9, 1955.

19. Garnet J. Wolseley, *The Soldier's Pocket-Book* (London, 1869); cf. E. S. Turner, *op. cit.*

20. Cmnd. 570 (1958), par. 258; and "Radix," "How 'Military' Is The R.A.F.?" *Journal of the Royal United Service Institution* (November, 1958).

21. Rear Admiral Thursfield, "The Making of an Officer," *Brassey's Annual*, Vol. II, (1952).

22. House of Commons, *Official Report*, April 4, 1948, speech of Secretary for War; cf. *ibid.*, July 1, 1946 (democratization) and January 3, 1947 (education of officers).

23. The original inspiration of "Parkinson's Law" was the British Admiralty: cf., *Report on the Admiralty Headquarters Organization* (H.M.S.O., 1960); *1952 White Paper on Defence;* David C. Marsh, *The Changing Social Structure of England and Wales* (London, 1956).

24. The emphasis here is on "relatively": the service was successful enough, but no more than a quarter of the whole body of retiring officers was making use of it.

25. *The Times*, September 3, 1955, and subsequent correspondence.

26. *Defence White Paper*, Cmnd. 124 (1957), *The Central Organization for Defence*, Cmnd. 476 (1958); also cf. *The Future Organization of the Army*, Cmnd. 230 (1957); House of Commons, *Official Report*, April 4, 1957, and May 14, 1957, speech of Secretary for War; Editorial and appendices to *Brassey's Annual* (1957); and, e.g., R. Goold-Adams, "The Organization of Defence," *Journal of the Royal United Service Institution* (May, 1960) and *Report on Defence*, Cmnd. 952 (1960), and *Progress of the Five Year Plan*, Cmnd. 662 (1959).

27. Admiral J. Hughes-Hallett, "The Central Organization for Defence," *Journal of the Royal United Service Institution* (May, 1958); Air Vice Marshal E. J. Kingston-McCloughry, *The Direction of War* (London, 1955).

28. "Centurion," "Defence—A New Look for Nuclear War," *Brassey's Annual* (1957); Group Capt. J. R. Morgan, "Education in the Armed Forces," *ibid.;* and "Seaborne," "Regular Careers and Future Planning," *Journal of the Royal United Service Institution* (February, 1955).

29. Cf. Admiral J. Hughes-Hallett, *loc. cit.; Report on Defence*, Cmnd. 952 (1960), pars. 7 and 8; and Brigadier C. N. Barclay, "Selection and Training for High Command," *Brassey's Annual* (1958).

30. House of Commons, *Official Report,* March 3, 1959, speech of Secretary for War.

31. *The Times,* September 3, 1955.

32. House of Commons, *Official Report,* March 3, 1959, debate on Army Estimates; *Progress Report of the Resettlement Advisory Board,* Cmnd. 789; Sir Ronald Ivelaw-Chapman, "The Regular Forces Resettlement Service," *Brassey's Annual* (1959); and Major General B. T. Wilson, "The Modern Relationship of Statesmen and Military Leaders," *ibid.* (1958).

33. Cf. *Survival* (journal of the Institute of Strategic Studies), I, and the lectures to R.U.S.I. audiences by the directors of the I.S.S. and by R. Goold-Adams (1960) and D. McLachlan (1956), in particular the discussion following these lectures as reported in the *Journal.*

34. Brigadier C. N. Barclay, *loc. cit.;* Major General B. T. Wilson, "Back to a Long Service Professional Army," *The Army Quarterly* (April 1958).

35. Lt. General Sir John Cowley, "Future Trends in Warfare," *Journal of the Royal United Service Institution* (February, 1960). General Cowley was at that time Controller of Munitions in the Ministry of Supply. Cf. House of Commons, *Official Report,* November-December, 1959. The lecture was delivered on November 4, 1959; on December 30th General Cowley was appointed Master-General of the Ordnance and an additional member of the Army Council.

36. *Brassey's Annual* (1959), pp. 292, 313; House of Commons, *Official Report,* May 14, 1957; *Compensation for Premature Retirement,* Cmnd. 230 (1957) and Cmnd. 231 (1957).

37. Group Capt. J. R. Morgan, *loc. cit.*

38. Cmnd. 545 (1958), par. 186.

39. *Ibid.*

40. Introduction, Cmnd. 789 (1959).

41. Cmnd. 952 (1960), and House of Commons, *Official Report,* February 29, 1960, speech of the Minister of Defence.

42. *Ibid.,* and Sir Ronald Ivelaw Chapman, *loc. cit.*

43. *Ibid.*

44. *Ibid.,* pp. 14-16. It was not so much that the Ministry of Labour was disreputable in any objective sense, of course, but that many officers had a "traditional" and "emotional" reluctance to make use of it.

45. Sir Ronald Ivelaw-Chapman, *loc. cit.*

46. Cmnd. 789 (1959), p. 14.

47. *Annual Report of the Officers Association* (1958-59), p. 12.

48. Ministry of Labour and National Service, *Employing the Ex-Regular,* p. 5.

49. Ministry of Labour and National Service, *Business Training Courses for Service Officers,* p. 5.

50. Cmnd. 231 (1957), Cmnd. 545 (1958), *Service Pay and Pensions,* Cmnd. 945 (1960), and Cmnd. 952 (1960); also *Brassey's Annual* (1958), and 1959 reference section, and the announcement by the Minister of Defence on February 29, 1960, in House of Commons, *Official Report.*

51. House of Commons, *Official Report,* March 15, 1955, and cf. March 3, 1959, and in particular the debate of February 29, 1960.

52. Pinero, quoted with some effect in the House of Commons debate of February 9, 1955; it moved at least one officer-M.P. to considerable anger.

53. Information for this section from *The British Imperial Calendar and Civil Service List,* 1960, *Commonwealth Relations Office List,* 1960, *Colonial Office List,* 1960, *Who's Who,* 1960, and a one in ten sample of names in "The Aeroplane Directory of British Aviation, 1958-59," in *Who's Who in British Aviation.*

54. R. Goold-Adams, "The Organization of Defence," *Journal of the Royal United Service Institution* (May, 1960).

55. Lt. General Sir John Cowley, *loc. cit.*

56. The *Guardian,* September 7, 1960.

57. Information from a one in ten sample of the names in the *Directory of Directors,* 1960, from G. H. Copeman, *Leaders of British Industry* (London, 1955), and from *F.B.I. Register,* 1960.

58. Acton Society Trust, *The Men on the Boards* (London, 1951), and Clive Jenkins, *op. cit.*

59. *Punch,* March 13, 1957, and cf. the *Observer,* May 27, 1956.

60. E.g., *Railway Review,* February 7, 1958.

61. C. Jenkins, *op. cit., passim.*

62. Information from *The Banking Almanac and Year Book* (1958-1959) (London:

Skinner), *The Shipping World Year Book* (1960), and Kemps *Directory* (1958); from all officers retired since 1945 listed in *Who's Who* (1960), and from *The British Imperial Calendar and Civil Service List,* 1960.

63. Cmnd. 789 (1959), pp. 16-17.

64. The Officers Association, *op. cit.,* pp. 5-6, 11-12.

65. Colonel C. P. S. Denholm-Young, *Army Quarterly* (January, 1960), and cf. M.N.L.S., *Business Training Courses for Service Officers,* p. 12, and Cmnd. 789 (1959), p. 8. The information provided by the Officers Association is strictly comparable *(loc. cit.).* The starting salaries of the career regulars placed average £838 p.a.; of short service commissioned officers £702 p.a.

66. *Report of the Advisory Committee on Recruiting,* Cmnd. 545 (1958), *passim.*

67. C. P. S. Denholm-Young, *op. cit.,* and cf. Officers Association, *Annual Report* p. 6, and Cmnd. 789 (1959), p. 22; 72 per cent of the officers registered as unemployed for more than six months in March, 1959, were above forty-six years. Brigadier Sir Otho Prior-Palmer M.P., who has been active in the work of promoting resettlement, has been kind enough to confirm in correspondence the very hazardous situation of these older officers.

68. Information for this and the following paragraphs from analysis of all officers listed in *Who's Who* (1960).

69. Group Capt. J. R. Morgan, *op. cit., Brassey's Annual* (1957), "Centurion," *op. cit.,* Field Marshal Montgomery, "The Army of the Future," *Journal of the Royal United Service Institution* (1955), etc.; the most direct suggestion, however, came from the Advisory Committee on Recruiting, Cmnd. 545 (1958), and was not taken up by the government.

70. Cf. a rather bitter letter in the *Observer,* October 16, 1960: "How . . . would the average middle-aged civilian cope in peacetime with becoming, say, a member of a V-bomber crew and in addition competing with men who had been doing this all their adult lives? This is the sort of transition in reverse which faces retiring officers and most manage successfully." It is interesting to note that this writer cites an Air Force situation, however, and is in fact an R.A.F. officer.

71. Information from an analysis of all officers listed in *Who's Who* (1960).

72. As, for example, bishops, canons, fellows of the Royal College of Surgeons or similar professional bodies, professors, etc.

73. By and large these positions go to officers who have acquired civilian professional skills during their service careers—primarily medical and legal. The post of bursar is increasingly widely recognized as a retired officer's post; several Oxford and Cambridge colleges have taken on ex-officers in this capacity, and cf. an article on postservice careers in this field in *Journal of the Royal United Service Institution* (1956).

74. The emphasis is most marked in the distribution of the more traditional local dignities—justices of the peace and deputy-lieutenants, lord-lieutenants and sheriffs of counties; only twenty-eight of 100 positions are held by officers with middle-class backgrounds.

75. There are 400 major-generals in the *Who's Who* group: 227 have postcareer positions or dignities.

76. Information from *Journal of the Royal United Service Institution* and *Who's Who.*

77. Cf. n. 75; the combination of an upper- or upper-middle-class background and high military parentage seems to concentrate ambitions within the framework of military endeavor, to be the most favorable point of departure for reaching the heights of the profession and, for this generation at least, a guarantee of civilian eminence afterwards. Access to the professional "elite nucleus," in Janowitz' term, seems to depend quite remarkably on inheritance.

78. Janowitz, *op. cit.,* p. 6.

79. Cf. Lupton, Shirley-Williams, Jenkins, *op. cit.,* etc.

80. Information from *Who's Who,* Burke's *Peerage and Baronetage,* Burke's *Landed Gentry, The Directory of Directors,* and *Kelly's Handbook of the Titled Landed and Official Classes* (1960).

Militia Lobby in the Missile Age – The Politics of the National Guard

BY *MARTHA DERTHICK*

I: Introduction

IN POLITICS INFLUENCE is ascribed to the successful. Influence is ascribed particularly to the successful lobby, for opponents of the special interest often glorify their target the better to abuse it. The rhetoric of pressure politics that is used in Washington, which has been adopted to some extent by political scientists, tends to portray every successful group as the agent of its own success. It describes a political contest in which interest groups achieve victories, defeat opponents, and capture spoils. Not only do the opponents of particular interest groups, pursuing pejorative purposes, exploit this rhetoric, but so also do the leaders of successful groups, who claim maximum credit for their success in order to intimidate opponents and consolidate followers. The disinterested also play a role, in a search for the quickest and most readily comprehensible explanation of political events. Confronted with the facts of group success, they assume influence in the successful, often finding confirmation of this assumption in the existence of a lobby.

It is not surprising, therefore, that the National Guard and its lobby, the National Guard Association, have an enormous reputation for influence, for they have a long and imposing record of political success. Foremost among the victories that have served the interests of the Guard are the Militia Act of 1903, Militia Act amendments in 1908, the National Defense Act of 1916, and National Defense Act amendments in 1920 and 1933. The Guard's record of achievement is written as well in many substantive statutes of less import and in appropriations acts. Those scholars who have examined it have been incited by the subject to vivid metaphor. Elias Huzar called the Guard the military establishment's closest thing to a "sacred cow" on Capitol Hill.[1] Samuel Huntington characterized its lobby as a "Frankenstein monster."[2] In Washington, where allies, opponents, and rivals assay its strength,

The author acknowledges, with thanks, the assistance of an Irma E. Voigt Fellowship from the American Association of University Women.

the Guard inspires a mixture of jealousy and awe. Its rank as the most effective of the military interest groups is acknowledged without challenge.

First chronologically in any listing of the Guard's political assets must come its foundation in the country's colonial past. The more exuberant historians of the Guard have even traced its origin to the troops assembled by Ponce de Leon in Puerto Rico early in the sixteenth century. A more realistic point of departure for contemporary inquiry is Philadelphia in 1787. The militia clauses authored by the Constitutional Convention provide that Congress shall have power

> To provide for calling forth the Militia to execute the Laws of the Union, suppress Insurrections and repel Invasions;
> To provide for organizing, arming, and disciplining the Militia, and for governing such Part of them as may be employed in the Service of the United States, reserving to the States respectively, the Appointment of Officers, and the Authority of training the Militia according to the discipline prescribed by Congress . . . .

Besides grounding the Guard in the country's fundamental law, this language links it to the state governments, assuring that it will be commanded by the states in peacetime. Though the Constitution does not say so, the Guard is also a community institution. Spreading out from the state capitals, it has become rooted in the village and the city. In 1960 the Army Guard had units in 2,534 communities.

As citizens first, soldiers second, the men who constitute this group are under no compulsion, as is the professional soldier, to refrain from partisan political activity. On the contrary, they have shown a special affinity for it. Militia officers spoke frankly and confidently in the late nineteenth century of their potential influence as voting citizens. In 1898 a worried Theodore Roosevelt, running for governor of New York, complained to Cabot Lodge that "the National Guard will give a majority against me . . . ."[3] For many a Guard officer, militia service has paralleled a career in politics.

The archetype of the political Guardsman is the adjutant general, an appointee of the governor in all of the states except South Carolina, where he is popularly elected, and Vermont, where he is elected by the legislature. A full-time soldier of the states, the adjutant general functions as chief of staff to the governor, who is commander-in-chief of the Guard. He makes it his business to know the congressmen from his state, a task that is often eased by friendships formed in the state capitol. The office has notoriously been a reward of the spoils system, with a hoary reputation for attracting the politically wise.

Since 1916 the federal government has prescribed standards for Guard officer personnel. Federal recognition is extended by decision of a three-man board that is customarily composed of two Guard officers and one Regular officer. That this process is not immune to political pressures is suggested by the following excerpt from a General Staff memorandum written in 1948:

> Experience since the war has demonstrated that governors will not accept the decision of a Federal Recognition Board. Men have been selected by governors for general officer positions in combat units who have had no command experience whatsoever . . . .

Refusal to give federal recognition has resulted in continual political pressure on the Department.[4]

Among 124 general officers in the Guard in 1960, twenty-eight were employed in the Veterans Administration, Post Office, Internal Revenue Service, or other civil agencies of the federal and state governments.

Not only have Guardsmen been active in the partisan politics of state and nation; they have also been politically active on their own behalf. The National Guard Association was founded by militia officers in 1879. By the turn of the century the "militia lobby" was a well-known Washington institution.

From such phenomena has derived the common explanation of the Guard's political success. The Guard, it is said, has formed part of the intricate and subtle political chain that laces the country, running through village council rooms, county courthouses, and state capitols to Congress and the White House, engaging them in relationships of influence. The folklore of the Guard's power is summarized in such phrases as: "It has votes"; "It has a strong lobby"; "Of course it has power, it's full of politicians"; "The governors like it." It was, presumably, some such conception of the Guard's power that President Truman had in mind in 1948 when he warned his Secretary of Defense against the Gray Board report, with its recommendation for placing the Guard under federal control: "It is a most interesting document and one that deserves a lot of study but, at this time, it is filled with political dynamite, and during a presidential campaign can defeat its own purpose."[5]

The political scientist, viewing the same phenomena, assesses them with less pragmatism and more sophistication. Huntington's analysis of the Guard's power stresses, not the electoral weight of the citizen soldier, but his constitutional symbolism. It stresses the importance of the Guard's state foundations not simply because they underlie the political activity of the adjutants general, but because they have enabled the Guard to exploit the conflict of interest between federal and state governments. Despite these differences, however, the lay and sophisticated analyses of the Guard's power agree fundamentally that the Guard has been the agent of its own success. In common they conclude that its victories are the fruit of influence—of its ability to persuade persons in power to act more or less as it wants. "Within its sphere of interest its word is law, or becomes law very quickly."[6]

For a group to achieve objectives through influence, it must have a capacity to formulate goals and a capacity to make individuals or other groups respond to its will. These capacities are acquired through organization. Organization is the means by which goals for the group are sanctioned and the action of the group concerted in support of them. The argument that the Guard's influence explains its success therefore depends upon the Guard's having possessed an organization adequate to formulate agreed goals and to realize them through concerted political activity. In fact, however, the Guard did *not* possess such an organization before World War II. Until the mid-1940's, the National Guard Association was impecunious, haphazardly run, and unable at crucial moments to speak authoritatively for the Guard. The most important political successes of the Guard are less the product of its own agency than of fortuitous circumstances in an environment that for most of its history has been predominantly favorable to the realization of its interests.

The Guard's environment has been favorable to it in two ways. First, the institutional setting of the Guard has been an advantageous one. The Constitution made the Guard an instrumentality of both the states and the federal government. As a result, both the state governments and the federal government have had an interest in its development. Nongovernmental groups with an interest in increasing the military power of the state and federal governments also are potential allies of the Guard. Another result of the Guard's dual institutional foundation is that the Guard is made a beneficiary of conflict between federal and state interests. Though they have in some respects a shared interest in its development, the federal and state governments are necessarily rivals for control over it.

Second, certain predominant values in American society have importantly served the interests of the Guard. Among these, two stand out: a bias in favor of dispersion of power and a bias against military professionalism. The militia clauses themselves reflect the attachment of the Founding Fathers to dispersion of power, an attachment that has remained strong in succeeding generations of Americans. As an institution peculiarly suited to serve that value—designed, in fact, for just that purpose—the Guard has had a major advantage as an interest group. There can be little doubt that this is so, despite the fact that it is not often possible in a survey of the Guard's political history to discern the force exerted by this value, for its effects are obscured by the more readily discernible workings of groups, including the Guard, with a manifest interest in preserving the state status of the Guard against federal encroachment. Where "state interests" in the Guard leave off and genuine, rather than rationalized, attachment to the "value of dispersion of power" begins is usually indistinguishable, and no sustained attempt will be made in the following analysis to make the distinction. Generally, when some such term as "states' rights sentiment" is used, it is meant to encompass both phenomena.

More readily distinguishable in its effects has been the profound American bias against military professionalism. The authoritarian, elitist values of the professional soldier have long placed him at odds in the United States with a liberal and egalitarian society. He also has been scorned because he is not materially productive. By contrast, the amateur and voluntary character of the Guard, its early practice of electing officers, its tradition that men must work their way up through the ranks, and the productivity of its members in private life all served to demonstrate the inherent patriotism, egalitarianism, and initiative of the citizen soldier, endearing him to a society in which those values have been much prized. One of the hoariest of American maxims is that standing armies are a "menace to liberty" and a citizen militia "the safe reliance of a free people." This is the classic American theory of civil-military relations.

The attachment of Americans to the symbol of the citizen soldier can be exaggerated. In much of the nineteenth century the militia was as much an object of national ridicule as of national admiration. Even when the citizen soldier has been extolled with maximum vigor, there has been a suggestion of some expediency about this particular political rhetoric. The citizen soldier, in addition to his other virtues, is some congressman's constituent. Still another consideration more mundane than liberal ideology is that a part-time warrior is a better bargain than a full-time one. Many can be supported with relatively little money. Though they mitigate the traditional image of American society's devotion to the citizen soldier, these factors do not mitigate its hostility to the professional one.

States' rights sentiment and antimilitarism (meaning, hereafter, anti-military professionalism) have been strongly represented in Congress during much of the Guard's political history. Insofar as they have been favorable to realization of the Guard's interests, they have tended to make Congress an ally of the Guard.

The interests of the Guard have always been to secure a federal reserve role and federal assistance while preserving a state status and freedom from federal supervision in peacetime. To say that the Guard has been successful is to say, then, that it has done these things—that it *has* obtained a federal reserve role and a large amount of federal support, and that it *has* preserved its freedom as a state force. Its success is reflected primarily in two major statutes: the Militia Act of 1903, which established it as a reserve to the Army, and the National Defense Act of 1916, which confirmed it in this role, despite major opposition from the War Department. To this day these two statutes form the foundation for much of the federal law that pertains to the Guard.

Pursuit of the Guard's interests engaged the NGA from its founding in relationships with the War Department and Congress. Both were objects of its activity, governmental institutions from which responses were sought as the means for realization of the Guard's interests. The common view is that the Guard's success is attributable to the ability of the NGA to elicit favorable action from Congress. It stresses the role of Congress as respondent to the Guard. In doing so, it ignores the role of both the War Department and Congress as allies of the Guard, impelled by interests distinct from but at least partially compatible with those of the Guard. The interest of the War Department in establishing a reserve for the Army first led to the Guard's receiving federal status and a substantial amount of federal aid. Subsequently, when the Army sought to abandon the Guard, the predominance of anti-militarist and states' rights groups in Congress, as well as the institutional interest of Congress vis-à-vis the War Department, preserved the Guard as a federal force. In general, the Guard's objectives were promoted in the early years of its activity by a process of competition and compromise between governmental and nongovernmental groups favoring an increase in federal military power and others opposing such an increase. Fortuitous events, in particular the Spanish-American War and World War I, stimulated this process. The Guard was, of course, a participant in it, but notwithstanding its success and its reputation for influence, it was not a dominant participant.

To argue that the Guard has not been the agent of its own most valued victories is not to deny the reality of its political power. If power is the capacity for the realization of interests, the Guard has had power in impressive measure. Its power has not, however, been primarily a function of influence—that is, the capacity for imposing its will on others. Instead, it has been a function of the Guard's capacity to serve values and interests prevailing in its environment. The Guard has been successful, in other words, not because of what it has done, but because of what it has been. Because it is a military force available for federal use, it has benefited from the interest of the federal government and allied nongovernmental groups in developing federal military power. Because it is a state force, it has benefited from the interest of the state governments and allied groups in developing it and preserving it from War Department control. Because it is a citizen military force, it has benefited from the traditional American hostility to military professionalism. These characteristics have constituted intrinsic attributes of power. Given the issues in which the Guard has been involved and the setting in which those issues have been contested, they have assured its success.

The success of the Guard as a beneficiary of environmental circumstances has been dependent upon the flexibility of its interests. In pursuit of one of its interests, federal status and aid, the Guard has sacrificed its other interest, autonomy. The pattern of this trade was established by the acts of 1903 and 1916. As Professor Riker has emphasized, this pattern has recurred throughout the political history of the Guard.[7] The capacity of the Guard to make the trade without incurring crucial damage at any given time has been essential to its record of political success.

Emphasis on what might be called the passive qualities of the Guard's power—on its inherently advantageous characteristics as an interest group and the flexibility of its interests—is not meant to suggest that the Guard has had no influence or that its influence was without effect in the achievement of its most important successes. Though the influence of the Guard does not account for its major victories, within discernible limits it did contribute to them. The Guard was more influential in preventing unfavorable action than in obtaining favorable action. Whereas achievement of new legislation required concerted activity that was beyond its capacity, defensive activity tended both to produce cohesion and to require less of it. Despite its weak political organization, the Guard could help protect itself, given the fundamentally antimilitarist nature of its environment, from such threats as increases in the Regular Army and creation of a federal reserve. Its political activity reinforced its environmental advantages and tended to inhibit its potential opponents from proposing actions adverse to it. Also, the NGA could win small offensives when it could not win big ones. It could obtain additional appropriations for the Guard even when it could not achieve major acts of substantive legislation. And, even though it could not achieve major substantive legislation, it helped to propagate ideas for action that would be favorable to the Guard and to assure, simply by its existence, that the Guard's interests would be considered if action should be taken within its sphere of interest by Congress or the War Department.

The passage of time has produced major changes in the favorable environment that once guaranteed the interests of the Guard. Formally, the institutional setting of the Guard has not changed. The Guard remains a creature of both the states and the federal government, founded in the Constitution and laws of long standing. But federal military power has expanded so greatly, especially during the Cold War period, that the Guard has become almost wholly dependent upon federal action. State power, having declined generally in relation to federal power, especially in the sphere of military affairs, does not check as strongly as it once did the extension of federal control over the Guard. Only technically does the Guard remain primarily a state force; in practice, little is left of state control but the hard shell. This situation is the more serious for the Guard because federal interest in it is declining. Though the interest of the federal government in developing military strength has never been greater, the relative capacity of the Guard to contribute to that strength has been reduced by the arrival of the nuclear age. Finally, the decline of antimilitarism in American society since World War II has robbed the Guard of one of its major environmental advantages. The country has accepted the maintenance of large professional forces, and the concept that the Guard should safeguard the liberties of American citizens by checking the military power of the professional army has been relegated to the closet of our quaint constitutional lore.

As the environment of the Guard has changed, so has the Guard. Its amateur and voluntary character has been considerably tarnished as its federal pay and incentives have increased. These changes, however, probably do not reduce the Guard's contemporary political appeal, since its increasing professionalism is in keeping with contemporary trends. More significant in its implication for the political success of the Guard has been the decline in the flexibility of its interests. It has been decreasingly able to trade its autonomy for federal support: it has had less and less autonomy to trade. In the Cold War period its dominant aim has been to maintain the status quo in its sphere of interest. Consequently, there has developed increasing tension between the interests of the Guard and the demands of its environment, which has become highly dynamic. The response of the Guard to this situation is reflected in the sophisticated development of its political organization. The National Guard Association has become prosperous, united, articulate, and highly active. In defense of the Guard's interests, it systematically exploits the Guard's political assets. Through propaganda it attempts to perpetuate the advantages of the Guard's states' rights and citizen-soldier symbolism.

Analysis of the political history of the Guard suggests that its extraordinary capacity for success has been a function of two dimensions of group power: *intrinsic attributes of power*, defined as the capacity of the group to realize its interests by serving values and interests in its environment; and *acquired attributes of power,* defined as the capacity of the group to realize its interests through the imposition of its will upon other groups.

Intrinsic attributes of power are a function of inherent characteristics of the group—those characteristics that, taken together, are peculiar to it and give it identity as a group. Its dual federal-state status, its military purpose, and its amateur, citizen character are the essential characteristics of the Guard, for example.

The characteristics of a group are the primary determinants of its interests —that is, they account fundamentally for the nature of the demands that it makes upon other groups. The Guard, being a citizen military force, has demanded that the nation's military policy be based on the principle of maintaining large citizen reserves. The most fundamental interest of any group is simply the preservation of its essential characteristics. The Guard cannot yield completely to federal control, or become a full-time, professional military force, or become, say, a highway police force, without ceasing to be the Guard. The degree of compatibility between the characteristics and hence the interests of a group and the environment of the group determines its intrinsic attributes of power.

The environment of a group is not monolithic. It consists of a variety of other groups and institutions with interests of their own. It consists also of the values and attitudes held by whatever public is relevant to the group's existence. A group that enjoys a high level of the intrinsic attributes of power has characteristics and interests that are highly compatible with the dominant interests and values in its environment.

This compatibility is bound to fluctuate over time. The interests of no group are perfectly static; rather, group demands change in response either to developments within the group or in its environment. If a group is to sustain a high level of the intrinsic attributes of power, its interests must change in harmony with changes in its environment. The flexibility of the Guard's interests, for example, has been demonstrated by its ability to adjust to a steady increase in federal military power, obtaining the benefits of greater federal support while maintaining its basic identity as a state force.

The rewards of the intrinsic attributes of power are realized passively. They are not realized by conscious action of the group. Theoretically, a group with a high level of the intrinsic attributes of power may achieve some measure of success without engaging in organized action at all. The most successful groups, however, are those whose power is enlarged by their having acquired, through organization, a capacity for purposeful action in pursuance of their interests. Organization enables them to exercise influence.

The two dimensions of group power are distinct only in theory, of course. The efficacy of the deliberate efforts of any group to enhance its interests is conditioned by the compatibility of those interests with its environment. Organized, purposeful political activity—by articulating group goals and deliberately adapting them to environmental demands, by encouraging allies, and by discouraging opponents—can exploit the favorable elements in the environment of a group and minimize the unfavorable ones. It cannot produce success in a wholly unfavorable environment.

Influence itself is therefore a function, among other things, of the

compatibility of the interests of a group and its environment. It is also, and
more obviously, a function of the real or presumed ability of the group to
reward its supporters and impose penalties on its opponents. When group
success is equated with group influence, it is usually equated with this ability.
Thus, the National Guard's long record of success has led to a widespread
assumption in Washington that the NGA has the capacity to punish its
opponents effectively. In an interview in 1960 a veteran congressional staff
member familiar with both the American Legion and the Guard contrasted
their power by observing that an Ohio Senator had dared to criticize the
Legion and apparently had suffered no serious repercussions. "If he had done
that to the Guard," said this man, "he would have been slaughtered."

It may be true that the Guard has influence in this sense. At any rate, the
fact that people on Capitol Hill and in the Pentagon think so has given it
influence in the Cold War years. The following analysis will show, however,
that the Guard's success has been assured throughout most of its history less
by its influence than by an environment that has been favorable to the
realization of its interests.

The political history of the Guard will be divided into four periods. In
the first period, ending in 1916, the Guard realized its major offensive goals.
During the second period, 1920-1939, it made few claims either defensive or
offensive. In the third period, 1940-1947, it began to assert defensive claims
in an environment that threatened its interests without, however, seriously
affecting them. In the Cold War period, beginning in 1948, its defensive
activity has intensified as adverse trends in its environment have developed at
rapid pace.

II: Political History of the Guard

SATISFACTION OF THE GUARD'S OBJECTIVES, 1879-1916

The modern National Guard and the National Guard Association are
products of the last quarter of the nineteenth century. Before then the
militia had not been an organized force except for scattered units that
largely sustained themselves; the Militia Act of 1792, which obligated every
male citizen between eighteen and forty-five to serve in the militia, was a
national joke. In the late 1870's the militia suddenly became serious business. Within twenty years a reform movement turned it into a genuine
military force. Every state in the Union revised its military code between
1881 and 1892 to establish an organized militia. Many states also provided
their militias with arms, uniforms, armories, and camp sites. In 1896 state
military appropriations totaled $2,799,549. With 115,000 officers and men,
the Guard was four times the size of the Regular Army. Whether it would
supplant the Army was seriously discussed in periodicals.[8]

The chief impetus for a reform movement appears to have been the labor
riots of 1877. Employer groups, threatened by labor's hostility, spurred state
governments to strengthen the Guard as an assurance that domestic order
would be preserved. Some Guard units were even supported directly by

businessmen. Industrial violence, however, does not wholly account for the sudden growth of the Guard. Animating the movement as well was a good deal of spontaneous martial enthusiasm among the nation's young men. The founding of the NGA in 1879 was associated with the movement for reform. The primary aim of the Association was to obtain passage of a federal law that would recognize an organized militia. This goal was fulfilled by the Militia Act of 1903, which transformed the Guard from a heterogeneous set of military units, unevenly supported by the states, into the recognized militia of the Constitution, uniformed and equipped by the federal government and trained for its use as a reserve to the Army.

Acquisition of a reserve was a major interest of the tiny late-nineteenth century Army of the United States. Professional journals carried numerous plans for creation of such a force, almost all of them based on adoption of the Guard. Generals William T. Sherman and George B. McClellan both argued from retirement for militia reform. The movement was officially supported by the Chief of Ordnance, the Adjutant General, and the Secretary of War, who year after year recommended that Congress increase federal assistance to the Guard. Professional officers in the field informally provided advice and conducted inspections for militia units. In 1885 militia officers were admitted to associate membership in the Military Service Institution.

Not even with War Department support, however, was the NGA able to get its reform proposals through Congress in the nineteenth century. In 1887 it obtained an increase in federal appropriations for the militia to $400,000, double the figure of $200,000 that had been authorized in 1808, but its more substantial objectives were frustrated by congressional apathy, by opposition from states' righters, who objected to extension of federal authority over state forces, and by opposition from antimilitarist congressmen, who objected to any expansion of federal military power. The support of the professional Army for the Guard's proposals, by antagonizing these antimilitarist congressmen, appears actually to have impeded passage of a militia reform bill.[9]

The Spanish-American War shifted the legislative mood toward acceptance of a militia act. Congressional interest was stirred; states' rights and antimilitarist opposition was relieved. In 1900 the NGA took advantage of the new mood to obtain an increase in federal appropriations for the militia to $1 million a year. It was not the NGA, however, that took the postwar initiative toward a militia reform act. The Guard could not agree on what it wanted. Officers in New York, whose Guard was the biggest and best financed in the country, argued that the Guard should be used by the federal government as a stopgap force, which in war would return to the office and the armory as soon as the volunteers were ready. An opposing group, whose leadership was centered in Illinois, wanted an unrestricted fighting role for the Guard. When Secretary of War Elihu Root determined to seek militia reform legislation as a means of creating an Army reserve, his chief task was to obtain agreement on a bill from both of these factions.[10]

Root would probably have preferred a reserve entirely under federal control, organized under the army clause of the Constitution, but the idea was too radical to be proposed to Congress in 1902. Furthermore, the Guard, having been strengthened by support from the states in the preceding quarter century, was the obviously available vehicle for Root's purpose. Inviting militia officers to a meeting at his home in Washington, he obtained agreement on a bill that authorized the President to call forth the militia for the purposes prescribed in the Constitution for a period not to exceed nine months. He did include in the bill authorization for a national volunteer reserve to form a third line behind the Guard, but that provision was removed by southern Senators, even though it had the support of the official leadership of the NGA. Root placed a high value on the federal reserve provision but agreed to its sacrifice for the sake of achieving militia reform.[11] Otherwise the bill remained intact. Root fended off a variety of amendments, explaining to each proponent that he feared to upset the compromise. The veto power of factions within the Guard had been demonstrated in 1898, when officers from the Middle West managed to emasculate a bill providing for an increase in the Regular Army.

The political activity of the Guard did, therefore, contribute in a limited way to the operation of the forces that produced the Militia Act. The NGA's agitation for some measure of militia reform, begun in 1879, eased Root's advocacy in 1902-1903, while the potential ability of Guard officers to exploit states' rights and antimilitarist sentiment in Congress was one factor that kept Root from proposing a federal reserve in lieu of the Guard. But the act was not the Guard's achievement. On one hand, the Guard benefited from the nationalist philosophy of Root, whose perception of a national interest led to its receiving federal aid and recognition; on the other hand, it benefited from the states' rights philosophy of southern Senators, who prevented Root from creating even a third-line federal force to serve after the Guard. The Militia Act was essentially the work of the War Department, whose initiative and support it required. Behind it lay the Army's assumption, developed over the preceding quarter-century, that adoption of the Guard as a reserve force was in its interest.

The momentum that Root gave to militia reform continued for several years. In 1906 the War Department and the NGA cooperated in obtaining an increase in the Guard's annual federal appropriation to $2 million. In 1908 they again cooperated in obtaining an act that explicitly authorized foreign service for the Guard, specified that it must be called in advance of a volunteer army, removed the nine-month limit on its service, and increased its federal appropriations to $4 million a year. The continuing development of the Guard as a front-line reserve aroused some dissent among New York Guardsmen, but theirs was a diminishing voice in the affairs of the NGA. It also aroused objections in Congress, where a substantial minority protested the steady rise in federal expenditures for the Guard and its growing identification with the professional army. The War Department, not Congress, continued to be the Guard's best ally.

Passage of the acts of 1903, 1906, and 1908 did not greatly diminish the Guard's autonomy, despite the fears of Congress. State appropriations in 1908 remained greater than those of the federal government. Furthermore, the War Department was making no special effort to exert control over the Guard. Because the Assistant Secretary of War in 1903 was a former Guardsman and a student of militia affairs, he took charge of militia administration rather than leaving it to the newly formed General Staff. His successor brought the same qualifications to office, having been picked by President Roosevelt with the express purpose of satisfying the Guard. Not until 1908 was a separate militia-affairs division established in the War Department, and then it was made responsible to the Secretary of War rather than to the General Staff.[12]

In 1910 the political alliance between the War Department and the Guard began to disintegrate. The balance of political forces that had produced militia reform was disturbed by the steady development of nationalism. Increasingly dissatisfied with a reserve that it could not control, the War Department began to consider the possibility of creating a wholly federal reserve, an idea that no longer seemed as radical as it had in 1903. Simultaneously, the Department sought to extend its control over the Guard. The source of this movement was the General Staff, charged with central direction of the Army and hence a natural antagonist of the Guard, an adjunct of the Army that was inherently resistant to central direction. Conflict between the two had been delayed because the General Staff, created in 1903, was slow to develop its functions and to assert its authority over militia affairs. Not until Leonard Wood arrived as chief of staff and took charge of the militia-affairs division did their antagonism develop. Under the administration of Wood and, after 1913, that of Lindley M. Garrison, President Wilson's Secretary of War, the Department was constantly embroiled with the NGA.

Among many sources of controversy between the Army and the Guard in this period the most persistent was the Guard's pay bill. In 1910, just as Wood took office, the NGA opened a campaign for armory drill pay. For the next five years it struggled to obtain the support of the War Department for its bill. At issue was not the principle of pay but what the federal government was to obtain in return. Wood and Garrison held out for strong measures of federal control over the Guard. The Department's position was greatly strengthened in 1912 by an opinion of the Attorney General holding that use of the Guard outside of the United States, except incidentally to repel invasion, was unconstitutional. To retain its federal reserve role, the Guard had to agree to surrendering its militia status in wartime. Even after it had conceded this much, Secretary Garrison declined to give an official endorsement to the pay bill. Without such an endorsement the NGA was not willing to seek passage, although Secretary Garrison explicitly invited it to do so. As in 1902, the NGA was weakened by division. One faction favored yielding to the demands of the War Department; another, which dominated the executive committee of the NGA until 1914, stood against the Department in the name of states' rights.[13] Once more the NGA lacked the capacity to pursue its major goal through positive, independent action. Its pay bill was still pending when the preparedness movement began.

World War I completed the rupture of the Army-Guard alliance. Encouraged by public demands for preparedness, the War Department

decided in 1915 to essay disposal of the Guard as a first-line reserve force.
Under instructions from the Secretary of War to draw up a preparedness
program, the General Staff developed a proposal for a 400,000-man
volunteer federal reserve, the continental army, which President Wilson put
before Congress in December. The ensuing contest yielded a major victory
for the Guard. In the National Defense Act of 1916 Congress reaffirmed its
federal reserve role and provided it with armory drill pay.

Like the Militia Act of 1903, the National Defense Act was molded by
pressures for an increase in federal military power and counterpressures
exerted by antimilitarist and states' rights groups in Congress. As in 1903, a
combination of the two forces produced legislation that was highly favorable
to the interests of the Guard. Once more the NGA played a limited role in
stimulating both forces. Since 1910 it had been promoting new federal action
on behalf of the Guard. Unable by itself to obtain such action, it was nonetheless well prepared to reap benefits from a broad movement for an increase
in federal military strength. It was also prepared to mobilize opposition
to the continental army plan. Early in January, 1916, the NGA executive
committee chairman issued a circular to Guard officers containing instructions for defeat of the continental army. He remained in Washington to
follow the progress of the bill and to direct, through letters and telegrams,
the response of Guard officers in the states to issues arising before Congress.
His enterprise itself became an issue in the debate. The chairman of the
Senate Military Affairs Committee denounced the NGA from the floor,
urging that the Guard be eliminated entirely if it was to become a "political
force."[14] Leonard Wood warned against growth of the Guard lobby in a
private memorandum to Colonel House. To provide the Guard with pay,
he declared, would make it "solid and effective in only one line, and that
will be in a raid on the federal treasury."[15] Cries of "pork-barrel politics"
rose from the preparedness advocates.

If the political strength of the Guard appeared especially menacing in
1916, it was partly because the continental army plan had driven Guard
officers together in self-defense. The determination of the Regular Army to
dispense with the Guard alienated even its friends in the NGA. Even so,
efforts of this group to avoid an open break with the Army delayed development of Guard opposition to the continental army. Meeting with Secretary
Garrison late in October, 1915, the NGA executive committee, then
commanded by the moderates, tentatively agreed to support the continental
army if in return the Secretary would back the Guard's pay bill. Two weeks
later, the 1915 convention of the NGA declined to endorse the continental
army but at least refrained from attacking it, urging instead adoption of a
constitutional amendment that would remove obstacles to federal control of
the Guard.[16] The refusal of the Department even to consider this proposal
finally forced the Guard's moderates into a fight against the Department's
program.

It is not likely that the NGA's rather belated activity was decisive in
defeat of the continental army. In the first week of December, before the
Guard openly opposed the plan and even before it had been sent to Congress

by President Wilson, the chairman of the House Military Affairs Committee, James Hay, informed the War Department that he would draw up his own preparedness bill rather than use its draft.[17] Though Hay did not declare his preference for a program based on the Guard until January 11, his whole record in Congress foreshadowed opposition to the continental army. A Virginian, veteran of eighteen years on the Military Affairs Committee, he was one of the large bloc of southern and western Democrats who opposed on principle any aggrandizement of federal military power, especially its concentration under professional control in the War Department. From this group had come sharp opposition to the Guard's pay bill when it was before Congress in 1912. Existence of this bloc, constituting a majority of the Administration party in the House, made adoption of the continental army plan unlikely. Additionally, there were strong practical objections to it. Persons not otherwise friendly to the Guard, among them Leonard Wood, doubted that the continental army could be raised from volunteers and advocated instead a program of universal military training, the very suggestion of which outraged the antimilitarists. The Guard, of course, had the advantage of being already in existence, a convenient vehicle for compromise between the extreme preparedness advocates and the extreme antimilitarists. Recommending a bill based on Guard reform, Hay privately admonished President Wilson in February:

. . . how important it is that we should have a plan which will not only unite our own party, but which will bring the opposition to the support of your policies. . . . It will, if you will permit me to say so, be a very great triumph for you, if the entire Congress shall adopt what you propose. Mr. Kitchin [the Democratic majority leader in the House] informed me on Saturday last that he would not oppose the National Guard plan. . . .[18]

Though it meant the sacrifice of his Secretary of War, Wilson acquiesced in Hay's proposal. He sent warm congratulations to Hay when it passed the House by the generous margin of 402 to 2.

Defeat of the continental army, therefore, cannot be laid solely or even largely to the activity of the NGA. Nor does the act as passed bear specific marks of NGA influence, despite its generally favorable effect on the Guard. Representative Hay, its chief author, was no more a prisoner of the National Guard than was Elihu Root. As chairman of the Military Affairs Committee after 1911, he had declined to introduce its pay bill in the House. The chief of the Division of Militia Affairs, one of the Army's most distinguished generals, adjudged him "a strong man [who] does his own thinking and comes to his own conclusions."[19] The bill that he produced in 1916 fully satisfied no element in the Guard. It was bitterly criticized by the leader of the strong states' rights faction in the NGA for its broad extension of federal power over the Guard. Although they acquiesced in most of the new provisions for federal control, the NGA's moderates circulated a list of thirty amendments that they desired. They lobbied especially for Guard representation on the General Staff, but Hay objected, preferring to take militia business away from the General Staff entirely. The Division of Militia Affairs was one of three divisions in the General Staff, out of a total of four, that his bill either abolished or (as in the case of Militia Affairs) transferred to the Secretary of War. This and other important provisions reflected the influence of Hay's chief collaborator, Major General Fred C. Ainsworth, who had grievances against the General Staff to match those of the Guard. As Adjutant General of the Army and one of the most adroit wielders of power that Washington had known, Ainsworth had tried to set his domain against the expanding realm of the General Staff. Following his departure from the War Department in 1912 under threat of a court-martial, he pursued his vengeance on Capitol Hill. He was, Hay wrote, "my adviser and helper throughout" preparation of the National Defense Act.[20] The act strongly reflects their joint purpose to circumscribe the authority of the General Staff. The Guard was a beneficiary of their work.

With the Act of 1916, Congress supplanted the War Department as the Guard's chief institutional ally. The War Department itself forced consolidation of this alliance with its proposal of the continental army plan. Under pressure for creation of a federal reserve, states' rights and antimilitarist groups in Congress ended their resistance to new federal action on behalf of the Guard. As of 1916 the Guard ceased to have opponents in Congress; thereafter it had only friends. The continental army proposal also encouraged consolidation of a congressional alliance with the Guard by threatening the role of Congress in military affairs. At stake in the debate of 1916, more subtly but no less surely than the reserve role of the Guard, were the relative powers of Congress and the War Department. It was the view of Secretary Garrison and some of his fellow nationalists of this era that military policy should be determined by professional military men (specifically, the General Staff) in the light of an "objective" national need and ratified more or less automatically by Congress. This view had led Garrison into conflict with the chairmen of both Military Affairs Committees even before 1916, but it was the continental army proposal that put Garrison's principles to a crucial test. For Congress to have passively accepted the continental army plan would have been a major surrender to the authority of the War Department —a surrender that, furthermore, would have greatly enlarged the scope of War Department power with respect to the reserve forces of the Army. By rejecting the continental army plan, Congress asserted its authority over military affairs and established the Guard as peculiarly its own makeweight to the growing power of the War Department. Ever since, Congress has had an institutional interest in the preservation of the Guard.

Passage of the National Defense Act, by providing the Guard with armory drill pay, satisfied the major goals of the NGA. In 1916, as in 1903, it had profited from someone else's purpose. In 1903 the purpose was Secretary Root's, to create some kind of reserve for federal use. In 1916 the purpose was Representative Hay's, to satisfy demands for preparedness without aggrandizing the power of the General Staff or splitting the Democratic Party. The successes of the Guard obscured the weakness of its political organization. The early NGA had no headquarters or staff. It had no membership list. The Association did not collect dues systematically from individuals but relied for its income on contributions from the fifty to 100 officers who came to its conventions. Miscellaneous voluntary contributions bolstered it at moments of unusual activity. In 1902, when the Militia Act was under consideration, the executive committee chairmen of the NGA received $1,030 in contributions from Guard officers, ranging in individual amounts from $1 to $100. He also received $200 from manufacturers of firearms. The budget of the NGA after 1900 was usually between $1,500 and $2,000, and even in the year of the National Defense Act it did not exceed $4,000. Between annual conventions, which met regularly after 1902, its business was directed by the chairman of its executive committee, an elected official who received no salary and who was not necessarily a resident of Washington. This official spent as much effort on the Guard as his devotion might dictate and his time and cash on hand might allow. Even with so haphazard a political organization the Guard was able to produce strong pressures on Congress. It took no more than one determined man in a Washington hotel room to stimulate telegrams from Guard officers in each of the states to their representatives in Congress. Still, this was a modest organization, poorly able to guide the Guard in effective political activity.[21]

THE INTERWAR EQUILIBRIUM, 1920-1939

The period between the world wars was the most tranquil in the political history of the Guard. After the National Defense Act of 1920 was passed, concluding the postwar policy debate, Army-Guard relations reached an equilibrium. Its major goals having been satisfied in 1916, the NGA had few demands to make. With the Army's acquiescence, it obtained in 1933 an act that made the Guard at all times a reserve component of the Army, liable to be "ordered" to duty rather than "drafted" in time of war. The act did not really alter the principles of 1916, although its language has subsequently been very helpful to the Guard in its constant effort to gain federal perquisites without surrendering its state status. The Army, for its part, did nothing to disturb the course of coexistence with the Guard. There were no Leonard Woods in the War Department during this era of peace, parsimony, and isolation.

One new and potentially disruptive element did develop in the Guard's environment during this period—the Officers' Reserve Corps and its political adjunct, the Reserve Officers' Association. Authorization for the ORC was enacted initially in 1916, a residue of the continental army proposal, and re-enacted in 1920. The ROA was founded in 1922. There were no significant conflicts between it and the NGA in the interwar period, although the NGA did oppose in 1928 a bill that would have established a War Department agency for administration of the Reserves. As long as the federal reserve organization remained simply an officer pool, it did not seriously endanger the Guard.

The Act of 1920 confirmed the results of 1916. After the war as before, the War Department put forth a proposal that would have ended the Guard's first-line reserve role, this time by increasing the size of the Regular Army and establishing a system of universal military training. Discarding this plan,

Congress debated the issue of control over the Guard. Antagonism between the Army and the Guard, having been deepened by the war, demanded relief. Conflicting solutions for the problem came from the Guard, badly disorganized after the war and as usual divided into pro- and anti-Army factions. One faction argued for abandoning the militia clause, organizing the Guard as a federal reserve, and giving it representation on the General Staff. Friction with the Army would be cured by integration with it. The author of this view was Major General John F. O'Ryan of New York, the only Guardsman to command a division in World War I. It was endorsed by the National Guard Association of New York and by a small minority of Guard officers who testified before the Military Affairs Committees in Congress. The other group, which was dominated by the adjutants general, argued with opposite logic for greater separation from the Army. It proposed that the Guard be administered by a National Guard Bureau in the War Department, to be headed by a Guard officer and advised by a council of Guard representatives from the states. In defiance of logic, Congress combined these conflicting views, giving the Guard much of the best of both. A Guard officer was placed at the head of the Militia Bureau, successor since 1916 to the Division of Militia Affairs, and Guard representatives were added to the General Staff to participate in determination of policies affecting the "organization, distribution, and training" of the Guard. The proposal to turn the Guard over to the federal government, having been passed by the Senate, was vehemently rejected by an antimilitarist and states' rights majority in the House.[22]

By freeing the Division of Militia Affairs from the General Staff and turning it into a bureau with a Guard officer as chief, the Acts of 1916 and 1920 went far to compensate for the Guard's increasing subjection to federal control. The Act of 1916 had made federal administration of the Guard a large undertaking. Not only did it provide pay for forty-eight armory drills a year but it also prescribed standards for Guard officer personnel and authorized the federal government to prescribe the units, by branch and arm, that the Guard should maintain. These functions, along with the issue of uniforms and equipment, constituted a broad area of federal responsibility for the Guard. This threat to the Guard's autonomy was considerably reduced by development of the Militia Bureau as an enclave of its interests within the War Department. Henceforth, autonomy for the Guard was to depend not only on its freedom from federal control, but also on the autonomy of its bureau within the executive branch. In the interwar years the Bureau developed into a little War Department within the larger one. Under threat of an NGA-sponsored bill that would have defined functions of the Bureau in law, the Department in 1926 yielded a broad administrative charter to it. The Bureau chief was given "general administrative control of all War Department activities incident to the relationship established by law and custom between [the] National Guard and the Federal Government, except when the Secretary of War definitely assigns such functions elsewhere."[23] Thereafter the Bureau dealt almost exclusively with an Assistant Secretary of War, independently of the General Staff and the Adjutant

General. It prepared and defended the Guard's budget. It administered Guard funds, which were appropriated by Congress to its account. It had custody of Guard personnel records and handled correspondence relating to the Guard. In the later words of one Regular Army general, it became an "organizational monstrosity."[24]

The NGA, viewing the Bureau with jealous pride, developed the technique of playing "Mr. Outside" to its new "Mr. Inside." They both appeared at appropriations hearings, one to present the official budget with restrained hints of dissatisfaction, the other to amplify those hints into candid requests. Other than at appropriations hearings, the NGA behaved inconspicuously in these years. It continued to function without a national headquarters, a staff, a publication, or a system of individual memberships. In Milton A. Reckord, the Maryland adjutant general, it had a lobbyist of extraordinary skill and personal influence, but his was a one-man, voluntary operation. In 1931 an Army general addressing the NGA observed that "this organization needs to be stirred up a bit as to its history." He had been unable to learn anything about it. In 1939 it had only $7,217 in the bank. A Princeton senior, at work on his honors thesis, concluded from Washington interviews that the Guard had ceased to be a force in military politics.[25]

THE CHALLENGE OF WORLD WAR II, 1940-1947

That was an illusion. On the contrary, the Guard was yet to attain a high level of effective group activity. With the beginning of World War II it entered a new phase in its political life. The equilibrium of the interwar period would not be restored. Henceforth the Guard would be engaged in defending its victories of 1903-1933 against change.

The challenge came initially from the Selective Service and Training Act of 1940, which threatened to supplant the Guard in the short run with a force of drafted men and in the long run with a trained federal reserve of dischargees. Pressures for an increase in federal military power, which hitherto had worked to the benefit of the Guard, now began to work against it. As the price of Guard support for the draft act General Reckord procured the "National Guard protective clause," which guaranteed continuation of the Guard's front-line role. But he remained uneasy. In the fall of 1940 he warned a small NGA convention that

the future of the National Guard is so definitely tied up in this thing that you have got to keep your powder dry, you have got to keep men here . . . who will carry the fight, if necessary, to Congress . . . to protect the National Guard as an institution.

The war compounded the challenge by promising to reopen the policy issues that earlier in the century had been settled in favor of the Guard. In 1943 proponents of universal military training, hoping to take advantage of favorable wartime opinion, began to promote a bill that the Guard considered inimical to its interests. Faced with these dangers, the NGA followed General Reckord's advice and picked a fighting political leader. Major General Ellard A. Walsh, the adjutant general of Minnesota, brought an apocalyptic fervor to the NGA president's office in 1943. The Guard had been the absorption of his life since he joined it in 1905 at the age of eighteen. Under his leadership, the NGA would become prosperous, united, and articulate.

General Walsh rallied the "new" National Guard Association in 1944 with rhetoric so extreme that it would be hard to match in the entire history of American civil-military relations. Condemning professional Army officers variously as "Brahmins," "Bourbons," and "Samurai," he charged them with "undiluted and undisguised hate of us." For 145 closely printed pages covering 155 years (and condensed for delivery), he recounted villainous abuses of the Guard and its heroic endurance under the leadership of the NGA. Conspiracy, he concluded, was at that very moment threatening destruction of "a great citizen force." He had spent nine months preparing the speech. Its contents were distributed as widely as possible to Guard officers in the United States and overseas, along with requests for contributions to finance the NGA's first Washington office. Within a year $24,694 had been raised. In the meantime, General Walsh operated the office out of his personal savings.[26]

His first active step in defense of the Guard was the conclusion of some alliances. In a series of meetings in 1943 and 1944 he obtained agreement from the American Legion not to support any UMT bill that would be harmful to the Guard. This was not a difficult task, inasmuch as the Guard and the Legion had always been informal allies with much common membership. He also made a formal pact with the Reserve Officers' Association, pledging mutual cooperation. The result of this activity was an early consolidation of the citizen-soldier interest against any attempt by the War Department to reduce the role of the civilian components.

General Walsh also fought the danger to the Guard with propaganda. Copies of the 1944 convention proceedings were distributed throughout the country. A formal statement of NGA policy was prepared, demanding continuation of the front-line role and dual status of the Guard, and distributed separately. In May, 1944, the statement was formally presented to the House Select Committee on Postwar Military Policy, along with a complaint that contrary to law the War Department was planning National Guard policy without participation of Guard representatives. The NGA inspired, printed, and distributed a speech by the Iowa governor at the Governors' Conference in 1944 as well as a conference resolution that supported its position. It began the practice of replying systematically to all adverse publicity about the Guard. All of this material was designed to exploit the Guard's ancient assets as a citizen force organized in the states' rights tradition. Through it all ran bitter strains of hostility to the professional officer, warning the War Department of wounds that it might suffer if it chose to contest the Guard.

The political danger to the Guard in the war years does not appear to have warranted the violence of General Walsh's reaction, although it is true that the Army would have liked to dispense with the Guard and that General Walsh's activity discouraged it from an attempt to do so. Plans for the postwar Guard were a responsibility of the Special Planning Division, a unit of the special staff that was established by the War Department in mid-1943 to conduct planning of postwar policy and demobilization. The man who had for years been the most devoted and articulate expounder of the organized reserve concept, Brigadier General John McAuley Palmer of the Regular Army, was attached to the Division as a special adviser on organization of the civilian components, having been recalled to active duty by Chief of Staff George C. Marshall, his close personal friend, in November, 1941. Through 1942, 1943, and early 1944 Palmer argued in letters and memoranda that the Guard should be dispensed with as a federal reserve component, although he suggested that it be developed for use in home defense. It was assumed within the General Staff in this period that a dual-status Guard would not be revived after the war but would be replaced by a single federal reserve force.[27]

Palmer began to change his mind in the spring of 1944 following a meeting on February 28-29 with General Walsh, other senior Guard officers, and officers of the Special Planning Division, including its director, Brigadier General William F. Tompkins. He was impressed with General Walsh's argument that the Army could make the Guard an adequate reserve if it made fuller use of power available within the limits of the militia clause. Among other things, General Walsh hinted that the Guard might accept Regular Army officers as commanders of major troop units. General Tompkins was also impressed by this argument, and perhaps even more by the implied threat of the NGA to kill universal military training unless the Guard system was retained. UMT was regarded as the foundation of postwar military planning, a goal not worth sacrificing in an endeavor to be rid of the Guard. Besides, to abandon the Guard as a combat reserve would require amendment or repeal of existing law, which, it was recognized, would be impossible to obtain from Congress in view of the militant attitude displayed by General Walsh in the meeting. By early March, two months before Walsh's vitriolic speech, both Palmer and Tompkins were therefore reconciled to retaining the Guard. The Secretary of War concurred in this view.[28]

Postwar policies for the Guard were drawn up by a six-man joint General Staff Committee, composed equally of Guard and Regular Army officers, which was appointed in August, 1944, in response to protests from General Walsh and the advice of General Palmer. Later this committee was broadened to include a panel of Reserve officers. Dominated by the Guard members, it produced a reaffirmation of the Guard's dual status and front-line role in language that exceeds the Washington average for force and lucidity. It also prescribed a broad charter for the National Guard Bureau, assuring its full restoration after four years of wartime obscurity. A policy of organizing Reserve units was set forth, but the Reserves were clearly subordinated to the Guard. The Reserve troop basis was to be determined by subtracting Regular Army and Guard units from the total War Department troop basis. When the Secretary of War approved the statement on October 13, 1945, the war's danger to the Guard passed without ever having really materialized.

There was nothing in the experience of the war to produce a serious challenge to the basic interests of the Guard. The war merely opened the policy issues that involved the Guard, creating the potential for change; it did not create the pressures that would produce change. Specifically, it did not demonstrate that the country should modify its customary reliance on reserve forces. Although planners recognized that the United States would henceforth be immediately engaged in any major war, probably by air attack, it was thought feasible through a program of universal military training to increase the level of reserve readiness sufficiently to compensate for reduced mobilization time. On the assumption that UMT would be adopted, the War Department rationalized re-establishment of the Guard.[29]

Nor did the war produce a nationalist trend so strong as to support a radical extension of federal control over the Guard. Rapid demobilization in 1945-1946 demonstrated the determination of the country to restore a normal peacetime military establishment, which meant a small Army combined with the Guard in its dual status. The NGA was agitating in this period for conversion of West Point into a two-year graduate school, an idea that had occurred also to the President of the United States.[30] In 1947 there began to appear from Reserve sources proposals for consolidation of the Guard and the Reserves under federal control; but when a Defense Department committee (the Gray Board) made such a recommendation in mid-1948, the idea seemed politically so farfetched that it stirred little public controversy. The Army never even tried to carry it out. The Air Force tried briefly, encouraged by the dissidence of some Air Guard officers, but it soon yielded to the opposition of the NGA.

Though the Guard's environment remained relatively favorable, the immediate postwar period did present it with the difficult problems of reorganization. These problems were handled by General Walsh, President of the NGA, and General Reckord, chairman of its committee on legislation. Together the two men were able for several years to dominate federal decision-making with respect to the Guard. No other period demonstrates so clearly the influence of the Guard at work.

The NGA was still an embryonic organization, just beginning to develop under General Walsh's leadership, but even before its development was completed he was able, through sheer aggressiveness, to consolidate Guard officers into a united group and to speak for them with an authority that none of his predecessors possessed. Though he continued to serve as adjutant general of Minnesota, he was nearly as often in Washington as in St. Paul. A gregarious, hyperactive Irishman, he waged a steady verbal campaign on behalf of the Guard. In the words of a man who watched him on Capitol Hill, "He was always after that rabbit." His partner in political activity, General Reckord, was a man of quite different talents and temperament. Less verbal than General Walsh, he was more prestigious, combining an awesome mixture of dignity and will. Like General Walsh, he had spent a lifetime in the Guard, having joined in 1901 at the age of twenty-two. After an outstanding record in World War I, he became Maryland's adjutant general and the NGA's lobbyist. Proximity to Washington plus an uncanny political talent made him an extremely powerful individual, friend to congressmen and chiefs of staff. Not only the NGA but also the American

Legion and the National Rifle Association benefited from his talents. The influence of the NGA in the late 1940's was in large part his personal influence.

Generals Walsh and Reckord concentrated their activity on Capitol Hill. When Guard strength was lagging late in 1946, they persuaded Chairman John Taber of the House Appropriations Committee to allow the expenditure of $1 million for a recruiting campaign. In this task they enlisted the aid of Representative Bernard W. Kearney, a retired major general in the Guard and one of Taber's fellow Republicans from upstate New York. Guard strength jumped by 81,648 in the featured month of the campaign. In 1948, when the Selective Service and Training Act was passed, they obtained from Congress a draft exemption for Guard members as of the date of the act and men subsequently enlisting between the ages of seventeen and eighteen and a half. The Defense Department had asked that only members as of the date of the President's draft message to Congress be exempted. In the month before passage of the act, 68,002 men joined the Guard, bringing it to a new peak strength of 317,857.[31] For the next nine years the seventeen- to eighteen-and-a-half-year-olds would be the major source of Guard strength. The two men were equally successful in obtaining appropriations. In 1947 and 1948, which were stringent years for American military forces, they added a total of $79 million to the budget requests for the Guard. In cooperation with the ROA, they were successful in securing passage in 1948 of an act that authorized retirement pay for nondisabled reserve officers. (General Reckord had secured retirement pay for disabled reserve officers in 1939 by attaching an amendment to a major piece of army legislation, part of the President's program, that was certain not to be vetoed.) In pursuing objectives on Capitol Hill, Generals Walsh and Reckord drew when necessary on the grass-roots resources of the Guard, calling for telegrams from the adjutants general. When the Selective Service Act was under consideration, General Walsh summoned nearly all of the adjutants general to Washington to lobby in person, although by the time they arrived a settlement had been reached. For most purposes, however, General Walsh and General Reckord alone needed to speak for the Guard; their domination of the NGA was unquestioned.

Their success with Congress was in turn facilitated by the effectiveness of Guard administration, performed through the Bureau. Money appropriated to the Bureau constituted money quickly available to the states for Guard pay, though it was not always available quickly enough to satisfy the leaders of the NGA. Prodding the Bureau was a normal part of their activity. Whether or not it matched goals, progress with reorganization helped strengthen the Guard's claim for more money from Congress. "The National Guard is always very dependable in doing what they say they will do," Representative Albert J. Engel gratuitously observed to General Reckord in 1946.[32] The Guard's administrative performance appeared the more dependable by comparison with that of the Reserves. Control over the Reserve program was scattered among sections of the General Staff and the Office of the Executive for Reserve and ROTC Affairs, hampering effective

administration. Nor were the Reserves' problems helped by the determination of Generals Walsh and Reckord to protect the Guard from competition.
In 1946, when ROA officials were promoting a bill that would have
authorized forty-eight armory drills a year for all Reserve units—the same
as authorized for the Guard—General Reckord threatened to kill it in
Congress unless it was modified to provide fewer drills for Reserve units
of low mobilization priority. The ROA thereupon settled for a bill that
authorized twelve armory drills for some Reserve units, twenty-four for
others, and forty-eight for still others. It passed Congress in July, 1948; but
even after it passed, five months elapsed before any money reached the
Reservists. A House Appropriations Committee report in 1948 contrasted
the Guard's success and the Reserves' failure.

In addition to Congress and the Bureau, Generals Walsh and Reckord
concentrated attention on the offices of the Chief of Staff and the Secretary
of War, which were freely open to them as courts of appeal in case of
trouble. When competition threatened with the Reserves in 1946, General
Reckord persuaded Chief of Staff Eisenhower to issue a "clarification" of
War Department reserve policies that restated the primacy of the Guard.[33]
It was thereby assured of priority receipt of materiel.

It would be hard to overestimate the Guard's dependence on its extraordinary pair of leaders in these years. They and they alone defined its
interests. In 1946, when the Chief of the National Guard Bureau, contrary
to the position of the NGA, asked Guard division commanders to support
a universal military training program of six months, General Walsh: (1)
wired the Secretary of War condemning the chief's action; (2) wired the
chief demanding that he withdraw his telegram; (3) wired officials of the
American Legion, the leading promoter of UMT, saying that the Guard's
position was unchanged; and (4) wired all Guard division commanders and
adjutants general telling them to ignore the chief's request.[34] In 1948 the
two men overturned a draft directive, agreed to by the Chief of the National
Guard Bureau and by a majority of adjutants general and Air Guard
commanders, that gave the Air Force "tactical as differentiated from administrative command" over Air Guard units while in training for their federal
mission. The directive had been drawn up at a meeting in San Antonio while
they were in Washington testifying before the Gray Board. Receiving a
copy for his approval as adjutant general of Minnesota, General Walsh
condemned it as "unconstitutional, illegal and a wholly wrong approach
to the problem." The draft was replaced by another, drawn up by General
Reckord, that gave the Air Force "training supervision as differentiated
from command jurisdiction" over the Air Guard, thereby preserving the
principle of state command in pristine clarity.[35] No Bureau chief was driven
from office by Generals Walsh and Reckord in this period, nor was the
choice of a chief dictated by them. It has been the policy of the NGA, for
reasons of internal harmony, not to become involved in the selection of a
chief by the Secretary of the Army. In practice, however, the activity of the
two generals greatly restricted the authority of the Bureau chief. As late as
1957, when General Reckord, nearly eighty, had been out of NGA office

for several years, he remained sufficiently active and influential that an embarrassed Defense Department official mistakenly identified him before a congressional committee as chief of the Bureau's Army Division.

The period of the Walsh-Reckord ascendancy demonstrates the practical meaning of the Guard's autonomy. Two men were able to dominate the processes of policymaking for the Guard in the late 1940's because of an institutional setting that maximized their opportunities for the exercise of influence. As the unchallenged leaders of the NGA, they were able to embody the interests of forty-eight state governments in the Guard and to obtain access at the federal level to all of the points at which decisions importantly affecting the Guard were made. In the offices of a few congressmen, the Secretary of War, the Army Chief of Staff, the Chief of the National Guard Bureau—at so few points was concentrated the exercise of formal authority over the Guard. This simple system was readily susceptible to exploitation. Thus the leaders of the NGA directed an autonomous structure of power—"an empire within an empire," General Walsh liked to call it— transcending the federal-state and executive-legislative divisions of power that were contrived by the authors of the United States Constitution.

DEFENSE IN A DYNAMIC ENVIRONMENT, 1948-1960

For the Guard the Cold War began in 1948 with passage of the Selective Service Act. Since then the environment of the Guard has changed radically. When the isolationist security of the nation ended, so eventually did its traditional antimilitarism and its traditional adherence to a balance of federal and state power in the military sphere—traditions of which the Guard had been the beneficiary. The sudden expansion of federal military power that stemmed from the Cold War has so broadened federal responsibility for the Guard that its state status has become almost a technicality. Simultaneously, new administrative agencies have burgeoned around and above the National Guard Bureau, greatly restricting the ability of the Guard to influence federal decisions in which it has an interest.

The development of federal military power since 1948 has affected the Guard's interests ambiguously, as did such movements earlier in the century. The Guard has received a level of federal support that would have seemed fantastic in any previous period, but with this support has come almost total dependence on the federal government. Before World War II appropriations to the National Guard Bureau were approximately $33 million per year, a little over twice as much as the states were spending for the Guard. As of 1959 federal appropriations were nearly $600 million, approximately eighteen times the prewar figure, while state expenditures had tripled. Except for armory maintenance, no significant responsibility for support of the Guard remained with the states. At its own insistence, the Guard has become almost wholly dependent on the federal government for provision of its armories. Before 1950 its armories were built by the states, except for about 200 that were erected by the Public Works Administration during the Depression. Since passage of the National Defense Facilities Act in 1950, the federal government has assumed 75 per cent of the cost of new armory construction. More importantly, the Guard's autonomy has been reduced by assertion of federal authority over the military manpower supply. Until passage of the Selective Service Act in 1948, the Guard had always relied in peacetime on voluntary enlistments. Since its passage the Guard has depended on federal action to provide incentives for its recruits. Along with these incentives have come federally imposed conditions for recruitment that further reduce the Guard's freedom. It has become the prisoner of federal military manpower policies.

Besides producing a major extension of federal control over the Guard, the Cold War produced a federal reserve to rival it. In 1960, 300,000 Army Reservists were receiving drill pay, compared with 400,000 Army Guardsmen. The Guard retained mobilization priority over the Reserves, and in general its units were better equipped than Reserve units. It was in no immediate danger of being supplanted. Growth of a competitor, however, has definitely compounded the Cold War's perils to the Guard, primarily by increasing pressure on it to yield to federal control.

Expansion of federal responsibility for the Guard has made more important than ever its retention of autonomy within the federal administrative structure, but the Cold War has damaged the Guard especially in this respect. Authority for decisions affecting it has been dispersed throughout a complex bureaucratic hierarchy to which the NGA has only limited access. Development of this hierarchy began with passage of the National Security Act in 1947, which divided interest in the Guard between the Army and the Air Force and added the Secretary of Defense as another layer of authority with which the Guard had to deal. (The adverse effects of the act on the Guard were mitigated by an NGA-sponsored provision that required the Air Force to operate through the Bureau in the same manner as the Army.) Since then, the Office of the Assistant Secretary of Defense (Manpower, Personnel and Reserve), formally established in 1952, has developed as the chief overseer of reserve policy. Also in the Office of the Secretary of Defense is the Reserve Forces Policy Board (initially the Civilian Components Policy Board), which was established in 1949 to advise the Secretary on reserve policy. The Guard has four representatives among its nineteen members, of whom reservists constitute a majority. In addition to these agencies, there are others in the Office of the Secretary of Defense that make decisions importantly affecting the Guard, especially the Office of the Comptroller.

Within the Army and the Air Force, assistant secretaries have also been established with authority over manpower and reserve affairs. Of most significance for the Guard, an assistant chief of staff for reserve components has been created in both the Army and the Air Force. These offices developed out of an executive order issued by President Truman in October, 1948, along with a letter to the Secretary of Defense, directing that a high-ranking officer be named to head the reserve program in each department. Beginning simply as "special assistants"—one-man offices for liaison between the reserves and the administration of the regular services—they burgeoned into full-fledged staff operations. By 1956 the Army's special assistant had grown sufficiently to menace the authority of the National Guard Bureau. For months the Bureau fought suggestions for a deputy chief of staff's office to which it would be subordinate. It emerged from the 1956 controversy with its operational functions unimpaired but its staff functions somewhat diminished. An assistant chief of staff was established with authority for planning the "major force, installation, and materiel objectives for the National Guard [and] the Army Reserve," though a footnote to this regulation safeguarded to the Bureau and to the Chief, Army Reserve and ROTC Affairs "staff responsibility" for reserve programming under "coordination" of the assistant chief of staff.[36] In addition to the growth of reserve forces administration, creating new centers of authority, the Guard has suffered from reduced access to long-established authority. No longer can the Chief of the National Guard Bureau or the president of the NGA, no matter who he may be, obtain casual entry to the office of the Army chief of staff, who has become a busy man.

All these developments have circumscribed the ability of the Guard to influence federal action in which it is interested. The National Guard Bureau continues to operate as a relatively autonomous agency committed by tradition to the service of the Guard's interests, but it is in no position to dominate the formulation of Defense Department policies on reserve forces. The General Staff Committee on National Guard policy, supposedly the vehicle by which the Guard participates in policy formulation, has been ineffective. The Committee originated in Section Five of the National Defense Act, the provision of 1920 that policies affecting the organization, distribution, and training of the Guard should be determined by General Staff committees composed equally of Regular Army and Guard members. Between the two world wars there was no regularly functioning committee based on this provision although several Guard officers, usually lieutenant colonels or colonels, were ordinarily on duty with the General Staff. A standing Section Five Committee, as it is called, was established after World War II. The committee was to meet "semi-annually and at such other times as may become necessary," according to the postwar policies drafted for the Guard by General Reckord's committee in 1945. It was provided that between sessions of the committee one National Guard member would remain on active duty in order to watch over business and keep the other members informed. The assumption appears to have been that a high-ranking group could handle formulation of policy for the Guard on a part-time basis. (Although the policy statement did not specify the rank of committee members, all have been generals except the resident member, who is a colonel.) Events quickly outran the assumption. The committee simply has not had the capacity for its job. Its meetings, subsequently increased to four a year, have been occupied with the review of policies developed elsewhere in the General Staff. It has not had enough authority to block Army actions inimical to the Guard. Furthermore, since it normally meets in combination with its Reserve counterpart, forming a General Staff Committee on National Guard and Reserve Policy (with a single panel of Regular Army members), the Guard runs the danger of being outvoted. Nonetheless, the committee is of value to the Guard as an outlet for its views within the Army Department, and an alert resident member can be a useful source of Pentagon intelligence. The Air Force Section Five Committee functions much as the Army Committee.

The significance of recent administrative developments for the Guard may be discerned in the formulation of several policies in which it has had a major interest. The Armed Forces Reserve Act of 1952 was developed by the Reserve Forces Policy Board. The NGA president testified before the Board during its preparation, and the Guard's representatives on the Board were able to keep the NGA informed of what was being considered. Still, the Guard was a relatively remote participant in the formulation process, the outcome of which was unsatisfactory to it. Even less was the Guard a participant during 1953 and 1954 in the formulation of the National Reserve Plan, which developed out of the efforts of the National Security Training Commission, the Office of Defense Mobilization, the National Security Council, and *ad hoc* committees within the Defense Department more than efforts of the Reserve Forces Policy Board. The result was to exclude the reserve interest groups from a direct share in authorship, although the Director of Defense Mobilization did allow the presidents of the Reserve Officers' Association and the NGA to comment on a classified version of the plan before it went to the NSC.[37] Exclusion of the Guard from effective participation in policymaking is illustrated also by development of the Army directive of January, 1957, ordering that all Guard recruits take six months of active duty. The immediate inspiration for this action was a memorandum of November 26, 1956, from the Secretary of Defense to the service secretaries instructing that after April 1, 1957, all reserve recruits must receive basic training of at least four months. In response the Army Staff developed plans calling for an uninterrupted six-month period of training. The National Guard Bureau asked for one or two three-month periods so that the Guard's seventeen to eighteen-and-a-half-year-old recruits, the major source of its manpower, would not be discouraged from enlistment by interruption of the school year. The chief of staff decided on the six-month plan. On December 27, after his decision was made, the plan was submitted to the Section Five Committee meeting with Regular, Reserve, and Guard members, who approved it thirteen to seven—the Regulars and Reserves voting solidly for it, the Guard solidly against. On December 29 the Army's reply went forward to the Secretary of Defense, who approved the six-month plan, and it was announced on January 14. The Guard was forced to wage its fight against the directive in public, at what appear to have been some costs to its prestige.[38]

The burgeoning of reserve forces administration has not been an unalloyed menace to the Guard. Like the broadening of federal responsibility for the Guard, to which it is of course related, this development is accompanied by compensatory advantages. Though they naturally strive to subject the Guard to their control, the offices of reserve administration in the Pentagon also have an interest in protecting its existence. In general, they have developed in response to pressures from Congress and the ROA for enlarged representation of reserve interests within the Defense Department. When occupied by men of kindly disposition toward the Guard, they can be of help to it.

Threats to its autonomy constitute only one dimension of the Cold War's danger to the Guard. More fundamental is the challenge to its federal reserve role, a challenge that has grown as the atomic age has evolved. The issue of readiness has plagued the Guard throughout the Cold War years. Because of the repeated failure of Congress to enact UMT or a substitute that might assure trained manpower for the Guard, it depended until 1958 almost entirely on recruits who received no basic training. The dangers of this situation to the Guard were demonstrated by the Korean War. Within five days after the invasion of South Korea, Congress hastily suspended the Guard's protective clause to allow the President to order all members and units of the reserve components to active duty. The flimsiness of the Guard's guarantee of a front-line role was thus revealed at imponderable damage to its prestige. Eight divisions, three regimental combat teams, and 714 company-size units of the Army Guard, as well as two light bomber wings, nineteen fighter wings, and one tactical reconnaissance wing of the Air Guard, were eventually mobilized, but it took seven to nine months to prepare the divisions for combat.[39] In 1957 the readiness issue was eased by the Army's requiring Guard recruits to take six months of active duty. Notwithstanding this palliative, the rapid advance in the technology of warfare continued to jeopardize the Guard. All of the reserves were threatened by a trend toward emphasis on forces in being, while the Army reserve forces, including the Guard, were threatened additionally by de-emphasis of ground forces either in being or in reserve. The immediate result of these developments was an attempt by the Department of Defense to cut the strength of the Army Guard. These challenges to its military role present the Guard with a problem unique in its experience. For the first time, heightened national awareness of military need does not work automatically to the Guard's advantage. The Guard must prove that it can help satisfy that need.

III: Growth of the NGA

The response of the Guard to the worsening of its environment is reflected primarily in the sophisticated development of its political organization. Through the modern NGA the Guard has fully mobilized its political strength. Its annual expenditures jumped from $62,519 in 1948 to $198,000 in 1952, $336,000 in 1955, and $464,500 in 1957. Its activities are managed no longer by officers of the Association receiving little or no salary but by a professional staff headed by an executive assistant (to the president), general counsel, and public relations director. In all, twenty-five employees draw an annual payroll of $125,000. In 1959 the NGA moved into a $2 million headquarters at the foot of Capitol Hill, construction of which was financed largely by the membership. Not only are all of the Guard's active officers regularly enrolled in the Association, but retired officers also are organized in an "old Guard" in order to increase the financial and political resources of the organization and assure its continuity in case of mobilization.

This growth is not wholly attributable to the demands of the Cold War. To some extent it represents simply the natural development of the organization that General Walsh launched in 1944. New staff members were added as the organization acquired a stable income and a financial reserve. On the other hand, only a full-time staff could possibly handle the number and variety of problems that are involved in contemporary defense of the Guard's interests. By 1949 the demands of the NGA were so great that General Walsh resigned as adjutant general of Minnesota to spend full time in the Washington office. General Reckford's activity in the NGA began to diminish soon after that, and only by drawing on the assistance of personnel in the National Guard Bureau was General Walsh able to handle the problems that preceded passage of the Armed Forces Reserve Act of 1952. In January, 1953, a member of the Senate Armed Services Committee staff was hired to handle legislation for the NGA. The other principal staff members, both of whom had served in the National Guard Bureau, were added in 1955 and 1958. The decision to employ a public relations man was a direct outgrowth of the training controversy in 1957, during which the Guard suffered an unusually bad press.[40]

In 1948 the NGA began, through the adjutants general, to collect dues of $5.00, $7.50, and $10.00 from individual Guard officers. Only 48 per cent of the eligible members joined that year, leaving finances in so unstable a condition that there was talk of closing the Washington office. Prodded by Major General Leo M. Boyle, the adjutant general of Illinois and membership chairman of the NGA, the adjutants general managed by 1953 to push the enrollment figure to virtually 100 per cent, where it has remained. It is standard practice for the adjutants general to require payment of NGA dues along with an application for a commission in the Guard. From 48,000 Guard officers in 1959 the NGA received $259,735. At the 1959 convention dues were raised to $7.00, $10.00, and $20.00 to meet rising costs of operation.

Indoctrination of the membership has become a major concern of the modern NGA. For several years General Walsh delivered lengthy annual reports, descendants of the expansive discourse of 1944, in which he repeated his highly partisan version of the Guard's political and military history. Since 1947 dogma has been dispensed through the *National Guardsman,* official monthly publication of the NGA. Pamphlets and various symbolic devices also have been used to stimulate loyalty to the Guard and its Association. Since 1950 an NGA distinguished service medal has been awarded annually to one or more senior Guard officers, usually those with records of distinguished service to the NGA, although in 1955 pressure from New York produced a medal for General O'Ryan, in recognition, presumably, of his record as a division commander in World War I. One non-Guardsman has received the medal—General Lewis B. Hershey, the Director of Selective Service.

The cohesiveness of the NGA is rated highly on Capitol Hill and in the Pentagon. "They're disciplined," "they stick together," they're very clannish,"

"I can't remember when they've been divided"—so run the comments of congressmen, Army officers, and civil servants who have watched and worked with the Guard. Officers who appear for the Guard on Capitol Hill and in the Reserve Forces Policy Board or Section Five Committees generally come prepared with an NGA position and stick to it. This solidarity is achieved despite the fact that several potential conflicts of interest exist within the Guard. The NGA might divide between the adjutants general, who have traditionally been the conservators of state control, and division commanders, who have often been more amenable to federal control. Or it might divide into Army and Air Force factions. Or, most serious of all, it might divide North against South (that is, commanders of units not racially segregated against commanders of segregated units). Internal conflicts have in fact occasionally disturbed the Guard during the Cold War. In 1948 some Air Guard officers, imbued with loyalty to the Air Force and indifferent to the niceties of the militia clause, sided with the Air Force in support of the Gray Board report. In 1957 one division commander testified before the House Armed Services Committee in opposition to the NGA stand on the Army's training directive. In 1952-1953 the NGA suffered a serious sectional schism over whether to seek a federal law that would authorize the Guard to procure men through Selective Service. The proposal was pushed hard by New York, the NGA's traditional renegade, with some support from other northern states. Opposed to it was the South, led by General Reckord with his customary intransigence. Though a majority of the NGA Executive Council favored the proposal, opposition was so bitter that it had to be dropped.[41] The controversy split the NGA badly, producing threats from contenders on both sides to quit the Association, but scant knowledge of the trouble appears to have spread outside the Guard. At such moments of stress, the NGA is sustained by the traditional loyalty of Guardsmen to the Guard. This loyalty helps to account for the perpetuation of the NGA through many years of weak direction. It also helps to explain its recent success in obtaining devoted leadership, first in General Walsh and after 1957 in his hand-picked successor, Major General William H. Harrison, the adjutant general of Massachusetts. Finally, the loyalty of its members helps to account for the ability of the Guard both to minimize the number and intensity of its internal quarrels and to keep private such quarrels as it has. The sources of this loyalty are not precisely identifiable, though it is probable that the military and patriotic character of the Guard accounts for it in part. As members of a military organization with a patriotic purpose, Guardsmen not only stick together in support of their interests but do so with self-righteousness born of confidence that what is good for the Guard is good for the country. A defensive mentality also has helped to cement the organization, especially during the Cold War. This attitude has been cultivated by NGA presidents, who habitually denounce even the mildest of Pentagon moves as attempts to "destroy us." Impending martyrdom has become the Guard's normal state. Solidarity on political issues seems to follow as a consequence.

The techniques of the NGA during the Cold War have been the standard lobbying techniques. (It should be noted that technically, according to the interpretation of the Justice Department, the NGA is not a lobby; it is not required to register under the Regulation of Lobbying Act.) The NGA relies on personal contacts with congressmen in Washington; letters, telegrams, and phone calls from the grass roots; and propaganda. The skill with which the Guard has used these techniques, as well as the excellence of its grass-roots resources, distinguishes it from many other lobbies.

The NGA's personal contacts in the Capitol were greatest when General Walsh was running its office. After the NGA moved to headquarters on Capitol Plaza in 1953, congressional offices were only a four-minute walk away. The walk and some conversation on the Hill were part of the General's daily routine. After he left in 1957, the Guard's contacts in Congress considerably diminished, although the executive assistant of the NGA retained some advantages of personal acquaintance on the Hill from six years' service as a member of the Senate Armed Services Committee staff. His experience as a congressional staff member also has contributed to the sophistication of the NGA's techniques. The NGA has not, like some other lobbies, fallen into the error of the stereotyped telegram. Its pressures on Congress have been highly personalized. When the NGA testifies before a congressional committee, its witnesses are likely to include adjutants general from states represented on the committee, although care is exercised that only the more able adjutants general make these appearances. Members of the professional staff avoid appearing as witnesses themselves.

The NGA's reliance on personal, grass-roots pressures on Congress is not new. What is new is the systematic way in which these pressures are applied. Defense of the Guard's interests has become a methodical process planned at NGA headquarters and pursued through calculated exploitation of the Guard's political resources. How this process works is illustrated by the following excerpt from the NGA operations plan that was developed at the time of the six-months' training controversy:

Recent actions and proposals by the Department of Defense make it clear that the Department is prepared to make a final and determined effort to reduce the National Guard in strength and relegate it to a secondary position in the military reserve estab-lishment. The most critical proposal, that which would make six months active duty training a condition of National Guard enlistment, is now awaiting approval of the Secretary of Defense. While the National Guard is willing and anxious to accept a workable plan to increase the mobilization readiness of its units, it does not feel that the six months program can be successful and, if it is imposed on the Army National Guard, the result will be a drastic reduction in strength in the next year.

It is apparent that the Department of Defense is of a mind to test the political strength of the National Guard Association of the United States and force through its proposals, and thereby reduce the strength and effectiveness of the Army National Guard. Aware, as we are, that the Department of Defense is determined to put into effect these proposals despite the opposition of the National Guard Association of the United States, it is imperative that the Association take immediate and constructive action in two areas—legislative (political) action, and public relations. Purpose of the action is to force re-consideration of the six months proposal, or to delay finalizing the proposal until Congressional appeal may be made to protect the status of the Army National Guard. It is recommended that the following actions be taken by the National Guard Association and the Adjutants General Association:

a. [That] a statement be issued immediately by General Walsh, citing the effect of the proposal on the Army National Guard, expressing concern of the entire National Guard over the proposal, and announcing that an emergency meeting of Adjutants General and senior Guard Commanders will be held in Washington on January 23, 1957, to consider implications of the proposal.

b. That the Adjutants General and Division Commanders be briefed at a session at Old Point Comfort on the night of January 22nd by General Jones, on armory construction problems, and by General Sage on the training and recruiting problems.

c. That the same group come to Washington on January 23rd for an emergency meeting, to be given the widest possible publicity.

d. That following the morning meeting on January 23rd, the individual General Officers contact their various Congressional representatives and express to them their grave concern over the future of the Guard and prompt a flood of inquiries by Members of the Congress to the Department of the Army and Department of Defense.

e. That immediately a number of key Governors wire key officials in the Executive Branch of the Government, expressing concern and requesting explanations and assurance that finalizing proposals affecting the Army National Guard will be delayed for further study.

f. That continued inquiries from Congressional, State and community sources be made regarding specific armory projects.

g. That the National Guard Association institute and continue an aggressive political action and public relations campaign, in a determined effort to protect the status of the Army National Guard.

h. [That] a letter [be sent] from General Walsh to each member of Congress, citing the concern of the National Guard over the proposed six months training restriction.

i. [That] a Senator and Representative rise in the Congress and call attention to the concern of the National Guard over the effect of the proposed Department of Defense action.[42]

New to the NGA, in addition to the systematization of its techniques, is the broadening of those techniques to include propaganda. Before 1944 the NGA published virtually nothing other than its convention proceedings. Since General Walsh's presidency, the NGA has been much concerned with the problem of public persuasion, though its staff did not include a public relations specialist until 1958. General Walsh was his own public relations man, untiring in repetition of the Guard's history to congressional committees. He also viewed the *National Guardsman* as a propaganda vehicle: besides circulating among the NGA membership, the magazine has made its way since 1948 into the office of every congressman. In 1954 the NGA's committee on public relations issued a brief history of the Guard in book form, and in 1955 it issued an attractive pamphlet, "Know Your National Guard," which has had several printings. Since the hiring of a public relations man, the NGA's propaganda output has noticeably increased. Speeches have been provided for use of Guard commanders throughout the country, and an occasional brochure is issued to bolster the Guard's position. The NGA has begun to sponsor essay contests for high school students, offering substantial cash prizes. Its public relations budget has not been large, however. An auditor's accounting of NGA expenditures in 1959 showed an outlay of only $6,459.81 for public relations purposes (not including the public relations man's salary, $120,358 that was spent on the *National Guardsman*, or expenditures for guests at the NGA convention).[43]

The need for propaganda activity by the NGA has been mitigated by the functioning of the public information office in the National Guard Bureau. The purpose of the Bureau's program is recruiting, but it does not require a very broad interpretation of that purpose to justify advertising devices that create a favorable "public image" for the Guard. The million-dollar recruiting campaign that was conducted by the Bureau in 1947 and 1948 featured a series of full-page advertisements in *Life, Look, Collier's,* and the *Saturday Evening Post* that exploited the patriotic symbolism of the citizen soldier. In this period General Walsh participated in selection of the agency to handle the Bureau's account. The public relations budget of the Bureau subsequently was reduced to about $300,000 a year, eliminating mass-circulation advertising; but TV and radio commercials have continued, with themes broad enough to impress the general public. Through the Bureau are planned annual musters and alerts of the Guard for public relations purposes. From it came the most favored item of NGA propaganda, a prosy pastiche of historical symbolism entitled "I Am the Guard." The public relations program of the Bureau has consistently been aided by donations of media space and time for public services purposes.

The NGA's lobbying techniques and propaganda appeals reflect its purpose to exploit and perpetuate the environmental advantages that the Guard has traditionally enjoyed. Specifically, this purpose is reflected in: (1) exploitation of the Guard's state ties, (2) propagandizing of the Guard's value as a federal military force, and (3) propagandizing of the citizen soldier symbol.

Its foundation in the states has become the prime political asset of the Guard. NGA propaganda dwells heavily on the theme of the Guard's dual status, explaining the practical and theoretical merits of a system that places the Guard under command of the states in peacetime. In the Cold War years the Guard's best friends in Congress have been southerners and former governors. The influence of these groups in the Appropriations and Armed Services Committees has been of great help to the Guard, giving it security against attempts by the executive branch to subject it completely to federal control or radically reduce its size.

The NGA has recently found a new and valuable source of strength in the governors. Despite its foundation in the states, the Guard had never, before 1958, received much organized help from the governors. A speech was made on its behalf at the Governors' Conference in 1944. Subsequent Conferences passed perfunctory resolutions about it, and in 1948 the executive committee of the Conference condemned the Gray Board report in perfervid language. None of this, however, indicated a very lively interest in the Guard. From 1946 through 1957 it was barely mentioned in the official publication of the Council of State Governments. Professor Riker, writing in 1957, even ventured that the states might be glad to get rid of the Guard if only the federal government would make them an offer.[44] Such a notion would have seemed less credible in 1958, when threatened cuts in both the unit and numerical strength of the Guard brought the governors to life in its defense. The controversy of that year engaged their attention as a matter of course, because federal law provides that "no change in the branch, organization, or allotment of a [National Guard] unit located entirely within a state may be made without the approval of its governor." But the governors would not have responded as vigorously as they did if NGA headquarters had not decided that they should. The NGA's executive assistant had been eying the governors for several years as a potential source of help. In 1958 his hopes were rewarded when several months of gubernatorial activity on behalf of the Guard helped to save it from both of the threatened cuts. The problems of the Guard were a major topic of discussion at the 1958 Governors' Conference. Two strongly worded resolutions were passed in its support, and a special committee on Guard affairs was formed whose members visited Washington to aid on the spot in the Guard's defense. They were instrumental in obtaining a House resolution that called for maintaining the Army Guard at a strength of 400,000. The committee has continued in existence, a convenient vehicle for assistance to the NGA and an outlet for its propaganda.

Only slightly less prominent than states' rights as a theme of NGA propaganda is the value of the Guard as a federal reserve force. This theme was intensified in 1958, when cuts in the Guard were threatened. The NGA, which has usually been concerned more with political than with military strategy, then became a devoted exponent of the limited-war doctrine. Statements of NGA officials before congressional committees, as well as NGA brochures and speeches, warned of the dangers to national security in reduction of ground forces. They also stressed the potential role of the Guard in home defense in case of nuclear attack.

The citizen soldier is perhaps the handiest theme of NGA propaganda because the most readily symbolized. The reader of NGA literature can expect with confidence to be met by a stolid minuteman, his musket in hand, his triangular hat juxtaposed with square jaw. In 1959 the NGA was collecting money for a minuteman statue for its headquarters, and studying the possibility of decorating its "hall of the states" with busts of United States presidents, beginning with Washington, who have been militiamen.

The NGA's propaganda efforts clearly reflect the adverse changes in its environment. In an earlier day, the Guard's public did not have to be reminded of the value of states' rights or the virtues of the citizen soldier. Before the age of the airplane and the missile, the ground reservist did not have to rationalize his role.

IV: Tests of NGA Influence

The major tests of the Guard's influence have come since 1951. Pressures for change in reserve policies have been constantly at work since then, stemming variously from Congress, the Department of Defense, and reserve interest groups besides the Guard. In the face of these pressures, the Guard has been a steady and sometimes frank defender of the status quo. "All the Guard needs," General Reckord told Congress in 1951, ". . . is to be left alone."[45] The plea was futile; far from being left alone, the Guard has been repeatedly disturbed. The results of the Guard's defensive activity in this period illuminate the contemporary dimensions of its power.

In general, the responses of the NGA to developments since 1951 have been cautious and limited, though the intensity of NGA activity and the hyperbole that often accompanies it obscure this fact. The NGA as a rule has committed its strength only on issues that clearly engage the immediate interests of the Guard. It committed itself most heavily in the controversy of 1957 with the Army over the six-month training directive and in the controversy of 1958 with the Defense Department over the proposed reduction in Guard strength. These controversies involved specific issues of manifest import to the Guard. The NGA's habit of caution is best illustrated by its reaction to the Defense Reorganization Plan in 1958. While indicating distrust of the plan and assailing the principle of centralization of power, the NGA did not announce formal opposition. It did ask successfully for amendments that would protect the National Guard Bureau. The same caution is illustrated, though ambiguously, by the attitude of the NGA toward the Armed Forces Reserve Act of 1952 and the Reserve Forces Act of 1955. Neither of these Acts promised anything that the Guard was eager to obtain. Neither was in any sense initiated by it. Both were significant primarily as measures for improvement of other reserve components and, as such, represented a threat to the interests of the Guard; yet the NGA did not seriously attempt to kill either one. It was mainly concerned to exorcise from both any language that might undermine its state status or its front-line role. However, it did oppose the Armed Forces Reserve Act before the Senate Armed Services Committee in May, 1952, after having endorsed its passage by the House seven months earlier. Proponents of the bill, who had been hailing it as a "magna carta" for the Reserves, were furious. The Reserve Officers' Association charged that the NGA was acting out of simple, self-interested malice. In fact, the primary aim of the NGA appears to have been not defeat of the bill but inclusion of a blanket draft exemption for enlistees in the Guard. In late 1951 and early 1952 the Guard had begun to suffer from an acute shortage of strength, in part because of a provision in the Universal Military Training and Service Act of 1951 that discouraged the Selective Service System's extralegal practice of deferring all enlistees in the Guard, even those who joined after the age of eighteen and a half. Because its strength was falling far short of its fiscal year 1952 program, the Guard received an extraordinary verbal and fiscal beating in the spring of 1952 from the House Appropriations Committee, which cut $66.7 million from its budget request. The NGA's sudden opposition to the Armed Forces Reserve Act appears to have been a response to this situation rather than to the content of the bill itself.[46] It is the only action in the 1950's that suggests a profligate use of NGA strength.

The NGA has been reluctant to redefine the interests of the Guard in order to accommodate them to environmental demands, but in self-defense it has made several attempts at accommodation. The first was the controversial proposal for a draft of men into the Guard. Despite the division this had caused within the NGA in 1953, it was officially proclaimed as policy in 1954, with the careful proviso that inductees should serve in the Guard only with the consent of the governors. Preparation of the National Reserve Plan by the Defense Department had made some declaration by the NGA advisable. Though a draft would have greatly increased federal control over the Guard, it at least offered the advantage of lodging control over its manpower procurement in the friendly hands of Congress and the Selective Service System. Again, in anticipation of Defense Department action, the NGA late in 1956 advanced a proposal that its recruits undergo training in two periods of three months each during consecutive summers. An accommodation of another sort was attempted by the NGA in 1958, when it began claiming a "recovery" mission for the Guard. Arguing against the proposed decrease in Guard strength, it summoned the image of a country ruined by nuclear attack and deprived of a federal government, leaving only the Guard, under command of the governors, to restore order. Until 1958 the NGA had been adamant about nothing so much as opposition to a wartime civil defense role for the Guard. Hints of a home defense mission, emanating from the Defense Department in the winter of 1953-1954, had brought a threat of "war" from General Walsh.[47] His retirement in 1957 made possible the change in 1958. An advantage of this accommodation was that it facilitated political support for the Guard from the governors.

The Guard's efforts to combat an unfavorable environment have met with mixed sucess. The NGA has demonstrated an impressive ability to eliminate or reduce specific threats to the Guard, but it has not been able to arrest, or even clearly to retard, the environmental trends from which threats to the Guard's interests stem. The evidence for this proposition is largely of a negative sort, for, as has been stated, the NGA has generally limited itself to the pursuit of specific defensive goals. Presumably it is not able to do any more than it attempts to do. But the point may be illustrated additionally by the fact that the NGA was unable, though willing, to assist the Army in combatting the post-1953 reductions in ground forces. In 1955, as the Army began suffering under the impact of the "New Look," Chief of Staff Matthew B. Ridgway confidentially appealed to General Walsh for political help on the supposition, according to General Walsh's diary notes, that the NGA was "the only agency that was strongly organized, thoroughly disciplined, and had the strength, influence, and potency to undertake the mission. . . ."[48] Ridgway's successor, Maxwell D. Taylor, continued conversations with General Walsh on the subject. The Guard was no less interested than the Army in combatting the "New Look" philosophy, which, by emphasizing air power, threatened to relegate the Army to a subordinate role in combat and the Guard to a role in home defense. There is no evidence, however, that the Guard was able to do anything for the Army on this issue. Sometimes, with a phone call to the Hill, it has helped the Army expedite a piece of legislation, but on major issues of military policy its influence does not extend beyond the sphere of the Guard's immediate interest. Even though it could not help to prevent cuts in the Army, the Guard was successful in preventing cuts in its own forces in 1958. Not only did it persuade Congress to appropriate funds for 400,000 Army Guardsmen (instead of 360,000 asked by the Administration), but it also obtained language making maintenance of 400,000 men mandatory upon the executive branch.

The NGA has not been able to halt the steady broadening of federal authority over the Guard. When the Army announced the requirement of six-months training for Guard recruits, the NGA was able, through an appeal to Congress, to delay the effective date of the directive by nine months and also to obtain an informal guarantee of Guard strength. This was a solid testimonial to its effectiveness, but that should not obscure the basic victory of the Army. Sometimes the NGA has not even tried to combat new extensions of federal power. In December, 1955, the Defense Department announced that Guard recruits who entered the six-month program (some were doing so voluntarily) must undergo training in a federal status rather than a militia status. General Walsh announced that the NGA would fight the order, but, finding himself without support in the NGA for the fight, he yielded to the Department.[49]

The Guard's attempts at accommodation of its interests have been less successful than its more forthright defensive efforts. The Defense Department ignored its proposals for a training program in 1956. Its proposal for a draft of men into the Guard, never pushed by the NGA leadership, did not receive serious consideration on Capitol Hill. When a draft for reserve service was proposed by the Defense Department in 1955, Congress rejected it. The idea had been no more palatable when it issued from the NGA. Nor did the argument for a recovery mission appreciably improve the Guard's position. At most it stimulated additional support from the governors, and hence from Congress, where the Guard's strength was not in doubt. It did not relieve pressure at its source in the executive branch. These attempts at accommodation illustrate the Guard's need to associate its own position with the interests of actual or potential allies. "Recovery" would be a rewarding accommodation only if there existed in the executive branch an influential group with an interest in promoting development of the Guard as a civil defense force. Independent policy proposals are difficult for the Guard also because of the monopoly exercised by the Defense Department over the channels of military policy formulation. Even minor items of legislation desired by the NGA must be cleared by the Defense Department. The Guard is condemned to perpetual defense. Opportunities for offense have been virtually closed to it.

The results of NGA activity are, of course, not the only criteria by which its power must be judged. The problem remains of assessing the threats that its potential opposition may have forestalled. After the Gray Board report of 1948, neither the state status of the Guard nor its federal reserve role was directly and overtly challenged. There can be little doubt that any such challenges would have been futile. That these interests have been secured simply by the influence of the NGA is doubtful, however. The Guard's most basic interests have continued to be buttressed by the complementary interests of its allies—by the interest of the states and Congress itself in perpetuating the Guard's dual status and by the interest of the Army in perpetuating its combat role.

State interests in the Guard are not as strong as they were before World War II, when use of the Guard in labor riots was common. Though governors once were said to be strongly attached to the Guard as their "private little army" (a phrase long favored by the Guard's critics), many have become so busy that they rarely see their adjutants general. The expense of the Guard, though small in relation to federal expenditures, is regarded as burdensome by some of the states. For the sake of economy, Governor William G. Stratton of Illinois decided not to reactivate the 44th Division when it was released from federal service after the Korean war. Nevertheless, the Guard still serves state interests in times of domestic disaster. Floods, fires, hurricanes, prison riots, and the like cause it to be used fairly often. Governor Orval E. Faubus of Arkansas found it useful in preventing integration at Little Rock High School in 1957. In 1958, at the urging of the NGA, the governors seized upon it as a civil defense force. Their interest in retaining the Guard remains sufficiently strong to be of major assistance to the NGA.

Congress also remains an ally of the Guard, both because of the continuing strength of states' rights sentiment within it and because the Guard continues to serve the institutional interests of Congress vis-à-vis the Defense Department. On issues involving the state status of the Guard, the NGA needs to exercise little or no persuasion on Congress. When the NGA cries "federalization," Congress responds. So true is this that the NGA tends to cry "federalization" frequently, using it as a synonym for "help." In 1949, when the NGA suspected an attempt by the Air Force to absorb the Air Guard through language in the Army and Air Force Authorization Act, it obtained from Congress a statutory proviso that nothing in the Act should be construed as modifying the Air Guard's status. When it opposed the Armed Forces Reserve Act of 1952, the NGA condemned it as "one more attempt to federalize the National Guard." In response, the Senate Armed Services Committee explicitly declared in its report of the bill that nothing in the law was intended to alter the status of the Guard. In 1955 the House Armed Services Committee changed the departmental draft of the Reserve Forces Act to provide that reserve obligors should be "transferred" to the Guard rather than "assigned" to it "for training"—a change intended to assure that such men would form part of the Guard in its state status. The committee also removed from the bill a provision that would have prohibited the states from employing the Guard during a federal emergency. Members of Congress are sometimes more zealous than the NGA itself in protecting state interests with respect to the Guard. The NGA has throughout its history shown a willingness to compromise state interests either on its own initiative, in order to gain federal benefits, or under pressure from the executive branch, in order to protect itself against adverse actions. Thus the NGA proclaimed support of a draft for the Guard, but within Congress there was strong opposition to it. Similarly, a member of

Congress in 1948 warned General Walsh against the principle of a common commission for the Guard and the Reserves, which the Guard was supporting. Incorporated in the Armed Forces Reserve Act of 1952, the common commission has considerably facilitated extension of federal control over the Guard. Though southerners and former governors are the staunchest defenders of the Guard's state status in Congress, a sensitivity to state interests with respect to the Guard is inevitably shared in some degree by a large majority of congressmen. Beyond their sensitivity to state interests as such, there still exists among congressmen, northerners as well as southerners, an attachment to the Guard because it serves the value of decentralization of military power. Its service has become largely symbolic, since the power represented by the Guard in terms of military expenditures, command responsibilities, or any other criterion is relatively insignificant; but Congress still likes to manifest its respect if only to a symbol.[50]

Because it tends to enlarge the scope of congressional power with respect to issues of military policy that involve the Guard, the existence of the Guard as a state force serves the interests not only of the states, as reflected in Congress, but also the interests of Congress as an institution vis-à-vis the Defense Department. The idea that the Guard "belongs" to Congress has endured. In the training controversy of 1957 the real "winner" was neither the Army nor the Guard, but Congress, which exercised informal powers as a mediator. The executive branch more or less openly acknowledges the special interest of Congress in all of the reserve components and the Guard in particular. In 1958, when Congress was threatening to place strength floors under the Army Guard, the Army Reserves, the active Army, and the Marines, the White House sought removal of the floors with the promise that reserve strengths would be maintained at the figures appropriated for by Congress, but it would make no such commitment with respect to the regular forces.[51] Despite objections from the White House, Congress enacted the floors for the Army Guard and the Army Reserves. In 1959 it removed the floor from the Reserves but continued it for the Guard. "[T]he logic behind our action in this case," explained the chairman of the House Defense Appropriations Subcommittee, "was that the National Guard is more of a state organization than is the Army Reserve. . . ."[52]

By providing Congress with information and ideas, the NGA facilitates and exploits the interest of Congress in the Guard. The proposal of the strength floor in 1958 came from NGA headquarters. Information from the NGA provides the basis for congressional inquiries to the Defense Department and the Bureau of the Budget. Questioning the Secretary of Defense in 1959 with the help of data from the NGA, Representative Porter Hardy angrily complained, ". . . that is the only way we can get a basis on which to ask you people questions, because you don't give us anything except what supports your position."[53] It has long been part of the theory of American civil-military relations that one role of the citizen soldier is to provide Congress with an alternate channel of advice on questions of military policy. This theory, like the theory of decentralization of military power through the Guard, is scarcely operative today in realistic fashion; yet there remains in Congress an attachment to the Guard as a channel of information if not advice—a pipeline into the Pentagon whose flow is not regulated by the Secretary of Defense or anyone responsible to him. This flow facilitates the performance of Congress' critical functions.

For all of these reasons, Congress protects the dual status of the Guard. On other kinds of issues it is less responsive to the NGA. In the face of opposition from church, farm, labor, education, and women's groups, it declined in 1952, as earlier, to adopt universal military training, which would have provided the Guard with a source of trained manpower. More than once it refused to provide a draft exemption for all enlistees in the Guard. In 1955 it failed to include the Guard in the six-month training program authorized by the Reserve Forces Act, after attachment of anti-segregation amendments made passage of provisions on the Guard impossible. Though this result was not at the time unwelcome to the NGA, it proved to be highly detrimental to the interests of the Guard. Congressional default invited the Army's training directive in 1957, which constituted a radical assertion of executive authority over the Guard. Many members of Congress, it would appear, reacted coolly when the Guard opposed the directive. The chairman of the House Armed Services Committee proposed initially to settle the controversy with a concurrent resolution that would have provided for an eleven-week training program and maintenance of the Army Guard at a strength of 405,000. Thirteen days after conceiving this plan, according to General Walsh's account, he abandoned it "for the simple reason that he doubted he could obtain the necessary number of votes. . . ."[54] Thus group interests conflicting with those of the Guard, or perhaps Congressional conceptions of a national interest, circumscribe the action of Congress on behalf of the Guard. To the detriment of the Guard's interests, though not over its active opposition, Congress pays much friendly attention to the other reserve components who are the Guard's competitors. In fact, it has sometimes seemed more eager to help the Reserves than to help the Guard, apparently for the reason that the Reserves have been more badly in need of help. The various Defense Department offices of reserve administration were established on a statutory basis in 1952 at the urging of the ROA and despite protests from the Defense Department and the NGA.

Comparable to the assistance of Congress in maintaining the Guard's dual status is the assistance of the Army in maintaining its federal reserve role. In the face of a threat to their common role as ground combat forces, the Army and the Guard have joined more firmly than at any time since the turn of the century (though conflicts have continued between them on issues involving the degree of Army control over the Guard). When the authors of the "New Look" were contemplating conversion of the Guard into a home defense force in the winter of 1953-1954 the Army fought the idea within the Pentagon while the NGA attacked it publicly. General Walsh attributed success to the "united front" they presented.[55] His judgment seems to be supported by the remarks of Assistant Secretary of Defense

John A. Hannah to a convention of the adjutants general in February, 1954. Hints of plans for its conversion to a home defense role had come to the Guard through Hannah's speeches. The adjutants general therefore were startled when he addressed them with plans for improving the combat readiness of the Guard. "I do not know as I have changed my mind," he replied to a question. "I have an increasing appreciation of the fact that it is so difficult as to be almost impossible for the Army to come up with an adequate reserve program that isn't based on the National Guard."[56] Ignoring executive discipline, the Army in 1958 publicly asked Congress to maintain a 400,000-man Guard, while privately the Secretary of the Army was exhorting the NGA staff to greater lobbying efforts. The Army's declaration assuaged the normal congressional reluctance to alter presidential recommendations on force levels.[57]

The willing support that the Guard receives from Congress and the Army lightens the burden of persuasion that falls on the NGA. To emphasize the value of the Guard's allies is not, however, to detract from the assets that the Guard brings to these alliances. The NGA's reputation for power facilitates the Army's support for the Guard inside the Pentagon. Under pressure from the Department of Defense to take actions adverse to the Guard, the Army can resist on the grounds of political infeasibility. Congress needs no excuse to act on the Guard's behalf, but the alert and aggressive performance of the NGA animates the functioning of their natural alliance.

V: Conclusion

Despite the development of its political organization, the success of the Guard continues to depend to an important extent on its capacity to serve values and interests in its environment—that is, on what were termed at the outset its intrinsic attributes of power.

This dimension of its power is seriously jeopardized, however. The problem for the Guard is not only that the strength of states' rights and anti-militarist values and interests has diminished. Another major problem of the Guard in the Cold War has been the limited capacity of its allies to help it. Congress at one time dominated the Guard's sphere of interest. This was true in 1916 and 1920, when congressional decisions on major issues of military policy resolved those issues in favor of the Guard. Though Congress can still protect the dual status of the Guard, neither Congress nor the Army can provide equal assurance that it will be maintained at a high level of strength.

The Guard's protective clause, itself jealously protected by the NGA, remains in the U.S. Code, declaring it "essential that the strength and organization of the National Guard . . . as an integral part of the first line defenses of the nation be at all times maintained and assured." It does not say how much strength must be maintained and assured. Congress demonstrated in 1958 the requisite will and authority to enforce a floor under the Guard, but this victory for the Guard could not obscure the fact that development of executive pressure for a reduction in its strength constituted a major blow to its interests, one that the Army could not prevent. In the long run the advantages in any budgetary issue between Congress and the President lie with the President. The executive branch is the planner, proposer, and executor of the budget; the President is commander-in-chief. Even after the floor under the Guard had been set by Congress and carried out by the President, the weight of precedent continued to favor the President's position that he should be free, as commander-in-chief, to determine force levels within ceilings set by Congress. A substantial and influential minority of congressmen on the Appropriations and Armed Services Committees agreed in 1958 with the President's position on this constitutional issue.[58] The Guard's victory on the question was attributable in large part to special circumstances prevailing at that time. The proposal to cut the Guard was but one among a series of proposed reductions in ground forces. Because the Administration had previously justified cuts in active ground forces on the basis of increases in the reserves, it exposed its expertise to congressional skepticism when it proposed cuts in both at the same time. By placing a floor under the Guard, Congress registered its protest against the whole policy of reducing ground forces. It also placed a floor under the Army Reserves, and it voted extra funds not only for the Guard and the Reserves but also the active Army and the Marines. The Guard enjoyed another circumstantial advantage in the terms of the memorandum of understanding that had ended its dispute with the Army in 1957. Reflecting the interests of Congress, this memorandum provided that the strength of the Army Guard should be maintained through Fiscal Year 1958 at 400,000 "and thereafter at such greater or lesser strength as may be determined in annual appropriations of the Congress. . . ." It was signed by the Secretary of the Army and informally endorsed by the President and the Secretary of Defense.[59] Existence of this memorandum— not yet a year old when the reduction in the Guard was proposed—had the effect of engaging the extraordinary prestige of its author, House Armed Services Committee Chairman Carl Vinson, on the side of the Guard. The Armed Services Committee, through its Reserves Subcommittee, held hearings on the proposed cut; the full committee, at Mr. Vinson's urging, passed a strong resolution opposing it; and two committee members, delegates of Mr. Vinson, argued on the Guard's behalf before the House Appropriations Committee. The NGA owed much in 1958 to the timely support of this peculiarly powerful man.

Not only the questionable ability of Congress to protect its interests is troublesome to the Guard. So also is the danger that the institutional interest of Congress in the Guard will diminish as the Guard's relative significance for U.S. military policy declines. In 1916, by asserting a protectorate over the Guard, Congress made a substantial gain vis-à-vis the executive branch. The policy issues that involved the Guard were then the major issues of military policy. In the Cold War, however, they have become minor issues, with the result that the interests of Congress may no longer be significantly served by the exercise of its protectorate over the Guard. Though Chairman Vinson apparently welcomed a mediator's role in the Army-Guard dispute in 1957, a younger member of the Armed Services Committee, Frank C.

Osmers, complained to the NGA in 1958 about the Committee's having to spend so much time on the Guard's problems.[60] Congressmen have been increasingly occupied with issues of greater import, or at least of greater glamour, than the Guard.

These adverse developments suggest that the Guard must find new resources of strength if it is to maintain its capacity for success. However, the most obvious form of response and the one that the Guard followed in the recent past—intensification of its political activity—is scarcely practicable. The NGA is as fully organized as it can be, with 100 per cent of its potential membership enrolled and paying sizable dues. By including enlisted men in its membership (a possibility that has several times been considered and rejected), the NGA might increase its budget considerably, but it is difficult to see what more the NGA could do than it has done, except possibly increase its propaganda. NGA officials and interested observers of the NGA alike agree that it is already exploiting its political assets to the maximum. If adverse trends in its environment continue, diminishing the "intrinsic" dimension of its power, its capacity for success is therefore likely to be reduced. Not only are compensatory increases in the "acquired" dimension of its power impracticable, but they might not be efficacious. Strongly organized and highly active as the NGA is, it has not been able to prevent serious damage to the Guard's interests in the Cold War, damage that is reflected chiefly in the Guard's steady subjection to federal control and attempts by the executive branch to reduce its strength. Nevertheless, the effectiveness of the NGA on those specific issues that it has chosen to contest has sustained its reputation for influence. A few political reverses, by destroying its image of political invincibility, could significantly diminish its power, which has been based to an immeasurable (and probably great) extent on a reputation for influence that derives from its long record of political success. Throughout its early history and even down to the present, however, the Guard's success has not been fundamentally attributable to its influence.

NOTES

1. Elias Huzar, *The Purse and the Sword* (Ithaca, N. Y., 1950), p. 271.
2. Samuel P. Huntington, *The Soldier and the State* (Cambridge, Mass., 1957), p. 177.
3. Elting E. Morison (ed.), *The Letters of Theodore Roosevelt*, II, *The Years of Preparation, 1898-1900* (Cambridge, Mass., 1951), 887.
4. Memo, Lieutenant General W. S. Paul, Director of Personnel and Administration, for Deputy Chief of Staff, "Report of the Committee on Civilian Components, 'Reserve Forces for National Security,'" October 25, 1948, copy at NGA headquarters (hereafter, "Paul memo").
5. Memo, President Harry S. Truman to Secretary of Defense James Forrestal, August 12, 1948, quoted in Charles D. Story, "The Formulation of Army Reserve Forces Policy: Its Setting Amidst Pressure Group Activity," Ph.D. dissertation, University of Oklahoma, 1958, p. 225.
6. Huntington, *op. cit.*, p. 172.
7. William H. Riker, *Soldiers of the States* (Washington, D. C., 1957), p. 67. This case study in federalism is the only monograph on the Guard.
8. Francis V. Greene, "The New National Guard," *Century,* 21 (February, 1892), 483-498; War Department, Adjutant General's Office, Military Information Division, *The Organized Militia of the United States in 1896* (Washington, D. C., 1897), p. 5; and H. R. Brinkerhoff, "The Regular Army and the National Guard," *United Service,* New Series, 13 (June, 1895), 501-507.
9. *Congressional Record,* 26, 8347.

10. *Annual Reports of the Secretary of War, 1899-1903*, pp. 289-290; Root to J. C. Boyd, April 12, 1902, Box 290, Root Papers, Library of Congress.

11. Root to Redfield Proctor, December 12, 1902, January 7 and 20, 1903, Box 291, Root Papers; *Congressional Record*, Vol. 35, p. 7721, and Vol. 36, pp. 354, 395, 782; and William H. Carter, "The Organized Militia—Its Past and Future," *United Service*, Third Series, 3 (February, 1903), 789-794.

12. *Creation of the American General Staff, Personal Narrative of the General Staff System of the American Army by Major General William Harding Carter*, S. Doc. 119, 68 Cong., 1 Sess. (1924), p. 58; Morison, *op. cit.*, III, *The Square Deal, 1901-1903*, p. 507; and *War Department Annual Reports, 1908*, I, 37.

13. The negotiations between the NGA and the War Department over the Guard's pay bill are chronicled in detail in the NGA convention proceedings for 1910-1914. On the NGA's internal troubles, see File 080, "National Guard Assn. of the U. S., Meeting, 1914," Record Group 168, National Archives.

14. *Congressional Record*, Vol. 53, p. 5530.

15. Wood to E. M. House, Series II, Box 96, Woodrow Wilson Papers, Library of Congress.

16. Hugh L. Scott to John F. McGee, November 2, 1915, Scott Papers, Library of Congress; Memo, Capt. H. A. Hanigan to Chief, Division of Militia Affairs, "National Guard Convention at San Francisco," November 15, 1915, File 080, "National Guard Association, Meeting, 1915," R. G. 168, National Archives.

17. H. L. Scott to Leonard Wood, December 1, 1915, Scott Papers.

18. MS, "Woodrow Wilson and Preparedness," no date, Hay Papers, Library of Congress (hereafter "Hay memoir").

19. Albert L. Mills, Chief, Division of Militia Affairs, to W. F. Sadler, Jr., Adjutant General of New Jersey, October 9, 1914, File 011.6, "Revision of the Militia Laws (Pay Bill)," R. G. 168, National Archives.

20. Hay memoir.

21. The basic record of NGA activity is the *Proceedings* of its annual conventions. NGA headquarters in Washington has a set that is complete from 1905. Only a few records are available there or elsewhere for earlier years.

22. *Congressional Record*, Vol. 59, p. 4036, 5190, 5829-5830; U. S. Congress, Senate, *Reorganization of the Army*, Hearings before Subcommittee of the Committee on Military Affairs, 66 Cong., 1 Sess. (1919), pp. 517-518, 1803-1817, 1840-1843, 1915-1920, 1934; and John Dickinson, *The Building of an Army* (New York, 1922), ch. IX.

23. War Department General Orders No. 6, March 10, 1926; NGA Convention *Proceedings*, 1926, pp. 23-25; Memo, Chief, Militia Bureau, to the Adjutant General, "Report on H.R. 9571," February 26, 1926; and other memoranda in File 321.15 (2-24-26) R. G. 94, National Archives.

24. Paul memo.

25. E. Brooke Lee, Jr., *Politics of Our Military National Defense*, S. Doc. 274, 76 Cong., 3 Sess. (1940), p. 130.

26. NGA Convention *Proceedings*, 1944, pp. 25-170, and 1945, pp. 56-57; interview with General Walsh, April 7, 1960.

27. Memo for President, Post-War Planning Board, "Outline of Post-War Military Policy," November 24, 1942, and other memoranda by Palmer in the Palmer MSS, Library of Congress; Memo, Colonel William E. Carpenter, GSC, for Director, Special Planning Division, "Post-War Reserve Organization," January 3, 1944, File WDSSP 325 National Guard, National Archives, World War II Records Division.

28. Memo, Brigadier General John McA. Palmer for Director, Special Planning Division, "Conference on Post-War Status of the National Guard, February 28-29, 1944," March 3, 1944; and Memo, Director, Special Planning Division, for Chief of Staff, "Post-War Status of the National Guard," March 8, 1944, File WDSSP 325 National Guard, National Archives, World War II Records Division.

29. U.S. Congress, House of Representatives, *Universal Military Training*, Hearings before the Select Committee on Post-War Military Policy, 68 Cong., 2 Sess. (1945), pp. 499-501, 577.

30. Walter Millis (ed.), *The Forrestal Diaries* (New York, 1951), p. 89.

31. *Annual Report of the Chief of the National Guard Bureau, 1948*, p. 2 (this series hereafter "*CNGB Report*"); U. S. Congress, House of Representatives, *Selective Service*, Hearings, Armed Services Committee Serial No. 265, 80 Cong., 2 Sess. (1948), p. 6522; and H. Rept. 2438, 80 Cong., 2 Sess. (1948).

32. U.S. Congress, House of Representatives, *Military Establishment Appropriation Bill for 1947*, Hearings before Subcommittee of Committee on Appropriations, 79 Cong., 2 Sess. (1946), p. 1150.

33. NGA Conference *Proceedings,* 1947, p. 175; U.S. Congress, House of Representatives, *Military Establishment Appropriation Bill for 1948,* Hearings before Subcommittee of Committee on Appropriations, 80 Cong., 1 Sess. (1947), pp. 1131-1132.

34. Official diary of Major General Ellard A. Walsh, entry for October 1, 1946. This diary, which was begun by General Walsh in 1946 and kept through the close of his presidency in 1957, is at NGA headquarters. I am very grateful to him for unconditional access to it.

35. NGA Conference *Proceedings,* 1948, pp. 39-44; and *CNGB Report,* 1949, pp. 21-22.

36. Army Regulation 11-1, Dec. 31, 1956.

37. U.S. Congress, House of Representatives, *Reserve Components,* Hearings before the Committee on Armed Services, 82 Cong., 1 Sess. (1951), pp. 188, 216, 219, 326, 373-374, 475; and *National Reserve Plan,* Hearings, Armed Services Committee Serial No. 11, 84 Cong., 1 Sess. (1955), pp. 1408, 1449, 1536, 1694-1695, 2223-2234.

38. U.S. Congress, House of Representatives, *Review of the Reserve Program,* Hearings, Armed Services Committee Serial No. 22, 85 Cong., 1 Sess. (1957), pp. 665-666, 686, 692, 713, 772-773, 825; and *New York Times,* January 15, 1957, p. 1.

39. *Semiannual Report of the Secretary of Defense, January 1 to June 30, 1953,* pp. 67-68; and *Review of the Reserve Program,* Hearings, *op. cit.,* p. 706.

40. NGA Conference *Proceedings,* 1958, p. 228.

41. Walsh Diary, February 22, 1953; Transcript, Meeting of the NGA Executive Council, April 25-26, 1953, p. 327 (NGA headquarters).

42. "Presentation of Major General Ellard A. Walsh . . . at a Special Closed Meeting of the Adjutants General . . . and General Officers of the Line of the Army National Guard, Washington, D. C., 23 January 1957," MS at NGA headquarters.

43. NGA Conference *Proceedings,* 1959, pp. 227-228.

44. Riker, *op. cit.,* p. 100.

45. U.S. Congress, House of Representatives, *Full Committee Hearing on H. R. 5426,* Armed Services Committee Serial No. 49, 82 Cong., 1 Sess. (1951), p. 1968.

46. U.S. Congress, Senate, *Armed Forces Reserve Act,* Hearings before Subcommittee of Committee on Armed Services, 82 Cong., 2 Sess. (1952), p. 110; NGA Conference *Proceedings,* 1952, pp. 267, 272; U.S. Congress, House of Representatives, *Department of the Army Appropriations for 1953,* Hearings before Subcommittee of the Committee on Appropriations, 82 Cong., 2 Sess. (1952), pp. 470-477, 506-509; and H. Rept. 1685, p. 5.

47. *Time,* 63 (March 1, 1954), 18.

48. Walsh Diary, May 27, 1955.

49. *Army Times* (res. ed.), January 21, 1956, p. 2; and Walsh Diary, January 25, 1956.

50. For example, see the remarks of Representative James Devereux in U.S. Congress, House of Representatives, *Department of Defense Appropriations for 1959,* Hearings before Subcommittee of Committee on Appropriations, 85 Cong., 2 Sess. (1958), p. 1034 of volume on Advanced Research Projects Agency *et al.*

51. Interview with Bryce N. Harlow, Deputy Assistant to the President, April 13, 1960.

52. *Congressional Record,* Vol. 105 (daily ed.), p. 13797.

53. U.S. Congress, House of Representatives, *Military Posture Briefing,* Armed Services Committee Serial No. 16, 86 Cong., 1 Sess. (1959), p. 865.

54. Walsh Diary, February 5 and 18, 1957; transcript, Annual Meeting of the Adjutants General Association, 1957, NGA headquarters.

55. Walsh Diary, February 16, 1954.

56. Transcript, AGA Meeting, 1954, NGA headquarters.

57. U.S. Congress, House of Representatives, *Proposed Reduction in the Strength of the National Guard,* Hearings, Armed Services Committee Serial No. 77, 85 Cong., 2 Sess. (1958), pp. 5647-5648; interview with Brigadier General Mark H. Galusha, executive assistant, NGA, April 28, 1960.

58. Interviews with Congressman James E. Van Zandt, March 30, 1960; Congressman Robert L. F. Sikes, April 1, 1960; Robert L. Michaels of the House Defense Appropriations Subcommittee staff, April 14, 1960; and Robert W. Smart, chief counsel, House Armed Services Committee, April 14, 1960; *Congressional Record,* Vol. 105 (daily ed.), pp. 13789, 13795.

59. U.S. Congress, House of Representatives, *Action of Committee on Armed Services . . . on U.S. Army-Army National Guard Reserve Training Requirements,* Armed Services Committee Serial No. 16, 85 Cong., 1 Sess. (1957), pp. 437-439.

60. NGA Conference Proceedings, 1958, pp. 140-141.

Recent Writing in Military Politics – Foci and Corpora

BY *SAMUEL P. HUNTINGTON*

I: Introduction

IN THE 1950's a significant scholarly literature on military politics emerged in the United States. The rapidity of this development was striking. In 1952 the Social Science Research Council's newly established Committee on Civil-Military Relations Research undertook a bibliographical survey of the literature in the area between 1940 and 1952.[1] The results of that survey showed a large number of writings touching on many aspects of military affairs. As a whole, however, the writings tended to be diffuse, and to a large extent they were the product of World War II. Scholars, lawyers, and administrators whose primary and continuing interests were in other areas recorded their experiences in and reflections on the war or published studies deriving directly from their temporary activity in the military field. Individually the studies were often of a high order; only rarely, however, were they directly related to each other. Notably absent from the bibliography were the names of many of the frequent writers on military affairs in the following eight years: Osgood, Kissinger, Knorr, Janowitz, Kahn, Nitze, Kaufmann, Schelling, Hammond, Snyder, Masland, and Morton have no entries, Hilsman and Fox one each, Brodie two. Many of the categories into which the 1952 bibliography was divided and the items which they contained reflected concerns characteristic of World War II: "military government and occupation," "procurement, logistics, and transportation," martial law, legal aspects of total mobilization, and manpower mobilization. Insofar as there was a focus of interest, it was the problems of mobilization for total war. Reading through the bibliography, one is struck, however, by the heterogeneity of the literature and its lack of unity.

The outstanding aspect of the growth of social science literature in military affairs during the 1950's was the emergence of a number of distinct foci of scholarly interest and the development of reasonably substantial corpora of writings about many of these foci. The writings of any one corpus are distinguished by exactly what the earlier literature seemed to lack—a common focus and mutual relatedness. These are the hallmarks of a growing intellectual tradition. Studies do not exist in isolation but stand in an intellectually identifiable relation to earlier and later work. One can see the process of scholarship and research at work, as successive studies build upon, supplement, correct, or refute their predecessors.

The growth of the literature on the political aspects of military affairs was, of course, part of a broader development of concern over national security policy. The 1950's also saw the publication of scholarly writings dealing with many of the nonmilitary aspects of national security. This essay, however, will focus only on those writings dealing with military politics. These writings may or may not be concerned directly with problems of national security. Military politics, moreover, includes but transcends military policy, because it also encompasses non-policy-oriented studies of the nature of the military establishment and its relations with other social and political institutions.[2] A study of the role of military officers in business corporations is a study in military politics but not necessarily a study in military policy.

The foci of interest and scholarship mentioned in this bibliographical note are all concerned with the political uses of violence or with the political aspects of the management of violence. This is a common bond but a weak one. An analysis of the implications of a strategy of graduated deterrence is reasonably far removed from a study of the role of the army in Burmese politics or a study of Locke's ideas on war and peace. The first demands the logic and theory of the strategist and systems analyst, the second the perception and understanding of the student of social and political behavior, and the third the skills and insights of the historian of ideas. Each focus of study in military politics is also related to some other area of study or some other method of study. The analysis of Plato's theory of civil-military relations is a contribution to the large literature on Plato as well as to the small literature on civil-military relations. Martha Derthick's article on the National Guard in this volume should be as valuable to the student of interest groups as it is to the student of military policy. Some aspect of military politics is relevant to almost every traditional branch of political science. Yet students of the traditional branches have tended to ignore their military potentialities. The writers on interest groups have been more interested in the NAM than in the Navy League. Students of comparative politics have compared parliaments and political parties but not armies. The literature of public administration has much on the Bureau of the Budget but little on the Joint Chiefs of Staff. Students of political theory have been more concerned with ideas of how the public can control its government than with how the government can control its soldiers. A tendency to ignore the military aspect of politics once existed in international relations, but disappeared rather rapidly after World War II. Similar developments have now begun in the other branches of political science. These developments will enrich the study of both military politics and the traditional areas of concern. The multiplication and diversification of the foci of scholarly interest in military politics thus reflects its integration into the existing disciplines.

The purpose of this bibliographical essay is to give some idea of the size and diversity of the recent literature on military politics. In some areas the number of writings is so great that only a very few can be selected for inclusion, and inevitably the grounds for inclusion and exclusion are arbitrary. In cases of doubt, first priority has been given to representativeness rather than to excellence. In several instances foci or potential foci with a relatively small or even nonexistent literature have been mentioned, to draw attention to the gaps as well as the riches in the field. Selections are limited to studies produced or published in English from 1946 to the spring of 1961. The periodical literature is so large that primary emphasis is necessarily placed upon book-length works. Studies of the internal sociology of the military establishment are not included. The recent sociological literature on the military has been exhaustively surveyed and analyzed in Morris Janowitz, *Sociology and the Military Establishment* (Russell Sage, 1959). With one or two special exceptions, works dealing primarily or exclusively with World War II are also excluded because: (1) there are too many of them, and (2) the primary focus of this listing is not the conduct of war but the continuing problems of military politics in war or peace. For an excellent brief survey of the literature on World War II, the reader should consult Louis Morton, "Sources for the History of World War II," *World Politics,* 13 (April, 1961), 435-453.

PERIODICALS

Some general magazines and some scholarly journals carry articles on military politics. So also, at times, do the specialized or technical military publications, such as *Air Force, Army, Ordnance, Armor.* Only a relatively few journals, however, consciously and continuously devote attention to the area where politics and military affairs mix. Among these journals, official and unofficial, are the following:

Air University Quarterly Review
Airpower Historian
Bulletin of the Atomic Scientists
Foreign Affairs
Journal of Conflict Resolution
Journal of the Royal United Service Institution (U.K.)
Military Affairs
Military Review
Orbis
Survival (U.K.)
United States Naval Institute Proceedings
World Politics.

BIBLIOGRAPHY

Civil-Military Relations: An Annotated Bibliography, 1940-1952, prepared under the direction of the Committee on Civil-Military Relations Research of the Social Science Research Council, covers the English-language materials on the procedures and processes of policymaking for the years indicated. The "Military Library" of *Military Affairs,* quarterly publication of the American Military Institute, is a comprehensive, continuing listing of books and articles. Also extremely useful is the quarterly *Current Thought on Peace and War,* which contains brief summaries of the items included, but which unfortunately only began publication in the winter of 1960. The *Journal of Conflict Resolution* digests a select number of articles on problems of war and peace, and *Foreign Affairs* contains an annotated bibliography of books on military affairs and related areas in international politics. *International Political Science Abstracts,* published quarterly by Basil Blackwell for the International Political Science Association, includes articles from a large number of periodicals in different languages. The Department of the Army has issued many useful annotated bibliographies on special topics in military policy. These, together with other specialized bibliographies, are listed under the appropriate headings that follow.

II: Strategy and Strategic Theory

The most striking and possibly the largest corpus of writings on military affairs deals prescriptively with strategy. In this context "strategy" means the policy of the government on the size, composition, and use of its armed forces. In this sense, strategy is an element of military policy, and it should not be confused with "strategy" in the narrower sense of the direction of campaigns (in contrast to tactics) or "strategy" in the broader sense of over-all foreign and domestic policy (national strategy). The writings considered in this section are concerned primarily with the wisdom, rationality, and feasibility of alternative strategic choices. In many cases these writings also include much descriptive material of what strategy has been and how it is formulated. Writings concerned primarily with these questions, however, are listed in Sections III and IV below. By and large the studies in this section reflect a concern with what policy ought to be.

Before World War II the amount of prescriptive writing on military affairs was not only relatively small, but it was to a very high degree the product of military officers or retired military officers. One of the outstanding aspects of the post-World War II period was the extent to which the writings on strategy were the product of civilians. The civilian analysts, as two military strategists put it, "debouched" into strategy.[3] The civilian role was marked not only in terms of quantity but also in quality. After World War II no book on strategy produced by an American military officer reached the sophisticated level of analysis of the best books on strategy written by American civilians. The reasons for civilian interest undoubtedly were complex. Military officers, by definition, have to be members of one of the armed services; inevitably, they tend to analyze strategic problems through service prisms. Earlier in military history this was perfectly feasible: Mahan produced a strategy of seapower, and Douhet one of airpower. The Cold War, however, required strategies of massive retaliation, limited war, graduated deterrence. The strategic categories cut across service lines. Service doctrine couched in terms of land, sea, and air was more of a hindrance than a help in the analysis of many important strategic problems.

A civilian, on the outside, however, was free to discuss strategic issues without relating his discussion directly to service doctrine. Even where the civilians might be associated with a military service, they were still able to exercise an independent judgment and to make independent analyses of strategic problems. Many of the writings on limited war were produced by civilian strategists employed by the RAND Corporation, which did most of its work for the Air Force. Civilian writing on strategy was also encouraged by the appearance of research centers on foreign policy and international affairs at most of the major universities. Financed primarily by the great foundations, these centers made it possible for university social scientists to study strategic problems along with other foreign-policy issues. The Council on Foreign Relations also became a focal point for the study and discussion of strategic issues. Finally, British civilians and retired military men made a contribution to strategic analysis which, although small, was probably larger proportionately than their country's contribution of military power to the Anglo-American alliance.

Perhaps most important in stimulating civilian interest in strategy was the discovery by social scientists and governmental officials that the strategic questions were one subject where the distinctive skills of the social scientist were peculiarly relevant. This relevance, however, was achieved at the price of accepting the broad outlines of governmental policy. Civilian writings on foreign-policy issues in general may, in this connection, be contrasted with civilian writings on strategy. Prescriptive works on "American foreign policy" often tend to be more exhortatory, to have more passion and less tightly reasoned logic, than civilian writings on "strategy." Social scientists who are moved to the critical analysis of foreign policy normally deal with basic values, goals, and policy choices. Social scientists dealing with strategy, however, normally accept the framework of existing policy. General criticisms of the American strategy of deterrence, for instance, were seldom made by social scientists specializing in military problems. The social scientist tended to accept a deterrent strategy as "given" and to analyze the "requirements of deterrence." Strategic writing was thus more professional, more technical, more "expert," but also more limited than prescriptive writings on foreign policy in general. To the critic of deterrence most of the writing on strategy seemed to be based upon invalid assumptions. To the strategic specialist the attacks on deterrence usually seemed to be oratorical, amateurish, and lacking in analytical depth and sophistication. Given the general consensus within the American government and among the attentive elites on the necessity of a strategy of deterrence, the strategists undoubtedly performed a useful role in analyzing the best means of implementing that strategy. The relevance of much of their technical and, at times, esoteric analyses, however, depended upon the continued acceptance by the government of the assumptions upon which those analyses were based.

Compared to descriptively analytical studies, prescriptive writings on strategy have a relatively short life. They are directed to the key policy issues of the day, the character of which is shaped by a changing political environment and an even more rapidly changing technology. Even the best books on strategy are usually "dated" two years after publication.

The most frequently advanced alternative to deterrence was a system of negotiated disarmament. Until the mid-1950's most of the writings on disarmament fell outside the main stream of the writings on strategy. By 1957, however, it became clear that means of arms control, as distinguished from comprehensive disarmament, might play an important role in implementing a strategy of deterrence. Hence the civilians who had previously "debouched" into strategy now executed a turning movement and "debouched" into arms control and disarmament, areas which had previously largely been dominated by writers more inclined to pacifism than strategy.

The first significant work on the strategic problems of the nuclear age appeared in 1946—*The Absolute Weapon,* edited by Bernard Brodie and including among its authors Frederick S. Dunn, Arnold Wolfers, Percy E. Corbett, and William T. R. Fox. Significantly, it was a product of the Yale Institute of International Studies, one of the few major university research centers on international affairs established before World War II. After *The Absolute Weapon* civilian writing on strategy tended to drop off, until it received another stimulus from the Soviet acquisition of nuclear weapons, the Korean War, and the "new look" policies of the Eisenhower Administration. Beginning with *Military Policy and National Security,* edited by W. W. Kaufmann, in 1956, a steady stream of books on strategy was added to the already growing periodical literature. Much of this literature was devoted to analysis of the over-all requirements of American strategy. Certain specific problems, however, became the foci of substantial corpora of writings on their own. Outstanding among these were the problems of limited war, NATO strategy, arms control, the economic aspects of strategy, and the strategy of internal war. The relative importance of these foci changed over time. The mid-1950's saw a mushrooming literature on limited war. In 1960 arms control became the dominant concern: no less than ten serious book-length studies appeared in as many months. In 1961 the new area of attention seemed to be revolutionary war, para-military operations, "unconventional" warfare, and strategies of intervention. An Internal War Project was under way at the Princeton Center of International Studies; articles on these subjects were blossoming forth in the journals; several book-length manuscripts were in preparation; and one publisher was even considering a series of volumes on revolutionary war.

Strategic theory is the effort to develop models and concepts for the analysis of strategic problems. It bears about the same relation to the more specifically policy-oriented studies in strategy that economic theory bears to studies in economic policy. The line between strategy and strategic theory is appropriately a hazy one. Writings in strategic theory are obviously inspired by immediate policy problems. Their argument, however, is usually couched in more general terms, analyzing the effects of the logically possible courses of action in generalized situations. Since they operate on a high level of abstraction, strategic theorists frequently use tools and approaches, such as game theory or bargaining theory, applicable to the analysis of other types of problems also. Writings on strategic theory tend to be formal, logical, deductive, and analytical. They also tend to be brief. They do not include masses of facts or extensive consideration of all the ramifications of any particular policy move, such as giving long-range missiles to NATO, that would have to be covered in a study more directly related to policy. Hence, strategic theory is usually found in journal articles and relatively short memos from RAND, the Princeton Center for International Studies, and comparable institutions.

A. GENERAL STRATEGY (arranged chronologically)

Brodie, Bernard (ed.) *The Absolute Weapon.* Harcourt, Brace, 1946.
————. "Nuclear Weapons: Strategic or Tactical," *Foreign Affairs,* 32 (January, 1954), 217-229.
Finletter, Thomas K. *Power and Policy: U.S. Foreign Policy and Military Power in the Hydrogen Age.* Harcourt, Brace, 1954.
Slessor, Marshal of the Royal Air Force Sir John. *Strategy for the West.* Morrow, 1954.
Reinhardt, Col. George C. *American Strategy in the Atomic Age.* Oklahoma, 1955.
Smith, Brig. Gen. Dale O. *U.S. Military Doctrine: A Study and Appraisal.* Duell, Sloan & Pearce-Little, Brown, 1955.
Nitze, Paul H. "Atoms, Strategy and Policy," *Foreign Affairs,* 34 (January, 1956), 187-198.
Blackett, P. M. S. *Atomic Weapons and East-West Relations.* Cambridge, 1956.
Kaufmann, William W. (ed.). *Military Policy and National Security.* Princeton, 1956.
Hoag, Malcolm. "Is 'Dual' Preparedness More Expensive?" *Bulletin of the Atomic Scientists,* 13 (February, 1957), 48-51.
Kingston-McCloughry, Air Vice-Marshal E. J. *Global Strategy.* Praeger, 1957.
Kissinger, Henry A. *Nuclear Weapons and Foreign Policy.* Harper, 1957.
Osgood, Robert E. *Limited War.* Chicago, 1957.
Knorr, Klaus. *Is the American Defense Effort Enough?* (Memorandum No. 14). Center of International Studies, Princeton University, 1957.
Stern, Frederick Martin. *The Citizen Army: Key to Defense in the Atomic Age.* St. Martin's, 1957.
Rockefeller Brothers Fund. *International Security: The Military Aspect.* Doubleday, 1958.
Kennan, George F. *Russia, the Atom, and the West.* Harper, 1958.
Kecskemeti, Paul. *Strategic Surrender: The Politics of Victory and Defeat.* Stanford, 1958.
Acheson, Dean. *Power and Policy.* Harvard, 1958.
Miksche, F. O. *The Failure of Atomic Strategy.* Praeger, 1958.
King-Hall, Stephen. *Defence in the Nuclear Age.* Gollanz, 1958.
Wohlstetter, Albert. "The Delicate Balance of Terror," *Foreign Affairs,* 37 (January, 1959), 211-234.
Snyder, Glenn H. *Deterrence by Denial and Punishment* (Research Monograph No. 1). Center of International Affairs, Princeton University, January 2, 1959.
Backus, P. H. "Finite Deterrence, Controlled Retaliation," *U.S. Naval Institute Proceedings,* 85 (March, 1959), 23-29.
Kaplan, Morton A. *The Strategy of Limited Retaliation* (Policy Memorandum No. 19). Center of International Studies, Princeton University, April 9, 1959.
Washington Center of Foreign Policy Research. *Developments in Military Technology and their Impact on United States Strategy and Foreign Policy.* Study prepared for U.S. Senate Committee on Foreign Relations, 86th Cong., 1st Sess., December 6, 1959.
Aron, Raymond. *On War* (trans. Terence Kilmartin). Doubleday, 1959.
Knorr, Klaus (ed.). *NATO and American Security.* Princeton, 1959.

Brodie, Bernard. *Strategy in the Missile Age.* Princeton, 1959.

Morgenstern, Oskar. *The Question of National Defense.* Random House, 1959.

Wolfers, Arnold (ed.). *Alliance Policy in the Cold War.* Johns Hopkins, 1959.

Rowen, Henry. *National Security and the American Economy in the 1960s.* Study Paper No. 18, Study of Employment and Price Levels, U.S. Congress Joint Economic Committee, 86th Cong., 2nd Sess., January 30, 1960.

Liddell Hart, B. H. *Deterrent or Defense: A Fresh Look at the West's Military Position.* Praeger, 1960.

Turner, Gordon B., and Richard D. Challener (eds.). *National Security in the Nuclear Age: Basic Facts and Theories.* Praeger (paperback), 1960.

Kahn, Herman. *On Thermonuclear War.* Princeton, 1960.

Osgood, Robert E. "Stabilizing the Military Environment," *American Political Science Review,* 55 (March, 1961), 24-39.

Kissinger, Henry A. *The Necessity for Choice.* Harper, 1961.

Strausz-Hupé, Robert, William R. Kintner, Stefan T. Possony, *et al. A Forward Strategy for America.* Harper, 1961.

Collections of Previously Published Studies

Furniss, Edgar S. (ed.). *American Military Policy: Strategic Aspects of World Political Geography.* Rinehart, 1957.

Hahn, Walter F., and John C. Neff (eds.). *American Strategy for the Nuclear Age.* Doubleday (Anchor), 1960.

McClelland, Charles A. (ed.). *Nuclear Weapons, Missiles, and Future War: Problems for the Sixties.* Chandler, 1960.

Bibliography

Brody, Richard. "Deterrence Strategies: An Annotated Bibliography," *Journal of Conflict Resolution,* 4 (December, 1960), 443-457.

B. EUROPE AND NATO (arranged chronologically)

Wolfers, Arnold. "Could a War in Europe Be Limited?" *Yale Review,* 45 (Winter, 1956), 214-228.

Patterson, Gardner, and Edgar S. Furniss, Jr. *NATO: A Critical Appraisal. Report of Princeton University Conference on NATO.* 1957.

Hoag, Malcolm. "NATO: Deterrent or Shield?" *Foreign Affairs,* 36 (January, 1958), 278-292.

Moore, Ben T. *NATO and the Future of Europe.* Harper, 1958.

Howard, Michael. *Disengagement.* Penguin, 1958.

Gordon, Lincoln. "NATO in the Nuclear Age," *Yale Review,* 48 (March, 1959), 321-335.

Wolfers, Arnold (ed.). *Alliance Policy in the Cold War.* Johns Hopkins, 1959.

Knorr, Klaus (ed.). *NATO and American Security.* Princeton, 1959.

Osgood, Robert E. "NATO: Problems of Security and Collaboration," *American Political Science Review,* 54 (March, 1960), 106-130.

Buchan, Alastair. *NATO in the 1960s.* Praeger, 1960.

Wohlstetter, Albert. "Nuclear Sharing: NATO and the $N + 1$ Country," *Foreign Affairs,* 39 (April, 1961), 355-387.

C. LIMITED WAR (arranged chronologically)

Brodie, Bernard. "Unlimited Weapons and Limited War," *The Reporter,* 11 (November 18, 1954), 16-21.

Royal Institute on International Affairs. *On Limiting Atomic War.* 1956.

Schelling, Thomas C. "Bargaining, Communication, and Limited War," *Journal of Conflict Resolution,* 1 (March, 1957), 19-36.

Hilsman, Roger. "American Military Policy: The Next Phase," *Current History,* 33 (October, 1957), 208-215.

Kissinger, Henry A. *Nuclear Weapons and Foreign Policy.* Harper, 1957.

Osgood, Robert E. *Limited War.* Chicago, 1957.

Kaufmann, William W. "The Crisis in Military Affairs," *World Politics,* 10 (July, 1958), 579-603.

Baldwin, Hanson W. "Limited War," *Atlantic Monthly,* 203 (January, 1959), 35-43.

Schelling, Thomas C. *Nuclear Weapons and Limited War* (P-1620). The RAND Corporation, February 20, 1959.

Kissinger, Henry A. "Limited War: Nuclear or Conventional? A Reappraisal," *Daedalus,* 89 (Fall, 1960), 800-817.

Halperin, Morton H. "The Theory of Limited War." Ph.D. Thesis, Yale University, 1961.

Bibliography

U.S. Department of the Army. *Bibliography on Limited War* (Pamphlet No. 20-60). February, 1958.

Halperin, Morton H. "Limited War: An Essay on the Development of the Theory and an Annotated Bibliography." Center for International Affairs, Harvard University, February, 1961.

D. ARMS CONTROL (arranged chronologically)

Cavers, D. F. "The Challenge of Planning Arms Control," *Foreign Affairs,* 34 (October, 1955), 50-66.

U.S. Senate Subcommittee on Disarmament. *Final Report.* 85th Cong., 2nd Sess., 1958.

Pauling, Linus. *No More War!* Dodd, Mead, 1958.

Noel-Baker, Philip. *The Arms Race: A Programme for World Disarmament.* Oceana, 1958.

National Planning Association. *1970 Without Arms Control* (Planning Pamphlet No. 104), 1958.

Melman, Seymour (ed.). *Inspection for Disarmament.* Columbia, 1958.

Clark, Grenville, and Louis Sohn. *World Peace Through World Law.* Harvard, 1958.

Jessup, Philip C., and Howard J. Taubenfeld. *Controls for Outer Space and the Antarctic Analogy.* Columbia, 1959.

Nogee, Joseph. "The Diplomacy of Disarmament," *International Conciliation,* No. 526 (January, 1960), 235-303.

Osgood, Charles E. "A Case for Gradual Unilateral Disarmament," *Bulletin of the Atomic Scientists,* 16 (April, 1960), 127-131.

Kissinger, Henry A. "Arms Control, Inspection, and Surprise Attack," *Foreign Affairs,* 38 (July, 1960), 557-575.

National Planning Association. *Strengthening the Government for Arms Control.* 1960.

――――. *The Nth Country Problem and Arms Control* (Planning Pamphlet No. 108). 1960.

Benoit, Emile. *Economic Adjustments to Disarmament.* Institute for International Order, 1960.

Feld, Bernard T., *et al. The Technical Problems of Arms Control.* Institute for International Order, 1960.

Barnet, Richard J. *Who Wants Disarmament?* Beacon, 1960.

"Special Issue: Arms Control," *Daedalus,* 89 (Fall, 1960).

Summer Study on Arms Control. *Collected Papers.* American Academy of Arts and Sciences, January, 1961.

Hadley, Arthur T. *The Nation's Safety and Arms Control.* Harper, 1961.

Schelling, Thomas C., and Morton H. Halperin. *Strategy and Arms Control.* Twentieth Century Fund, 1961.

Frisch, David H. (ed.). *Arms Reduction: Program and Issues.* Twentieth Century Fund, 1961.

Singer, J. David. *Deterrence, Arms Control, and Disarmament: Toward a Synthesis in National Security Policy* (Preliminary draft). Mental Health Research Institute, March, 1961.
Brennan, Donald G. (ed.). *Arms Control, Disarmament, and National Security.* Braziller, 1961.
Bull, Hedley. *The Control of the Arms Race.* Praeger, 1961.
Henkin, Louis (ed.). *Arms Control: Issues for the Public.* Prentice-Hall, 1961.

Bibliography

Collart, Yves. *Disarmament: A Study Guide and Bibliography on the Efforts of the United Nations.* Nijhoff, 1958.
Wright, Christopher. "Selected Critical Bibliography," *Daedalus,* 89 (Fall, 1960), 1055-1070.
Coward, H. Roberts. "Bibliography on Arms Control and Related Problems," in Summer Study on Arms Control, *Collected Papers,* pp. 441-459.

E. ECONOMIC ASPECTS OF STRATEGY (arranged chronologically)

Colm, Gerhard. *Can We Afford Additional Programs for National Security?* National Planning Association (Planning Pamphlet No. 84), October, 1953.
Lincoln, George A., et al. *Economics of National Security,* 2nd ed. Prentice-Hall, 1954.
Knorr, Klaus. *The War Potential of Nations.* Princeton, 1956.
Colm, Gerhard, and Manuel Helzner. "General Economic Feasibility of National Security Programs." National Planning Association, March 20, 1957. (Published in U.S. Congress Joint Economic Committee, Subcommittee on Fiscal Policy. *Federal Expenditure Policy for Economic Growth and Stability.* Hearings, 85th Cong. 1st Sess., 1958.)
U.S. Congress Joint Economic Committee, Subcommittee on Fiscal Policy. *Federal Expenditure Policy for Economic Growth and Stability: Papers Submitted by Panelists.* 85th Cong., 1st Sess., November 5, 1957:
    Burns, Arthur E. "Military Expenditures, Economic Growth, and Stability," pp. 509-517.
    Fishman, Leo, and Betty G. Fishman. "Economic Effects of Postwar National Security Expenditures," pp. 518-522.
    Hildebrand, George H. and Norman V. Breckner. "Impacts of National Security Expenditures Upon the Stability and Growth of the American Economy," pp. 523-541.
    Novick, David. "Federal Spending for National Security," pp. 542-550.
    Smithies, Arthur. "Defense Budget," pp. 551-558.
Davenport, John. "Arms and the Welfare State," *Yale Review,* 47 (Spring, 1958), 335-346.
Tobin, James. "Defense, Dollars, and Doctrines," Yale Review, 47 (Spring, 1958), 321-334.
Committee for Economic Development. *The Problem of National Security.* (Statement by Research and Policy Committee). July, 1958.
Rowen, Henry. *National Security and the American Economy in the 1960s.* Study Paper No. 18, Study of Employment and Price Levels. U.S. Congress Joint Economic Committee, 86th Cong., 2nd Sess., January 30, 1960.
Schlesinger, James R. *The Political Economy of National Security.* Praeger, 1960.
Hitch, Charles J., and Roland N. McKean. *The Economics of Defense in the Nuclear Age.* Harvard, 1960.

F. DOMESTIC WAR (arranged chronologically)

Miksche, F. O. *Secret Forces: The Technique of Underground Movements.* Faber, 1950.
Papagos, Alexander. "Guerrilla Warfare," *Foreign Affairs,* 30 (January, 1952), 215-230.
Dixon, C. Aubrey, and Otto Heilbrunn. *Communist Guerrilla Warfare.* Praeger, 1954.
Pye, Lucien. *Guerrilla Communism in Malaya.* Princeton, 1956.
Ney, Virgil. "Guerrilla War and Modern Strategy," *Orbis,* 2 (Spring, 1958), 66-82.

Paret, Peter. "The French Army and La Guerre Révolutionnaire," *Journal of the Royal United Service Institution,* 104 (February, 1959), 59-69.

Strausz-Hupé, Robert, William R. Kintner, *et al. Protracted Conflict.* Harper, 1959.

Crozier, Brian. *The Rebels.* Beacon, 1960.

Atkinson, James D. *The Edge of War.* Regnery, 1960.

Kelly, George A. "Revolutionary War and Psychological Action," *Military Review,* 11 (October, 1960), 4-13.

Bjelajac, Slavko N. "Unconventional Warfare in the Nuclear Era," *Orbis,* 4 (Fall, 1960), 323-337.

Guevara, Ernesto. "La Guerra de Guerrillas." *Army,* 11 (March, 1961) 21-32; (April, 1961), 59-69; (May, 1961), 63-69.

Modelski, George. *The International Relations of Internal War* (Research Monograph No. 11). Center of International Studies, Princeton University, May 24, 1961.

Girardet, Raoul. "Civil and Military Power in the Fourth Republic," *supra,* pp. 121-149.

Huntington, Samuel P. "Patterns of Violence in World Politics," *supra,* pp. 17-50.

G. STRATEGIC THEORY

Burns, Arthur Lee. *The Rationale of Catalytic War* (Research Monograph No. 3). Center of International Studies, Princeton University, 1959.

————. "From Balance to Deterrence: A Theoretical Analysis," *World Politics,* 9 (July, 1957), 494-529.

————. "A Graphical Approach to Some Problems of the Arms Race," *Journal of Conflict Resolution,* 3 (December, 1959), 326-342.

————. "The International Consequences of Expecting Surprise," *World Politics,* 10 (July, 1958), 512-536.

Ellsberg, Daniel. "The Art of Coercion: A Study of Threats in Economic Conflict and War." Unpublished Manuscript, 1959.

Kaplan, Morton. "The Calculus of Nuclear Deterrence," *World Politics,* 11 (October, 1958), 20-43.

Rapoport, Anatol. *Fights, Games, and Debates.* Michigan, 1960.

Schelling, Thomas C. *The Strategy of Conflict.* Harvard, 1960.

Snyder, Glenn H. "Deterrence and Power," *Journal of Conflict Resolution,* 4 (June, 1960), 163-178.

III: American Military Policy, 1946-1960

This category includes writings dealing with the content of military policy between 1946 and 1960 and the processes by which specific military policies were made. These items differ from those under the previous heading in that they are not primarily prescriptive. They may, to be sure, suggest or even explicitly argue the merits and demerits of particular policies, but this is secondary to description and descriptive analysis. These items also differ from those in Section V because they focus on particular problems or areas of policy, not upon the generalized roles of particular participants in the making of policy. Many of the case studies in policymaking included in this section were written with the thought that they would contribute to generalizations about the policymaking process. They remain, however, case studies of particular issues of policy, and hence they are included here.

Numerous accounts exist of the evolution of American foreign policy after World War II. The searcher for a comparable description of American military policy will run into difficulties. Part II of Millis, Mansfield, and Stein, *Arms and the State,* covers all significant elements of military policy, but only for the period from 1945 through 1953. Huntington's *The Common Defense* provides a general framework for the analysis of military policy but within this framework specifically covers only the evolution of policy on force levels and strategic programs. The volumes by Col. Charles H. Donnelly of the Legislative Reference Service present the basic facts on military policy; prepared annually under official auspices, however, they do not furnish an over-all analysis and interpretation of the development of policy. The more inclusive accounts of the evolution of foreign policy, on the other hand, such as Rostow's *The United States in the World Arena,* cover the high points of military policy within the broader framework of foreign policy.

The paucity of over-all analyses and surveys of military policy reflects neither the absence of specific studies of particular issues nor the absence of sources. Military issues of almost every possible type have been treated exhaustively. Some issues, such as the conduct of the Korean War in 1950 and 1951, have been subjected to repeated analysis. In many cases detailed studies have included not only the evolution of policy—in terms of the statements, actions, and decisions of key officials—but also exhaustive description of the processes by which the policies were formulated. Outstanding among these are the case studies prepared for the Civilian and Military Perspectives Project of the Institute of War and Peace Studies at Columbia University under the direction of Professor William T. R. Fox and those prepared for the Twentieth Century Fund Civil-Military Relations Project under the direction of Dr. Harold Stein. The authors of these studies supplemented documentary sources by interviews with leading participants in the policymaking process. Even where extensive interviewing is not undertaken, however, it is often possible to reconstruct a reasonably complete account of the policymaking process on a specific issue from imaginative and diligent detective work in the press and congressional hearings. Particularly useful and authoritative are the newspaper analyses and accounts of: Hanson Baldwin, Anthony Leviero, and Jack Raymond *(New York Times);* Walter Millis *(New York Herald Tribune);* Joseph and Stewart Alsop *(Herald Tribune* Syndicate); Chalmers Roberts and John G. Norris *(Washington Post);* T. R. Phillips *(St. Louis Post Despatch);* and S. L. A. Marshall *(Detroit News).* The annual budget hearings before the House and Senate Appropriations Committees and the "military posture" briefings before the Armed Services Committees often contain extensive information. In addition, special congressional investigations produce substantial quantities of material on particular policy issues. An increasing number of memoirs by participants in the policymaking process are also appearing. In addition to secondary analyses, the listings which follow include some of the more useful primary sources.

A. AMERICAN MILITARY POLICY, 1946-1960, IN GENERAL

Baldwin, Hanson W. *The Great Arms Race.* Praeger, 1958.
Council on Foreign Relations. *The United States in World Affairs.* Annual Survey.

Donnelly, Charles H. *United States Defense Policies Since World War II.* H. Doc. 100, 85th Cong., 1st Sess., November, 1956.

———. *United States Defense Policies in 1957.* H. Doc. 436, 85th Cong., 2nd Sess., January 10, 1958.

———. *United States Defense Policies in 1958.* H. Doc. 227, 86th Cong., 1st Sess., July 10, 1959.

———. *United States Defense Policies in 1959.* H. Doc. 432, 86th Cong., 2nd Sess., May 27, 1960.

Huntington, Samuel P. *The Common Defense: Strategic Programs in National Politics.* Columbia, 1961.

———. "Radicalism and Conservatism in National Defense Policy," *Journal of International Affairs,* 8 (1954), 206-222.

Millis, Walter, Harvey C. Mansfield, and Harold Stein. *Arms and the State.* Twentieth Century Fund, 1958. Part II.

Rostow, W. W. *The United States in the World Arena.* Harper, 1960.

U.S. House of Representatives, U.S. Senate Committees on Appropriations. *Department of Defense Appropriations.* Annual Hearings.

B. STRATEGY, FORCE LEVELS, AND WEAPONS, 1946-1953

Bradley, Gen. Omar N. "A Soldier's Farewell," *Saturday Evening Post,* 226 (August 22, 1953), 20ff.; (August 29, 1953), 22ff.

Denfeld, Adm. Louis E. "Why I Was Fired," *Collier's,* 125 (March 18, 1950), 13ff.; (March 25, 1950), 32ff.; (April 1, 1950), 36ff.

Gavin, Lt. Gen. James M. *War and Peace in the Space Age.* Harper, 1958.

Green, Murray. "Stuart Symington and the B-36." Ph.D. Thesis, The American University, 1960.

Hammond, Paul Y. "Super-Carriers and B-36 Bombers: Appropriations, Strategy, and Politics." Twentieth Century Fund Project on Civil-Military Relations.

———. "NSC 68: Prologue to Rearmament," to be published in Warner R. Schilling, Paul Y. Hammond, Glenn H. Snyder, *Strategies, Budgets, and Defense Politics* (Columbia, 1962).

Millis, Walter (ed.). *The Forrestal Diaries.* Viking, 1951.

Reagan, Michael D. "Demobilization and Post-War Military Planning." Twentieth Century Fund Project on Civil-Military Relations.

Schilling, Warner R. "The Fiscal Fifty Military Budget," to be published in Warner R. Schilling, Paul Y. Hammond, and Glenn H. Snyder, *Strategies, Budgets, and Defense Politics* (Columbia, 1962).

———. "The H-Bomb Decision: How to Decide Without Actually Choosing," *Political Science Quarterly,* 76 (March, 1961), 24-46.

Sparrow, John C. *History of Personnel Demobilization in the United States Army.* Office of the Chief of Military History, 1951.

Teller, Edward. "The Work of Many People," *Science,* 121 (February 25, 1955), 267-275.

Truman, Harry S. *Memoirs,* 2 vols. Doubleday, 1955-1956.

U.S. Atomic Energy Commission. *In the Matter of J. Robert Oppenheimer* (Transcript of Hearings before Personnel Security Board). 1954.

U.S. House of Representatives, Committee on Armed Services. *The National Defense Program—Unification and Strategy.* Hearings, 81st Cong., 1st Sess., 1949.

C. MILITARY FORCE AND DIPLOMACY, 1946-1950

Byrnes, James F. *All in One Lifetime.* Harper, 1958.

———. *Speaking Frankly.* Harper, 1947.

Clay, Gen. Lucius B. *Decision in Germany.* Doubleday, 1950.

Davison, W. Phillips. *The Berlin Blockade.* Princeton, 1958.

Jones, Joseph M. *The Fifteen Weeks.* Viking, 1955.

Truman, Harry S. *Memoirs,* 2 vols. Doubleday, 1955-1956.
Vandenberg, Arthur H., Jr. *The Private Papers of Senator Vandenberg.* Houghton Mifflin, 1952.
Xydis, Stephen G. "The American Naval Visits to Greece and the Eastern Mediterranean in 1946: Their Impact on American-Soviet Relations." Ph.D. Thesis, Columbia University, 1956.

D. THE KOREAN WAR, 1950-1953

Berger, Carl. *The Korea Knot: A Military-Political History.* Pennsylvania, 1957.
Clark, Gen. Mark. *From the Danube to the Yalu.* Harper, 1954.
George, Alexander L. "American Policymaking and the North Korean Aggression," *World Politics,* 7 (January, 1955), 209-232.
Goodrich, Leland M. *Korea: A Study of United States Policy in the United Nations.* Council on Foreign Relations, 1956.
Higgins, Trumbull. *Korea and the Fall of MacArthur: A Precis in Limited War.* Oxford, 1960.
Joy, Adm. C. Turner. *How Communists Negotiate.* Macmillan, 1955.
Kaufmann, William W. *Policy Objectives and Military Action in the Korean War* (P-886). The RAND Corporation, June 26, 1956.
Kinkead, Eugene. *In Every War But One.* Norton, 1959.
Lichterman, Martin. "March to the Yalu." Twentieth Century Fund Project on Civil-Military Relations. n.d.
——. "Korea: Problems in Limited War," in Turner, Gordon B., and Richard D. Challener (eds.). *National Security in the Nuclear Age.* Praeger, 1960.
Lyons, Gene M. *Military Policy and Economic Aid: The Korean Case, 1950-1953.* Ohio State, 1961.
Neustadt, Richard E. *Presidential Power: The Politics of Leadership.* Wiley, 1960. Chs. 2, 6.
Poats, Rutherford. *Decision in Korea.* MacBride, 1954.
Ridgway, Gen. Matthew B. *Soldier.* Harper, 1956.
Rovere, Richard, and Arthur M. Schlesinger, Jr. *The General and the President, and the Future of American Foreign Policy.* Farrar, Straus, 1951.
Snyder, Richard C., and Glenn D. Paige. "The United States Decision to Resist Aggression in Korea: The Application of an Analytical Scheme," *Administrative Science Quarterly,* 3 (December, 1958), 341-378.
Spanier, John W. *The Truman-MacArthur Controversy and the Korean War.* Belknap-Harvard, 1959.
U.S. Senate Committees on Armed Services and Foreign Relations. *Military Situation in the Far East.* Hearings, 82nd Cong., 1st Sess., 1951.
Vatcher, William H., Jr. *Panmunjom: The Story of the Korean Military Armistice Negotiations.* Praeger, 1958.
Whiting, Allen S. *China Crosses the Yalu: The Decision to Enter the Korean War.* Macmillan, 1960.
Whitney, Maj. Gen. Courtney. *MacArthur: His Rendezvous with History.* Knopf, 1956.
Willoughby, Maj. Gen. Charles, and John Chamberlain. *MacArthur, 1941-1951.* McGraw-Hill, 1954.

E. STRATEGY, FORCE LEVELS, AND WEAPONS, 1953-1960

Donnelly, Charles H. *The United States Guided Missile Program.* Committee Print., U.S. Senate Preparedness Investigating Subcommittee, 86th Cong., 1st Sess., 1959.
Donovan, Robert J. *Eisenhower: The Inside Story.* Harper, 1956.
Gavin, Lt. Gen. James M. *War and Peace in the Space Age.* Harper, 1958.
Halperin, Morton H. "The Gaither Committee and the Policy Process," *World Politics,* 13 (April, 1961), 360-384.
Medaris, Maj. Gen. John B. *Countdown for Decision.* Putnam, 1960.

Murphy, Charles J. V. A series of articles on the Eisenhower Administration's defense
  policies appearing in *Fortune* as follows:
    "The Atom and the Balance of Power," 48 (August, 1953), 97+.
    "The U.S. as a Bombing Target," 48 (November, 1953), 118-121+.
    "Strategy Overtakes Mr. Wilson," 49 (January, 1954), 80-81.
    "Eisenhower's White House," 49 (February, 1954), 116-118+.
    "Is the H-Bomb Enough?" 49 (June, 1954), 102-103+.
    "America's New Strategic Situation," 50 (August, 1954), 70-71+.
    "Crisis in the Cold War," 51 (June, 1955), 86-87.
    "The New Air Situation," 52 (September, 1955), 86-87+.
    "The Eisenhower Shift," 53 (January, 1956), 82-87+.
    "Defense: The Revolution Gets Revolutionary," 53 (May, 1956), 101-103+.
    "Eisenhower's Most Critical Defense Budget," 54 (December, 1956), 112-14+.
    "Washington and the World," 55 (January, 1957), 78-83.
    "America's Widening Military Margin," 56 (August, 1957), 94-96+.
    "The White House since Sputnik," 57 (January, 1958), 98-101+.
    "The White House and the Recession," 57 (May, 1958), 106-109+.
    "The Budget and Eisenhower," 57 (June, 1958), 96-99+.
    "Defense: The Converging Decisions," 58 (October, 1958), 118-120+.
    "Embattled Mr. McElroy." 59 (April, 1959), 147-150.
    "U.S. Sea Power—The New Mix," 60 (August, 1959) 76-83.
    "Is the Defense Budget Big Enough?" 60 (November, 1959), 144-147.
Murray, Thomas E. *Nuclear Policy for War and Peace.* World, 1960.
Ridgway, Gen. Matthew B. *Soldier.* Harper, 1956.
Snyder, Glenn H. "The New Look," to be published in Warner R. Schilling, Paul Y.
  Hammond, Glenn H. Snyder, *Strategies, Budgets, and Defense Politics.* Columbia,
  1962.
Taylor, Gen. Maxwell D. *The Uncertain Trumpet.* Harper, 1960.
U.S. Senate Committee on Armed Services, Subcommittee on the Air Force. *Study of
  Airpower.* Hearings, 84th Cong., 2nd Sess., 1956.
U.S. Senate Committee on Armed Services, Preparedness Investigating Subcommittee.
  Inquiry into Satellite and Missile Programs. Hearing, 85th Cong., 1st & 2nd Sess.,
  1957-1958.
————. *Major Defense Matters.* Hearings, 86th Cong., 1st Sess., 1959.

F. MILITARY FORCE AND DIPLOMACY, 1953-1960

Adams, Sherman. *Firsthand Report: The Story of the Eisenhower Administration.*
  Harper, 1961.
Alsop, S. "How We Drifted Close to War," *Saturday Evening Post,* 231 (December 13,
  1958), 26-27+.
Barnett, Robert W. "Quemoy: The Use and Consequence of Nuclear Deterrence."
  Center for International Affairs, Harvard University, 1960.
Braestrup, Peter. "Limited Wars and the Lessons of Lebanon," *The Reporter,* 20 (April
  30, 1959), 25-27.
Campbell, John C. *Defense of the Middle East: Problems of American Policy,* rev. ed.
  Harper, 1960.
Childs, Marquis. *The Ragged Edge.* Doubleday, 1955.
Donovan, Robert J. *Eisenhower: The Inside Story.* Harper, 1956.
Drummond, Roscoe, and Gaston Coblenz. *Duel at the Brink: John Foster Dulles' Com-
  mand of American Power.* Doubleday, 1960.
Eden, Anthony. *Full Circle.* Houghton Mifflin, 1960.
Ridgway, Gen. Matthew B. *Soldier.* Harper, 1956.
Roberts, Chalmers. "The Day We Didn't Go to War," *The Reporter,* 11 (September 14,
  1954), 31-35.
————. "The Battle on 'The Rim of Hell': President vs. War Hawks," *The Reporter,* 11
  (December 16, 1954), 11-14.

Speier, Hans. *The Soviet Threat to Berlin* (P-1912-1). The RAND Corporation, April 15, 1960.
Tsou, Tang. *The Embroilment over Quemoy: Mao, Chiang, and Dulles.* University of Utah Monograph Series, 1959.

G. EUROPE AND NATO STRATEGY, 1946-1960

Ball, M. Margaret. *NATO and the European Union Movement.* Praeger, 1959.
Cheever, Daniel S., and H. Field Haviland. *American Foreign Policy and the Separation of Powers.* Harvard, 1952. Ch. 11.
Craig, Gordon. "NATO and the New German Army," in William W. Kaufmann (ed.). *Military Policy and National Security.* Princeton, 1956.
Ismay, Lord. *NATO: The First Five Years, 1949-1954.* North Atlantic Treaty Organization, 1955.
Martin, Laurence W. "The American Decision to Rearm Germany." Twentieth Century Fund Civil-Military Relations Project, n.d.
Murphy, Charles J. V. "New Strategy for NATO," *Fortune,* 47 (January, 1953), 80-85+.
———. "The NATO Alliance Goes Nuclear," *Fortune,* 57 (February, 1958), 98ff.
Osgood, Robert E. "NATO: Problems of Security and Collaboration," *American Political Science Review,* 54 (March, 1960), 106-129.
Thomas, Jack E. "SACEUR and SHAPE: A Study of Peacetime Preparation for Coalition Defense, 1950-1956." Ph.D. Thesis, University of California (Berkeley), 1959.
U.S. Senate Committee on Foreign Relations. *Assignment of Ground Forces of the United States to Duty in the European Area.* Hearings, 82nd Cong., 1st Sess., 1951.
Vandenberg, Arthur H., Jr. *The Private Papers of Senator Vandenberg.* Houghton Mifflin, 1952.
Warne, J. D. *N.A.T.O. and Its Prospects.* Praeger, 1954.

H. DISARMAMENT AND ARMS CONTROL

Barnet, Richard J. *Who Wants Disarmament?* Beacon, 1960.
Davis, Saville. "Recent Policy Making in the United States Government," *Daedalus,* 89 (Fall, 1960), 951-956.
Humphrey, Sen. Hubert. "Government Organization for Arms Control," *Daedalus,* 89 (Fall, 1960), 967-983.
Murphy, Charles J. V. "Nuclear Inspection: A Near Miss," *Fortune,* 59 (March, 1959), 122ff.
———. "The Case for Resuming Nuclear Tests," *Fortune,* 60 (April, 1960), 148ff.
Murray, Thomas E. *Nuclear Policy for War and Peace.* World, 1960.
Nogee, Joseph. "The Diplomacy of Disarmament," *International Conciliation,* No. 526 (January, 1960), 235-303.
Nutting, Anthony. *Disarmament: An Outline of the Negotiations.* Oxford, 1959.
Roberts, Chalmers M. "The Hopes and Fears of an Atomic Test Ban," *The Reporter,* 22 (April 28, 1960), 20-23.
U.S. Department of State. *The Intensified Effort, 1955-1958* (General Foreign Policy Series No. 131). July, 1958.
———. *Documents on Disarmament, 1945-1959,* 2 vols. (Department of State Publication No. 7008). August, 1960.

I. MILITARY ASSISTANCE

Brown, William Adams, Jr., and Redvers Opie. *American Foreign Assistance.* Brookings, 1953.
Furniss, Edgar S., Jr. *Some Perspectives on American Military Assistance* (Memorandum No. 13). Center of International Studies, Princeton University, June 18, 1957.
Jordan, Amos A., Jr. "Foreign Aid and Defense: United States Military and Related

Economic Assistance to Southeast Asia." Ph.D. Thesis, Columbia University, 1961.
Lieuwen, Edwin. *Arms and Politics in Latin America.* Praeger, 1960.
Liska, George. *The New Statecraft.* Chicago, 1960.
U.S. President's Committee to Study the United States Military Assistance Program. *Composite Report and Supplement,* 2 vols. August 17, 1959.
U.S. Senate Special Committee to Study the Foreign Aid Program. *The Military Assistance Program of the United States: Two Studies and a Report.* Committee Print., 85th Cong., 1st Sess., 1957.
Wolf, Charles, Jr. *Foreign Aid: Theory and Practice in Southern Asia.* Princeton, 1960.

    J. RESERVE FORCES POLICY

Derthick, Martha. "Militia Lobby in the Missile Age: The Politics of the National Guard," *supra,* pages 190-234.
Galloway, Eilene. *A Legislative History of the Reserve Forces Act of 1955.* U.S. House of Representatives, Committee on Armed Services, Rept. No. 82, 84th Cong., 2nd Sess., 1956.
Lyons, Gene M., and John W. Masland. *Education and Military Leadership: A Study of the ROTC.* Princeton, 1959.
"The Reserve of the Armed Forces: A Historical Symposium," *Military Affairs,* 17 (Spring, 1953).
Story, Charles D. "The Formulation of Army Reserve Forces Policy: Its Setting Amidst Pressure Group Activity." Ph.D. Thesis, University of Oklahoma, 1958.

    K. ORGANIZATION

Hammond, Paul Y. *Organizing for Defense: The American Military Establishment in the Twentieth Century.* Princeton, 1961.
Kintner, William R., *et al. Forging a New Sword: A Study of the Department of Defense.* Harper, 1958.
Legere, Lawrence J., Jr. *Unification of the Armed Forces.* Office of the Chief of Military History. n.d.
McClendon, R. Earl. *Changes in Organization for National Defense, 1949-1953.* Research Studies Institute, Air University, 1956.
————. *Unification of the Armed Forces: Administrative and Legislative Developments, 1945-1949.* Air University, 1952.
Millis, Walter (ed.). *The Forrestal Diaries.* Viking, 1961.
Stanley, Timothy. *American Defense and National Security.* Public Affairs, 1956.

    L. MOBILIZATION, PROCUREMENT, AND ECONOMIC POLICIES

Gordon, Bernard W. "Conflicts in Military Procurement," *Current History,* 38 (April, 1960), 234-39.
Miller, John Perry. *Pricing of Military Procurement.* Yale, 1949.
————. "Military Procurement Policies: World War II and Today," *American Economic Review,* 42 (May, 1952), 453-475.
Rosenberg, Herbert H. "ODM: A Study of Civil-Military Relations During the Korean Mobilization." Office of Defense Mobilization (mimeographed), 1953.
Snyder, Glenn H. "The Stockpiling of Strategic Materials: A Study of Civilian and Military Perspectives in the Formulation and Administration of National Security Policy." Ph.D. Thesis, Columbia University, 1956.
U.S. Congress Joint Economic Committee. *Background Material on Economic Aspects of Military Procurement and Supply.* 86th Cong., 2nd Sess., February 16, 1960.
U.S. Senate Committee on Armed Services. *Military Procurement.* Hearings, 86th Cong., 1st Sess., 1959.

IV: American Military Policy before World War II

Traditionally, military history has been the history of battles, campaigns, and wars. The political scientist, the public official, and the journalist made the principal contributions to the understanding of the evolution of American military policy after World War II. The new emphasis on military affairs, however, also stimulated historians and others to explore the ramifications of American military policy before World War II.

This section is devoted to this topic. The literature on World War II itself, of course, is immense. So is that on the Civil War, and the other wars in American history lag behind only in comparison. Wars, however, are extraordinary situations, and the emphasis here is on the history and formulation of military policy in peacetime as a continuing activity of government. Specifically excluded are works which deal primarily with wars or wartime policy.

Recent writings on peacetime military policy have concentrated on the twentieth century. This is most appropriate and reflects the gradual clearance of the records and documents for the pre-World War II years. Earlier aspects of American military policy, however, also offer many opportunities for fruitful research not only on subjects of interest in themselves but also on those that frequently have important implications for policy and the making of policy today.[4] The 1950's thus saw the appearance of specialized studies of specific issues of peacetime military policy and some general interpretative essays, such as those by Walter Millis and T. Harry Williams. Between these two levels of scholarship, however, a need still exists for detailed, authoritative, and yet comprehensive studies of the development of military policy and of the nature of the political forces shaping it, studies on the model of the classic prewar work of Harold and Margaret Sprout, *The Rise of American Naval Power, 1776-1918* (Princeton, 1939).

Another gap in the literature concerns the makers of military policy. Presidents and wartime generals, of course, do not lack biographies. The service secretaries, congressmen, and general officers shaping peacetime military policy, however, are not adequately covered. There is a great need for more biographies like Elting E. Morison's *Admiral Sims and the Modern American Navy* (Houghton Mifflin, 1942). As the study by Stanley Falk, listed below, indicates, even the life of a second-level military figure can produce many insights into the political environment and decision-making processes of the military establishment.

A. GENERAL WORKS

Bernardo, C. J., and Eugene H. Bacon. *American Military Policy: Its Development Since 1775.* Military Service, 1955.

Ekirch, Arthur A., Jr. *The Civilian and the Military.* Oxford, 1956.

Graber, D. A. *Crisis Diplomacy: A History of U.S. Intervention Policies and Practices.* Public Affairs, 1959.

Millis, Walter. *Arms and Men.* Putnam, 1956.

Williams, T. Harry. *Americans at War.* Louisiana State, 1960.

Bibliography

U.S. Department of the Army. *The Writing of American Military History: A Guide* (Department of the Army Pamphlet No. 20-200). June, 1956.

B. MILITARY POLICY, 1900-1940

Brown, Richard C. "Social Attitudes of American Generals, 1898-1940." Ph.D. Thesis, University of Wisconsin, 1951.

Greene, Fred. "The Military View of American National Policy, 1904-1940," *American Historical Review,* 66 (January, 1961), 354-377.

Millis, Walter, Harvey C. Mansfield, and Harold Stein. *Arms and the State: Civil-Military Elements in National Policy.* Twentieth Century Fund, 1958. Part I.

Morton, Louis. "Origins of Pacific Strategy," *Marine Corps Gazette,* 41 (August, 1957), 36-43.

————. "War Plan Orange: Evolution of a Strategy," *World Politics,* 11 (January, 1959), 221-250.

————. "Army and Marines on the China Station: A Study in Military and Political Rivalry," *Pacific Historical Review,* 29 (February, 1960), 51-73.

————. "Military and Naval Preparations for the Defense of the Philippines during the War Scare of 1907," *Military Affairs,* 13 (Summer, 1949), 95-104.

————. "National Policy and Military Strategy," *Virginia Quarterly Review,* 36 (Winter, 1960), 1-17.

Reinhardt, Col. George C., and Col. William R. Kintner. *The Haphazard Years: How America Has Gone to War.* Doubleday, 1960.

Rood, Harold W. "Strategy out of Silence: American Military Policy and the Preparations for War, 1919 to 1940." Ph.D. Thesis, University of California (Berkeley), 1960.

Vinson, J. Chalmers. "Military Force and American Policy, 1919-1939," in Alexander DeConde (ed.). *Isolation and Security.* Duke, 1957.

C. ARMY AND RESERVE POLICY

Craven, Wesley F., and James L. Cate. *The Army Air Forces in World War II: Plans and Early Operations.* Chicago, 1948.

Derthick, Martha. "Militia Lobby in the Missile Age: The Politics of the National Guard," *supra,* pp. 190-234.

Falk, Stanley L. "Soldier-Technologist: Major Alfred Mordecai and the Beginnings of Science in the United States Army." Ph.D. Thesis, Georgetown University, 1959.

Jacobs, James R. *The Beginning of the U.S. Army, 1783-1812.* Princeton, 1947.

Killigrew, John W. "The Impact of the Great Depression on the Army, 1929-1936." Ph.D. Thesis, University of Indiana, 1960.

Kreidberg, Marvin A., and Merton G. Henry. *History of Military Mobilization in the United States Army, 1775-1945.* GPO, 1955.

Ransom, Harry Howe. "The Air Corps Act of 1926: A Study in the Legislative Process." Ph.D. Thesis, Princeton University, 1953.

Riker, William H. *Soldiers of the States: The Role of the National Guard in American Democracy.* Public Affairs, 1957.

Rutkowski, Edwin H. "The Politics of Military Aviation Procurement, 1926-1934." Ph.D. Thesis, Columbia University, 1960.

Watson, Mark. *The Chief of Staff: Prewar Plans and Preparations.* GPO, 1950.

D. NAVAL POLICY

Braisted, W. R. "The Philippine Naval Base Problem, 1898-1909," *Mississippi Valley Historical Review,* 41 (June, 1954), 21-40.

Clinard, O. J. *Japan's Influence on American Naval Power, 1897-1919.* California, 1947.

Haugen, Rolf N. B. "The Setting of Internal Administrative Communications in the United States Naval Establishments, 1775-1920." Ph.D. Thesis, Harvard University, 1953.

Schilling, Warner R. "Admirals and Foreign Policy, 1913-1919." Ph.D. Thesis, Yale University, 1954.
Smelser, Marshall. *The Congress Founds the Navy, 1787-1798.* Notre Dame, 1959.
Stillson, Albert C. "The Development and Maintenance of the American Naval Establishment, 1901-1909." Ph.D. Thesis, Columbia University, 1959.
Wheeler, Gerald D. "Japan's Influence on American Naval Policy." Ph.D. Thesis, University of California (Berkeley), 1954.
———. "The United States Navy and the Japanese 'Enemy': 1919-1931," *Military Affairs,* 21 (Summer, 1957), 61-74.

E. ORGANIZATION

Hammond, Paul Y. *Organizing for Defense: The American Military Establishment in the Twentieth Century.* Princeton, 1961.
Legere, Lawrence J. *Unification of the Armed Forces.* Office of the Chief of Military History. n.d.
May, Ernest R. "The Development of Political-Military Consultation in the United States," *Political Science Quarterly,* 70 (June, 1955), 161-180.
McClendon, R. Earl. *Autonomy of the Air Arm.* Research Studies Institute, Air University, January, 1954.
Morton, Louis. "Interservice Cooperation and Political-Military Collaboration, 1900-1938," to be published in Harry L. Coles (ed.). *Total War and Cold War.* Ohio State, 1962.
Nelson, Maj. Gen. Otto L., Jr. *National Security and the General Staff: A Study in Organization and Administration.* Combat Forces, 1946.
Smith, Lt. Col. William Y. "The Search for National Security Planning Machinery, 1900-1947." Ph.D. Thesis, Harvard University, 1960.

V: The Military Policy Process and Civil-Military Relations

The writings in this section focus not on particular problems of policy but on the analysis of the roles of institutions and individuals in the general area of military affairs. The literature tends to concentrate about two foci— the policymaking process and civil-military relations. These two broad categories overlap in the many studies that are directly concerned with the roles of civilian and military bodies in the making of policy. Studies of the policymaking process, however, frequently are also devoted to other or broader concerns than simply the roles of civil and military bodies. Studies of civil-military relations, in turn, are frequently concerned with the general role of the military in society beyond the specific role that military men and organizations may play in the formulation of policy.

Analyses of the policymaking process often are derived from models that would be equally applicable to the analysis of policy outside the military area. Their concerns are often the familiar ones of political scientists: the role of Congress and of public opinion in the formulation of policy, the relation of formal organizational structure to the actual policy process, and the means of coordination within the executive branch. Frequently analyses of the policymaking process lead to explicit recommendations for improvement of the process.

Many theoretical models now exist for the analysis of civil-military relations. These models vary considerably in their level of generality and applicability. The theories of Andrzejewski, Feld, and Rapoport, for instance, attempt to encompass the varieties of civil-military relations possible in almost any organized society. The theories of Janowitz, Lasswell, and Huntington are oriented primarily to civil-military relations in modern industrial societies. Other theories may furnish categories peculiarly applicable to the analysis of civil-military relations in only one society.

The pioneering work on American civil-military relations was Pendleton Herring's 1941 study, *The Impact of War,* a reconsideration of traditional American practices in the light of the new threats from abroad. The first postwar works on civil-military relations tended to be concerned primarily with the need to protect liberal values and democratic institutions and with the threat of the "garrison state" to civilian control. Subsequently, other works analyzed American civil-military relations with a primary concern for the needs of national security. Many of the case studies in policymaking mentioned above in Section III are also concerned with civil-military roles in the context of a specific policy issue. Along with the new interest in American civil-military relations, American and English writers have also turned to the role of the military in other industrialized societies and the somewhat different role of the military establishment in the less highly developed societies (see Section IX).

A. AMERICAN MILITARY POLICY PROCESS IN GENERAL

Fox, William T. R. "Civilians, Soldiers, and American Military Policy," *World Politics,* 7 (April, 1955), 402-418.

Hilsman, Roger. "Congressional-Executive Relations and the Foreign Policy Consensus," *American Political Science Review,* 52 (September, 1958), 725-744.

————. "The Foreign Policy Consensus: An Interim Research Report," *Journal of Conflict Resolution,* 3 (December, 1959), 361-382.

Huntington, Samuel P. *The Common Defense: Strategic Programs in National Politics.* Columbia, 1961.

Millis, Walter. *The Constitution and the Common Defense.* Fund for the Republic, February, 1959.

Bibliography

U.S. Senate Subcommittee on National Policy Machinery. *Organizing for National Security: A Bibliography.* Committee Print., 86th Cong., 1st Sess., 1959.

B. EXECUTIVE ORGANIZATION FOR MILITARY POLICY

Brookings Institution. *The Formulation and Administration of United States Foreign Policy.* U.S. Senate Committee on Foreign Relations, Committee Print., 86th Cong., 2nd Sess., January 13, 1960.

Brown, Alvin. *The Armor of Organization.* Hibbert, 1953.

Hammond, Paul Y. *Organizing for Defense: The American Military Establishment in the Twentieth Century.* Princeton, 1961.

Hilsman, Roger. "Planning for National Security: A Proposal," *Bulletin of the Atomic Scientists,* 16 (March, 1960), 93ff.

Kintner, William R., *et al. Forging a New Sword.* Harper, 1958.

Kissinger, Henry A. "Strategy and Organization," *Foreign Affairs,* 35 (April, 1957), 379-394.

Macmahon, Arthur W. *Administration in Foreign Affairs.* Alabama, 1953.

Mosher, Frederick C., Paul Y. Hammond, and Laurence I. Radway, "Decision-Making in Defense: The Role of Organization," *Public Administration Review,* 18 (Summer, 1958), 169-188.

U.S. Senate Subcommittee on National Policy Machinery. *Organizing for National Security: Selected Materials.* Committee Print., 86th Cong., 2nd Sess., 1960.
_____. *Organizational History of the National Security Council.* Committee Print., 86th Cong., 2nd Sess., 1960.
_____. *The National Security Council.* Committee Print., 86th Cong., 2nd. Sess., 1960.
_____. *The Secretary of State and the National Security Policy Process.* Committee Print., 87th Cong., 1st Sess., 1961.
_____. *Super-Cabinet Officers and Super-Staffs.* Committee Print., 86th Cong., 2nd Sess., 1960.

Bibliography

U.S. Department of Army. *Select Bibliography on Administrative Organization* (Department of the Army Pamphlet No. 10-5). December, 1960.
Van Riper, Paul P. "A Survey of Materials for the Study of Military Management," *American Political Science Review,* 49 (September 1955), 828-850.

C. CONGRESS AND PUBLIC OPINION

Almond, Gabriel A. "Public Opinion and National Security Policy," *Public Opinion Quarterly,* 20 (Summer, 1956), 371-378.
Harrison, Gordon. "Wanted: More Politics in Defense," *Harper's Magazine,* 213 (September, 1956), 50-55.
Huzar, Elias. *The Purse and the Sword: Control of the Army by Congress Through Military Appropriations, 1933-1950.* Cornell, 1950.
McConaughy, James L., Jr. "Congressmen and the Pentagon," *Fortune,* 57 (April, 1958), 156ff.
"The 'Military Lobby'—Its Impact on Congress, Nation," *Congressional Quarterly Weekly Report,* 19 (March 24, 1961), 463-478.
U.S. House of Representatives Committee on Armed Services, Subcommittee for Special Investigations. *Employment of Retired Military and Civilian Personnel by Defense Industries.* Hearings, 86th Cong., 1st Sess., 1959.

D. THE BUDGETARY PROCESS

Gumz, Donald G. "The Bureau of the Budget and Defense Fiscal Policy," *U.S. Naval Institute Proceedings,* 85 (April, 1959), 80-89.
Huzar, Elias. *The Purse and the Sword: Control of the Army by Congress Through Military Appropriations, 1933-1950.* Cornell, 1950.
Katzenbach, Edward L., Jr. "Bubud's Defense Policy," *The Reporter,* 22 (June 23, 1960), 25-30.
Mosher, Frederick C. *Program Budgeting: Theory and Practice with particular reference to the U.S. Department of the Army.* Public Administration Service, 1954.
Smithies, Arthur. *The Budgetary Process in the United States.* McGraw-Hill, 1955. Chs. 11, 12.
U.S. Senate Committee on Armed Services, Preparedness Investigating Committee. *Major Defense Matters.* Hearings, 86th Cong., 1st Sess., 1959. Part II.

E. THEORIES OF CIVIL-MILITARY RELATIONS

Andrzejewski, Stanislaw. *Military Organization and Society.* Routledge & Kegan Paul, 1954.
Feld, M. D. "A Typology of Military Organization," *Public Policy* (Yearbook of the Harvard Graduate School of Public Administration), 8 (1958), 3-40.
Fox, William T. R. "Civilians, Soldiers, and American Foreign Policy," *World Politics,* 7 (April, 1955), 402-418.
Huntington, Samuel P. *The Soldier and the State: The Theory and Politics of Civil-Military Relations.* Belknap-Harvard, 1957.
_____. "Civilian Control of the Military: A Theoretical Statement," in Heinz Eulau,

Samuel J. Eldersveld, and Morris Janowitz (eds.). *Political Behavior: A Reader in Theory and Research*. Free Press, 1956. Pp. 380-385.

Janowitz, Morris. *The Professional Soldier and Political Power: A Theoretical Orientation and Selected Hypotheses*. Bureau of Government, Institute of Public Administration, University of Michigan, 1953.

————. *The Professional Soldier: A Social and Political Portrait*. Free Press, 1960.

Lasswell. Harold D. "The Garrison-State Hypothesis Today," *supra*, pages 51-70.

Rapoport, David C. "Praetorianism: Government Without Consensus." Ph.D. Thesis, University of California (Berkeley), 1960.

————. "A Comparative Theory of Military and Political Types," *supra*, pages 71-101.

Sapin, Burton, Richard C. Snyder, and H. W. Bruck. *An Appropriate Role for the Military in American Foreign Policy-Making: A Research Note* (Foreign Policy Analysis Series No. 4), Organizational Behavior Section, Princeton University, 1954.

F. AMERICAN CIVIL-MILITARY RELATIONS

Ekirch, Arthur A. *The Civilian and the Military*. Oxford, 1956.

Huntington, Samuel P. *The Soldier and the State: The Theory and Politics of Civil-Military Relations*. Belknap-Harvard, 1957.

Janowitz, Morris. *The Professional Soldier: A Social and Political Portrait*. Free Press, 1960.

Kerwin, Jerome G. (ed.). *Civil-Military Relations in American Life*. Chicago, 1948.

Lasswell, Harold D. *National Security and Individual Freedom*. McGraw-Hill, 1950.

Lyons, Gene M. "The New Civil-Military Relations," *American Political Science Review*, 55 (March, 1961), 53-63.

Masland, John W., and Laurence I. Radway. *Soldiers and Scholars: Military Education and National Policy*. Princeton, 1957.

May, Ernest R. (ed.). *The Ultimate Decision: The President as Commander-in-Chief*. Braziller, 1960.

"The Military and U.S. Foreign Policy Planning" (symposium), *Journal of International Affairs*, 8 (1954).

Mills, C. Wright. *The Power Elite*. Oxford, 1956.

Sapin, Burton M., and Richard C. Snyder. *The Role of the Military in American Foreign Policy*. Doubleday, 1954.

Schilling, Warner R. "Civil-Naval Politics in World War I," *World Politics*, 7 (July, 1955), 572-591.

Smith, Louis. *American Democracy and Military Power: A Study of Civil Control of the Military in the United States*. Chicago, 1951.

VI: Weapons, Technology, and Military Policy

First nuclear weapons and then sputnik made the role of science and scientists in government an issue of immediate importance. Much of the writing on this subject dealt either with the general relation of science to public affairs or with the specific implications of particular weapons for particular strategic choices. Works in the first category are excluded from the bibliography; works in the second are included in Section II. There were, in addition, however, two other principal foci of interest. One was the historical problem of how new weapons are introduced into military systems. Two notable early studies of weapons innovation were James Phinney Baxter, *The Introduction of the Ironclad Warship* (Harvard, 1933) and Bernard Brodie, *Sea Power in the Machine Age* (Princeton, 1941). In the years after World War II many comparable case studies were made of the innovation or noninnovation of other weapons. The continued accumulation of these studies should eventually permit some informed generalizations about the processes of innovation. The other principal focus of work was more directly policy-oriented on the proper role of the scientist in formulating military policy and the means of organizing the policy process to facilitate choice and to encourage the timely introduction of new weapons. A growing literature appeared, devoted to the specific problems of organizing "R. & D." Even a casual survey of this field, however, suggests that the greatest need is for integrating concepts and theoretical structures to provide a framework for relating hardware to policy and scientific specialists to political generalists.

A. THE INNOVATION OF WEAPONS

Amrine, Michael. *The Great Decision: The Secret History of the Atomic Bomb.* Putnam, 1959.

Baxter, James P., III. *Scientists Against Time.* Little, Brown, 1946.

Blair, Clay, Jr. *The Atomic Submarine and Admiral Rickover.* Holt, 1954.

Emme, Eugene M. *Hitler's Blitzbomber.* Research Studies Institute, Air University, December, 1951.

Green, Constance McL., H. C. Thompson, and P. C. Roots. *The Ordnance Department.* GPO, 1955.

Higham, Robin. *The British Rigid Warship, 1908-1931: A Study in Weapons Policy.* Foulis, 1961.

Holley, Irving B. *Ideas and Weapons: Exploitation of the Aerial Weapon by the United States during World War I.* Yale, 1953.

Jungk, Robert. *Brighter than a Thousand Suns: A Personal History of the Atomic Scientists.* Harcourt, Brace, 1958.

Katzenbach, Edward L., Jr. "The Horse Cavalry in the Twentieth Century: A Study in Policy Response," *Public Policy* (Yearbook of the Graduate School of Public Administration, Harvard University), 8 (1958), 120-150.

Ransom, Harry Howe. "The Politics of Airpower: A Comparative Analysis," *Public Policy* (Yearbook of the Graduate School of Public Administration, Harvard University), 8 (1958), 87-119.

Schilling, Warner R. "The H-Bomb Decision: How to Decide Without Actually Choosing," *Political Science Quarterly,* 76 (March, 1961), 24-46.

Smyth, H. D. *A General Account of the Development of Methods of Using Atomic Energy for Military Purposes under the Auspices of the United States Government, 1940-1945.* August, 1945.

B. SCIENTISTS AND WEAPONS IN MILITARY POLICY

Brewer, M. Carey. "Science and Defense: Military Research and Development in the United States." Ph.D. Thesis, Harvard University, 1956.

Bush, Vannevar. *Modern Arms and Free Men.* Simon and Schuster, 1949.

Gilpin, Robert G., Jr. "The Politics of American Scientists, 1945-1960." Ph.D. Thesis, University of California (Berkeley), 1960.

Klein, Burton. "A Radical Proposal for R. and D.," *Fortune,* 57 (May, 1958), 112ff.

Livingston, J. Sterling. "Decision Making in Weapons Development," *Harvard Business Review,* 36 (January-February, 1958), 127-136.

Ogburn, William F. (ed.). *Technology and International Relations.* Chicago, 1949.

Price, Don K. *Government and Science: Their Dynamic Relation in American Democracy.* New York University, 1954.

"Science and World Politics" (a symposium), *Journal of International Affairs,* Vol. 13 (1959).

Snow, C. P. *Science and Government.* Harvard, 1960.
U.S. House of Representatives Subcommittee on Military Operations. *Organization and Administration of the Military Research and Development Programs.* H. Rept. No. 2618, 83rd Cong., 2nd Sess., Aug. 4, 1954.
U.S. House of Representatives Subcommittee on Military Operations. *Organization and Administration of the Military Research and Development Programs.* Hearings, 83rd Cong., 2nd Sess., 1954.

Bibliography

U.S. Department of the Army. *Military and Strategic Implications of Technological Progress* (Special Bibliography No. 17). Aug. 1, 1958.

VII: Theory and Doctrine in Military Affairs

Studies of military policy and organization were many, studies of military ideas relatively few. Three foci of interest existed, but about none had there developed an extensive body of writings. One focus was the analysis of communist theories of war and strategy. Marxist theory, in this respect, received much more systematic treatment than any other single body of thought. A second focus was the analysis of the ideas of the traditional political thinkers on the problems of war and peace (Waltz) and the role of military institutions in society (Rapoport). The third was the study of the evolution of military ideas and doctrine as a part of intellectual history or from the viewpoint of the sociology of knowledge. The classic work on the development of modern military ideas was *The Makers of Modern Strategy,* edited by Edward Mead Earle (Princeton, 1943). The postwar years, except for the writings of Bernard Brodie and a few others, saw nothing comparable in scope or quality. This was a surprising deficiency, given the significance of military doctrine to foreign policy and the close relationship of military concepts to political ideas.

Atkinson, J. L. Boone. "Italian Influence on the Origins of the American Concept of Strategic Bombardment," *Air Power Historian,* 4 (July, 1957), 141-149.
Atkinson, James D. *The Edge of War.* Regnery, 1960.
Brodie, Bernard. *Strategy in the Missile Age.* Princeton, 1959.
———. "Strategy as a Science." *World Politics,* 1 (July, 1949), 467-488.
Cox, Richard H. *Locke on War and Peace.* Oxford, 1960.
Dexter, Byron. "Clausewitz and Soviet Strategy," *Foreign Affairs,* 28 (October, 1950), 41-55.
Garthoff, Raymond L. *Soviet Military Doctrine.* Free Press, 1953.
Garvey, James E. *Marxist-Leninist China: Military and Social Doctrine.* Exposition, 1960.
Greer, Thomas H., *et al. The Development of Air Doctrine in the Army Air Arm, 1917-1941.* Research Studies Institute, Air University, September, 1955.
Kintner, William R. *The Front is Everywhere.* Oklahoma, 1950.
Possony, Stefan T. *A Century of Conflict: Communist Techniques of World Revolution.* Regnery, 1953.
Rapoport, David C. "Praetorianism: Government without Consensus." Ph.D. Thesis, University of California (Berkeley), 1960.
Strausz-Hupé, Robert, *et al. Protracted Conflict.* Harper, 1959.
Tucker, Robert W. *The Just War.* Johns Hopkins, 1960.
Waltz, Kenneth N. *Man, the State, and War.* Columbia, 1959.

VIII: History and Analysis of War

An outstanding characteristic of the writing on military affairs in the 1950's was the shift of attention away from the specific problem of war to the more continuing problems of the requirements of military security and the political roles and relationships of military institutions and individuals. At the same time that this broadening took place, however, war was still studied; and certain wars, World War II in particular, were refought almost day by day and mile by mile. Nonetheless, some analysts maintained an interest in the general role of war in society, the evolution of the forms of combat, and the theoretical character of war. Much of the theorizing about war, of course, was prescriptively oriented and will be found under the headings "A. General Strategy" and "G. Strategic Theory" in Section II. Some of it, however, was more interpretative than prescriptive. The resurgence of interest in the sociology of conflict and the means of conflict resolution encouraged the analysis of war as one among many forms of social conflict. Significantly, however, despite the generosity of foundations and the prevalence of collective research, no effort was made to mount an investigation into war comparable to that which had produced *A Study of War* by Quincy Wright (Chicago, 1942) twenty years earlier.

Aron, Raymond. *The Century of Total War*. Doubleday, 1954.
Atkinson, James D. *The Edge of War*. Regnery, 1960.
Clark, Sir George. *War and Society in the Seventeenth Century*. Cambridge, 1958.
Falls, Cyril. *A Hundred Years of War*. Duckworth, 1953.
Fuller, J. F. C. *A Military History of the Western World*. Funk and Wagnalls, 3 vols., 1954-1956.
Huntington, Samuel P. "Patterns of Violence in World Politics," *supra*, pages 17-50.
Nef, John U. *War and Human Progress*. Harvard, 1950.
Preston, Richard A., Sydney F. Wise, and Herman O. Werner. *Men in Arms: A History of Warfare and Its Interrelationships with Western Society*. Praeger, 1956.
Richardson, Lewis F. *Statistics of Deadly Quarrels* (ed. Quincy Wright and Carl C. Lienau). Boxwood-Quadrangle, 1960.
Ropp, Theodore. *War in the Modern World*. Duke, 1959.

IX: Military Affairs of Other Countries

American research and writing on the military affairs of other countries has been spotty. Scholarship has followed the lead of policy. In the first decade after World War II American, English, and German writers analyzed the varied patterns of civil-military relations in modern Germany and the emergence and character of the new military establishment of the Bonn Republic. In contrast, Japanese militarism, which had been the subject of extensive study in the 1930's, received relatively little attention. This undoubtedly reflected difficulties in language and in the availability of documents and records. Undoubtedly it also meant that a resurgence of Japanese militarism was feared less than one of German militarism. Similarly, until 1958 only a few American writers studied civil-military relations in France.

Even fewer studies existed of British military affairs: success in war and harmony in peace provided little temptation to scholars. (Representative British writings on strategy are listed in Section II.) Outstanding among the works of Continental scholars were those of Gerhard Ritter *(Staatskunst und Kriegshandwerk*. R. Oldenbourg, vol. I, 1954; vol. II, 1960) and Raoul Girardet *(La Société Militaire dans la France Contemporaine, 1815-1939*. Plon, 1953) on the role of the military in their respective societies.

The single most important foreign country for research was, of course, the Soviet Union. English and American writings on Soviet affairs tended to cluster about three foci: the capabilities, weapons, and organization of the Soviet military forces; the role of the military in Soviet politics and the means by which the Communist Party maintained political and ideological control over its military forces; and the evolution of Soviet military doctrine. At the end of the 1950's the military affairs of Communist China were arousing a comparable interest. Also, in the mid-1950's the role of the military in the underdeveloped areas of the world began to attract increasing attention. In general, the focus was either upon the place of violence and revolution in the politics of the area (Latin America) or upon the role of the military establishment as an instrument of modernization (Middle East and southeast Asia).

Perhaps the greatest single deficiency was the almost complete absence of comparative studies of military policy, strategy, and civil-military relations in two or more countries. Modern societies face similar, although far from identical, security needs. Underdeveloped societies face similar, although not identical, pressures for modernization and development. Given these functional isomorphisms, the comparative study of military affairs would undoubtedly yield many valuable insights for comparative politics. Yet only a small number of comparative studies have been made. Outstanding among these are the efforts of Alfred Vagts to generalize on various topics in military policy and civil-military relations, based largely on European experience in the late nineteenth and twentieth centuries and the path-breaking study by Edwin Lieuwin of the role of the military in Latin American politics. During his tenure as director of the Defense Studies Program at Harvard University, Edward L. Katzenbach, Jr., taught a seminar in comparative military policy and attempted to stimulate interest in this field. His study of the slow disappearance of the horse cavalry and Harry Howe Ransom's analysis of the establishment of independent air forces in Great Britain, Italy, and the United States suggest some of the possibilities for fruitful comparative analysis.

A. GENERAL AND COMPARATIVE

Foot, M. R. D. *Men in Uniform: Military Manpower in Modern Society*. Praeger, 1961.
Howard, Michael, (ed.). *Soldiers and Governments*. Eyre & Spottiswoode, 1957.
———. "Civil-Military Relations in Great Britain and the United States, 1945-1958," *Political Science Quarterly*, 75 (March, 1960), 35-46.
Huntington, Samuel P. "Arms Races: Prerequisites and Results," *Public Policy* (Yearbook of the Graduate School of Public Administration, Harvard University), 8 (1958), 41-86.

Katzenbach, Edward L., Jr. "The Horse Cavalry in the Twentieth Century: A Study in Policy Response," *Public Policy* (Yearbook of the Graduate School of Public Administration, Harvard University), 8 (1958), 120-150.
Ransom, Harry Howe. "The Politics of Airpower: A Comparative Analysis," *Public Policy* (Yearbook of the Graduate School of Public Administration, Harvard University), 8 (1958), 87-119.
Richardson, Lewis F. *Arms and Insecurity* (eds. Nicholas Rashevsky and Ernesto Trucco). Boxwood-Quadrangle, 1960.
Turner, Gordon B. (ed.). *A History of Military Affairs in Western Society Since the Eighteenth Century*. Harcourt, Brace, 1952.
Vagts, Alfred. *Defense and Diplomacy: The Soldier and the Conduct of Foreign Relations*. King's Crown, 1956.
———. *A History of Militarism*, rev. ed., Meridian Books, 1959.

B. GREAT BRITAIN

Abrams, Philip, "Democracy, Technology, and the Retired British Officer," *supra*, pages 150-189.
Amery, L. S. *My Political Life*, 3 vols. Hutchinson, 1953-1955.
Eden, Anthony. *Full Circle*. Houghton Mifflin, 1960.
Ehrman, John. *Cabinet Government and War, 1890-1940*. Cambridge, 1958.
Hankey, Lord. *Government Control in War*. Cambridge, 1945.
———. *Diplomacy by Conference: Studies in Public Affairs, 1920-1946*. Putnam, 1946.
Johnson, Franklyn A. *Defence by Committee: The British Committee of Imperial Defence, 1885-1959*. Oxford, 1960.
Montgomery of Alamein, Field Marshal the Viscount. *Memoirs*. World, 1958.
Slessor, Sir John. *The Central Blue*. Praeger, 1957.
"Special Number on British Defence Policy," *Political Quarterly*, 31 (January-March, 1960).
Tunstall, W. C. B. *The Commonwealth and Regional Defence*. Oxford, 1959.
Wrinch, Pamela. *Winston Churchill's Military Strategy*. Boston University Bookstore, 1961.

C. FRANCE

Bankwitz, Philip. "Weygand: A Biographical Study." Ph.D. Thesis, Harvard University, 1952.
———. "Maxime Weygand and the Fall of France: A Study in Civil-Military Relations," *Journal of Modern History*, 31 (September, 1959), 225-242.
Brown, Bernard E. "The Army and Politics in France," *Journal of Politics*, 23 (May, 1961), 262-278.
Challener, Richard D. *The French Theory of the Nation in Arms, 1866-1939*. Columbia, 1955.
Domenach, Jean-Marie. "The French Army in Politics," *Foreign Affairs*, 39 (January, 1961), 185-195.
Earle, Edward Mead (ed.). *Modern France: Problems of the Third and Fourth Republics*. Princeton, 1951:
    Challener, Richard D. "The Military Draft of 1940 in Retrospect," pp. 405-420.
    Harvey, Donald J. "Contemporary Concepts of French Strategy," pp. 421-431.
    Katzenbach, Edward L., Jr. "Political Parties and the French Army since Liberation," pp. 432-446.
Girardet, Raoul. "Civil and Military Power in the Fourth Republic," *supra*, pages 121-149.
King, Jere Clemens. *Generals and Politicians: Conflict between France's High Command, Parliament and Government*. California, 1951.
Ryan, Stephen. "Petain and French Military Planning." Ph.D. Thesis, Columbia University, 1961.

D. GERMANY

Boenau, Arthur B. "Civilian Control of the Military by the West German Government, 1949-1956." Ph.D. Thesis, Columbia University, 1961.
Craig, Gordon A. *The Politics of the Prussian Army, 1640-1945*. Clarendon, 1955.
————. "NATO and the New German Army," in William W. Kaufmann (ed.). *Military Policy and National Security*. Princeton, 1956.
Deutsch, Karl W., and Lewis J. Edinger. *Germany Rejoins the Powers*. Stanford, 1959.
Edinger, Lewis J. *West German Rearmament*. Documentary Research Division, Research Studies Institute, Air University, 1955.
Goerlitz, Walter. *History of the German General Staff, 1657-1945* (trans. Brian Battershaw). Praeger, 1953.
Gordon, Harold J., Jr. *The Reichswehr and the German Republic, 1919-1926*. Princeton, 1957.
Muhlen, Norbert. "The New Army of a New Germany," *Orbis*, 1 (Fall, 1957), 278-290.
Ritter, Gerhard. "The Military and Politics in Germany," *Journal of Central European Affairs*, 17 (October, 1957), 259-271.
Speier, Hans. *German Rearmament and Atomic War*. Row, Peterson, 1957.
Taylor, Telford. *Sword and Swastika: Generals and Nazis in the Third Reich*. Simon and Schuster, 1952.
Wheeler-Bennett, John W. *The Nemesis of Power: The German Army in Politics, 1918-1945*. Macmillan, 1953.

E. JAPAN

Butow, Robert J. C. *Japan's Decision to Surrender*. Stanford, 1954.
Crowley, James. "Japan's China Policy, 1931-1938: A Study in the Role of the Military in Determination of Foreign Policy." Ph.D. Thesis, University of Michigan. 1959.
Maki, John M. "Japan's Rearmament: Progress and Problems," *Western Political Quarterly*, 8 (December, 1955), 545-568.
Maxon, Yale Candee. *Control of Japanese Foreign Policy: A Study of Civil-Military Rivalry*. California, 1957.
Morley, James W. *The Japanese Thrust into Siberia, 1918*. Columbia, 1957.
Morris, I. I. "Significance of the Military in Post-War Japan," *Pacific Affairs*, 31 (March, 1958), 3-21.
Storry, Richard. *The Double Patriots: A Study in Japanese Nationalism*. Houghton Mifflin, 1957.

F. SOVIET UNION

Capabilities and Organization

Berman, Harold J., and Miroslav Kerner. *Soviet Military Law and Administration*. Harvard, 1955.
Ely, Col. Louis B. *The Red Army Today*. Military Service, 1949.
Guillaume, Gen. Augustin. *Soviet Arms and Soviet Power*. Infantry Journal, 1949.
Kramish, Arnold. *Atomic Energy in the Soviet Union*. Stanford, 1959.
Lee, Asher (ed.). *Soviet Air and Rocket Forces*. Praeger, 1959.
Liddell Hart, B. H. (ed.). *The Soviet Army*. Harcourt, Brace, 1956.
Modelski, George A. *Atomic Energy in the Communist Bloc*. Cambridge, 1959.
Parry, Albert. *Russia's Rockets and Missiles*. Doubleday, 1960.
Saunders, Malcolm G. (ed.). *The Soviet Navy*. Praeger, 1958.
Stockwell, Richard E. *Soviet Air Power*. Pageant, 1956.
White, D. Fedotoff. *The Growth of the Red Army*. Princeton, 1944.

Military Policy Formulation and Civil-Military Relations

Brzezinski, Zbigniew. *Political Controls in the Soviet Army*. Research Program on the U.S.S.R., 1954.

Garthoff, Raymond L. *The Role of the Military in Recent Soviet Politics* (RM-1638). The RAND Corporation, March 1, 1956.
_____. "The Marshals and the Party: Soviet Civil-Military Relations in the Postwar Period," to be published in Harry L. Coles (ed.). *Total War and Cold War*. Ohio State, 1962.
_____. "The Military in Soviet Politics," *Problems of Communism*, 6 (November-December, 1957), 45ff.
_____. *The Soviet High Command and General Staff* (P-684). The RAND Corporation, May 27, 1955.
Mackintosh, M. "Party, Government and Army in the Soviet Union." Paper, 7th Round Table, International Political Science Association (Opatija, Yugoslavia), September, 1959.
U.S. Senate Subcommittee on National Policy Machinery. *National Policy Machinery in the Soviet Union*. Committee Print., 86th Cong., 2nd Sess., 1960.

Strategy and Doctrine

Dinerstein, H. S. *War and the Soviet Union*. Praeger, 1959.
Garthoff, Raymond L. *Soviet Military Doctrine*. Free Press, 1953.
_____. *Soviet Strategy in the Nuclear Age*. Praeger, 1958.
_____. *The Soviet Image of Future War*. Public Affairs, 1959.
Pokrovsky, Maj. Gen. G. I. *Science and Technology in Contemporary War* (trans. and annotated Raymond L. Garthoff). Praeger, 1959.

Bibliography

U.S. Department of the Army. *Soviet Military Power* (Pamphlet No. 20-65). 1959.

G. CHINA

Barnett, A. Doak. *Communist China and Asia*. Harper, 1960.
Garvey, James E. *Marxist-Leninist China: Military and Social Doctrine*. Exposition, 1960.
Hinton, Harold C. "Political Aspects of Military Power and Policy in Communist China," to be published in Harry L. Coles (ed.). *Total War and Cold War*. Ohio State, 1962.
Katzenbach, Edward L., Jr., and Gene Z. Hanrahan. "The Revolutionary Strategy of Mao Tse-Tung," *Political Science Quarterly*, 70 (September, 1955), 321-340.
Liu, F. F. *A Military History of Modern China, 1924-1949*. Princeton, 1956.
Mao Tse-tung. *Strategic Problems of China's Revolutionary War*. Foreign Languages Press, 1954.
_____. *On the Protracted War*. Foreign Languages Press, 1954.
_____. *Strategic Problems in the Anti-Japanese Guerrilla War*. Foreign Languages Press, 1960.
_____. *Problems of War and Strategy*. Foreign Languages Press, 1954.
Rigg, Robert B. *Red China's Fighting Hordes*. Military Service, 1951.
U.S. Senate Subcommittee on National Policy Machinery. *National Policy Machinery in Communist China*. Committee Print., 86th Cong., 1st Sess., 1959.
Whiting, Allen S. *China Crosses the Yalu: The Decision to Enter the Korean War*. Macmillan, 1960.

Bibliography

Halperin, Morton H. "Chinese Military Policy," in Summer Study on Arms Control, *Collected Papers*. American Academy of Arts and Sciences, 1961.

H. LATIN AMERICA

Alexander, Robert J. "The Army in Politics," in Harold E. Davis (ed.). *Government and Politics in Latin America*. Ronald, 1958.

Blanksten, George. "Revolutions," in Harold E. Davis (ed.). *Government and Politics in Latin America*. Ronald, 1958.
_____. *Constitutions and Caudillos*. California, 1951.
Fitzgibbon, R. H. "Armies and Politics in Latin America." Paper, 7th Round Table, International Political Science Association (Opatija, Yugoslavia), September, 1959.
_____. "Revolutions: Western Hemisphere," *South Atlantic Quarterly*, 55 (July, 1956), 263-279.
Fluharty, Vernon Lee. *Dance of the Millions: Military Rule and the Social Revolution in Colombia, 1930-1956*. Pittsburgh, 1957.
Kling, Merle. "Toward a Theory of Power and Political Instability in Latin America," *Western Political Quarterly*, 9 (March, 1956), 21-35.
Lieuwen, Edwin. *Arms and Politics in Latin America*. Praeger, 1960.
Stokes, William S. "Violence as a Power Factor in Latin American Politics," *Western Political Quarterly*, 5 (Summer, 1952), 445-468.
Wyckoff, Lt. Col. Theodore. "The Role of the Military in Latin American Politics," *Western Political Quarterly*, 13 (September, 1960), 745-763.

I. THE MIDDLE EAST

Berger, Morroe. *Military Elite and Social Change: Egypt Since Napoleon* (Research Monograph No. 6). Center for International Studies, Princeton University, 1960.
Khadduri, Majid. "The Role of the Military in Middle East Politics," *American Political Science Review*, 47 (June, 1953), 511-524.
Kedouri, E. "Soldiers and Politicians in the Middle East," Paper, 7th Round Table, International Political Science Association (Opatija, Yugoslavia), September, 1959.
Lerner, Daniel, and R. D. Robinson. "Swords and Ploughshares: The Turkish Army as a Modernizing Force," *World Politics*, 13 (October, 1960), 19-44.
Rustow, Dankwart A. *Politics and Westernization in the Near East*. Princeton, 1956.
_____. "The Army and the Founding of the Turkish Republic," *World Politics*, 11 (July, 1959), 513-553.
Sharabi, H. B. "Parliamentary Government and Military Autocracy in the Middle East," *Orbis*, 4 (Fall, 1960), 338-355.
Vatikiotis, P. J. *The Egyptian Army in Politics*. Indiana, 1961.

J. SOUTHEAST ASIA

Chatterjee, B. R. "The Role of the Armed Forces in Politics in Southeast Asia," *International Studies*, 2 (January, 1961), 221-233.
Dupuy, Col. Trevor N. "Burma and Its Army: A Contrast in Motivations and Characteristics," *Antioch Review*, 20 (Winter, 1960-1961), 428-440.
Pauker, G. J. "Southeast Asia as a Problem Area in the Next Decade," *World Politics*, 11 (April, 1959), 325-345.
Pye, Lucien W. "Armies in the Process of Political Modernization." Paper, Center for International Studies, Massachusetts Institute of Technology, July, 1959.

NOTES

1. Social Science Research Council, Committee on Civil-Military Relations Research. *Civil-Military Relations: An Annotated Bibliography, 1940-1952* (Columbia, 1954). See also William T. R. Fox, "Civil-Military Relations Research: The SSRC Committee and Its Research Survey," *World Politics*, 6 (January, 1954), 278-288.

2. See Laurence I. Radway, "The Study of Military Affairs," Paper prepared for the Annual Meeting, American Political Science Association (St. Louis, Mo.), September 4-6, 1958. Cf. Samuel P. Huntington, "The Challenge of Defense to Political Science," Paper prepared for the Annual Meeting, American Political Science Association, Washington, D.C., September, 1956.

3. Col. G. A. Lincoln and Col. R. G. Stilwell, "Scholars Debouch into Strategy," *Military Review*, 40 (July, 1960), 18-30.

4. On the relevance of history to current military policy problems, see Louis Morton, "*Historia Mentem Armet:* Lessons of the Past," *World Politics*, 12 (January, 1960), 155-164.

Index